AF607999

POWER AND LEGITIMACY

Law, Culture, and Literature

Power and Legitimacy

Law, Culture, and Literature

ANNE QUÉMA

UNIVERSITY OF TORONTO PRESS
Toronto Buffalo London

Toronto Buffalo London
www.utppublishing.com

ISBN 978-1-4426-4903-3

Library and Archives Canada Cataloguing in Publication

Quéma, Anne, 1960–, author
Power and legitimacy : law, culture, and literature / Anne Quéma.

Includes bibliographical references and index.
ISBN 978-1-4426-4903-3 (bound)

1. Law and literature. 2. Sociological jurisprudence. I. Title.

PN56.L33Q83 2015 809'.933554 C2014-907761-0

This book has been published with the help of a grant from the Federation for the Humanities and Social Sciences, through the Awards to Scholarly Publications Program, using funds provided by the Social Sciences and Humanities Research Council of Canada.

University of Toronto Press acknowledges the financial assistance to its publishing program of the Canada Council for the Arts and the Ontario Arts Council, an agency of the Government of Ontario.

Canada Council for the Arts Conseil des Arts du Canada

University of Toronto Press acknowledges the financial support of the Government of Canada through the Canada Book Fund for its publishing activities.

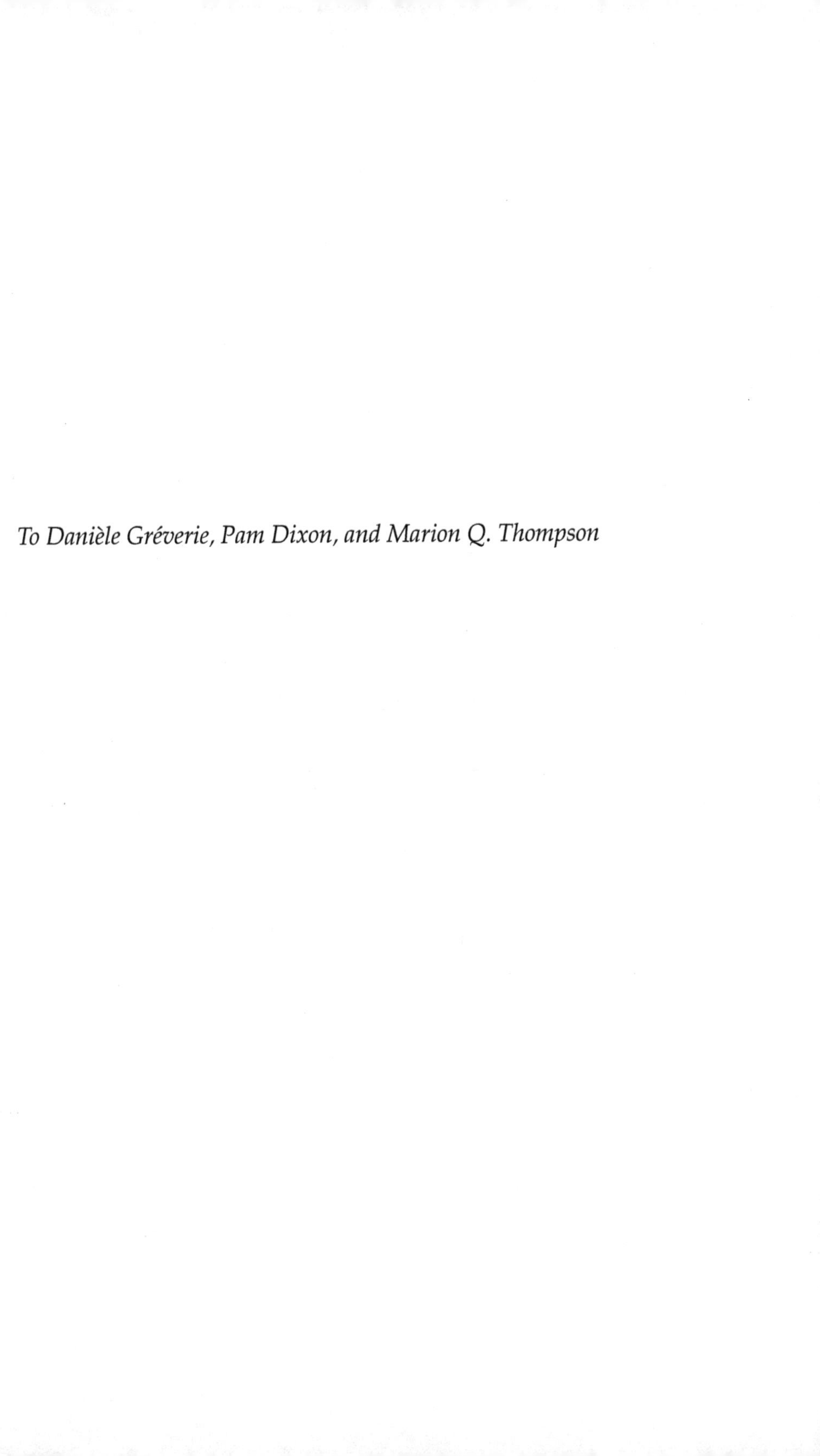

To Danièle Gréverie, Pam Dixon, and Marion Q. Thompson

Il faudra s'entendre sur les mots qui abrègent le désir, les mots qui empoignent nos vies, comme des tombeaux que l'on imagine avec un au-delà dans nos regards, tombeaux qui conviennent aux nuits d'amour, aux manuscrits, à l'attrait troublant que nous avons pour le soleil et la mer, tombeaux qui donnent la réplique à la plus audacieuse habitude que nous avons de justifier l'existence des planètes.

Nicole Brossard, *Langues obscures*

Contents

Acknowledgments

In writing this book, I crossed academic and linguistic borders and shared knowledge with friends and colleagues across continents and cultural practices. Thus, the interdisciplinary patterns of my work speak to a constellation of encounters with texts but also with individuals and their sensibility. In my mind, there is the unruly gang of the Canadian Initiative in Law, Culture and the Humanities (CILCH). The members of this scholarly group played a major role in encouraging me to pursue my research in law and cultural practices. I especially thank Diana Majury for her mentoring, hospitality, and generosity; this project would not exist without her trust and collaboration. Other major culprits include Logan Atkinson, Sheryl Hamilton, Neil Sargent, Peter Swan, Christiane Wilke, and Diana Young. I thank them all for their friendship and support as well as for inviting me to be a visiting scholar at the Department of Law and Legal Studies at Carleton University in Ottawa, where I completed my manuscript and had the honour of presenting the Chet Mitchell Memorial Lecture in 2010.

Through conversations and seminars, I also benefited from interaction with faculty members at Carleton, including Amy Bartholomew, Dianne George, Jane Dickson-Gilmore, Neil Gerlach, Ummni Khan, Vincent Kazmierski, Michael Mac Neil, Shoshana Magnet, Dawn Moore, Michael Mopas, Rosemary Warskett, and J. Barry Wright. Their welcoming was priceless. Throughout the years, I have participated in conferences and workshops organized by CILCH and have learned from the works of Charlene Elliott (University of Calgary), Rebecca Johnson (University of Victoria), Cheryl Suzack (University of Toronto), and Orit Kamir (Hebrew Union College/University of Michigan).

On the other side of the Atlantic, several scholars have been key to the development of my research in the United Kingdom, where I spent many hours working at the British Library. I particularly wish to thank Michael D.A. Freeman (University College London), whose early unconditional support played a determinant role. I remain indebted to his generosity and welcome to the interdisciplinary study of law and culture. I thank Anna Carline (Liverpool John Moores University) for her friendship and her willingness to read sections of the manuscript; Rosemary Auchmuty (University of Reading) for her encouragement; Julia J.A. Shaw (De Montfort University) for supporting my scholarship; Nicole Busby (University of Strathclyde), Felicity Kaganas (Brunel University), and Christine Piper (Brunel University) for including me in the Socio-Legal Studies Association Annual Conference at the University of Stirling; and David Gurnham (University of Southampton), with whom the dialogue continues.

Then there is the Gothic Studies gang of scholars, who through the years provided support and genuine interest. They include Sue Zlosnik (Manchester Metropolitan University), who weds knowledge with humour and warmth; Agnes Andeweg (Maastricht University), who offered friendship and scholarly collaboration; William Hughes (Bath Spa University), who embodies academic generosity; Jodey Castricano (University of British Columbia) and Karen Macfarlane (Mount Saint Vincent University), who offered support at earlier stages of the project; and Steven Bruhm and Peter Schwenger (Western University), who invited me to give a talk on things like Gothic biomechanoids at Mount Saint Vincent University. I also thank Fred Botting (Kingston University, London) and Catherine Spooner (Lancaster University) for supporting my scholarship, Eric Savoy (Université de Montréal) for a stimulating conversation on a train to Montreal, Paulina Palmer (Birkbeck College, London) for her knowledge and her dancing in Lancaster, Ardel Thomas (City College of San Francisco) for her feistiness and infectious humour, Antonio Alcalá González (National University of Mexico) for inviting me to give a plenary in Mexico, and Val Scullion (independent scholar) for intellectual exchange and a delicious lunch in Pimlico.

I would not have been able to carry out this project without the financial assistance of a Social Sciences and Humanities Research Council of Canada (SSHRC) Standard Research Grant (2005–08) and without the steady support of the University Research Fund from Acadia University. This funding was put to good use as I enlisted the help of research and technical assistants. Through the years, Janice Hudson,

Rebecca Jackson, Jennifer Knoch, Beth Lyons, Darrell Rhodenizer, Megan Sherman, Amanda Smallwood, and Tracy Tidgwell all contributed to the research process by participating in discussions, engaging in research and analysis, producing databases, and writing papers.

Finally, I am grateful to those individuals who through the years have offered their friendship or appreciation. Thanks to Romira Worvill, Paule Quéma, Sylvette Maniguet, Tricia Lootens, Julia Creet, Mary deYoung, Lynn Flocke, Kimberly Dark, Dianne Looker, Marlene Snyder, and Alison Smith.

This book has been published with the help of a grant from the Federation for the Humanities and Social Sciences, through the Awards to Scholarly Publications Program, using funds provided by SSHRC. I also thank Daniel Quinlan, who as editor at the University of Toronto Press offered patient guidance and an environment that fostered scholarly growth, and Stephanie Stone, who as copy editor demonstrated rigour and intellectual sharpness.

Earlier versions of chapter 7 were published as "Kinship, Sexuality, and Citizenship in the Civil Partnership Act 2004," *Contemporary Issues in Law* 10, no. 4 (Fall 2010): 313–29; and "'The Dangerous, Creative Act of Reading': Power, Family, and the Political Uncanny in Patricia Duncker's *The Deadly Space Between* and the Civil Partnership Act," in *Gothic Kinship*, edited by Agnes Andeweg and Sue Zlosnik (Manchester: Manchester University Press, 2013), 132–56.

POWER AND LEGITIMACY

Law, Culture, and Literature

Introduction

In the decade preceding the outbreak of the Second World War, a young man is accused of a crime on the basis of a single act of narration by a young female adolescent. In Ian McEwan's *Atonement* (2001), Briony's tale of Turner's victimization of her sister Cecilia and of the rape of her cousin Lola can be read as an act of usurpation of reality through the imposition of a single narrative, which the child wields like an incontrovertible means of control over glimpsed events. If Briony succeeds in convincing her relatives and law's representatives of the authority of her statements, it is not so much because of her talents for impersonation and tale-telling as that her tale captures and invokes some of the major values and norms governing the social microcosm of pre-war England that McEwan's novel stages. As a working-class, fatherless boy, dependent on an upper-class family's charity for his education, Turner is bound to be accused of the crime he has not committed. As soon as Briony tells her tale, the economic and cultural elements that form the social fabric of the lower- and upper-class characters fall into place and override Turner's and Cecilia's version of the events.

Thus, Turner's destiny is merely the materialization of a political *fatum* written in the institutions, practices, and bodies of Neville Chamberlain's England. Briony's presentation of the facts coheres with the dominant mythos of the society to which she belongs. As Briony invokes a wild body lashing out and inflicting its lubricity upon helpless virginal bodies, the law materializes and authorizes the heteronormative and political sociodicy that Briony's narrative has legitimized. Turner is condemned to a two-year sentence in Wandsworth Prison before he leaves for the front and ends up stranded on the beaches of Dunkirk. Briony spends the remainder of her life trying to atone for the injustice of her words and her acts.

At the centre of my reflection is the notion that as human beings, we seek to legitimize the social world and others through symbolic activities that are constitutive of a social organization and normative practices as well as productive of agonistic relations of social power. To develop this argument, I draw on Judith Butler's and Pierre Bourdieu's theories of social power, which both offer ways of conceptualizing the relationship between matter and meaning. In the elaboration of their respective theories, Bourdieu and Butler describe a social world where the emergence and sustenance of social governance occur at the heart of fundamental processes of meaning.[1] That symbolic representation engenders the social world is not just an assumption in their visions; it is an object of persistent demonstration. Not only is the self the materialization of beliefs and principles into a habitus, or the material effect of discursive and regulating norms, but, in both cases, the extreme mode of relationship between the socially constituted self and the symbolic organization of the social world is violence and injury.

The question of symbolic violence lies at the origins of Western philosophy, looming large in the *Republic*, where Plato establishes a social narrative based on fundamental axioms derived from a metaphysical system that has political implications for the organization of civic life and the community. In his critique, which betrays fascination for and resorts to censorship, Plato reveals the powerful role of art but also of symbolic systems of values, be they moral, political, or philosophical. Plato approaches the problem by devising an educational system that can shape future citizens according to the best divine and human qualities. Crucial to his reflection on power is the relation that he sees between the configuration of a social narrative and the determination of who has authority to legitimize the processes of representation. This agon between the constitution of the social world and symbolic power remains at the heart of the contemporary polis, whether we consider centripetal forms of state power or the daily activities of social agents in various social fields.

In the social competition for political ascendency, not all fields and symbolic activities are equally positioned. In particular, what Bourdieu refers to as cultural or symbolic capital is measured by the performative efficacy of symbolic representations in the social world, their practices, and structures. For him, "the form par excellence of the socially instituted and officially recognized symbolic power of construction is the legal authority, law being the objectification of the dominant vision recognized as legitimate, or, to put it another way, of the legitimate vision of the world, the ortho-doxy, guaranteed by the State."[2] Law seems to have the stronger performative ability to match words with deeds or, at the very least, to make its prescriptive utterances an unquestionable and legitimate means of social regulation. In fact, it is expected of the law to act according to its legal statutes, *obiter dicta,* and legal schedules even though the transition from the principles of legislation to the application of legal decisions is not as smooth as might be expected.

In contrast, art seems to wield a lesser symbolic power to the extent that its symbolic mediation does not function as an unquestionable and legitimate means of social regulation. Distinguishing between law and literature, Anne Barron cautions that "we need to tailor our theoretical frameworks to the specificities of the institution with which we are primarily engaged: that of law. Law is not literature, or art, or poetry, or even primarily a 'system of meaning,' though it verges on positivist heresy now to point this out. Law is a system of *prescriptions* which performs a particular function and is oriented towards a particular conception of legitimacy."[3] Furthermore, the symbolic capital of art is volatile, and the claim that it can achieve social efficacy is fraught with theoretical difficulties and historical examples of failure to live up to the claim. The debate is characterized by various claims and practices.

For instance, Plato's indictment of art in his musings on the creation of an ideal state is an unmistakable indication of the extent to which art as symbolic mediation and communication is suspected of political power. The persistent belief in this power is exemplified when Ngũgĩ wa Thiong'o states, "Political authoritarianism is terrified of the power of the word that has become flesh. It loves the word that has been dislodged from the flesh."[4] Or, countering Plato, Hélène Cixous argues that "in a manner that is strictly specific and reserved to writing, I think – I have always said it, I am reaffirming it – that the writers who are conscious are guardians, not only of the *res publica,* the common wealth, which is only one aspect of their work, but above all – it is their role, it is their mission – they are the guardians of language, that is to say of the richness of language, of its freedom, of its strangeness, strangerness."[5] Historically, the attempt by the communist regimes of the Soviet Union and China to enlist creative energies testifies equally to this potential power. From sacral music to painting and sculpture, art was also the mainstay of Christian political empires in Western Europe. Whether ousted or regimented, art is clearly something to lay one's hands on. However, the power of art to effect social and political change can seem at best ephemeral and at worst illusory. Diego Rivera remained powerless when in 1934 the managers of the Rockefeller Center ordered his politically offensive murals to be destroyed, while rock concerts to fight against AIDS and poverty in Africa have had limited effects on complex economic and geopolitical structures and practices of power.

The law-and-literature debate is inscribed in this dynamic of authoritative claims to legitimacy through symbolic power. Prominent in the historical evolution of the movement have been the two major claims – explicit or implicit – that the humanities offer a moral shield against legal manifestations of power and/or that literature acts as a subversive means of shattering law's aspiration to totality.[6] Consider Ian Ward's advocacy of what he calls "the active nature of literature": thus, "this 'doing' ambition has two components: first it seeks to educate, and second it seeks to present a socio-political agenda."[7] On this basis, he assigns to literature the pragmatic and performative role of "reconstituting the community."[8]

In another instance, Martha Nussbaum defends the literary imagination as "an essential ingredient of an ethical stance that asks us to concern ourselves with the good of other people whose lives are distant from our own."[9] In discussing which novels suit this purpose best, Nussbaum qualifies her general statement. "Many popular works entice the reader through crude sentiments and the evocation of fantasies that may involve the dehumanization of others. Ethical assessment of the novels themselves, in conversation both with other readers and with the arguments of moral and political theory, is therefore necessary if the contribution of novels is to be politically fruitful. We are seeking, overall, the best fit between our considered moral and political judgments and the insights offered by our reading."[10] That the study of literature is expected to play an ethical and educational role implies that one ascribes to it a didactic role. This claim leads directly into Platonic territory, for the pronouncement that literature always has a moral value will inexorably veer off into a discussion of the suitability and candidacy of texts: which texts best educate the polis? Good literature does not necessarily equate with the ethical standards of the day for the mere reason that nobody will agree on the definition of good literature. In addition, texts that are morally offensive – that is, by the moral standards of the society within which they were produced – have provided some of the best grounds for ethical inquiry.

The ascription of a subversive function to literature is exemplified by Shoshana Felman's analyses of law and literature. On the one hand, Felman seeks to destabilize the epistemological boundaries between law and literature by analysing them as two narratives of trauma, "two enigmas of emotional and physical destruction, two human responses to the shock of an unbearable reality of death and pain, and two linguistic acts of cultural and of social intervention."[11] On the other hand, in examining the law's unconscious repetition of sociopolitical traumas, she implicitly ascribes to literature a capacity to upset the law and its repressive effects. "Law is a language of abbreviation, of limitation and totalization. Art is a language of infinity and of the irreducibility of fragments, a language of embodiment, incarnation, and of embodied incantation or endless rhythmic *repetition*. Because it is by definition a discipline of limits, law distances the Holocaust; art brings it closer."[12] In the critical practice of law and literature, this analytical move is crucial for demonstrating the agonistic and heterogeneous relations among rhetorical fields and their political impact. But the practice becomes problematic when it ascribes to the literary text a universal ethos that is actually gainsaid by textual patterns of a political unconscious that may reinforce the very norms that the law legitimates and that jurors enact in their deliberations. As I see it, the problem is not so much whether literature has the capacity to subvert as whether we should ascribe to it an intrinsically subversive function and thereby create a hierarchy with subversion as the major jurisdictional criterion for the production, legitimacy, and effects of literature.[13]

If, however, we consider law and literature as social practices with varying performative effects of symbolic power and authoritative means of legitimizing, then we may be able to reconfigure the terms of their relationship without necessarily reproducing the various binaries that lock each field into hypostatized positions.[14] Law's symbolic power, or what various critics have identified as the rhetorical, poetic, literary, dialogical, or aesthetic dimension of law, is buttressed by the binding effects of its utterances, which give it the authority to legislate norms of being and doing things.[15] However, and to go back to Barron's distinction, while the notion that the law is a prescriptive system characterized by a particular conception of legitimacy is accurate, it does not take into account the complexities surrounding the performative process of legal utterances. That law functions as an institution masks the fact that its symbolic power derives not solely from its legitimizing authority but also from the assumption that the values under which its utterances are cloaked speak to the values that its addressees also perform through social structures and economic practices.[16]

Thus, the effects of law's institutional authority will spell normalization if not social coercion, but they can also aid and abet social aspirations for transformation depending on the social and economic contexts of its utterances and practices. Conversely, the imaginary and mythopoeic nature of literature is no insurance against the moral or political validity of the particular social nomos it may represent. As in the case of legalized social norms, there is no intrinsic value attached to the social process of narration, whose significance will remain determined by its historical, political, and economic context. Literature participates in social poiesis either by legitimizing existing norms through its representations, dismantling and demystifying them, or contributing to the social imagination with unthought-of forms of being, relationships, and practices that will be communicated to readers, who themselves define and are defined by the cultural sphere where social values are minted, stamped, and circulated.[17]

The pairing of law and literature derives from a literary and legal past in Western culture when both fields sought to establish themselves as disciplines of knowledge and truth. After years of legal and cultural criticism, it is timely to consider that law and literature constitute themselves as fields of symbolic power vying with other social practices for recognition and social authority and, as such, are potentially implicated in the exercise of symbolic violence in their production of social meaning.[18] So rather than lingering with the polarization between law and literature, it is productive to envisage the polis as a site of social poiesis in which law and literature engage to create norms of being and doing things while seeking to legitimate these norms through performative effects of authority. Law and literature interact at the level of discursive norms to the extent that, as modes of symbolization and communication, they share, swap, reconfigure, and disfigure beliefs and principles functioning as a normative substratum in constant evolution.[19] In this context, I propose to draw on the law-and-literature debate but also to re-inscribe it in the broader context of the agonistic processes of social poiesis that social agents generate as they vie for the legitimacy of their symbolic power and practices.

To examine this agon for legitimacy through symbolic agency, I have opened generic borders and disciplinary gates by selecting the fields of jurisprudence, philosophy, statutory law, and literature. Crisscrossing disciplinary borders and claiming hospitality in different fields of knowledge without settling in one or another, my argument moves from feminist and materialist critical analyses of the law, analytical philosophy of the law, and political science to statutory family law in England and Wales, legal commentaries, and Gothic narratives of the family of the late twentieth century and early twenty-first century. When I pursue such topics as jurisprudence, legal cases, charters, reports, Gothic novels, statutory law, and newspaper articles, I engage the reader in one and the same process: a reflection on what constitutes the poiesis of legitimate norms, their discursive and cultural authority, and their effects of symbolic violence in the struggle for political ascendency. Rather than assume a mirror relation among these various social fields, this study brings out the complex ways in which they interact through rupture, contradiction, subversion, and contestation at the discursive levels.[20] What fastens the analyses of these various discourses in the chapters of this book is the theoretical and dialogical framework I create out of a comparative analysis of Bourdieu and Butler, which enables me to examine the process of social poiesis and discursive performativity in interdisciplinary fields while identifying the manifestations of symbolic violence deriving from this process.

The method is therefore one of hybridity, yielding an unwieldy progeny that assembles and disassembles discursive bits and pieces while tracking down manifestations of symbolic power and the occasions for the dislocation of such patterns. I have used hybridizing tactics that call for a practice of reading that does not aim at interpretive and theoretical wholeness or at a formal elegance that would suppress the disruptive movement of thoughts, affects, practices, and what Stuart Hall identifies as "a proliferation of new points of antagonism."[21] These dialogical tactics consist not merely in transiting from one discipline to another but also in transplanting modes and concepts of analysis from one discipline to another. This is particularly the case in my use of social poiesis as a concept that enables the analysis of a semiotic governance across differentiated social fields as well as in my use of the uncanny as a device to examine the manifestation of symbolic violence in jurisprudence, legal statutes, and Gothic narratives.

In borrowing from other rhetorics, acts of analysis indirectly acknowledge the provisional status of their authority, letting in tropes and concepts from other fields, reining in any claim to cognitive purity and autonomy, and making room for the unthinkable. Further, and as indicated by my strategic use of Butler's and Bourdieu's heterogeneous analyses throughout the book, I have sought to break down intellectual silos by drawing on methodological frameworks as diverse as material and cultural feminism, analytical jurisprudence, queer theory, political science, literary critical analysis, and sociology.

In chapters 1 and 2, I develop a comparative analysis of Butler's and Bourdieu's reflections with a view to examining the performative effects of symbolic power on the polis and the claims of legitimacy associated with these effects. Language is material in that it consists in acts of mediation and communication that are always contextualized in historical, political, social, and economic terms. As such, language and other media participate in the shaping of what Bourdieu calls the social nomos, understood as the principles of social organization, be they institutional, collective, or individual. The capacity to tell, interpret, and communicate extends across and among the various fields constituting a social group, and this process of social poiesis carries with it claims of social legitimacy that lead these different fields and their social agents to compete for political ascendency and recognition.

I suggest that this broader sense of narrative disrupts both the legal appropriation of legitimacy and the literary appropriation of storytelling. On the one hand, symbolic practices of constituting the social world and claiming legitimacy for these practices are ubiquitous, and law is but the outcome of a particularized ascription to its authority to legitimize. Thus, in chapter 1, I reconfigure legitimacy as a fundamentally ontological and political mode of relationship to the world. On the other hand, narratives are socially ubiquitous, and literature is but the outcome of a specialization of social poiesis. Thus, in chapter 2, I suggest that the constitution of the social world into a nomos shares fundamental features with artistic poiesis, upon which depend symbolic power and its political claims to legitimacy. In both chapters, the objective is twofold: to thwart the dangers of a binary understanding of law and literature, while acknowledging their social and historical specificity, and to establish a comparative theoretical framework through which I elaborate, in the remainder of the book, my discussion of symbolic power, legitimacy, and the effects of symbolic violence.

It is in the redefined context of social poiesis as a multiplicity of symbolic practices vying for legitimacy that I examine conditions in which the law, as symbolic power, engages in social poiesis. I do so by focusing on the jurisprudential topic of the rule of law, which, according to Joseph Raz, constitutes law's singularity. In their elaboration of symbolic power and discursive performativity, Bourdieu and Butler are bound to consider the singular role that law plays in social poiesis. In the context of American repressive legal approaches to homosexuality and racism, Butler provides a searing critique of the legal institution and leans towards Robert Cover's critique of the law as an instrument of pain and death in "Nomos and Narrative" (1983) and "Violence and the Word" (1986).[22] However, her other strategy is to focus on juridical discourse and the voice of the law, as "implicated in a notion of *sovereign* power, power figured as emanating from a subject, activated in a voice, whose effects appear to be the magical effects of that voice. In other words, power is understood on the model of the divine power of naming, where to utter is to create the effect uttered. Human speech rarely mimes that divine effect except in the cases where the speech is backed by state power, that of a judge, the immigration authority, or the police, and even then there does sometimes exist recourse to refute that power."[23] In analysing the quasi-divine performativity of legal utterances, Butler indirectly addresses the binding power of law's voice, which the principle of the rule of law makes possible.

Bourdieu also acknowledges law's singularity, which he locates in its specific symbolic force. Thus, law "does no more than symbolically consecrate – by *recording* it in a form which renders it both eternal and universal – the structure of the power relation between groups and classes which is produced and guaranteed practically by the functioning of these mechanisms. ... The law thus contributes its own (specifically symbolic) force to the action of the various mechanisms which render it superfluous constantly to reassert relations by overtly resorting to force."[24] While the notion that the law participates in the production of power breaks down the boundaries between an autonomous institution and social fields, Bourdieu's use of the word *recording* implies that law is passively reinforcing social practices. However, if we agree that law is political insofar as it legitimizes principles organizing the social world, then it also participates in the social poiesis of reiterating, fashioning, and invoking these values and norms of being and doing things.

Thus, it can be argued that, operating according to the sovereign power of its symbolic force, the law legitimizes and constitutes dominant terms of a sociodicy.[25] In endeavouring to capture what constitutes the singularity of the law, Raz, Bourdieu, and Butler tend to focus on law's *institutional* capacity to make binding decisions, whether through authority, force, or sovereign performatives. In contrast, and in analysing law's symbolic power, I draw on Bourdieu's and Butler's considerations but also diverge from their conclusions by suggesting that, if we regard the law as a double helix of social norms and institutional rules, we can say that the law has the symbolic power to generate and legitimize social poiesis with the capacity to sanction in a sovereign way. Thus, in chapter 3, I begin with a succinct analysis of some of the major jurisprudential tenets of the rule of law. Taking Raz's, but also Hans Kelsen's and H.L.A. Hart's, reflections into account, I suggest that the specificity of modern law in the Western world does not lie in the formal criterion of the rule of law, but in the fact that it functions as a double helix, both rule-based and norm-based, both institutionally and socially constituted. In legitimizing the constitution of social beliefs, practices, and structures through its binding authority, the law is exposed to other practices of social poiesis in normative and symbolic terms.

Further, although the law derives power from its institutional autonomy, it nevertheless overlaps with social normativity, which it infiltrates through *jurisdiction* – that is, its capacity to say (*dicere*) the law (*juris*). On the one hand, and drawing on Butler, I show that the law is autonomously supreme in the sense that its performatives are binding. As I demonstrate, this binding capacity is invoked as a benefit by both positivists and feminist legal thinkers. On the other hand, and drawing on Bourdieu, I show that if law regulates and legitimizes social norms, and if it is in turn the historical product of material practices and processes, then its institutional and procedural framing of legal subjects and situations is bound to be criss-crossed by social normativity. It is in this context that seeking in law the signs of our legitimate existence, we expose ourselves to the symbolic violence of the social terms that the law legitimizes. We are both at home and expelled from the law and its language.

Bourdieu's concept of symbolic violence and Butler's concept of the exclusionary effects of normative discourses derive from the common assumption that social hegemony always takes the path of symbolic activity, which through performativity constitutes, organizes, and legitimizes the social world. While Bourdieu tends to emphasize the patterns of social, political, and economic conformity spawned by symbolic violence, Butler tends to focus on the exclusionary and abjecting effects of discursive power. However, in both cases, the concepts of social reproduction and discursive exclusion depend on a process of dematerialization to the extent that the principles of social organization lose their historical referents, social practices lose their temporal complexity through a truncated process of reiteration, and bodies are either marginalized or normalized to fit the dominant organization of a social field. Moreover, both Bourdieu and Butler ascribe to affect a major role in the social constitution of subjectivity. For the former, the costs of symbolic violence are "the tacit cruelties that sustain coherent identity, cruelties that include self-cruelty as well, the abasement through which coherence is fictively produced and sustained."[26] For the latter, the psychic life of power requires the creation of subjectivity through the enthralment of normative adherence for the sake of social survival.

In chapter 4, I propose to further the analysis of symbolic violence and the exclusionary effects of discourses by using the uncanny as an analytical device to demonstrate that the effects of symbolic violence indicate the operation of a political unconscious. In doing so, I uproot a concept that has been a staple of Freudian and Gothic studies and implant it in the political study of power and the effects of symbolic violence.[27] In the field of literary criticism, and Gothic studies in particular, critics have returned to Freud's essay "The Uncanny" (1919, originally titled "*Das Unheimliche*"), either by rehearsing and expounding the analytical categories of his text or by re-examining the concept in the context of the historical, social, and political significance of broader patterns of culture.[28]

It is with the latter endeavour that I am concerned, drawing on Freudian and critical insights while reconsidering the concept of the uncanny from a political standpoint. The notion that the unconscious is associated with a labyrinth of signifiers and metamorphoses of meaning that never sit still, or that it is not reducible to terms of narration and representation, does not evacuate the historical origins and political import of this chain of signifiers.[29] The challenge is to decipher the traces of social power in what Avery Gordon calls the "dense site where history and subjectivity make social life."[30] An analysis of the uncanny can be deployed to show how the production of subjectivity will be accompanied by proscription, which can be traced to historical, political, legal, and economic practices of subjectification.[31]

In this context, I propose a rereading of Butler and Bourdieu from the standpoint of the uncanny and suggest that they use tropes of the *(un) heimlich* – which can be translated as either "(un)homely" or "(un)hospitable" – to develop a vision of the ways in which social normativity is experienced as a conflict between that which makes the social subject at home in the world and that which renders the world unfamiliar to the subject, between that which establishes a plenipotentiary sense of identity and that which hints at an estrangement from one's psychic and historical origins. In my rereading of Freud's theory over Bourdieu's and Butler's shoulders, I seek to re-conceptualize the Freudian unconscious in the context of the relationship between symbolic violence and its psychosocial effects. Uncanny manifestations of symbolic violence gesture towards the operation of a political unconscious and derive from strategies of naturalization and dehistoricization that usurp symbolic means of constituting the world and delegitimize other possible ways of constituting this world.

Through these strategies of proscription and expropriation, this usurpatory process of social constitution creates a political uncanny sustained by repeated patterns of misrecognition. This usurpatory process produces effects of illegitimacy that can be analysed in terms of the spectralization and abjection of citizens, who either do not cohere with normative carvings of the social world or who do not recognize themselves in them. To this extent, the citizenship of these beings is held in abeyance, while social misfits and monsters are produced. Neither in nor out, spectralized and abjected citizens do not belong yet remain determined by the usurpatory terms of social categories, prescriptions, and propriety. The political uncanny can be defined as the return of that which was familiar but barred and silenced in the name of a dominant normativity and which is identified as the anomaly both haunting and sustaining the norms of the dominant nomos of a particular field.

I conclude the chapter by considering how sovereign forms of power clamp on our capacity to draw on symbolic agency – that is, our capacity through symbolic activity to constitute the social world, thereby engaging in historical processes of social poiesis. In their analyses of social power, both Butler and Bourdieu posit the creation of subjectivity through discursive and social techniques of repetition (performative citation and habitus) and through processes of affective adherence to structures, dogmas, and discourses of political power. However, in the midst of this exercise of symbolic power, and the violence it spawns, operates a different type of power whose effect is to interfere with these symbolic activities by seeking to deprive citizens of their very capacity for symbolic activity.

While in the case of techniques of biopolitical power (power over life) and practices of governmentality (norms of social regulation) the social subject is exposed to symbolic violence, in the case of what Giorgio Agamben calls sovereign power the social subject is exposed to bare life, stripped of the capacity to organize the world symbolically through norms and social practices. In her analysis of the suspension of international law and the exercise of unaccountable power by the US state after 9/11, Butler expands on and transforms Agamben's thesis by arguing that governmentality has not displaced the more traditional form of sovereign power, which actually nestles within the field of governmentality. "It is not, literally speaking, that a sovereign power suspends the rule of law, but that the rule of law, in the act of being suspended, produces sovereignty *in its action and as its effect*. This inverse relation to law produces the 'unaccountability' of this operation of sovereign power, as well its illegitimacy."[32] While Agamben concentrates on the juridical order, elaborating a theory of juridical and political state power, I refer to acts of sovereign power as acts of usurpation of the human capacity to organize the social world through symbolic activity. In this sense, each and every act of constitution of the world is a claim to symbolic legitimacy vulnerable to sovereign power and its strategies of abandonment. This rupture of democratic governance occurs whenever symbolic violence as the toxic effect of a dominant sociodicy switches to a violence that makes the creation of a sociodicy a unilateral and totalitarian exercise.

In chapter 5, I examine the mechanism by which the law is led to betray manifestations of a political uncanny, which derives from strategies of naturalization and dehistoricization that proscribe and delegitimize other possible symbolic means of constituting the social world. As argued in chapter 2, social poiesis cannot materialize outside time. Whether we consider norms of being and doing things from a historical, performative, and affective standpoint, we envisage various temporal aspects that make norms possible. If we agree that the law functions as a double helix – both rule-based and norm-based – then an analysis of the relation between legal time and social time is required to grasp law's intervention in social poiesis and its potential practices of proscription, which engender forms of the political uncanny. I suggest that the symbolic power of the law is materially deployed through the social temporality of its utterances. Specifically, intentionality endows legal utterances with a telos, mobilizing and stretching (which is the etymological origin of the word *intent*) performatives towards specific consequences whose significance for the legal subject or social field under its jurisdiction is binding.

Thus, law legitimizes social norms not only through the binding effect of its performatives, but also through its regulation of social time – that is to say, the everyday practices of being and doing things. It is through the conjunction of social norms and intentional utterances that the law engages in the agon for legitimacy as it draws lines and boundaries between the legal and the illegal, the legitimate and the illegitimate, the orthodox and the heretic. From this socio-institutional process of demarcation arises the potential for the law to evince effects of symbolic violence in the name of justice. In the latter part of the chapter, my rereading of Anna Carline's analysis of *R v. Zoora (Ghulam) Shah* demonstrates that, as an institution regulating and legitimizing the constitution of the social world, the law makes intentional utterances that may not only activate the spectralizing of legal subjects but also authorize it. In sum, the symbolic violence of the law and the operation of a political uncanny in its midst derive from the combined social temporality and intentionality of legal sovereign utterances.

In reflecting on the hybridizing of governmentality and sovereign power, Butler dodges a conception of power in centralized or hierarchical terms, a pitfall to which Agamben's thinking is vulnerable. In other words, the claim that sovereign power operates within the field of governmentality maintains a Foucaultian conception of the dispersal of power techniques and strategies. In chapters 6, 7, and 8, I mobilize my analysis of social poiesis and the political uncanny to examine the dispersal and hybridity of power in late twentieth- and early twenty-first-century family discourse in England, as regulated by family statutory law and narrated by two Gothic novels. This discourse presents itself in terms of cultural beliefs as well as legal regulation and circulates across various social fields, negotiating its claims over social configuration, constantly fashioning and refashioning the meaning of family and jostling to determine what Butler calls the intelligibility and viability of the subject and what Bourdieu refers to as the universe of possible discourse.

The slip of symbolic power into symbolic violence is implemented through *esprit de corps* and adherence to social norms of being and doing things as well as social recognition as the reward for normative adherence with concomitant illegitimacy for normative aberration. This implies that there is a cognitive and affective dimension to symbolic power and symbolic violence, which the analytical use of the uncanny is apt to explore. The uncanny more often than not initiates a crisis in the representation of the relation between practical knowledge of social norms and affect. These two elements Freud captured in his 1919 essay when he suggested that the uncanny signifies the transformation of the familiar into the unfamiliar – the known into the unknown – which is associated with the experience of dread. I suggest that, in instances of Gothic fiction, the subject under the spell of the uncanny is a subject of normative and practical knowledge who experiences dread whenever s/he contests normative power while still under the awe and psychic power of the norm and its forbidding effect. The subject of the uncanny is emblematized by Edvard Munch's figure of anxiety in *The Scream* (1893) reduced to the gaping hole of a mouth, which also constitutes a visual trope of all horror movies to this day. The very sight of the gaping hole is improper and grotesque, and it signals the crossing of the threshold from normative propriety to the abject, or what Kelly Hurley has named the ab-human.[33] A manifestation of political violence, the uncanny in these narratives operates at the level of affect and magic: drawing on violence, it works within power, not outside it. Hence, its rhetoric is one of excess and hyperbole.

In chapter 6, I seek to configure ways in which English family law and Gothic fiction participate in strategies of symbolic power, claiming legitimacy over the jurisdiction of the family, its naming and unnaming. Specifically, I argue that contemporary instances of family discourse are still caught in a historical nomos that linked the family head and the state through practices of *regia potestas*.[34] It is through this historical link that shifts occur from governmentality to sovereign power and from symbolic violence to power over bare life. To examine the revenance and spectrality of the patriarchal sociodicy linking family and state, I combine discursive analyses of statutory law concerning civil partnership and domestic violence with literary interpretations of Patricia Duncker's *The Deadly Space Between* (2002) and Lesley Glaister's *Honour Thy Father* (1990).

In my analysis of statutory law, I suggest that the uncanny and its dynamic of the familiar and the unfamiliar, the normal and the monstrous, the customary and the spectral, the territorial and the liminal are deployed whenever the nexus between patriarchal kinship and state power, whose historical origins are obscured by the process of naturalization and misrecognition, is made manifest by contradictions that turn the family nomos into social non-sense. In turn, the two novels stage confrontations with the symbolic violence of a haunting patriarchal kinship by turning the violence of norms against the characters that embody them. Moreover, these confrontations reach a paroxysm as the plots unfold towards states of exception in which protagonists are exposed to bare life, deprived of the ability to constitute their world through symbolic activity to mediate their experience of dread and the abject.[35]

In chapter 7, I argue that the transposition of the incest interdict to the United Kingdom's Civil Partnership Act 2004 re-inscribes a heteronormative regulation of gender identity revolving around an Oedipal interpretation of degrees of affiliation. In this sense, the political uncanny of the act derives from the Trojan horse of a sociodicy of heteronormative reproduction, whose power effect is to silence sexual bodies that do not fit. This usurpation of symbolic power and the ensuing agon for legitimacy originate in a legislating act of reading and interpreting bodies. In contrast, Duncker's *The Deadly Space Between* stages a first-person narrative through which, exposed to the symbolic violence of heteronormative kinship, the main protagonist generates a transgressive account whereby incest becomes the phantasmatic means of deregulating compulsory heterosexual norms. However, in this novel the desire for a new poiesis of gender and sexual norms clashes with and is eventually defeated by the recursive effects of a spectral form of sovereign power that reintroduces practices of *regia potestas* in the home.

In chapter 8, I examine practices of domestic violence as the manifestation of the political uncanny haunting the historical and social transformation of family practices in the West. Conceptualizing domestic violence as a symbolic type of violence as opposed to mere brute force, I argue that masculine domestic violence not only points to practices of domination but also indicates an undertow of power struggle undermining the nomos of a cohesive, benevolent, and egalitarian family. Thus, subjects of domestic violence struggle for the legitimacy of their account of a violence that jars with the social expectations created by the ways the family is told. In this context, Glaister's *Honour Thy Father* presents itself as a historicizing appropriation of symbolic power to lay bare the political uncanny haunting the home as site of domestic violence. At stake is the legitimacy of the first-person narrator's account of a violence that turns the familiar into the unfamiliar and sets up a regime of dread that compromises the regulating phantasm of and desire for a harmonious and caring home. However, from within the violence of the patriarchal household emerges a pattern of sovereign power over bare life that delegitimizes these subjects of domestic violence as they themselves become perpetrators of violence.

In the last section of the chapter, I consider this agon for legitimacy and the slips into sovereign power in statutory regulations of domestic violence. Family law has had paradoxical effects. On the one hand, it has engaged in a major poietic reconfiguration of the family insofar as it has legitimized members of the household – whether they be victims of domestic violence or not – beyond the rights of property that used to ensure patriarchal power in the home. However, in the late twentieth century, law reasserted the family nomos by upholding the principle of matrimonial unity that the very presence of domestic violence challenges. As a result, legitimacy switches hands from the tellers of domestic violence back to the state, which through the authority of family law exercises its sovereign power by intruding upon and controlling the space of the household in the name of safety.

From the analysis of these instances of family law and Gothic narratives emerges the fundamental ambivalence of the political uncanny. On the one hand, the uncanny in family law points to the proscription of modes of being shorn of legitimacy. On the other, the uncanny in the two Gothic narratives operates as a means of staging a crisis of orthodoxy that throws the family nomos into disarray. This fundamental ambivalence of the uncanny as sign of proscription and as sign of crisis enables a reflection on the shift from symbolic violence to a reappropriation of symbolic agency and transformation. The uncanny can actually be considered as the political sign of the failure of symbolic violence to the extent that normative injunctions lead to crises rather than performative compliance. Freud's fantastic expedition through dictionaries to trace the semantic transmogrification of the *heimlich* and the *unheimlich* indicates to what extent the uncanny taps the resources of ambivalence and the slipperiness of meaning in time – the time of a text, a practice, or a history.[36] The crises of the political uncanny generate an interplay between encoding and decoding, encryption and manifestation, the spook and the outspoken. Out of this interplay arises the possibility of a shift from misrecognition to cognition, proscription to poiesis, adherence to desire – all of which contribute to a process of signification subject to historical transformation.[37]

The desire to adhere obscures the fact that the relation among normative signs, beliefs, and practices is neither transparent nor straightforward and that the link between normative injunctions and practices is disrupted by daily aberrations of meaning and practices that do not fit normative frames. If this is the case, then social contestation in a material world symbolically shaped by material social beings motivated by desire does not consist in an exit from the symbolic domain but in the transformation of the norms of that domain. In particular, political possibilities arise when one considers that repetition can be not only a means of normative subordination but also a potential for transformation, that social power is both subordinating and constitutive, that fantasy is both hegemonic and a source of resistance. As Butler suggests,

"If the subject is *neither* fully determined by power *nor* fully determining of power (but significantly and partially both), the subject exceeds the logic of non-contradiction, is an excrescence of logic, as it were. To claim that the subject exceeds either/or is not to claim that it lives in some free zone of its own making. Exceeding is not escaping, and the subject exceeds precisely that to which it is bound. In this sense, the subject cannot quell the ambivalence by which it is constituted. Painful, dynamic, and promising, this vacillation between the already-there and the yet-to-come is a crossroads that rejoins every step by which it is traversed, a reiterated ambivalence at the heart of agency."[38] The political challenge is in part to work from within power and from within the uncanny moments of crisis, turning and twisting the terms of normative regulation.

In chapter 9, I examine the transition from the political uncanny as sign of proscription to the political uncanny as sign of productive crisis. To do so, I develop a comparative critique of the grounds for political resistance and social transformation in Butler's and Bourdieu's analyses, paying particular attention to the node where the social and the psychic converge. While both thinkers identify the social subject's experience of normative discordance through gaps between normative injunction and social performance, or between normative expectations and disappointment, I argue that Butler's politicization of the abject as a resource for a renewed process of legitimization presents advantages over Bourdieu's call for a forced congruence between self-reflexive reason and political transformation. In stating that "the unconscious is that excess that enables and contests every performance, and which never fully appears within the performance itself,"[39] Butler describes a normative world haunted by shadows of abjection charged with repressed desire. These figures of proscription threaten normative reality with disruption through the return of the repressed, which exceeds dominant norms of social self-identification. It is on this normative disruption that the political uncanny as productive crisis depends: the return of these abjected modes of being and practices is the political return of that which was once familiar – that is to say, familiar because belonging to symbolic representation and constitutive of the subject – and that becomes unfamiliar, scandalously disruptive of normative rhythms.

In the latter part of the chapter, I suggest that the social subject's ability to defeat normative domination lies partly in the capacity to practise symbolic agency across different fields of social organization. If symbolic violence succeeds in establishing a monological experience of time that masks the fact that social performance is characterized by discordance, interruptions, and tactics of deviance, then it is by translating from one social field to another that the subject not only reinforces the process of interruption and discordance but actually appropriates this process and defeats the autarchic effects of doxological modes of thinking and doing things. In other words, political resistance begins with normative border crossing.

In chapter 10, I suggest that this normative border crossing is brought to naught whenever the law authorizes terms of legitimacy that enact fetishization of the social subject and disconnection between social fields. I examine the effects of this particular symbolic violence by focusing on the topics of the private and public spheres, foetal rights, and contract, in which the law hijacks the competition for social meaning and normativity through recurrent patterns of fragmentation and partitioning. In contrast, one can envisage the integration of law's authority into a model of political interaction where exposure to heterogeneous norms of being and social relations prevails. The authority of the law derives not so much from an act of institutionalization that sets it apart from the polis as from its responsibility to codify and legitimize the community's competing normative interests. Although fundamental, this authority is never a given. Instead, law's authority is the effect of agents of social poiesis seeking legitimacy by resorting to the principles, practices, and structures of the law as an institution. Thus, law's authority remains inseparable from its capacity to be set in motion by a historically evolving community characterized by *dissensus* among nomadic citizens who engage in a symbolic praxis across and between among heterogeneous social fields.

Chapter One

Symbolic Power and Legitimacy

Thirteen years ago, Sara Crangle published in the *Globe and Mail*, a Canadian national newspaper, an article entitled "You Touch Mine, I'll Touch Yours." The subtitle to her journalistic piece indicates that in "the battle to outwit each other, prostitutes and undercover police officers are engaging in a sexual theatre of the absurd." Here are the details of her report.

HALIFAX – On a summer morning at 7:40 a.m., a 17-year-old girl is standing at the corner of Cunard and Maynard Streets in Halifax, waiting. A vehicle approaches, and she waves at the lone male driver. The car slows down and she climbs in.

"Are you a cop?" she asks the man.

"No."

"Can you prove it?" she asks, unbuttoning her pants. "Touch me here."

The man does so, but the girl is not convinced.

"Go further," she urges. He hesitates.

"Okay," she says. "What do you want?"

They haggle over price. She tells him she has a place they could go. They drive around the block. On Agricola Street, a car pulls up behind them. The vehicle, or the people in it, are familiar to the girl. She turns to the man beside her.

"Are you a cop?" she asks again. "Because the guy behind us is."

"Yes," he replies. The girl grabs the door handle and tries to get out of the car. The officer, Sergeant Tim Moser, head of the Halifax Regional Municipality Vice Squad, physically restrains her and places her under arrest.

> In court a few days after the arrest in July, 1998, the girl, known only as N.M.P., and Sgt. Moser agreed on every detail of their interaction. …
>
> Judge Castor Williams, who sentenced N.M.P., also used it in his ruling in order to congratulate Sgt. Moser on a job well done. He stated, "On the rules that [N.M.P.] set, the officer simply outwitted her." Judge Williams went on. "The duty of the police is to detect and to deter criminal activity. In doing so, they must act according to the law and any deviance from the legally established norm is not a valid public policy unless sanctioned by Parliament. Here, the touching was consensual. … Therefore, the touching was legal."[1]

This reported incident could be said to illustrate the hermeneutics of entrapment, whereby a young sex worker strives to match a man's sexual contact with the statement of his identity. The question hovering in the exchange between him and her is "Is there a cop in this car?" and her reasoning is as follows: if he touches, he may be a bona fide customer. On the other hand, the police officer uses the apparent congruence between his deed and his stated identity to catch her red-handed in the act of selling sex. Her interpretation puts her outside the pale of legitimacy, while his enables him to indict her as a prostitute within, paradoxically, the boundaries of sexual consent as regulated by law. In this scene, on which falls the shadow of law's authority, symbolic power can be defined as the ability to legitimize a normative interpretation of the social world and to act upon this world in accordance with this interpretation. The legitimacy of this interpretation and the social efficacy of the act depend on the endorsement of the interpretive norms governing the act.

In order to examine the socially constitutive role of symbolic power and the factors contributing to the legitimacy of symbolic representations, I turn to Pierre Bourdieu and Judith Butler, who have reflected at length on the relationship between symbolic representation and political domination. One could describe Butler's and Bourdieu's writings as the endeavour to let the nerves grow again between the subject, as defined in affective, physical, and cognitive terms, and the materiality of the social world. The demise of the transcendental, dualist conception of identity is a major characteristic of twentieth-century Western thought and has been the subject of numerous analyses. Among others, Giorgio Agamben singles out Martin Heidegger as a philosopher of facticity whose conception of subjectivity is no longer governed by dual oppositions between mind and body, consciousness and sensation, subject and object but situated in a material world, where the human task is to manufacture a self that rises from matter but is not necessarily determined by it. Thinkers such as Karl Marx, Sigmund Freud, Martin Heidegger, Hannah Arendt, and Michel Foucault ushered in biophilosophy to the extent that life, matter, and the body became major terms in their reflection on the ways in which we constitute the social world, our identities, and political relationships.

This material conception of what constitutes the basic terms of social subjectivity is encapsulated by Agamben's statement in the context of his analysis of Heidegger. "Man is not a living being who must abolish or transcend himself in order to become human – man is not a duality of spirit and body, nature and politics, life and *logos*, but is instead resolutely situated at the point of their indistinction."[2] This fundamental, ontological vision of our material origins has major implications for a conception of language as a symbolic activity with a performative function in the social and political world. In accounting for the way in which symbolic representation and mediation have the ontological function of creating social reality, Butler and Bourdieu provide models of analysis that transform traditionally established relationships among knowledge, power, politics, and aesthetics. In this and the next chapter, I present a critical and comparative analysis of their approaches while establishing the theoretical ground for my analysis of the political agon for social legitimacy through practices of symbolic power.

In general terms, Bourdieu's lasting allegiance is to two sets of principles: the causes of social domination are to be sought in material and structural conditions that embody principles of social organization; and reflexive and historical analysis is the principal means of unmasking material conditions of domination. In contrast, Butler's thinking remains grounded in the belief in the political and social validity of discursive analysis and in the possibility of social transformation by legitimizing social positions that have been abjected and repressed by dominant discursive norms. These positions constitute the cornerstones of two different world views, and one might conclude that a comparative analysis of the two will only increase the sense of their philosophical incompatibility.

This apparent divergence is no doubt reinforced by the fact that Bourdieu himself saw no connection between his materialist approach and theorists who focused on the relation between political power and discourse. Railing against discourse analysis and its inability to transform the material conditions of social domination, Bourdieu states,

"While it never does harm to point out that gender, nation or ethnicity or race are social constructs, it is naïve, even dangerous, to suppose and suggest that one only has to 'deconstruct' these social artefacts, in a purely performative celebration of 'resistance,' in order to *destroy* them. It amounts to ignoring that, while categorization by sex, race or nation is indeed a sexist, racist or nationalist 'invention,' it is inscribed in the objectivity of institutions, that is to say, of things and bodies."[3]

For her part, Butler actually articulated a direct critique of Bourdieu's approach, as exemplified in the translation of texts published as *Language and Symbolic Power*. In 1997, Butler argued that "[Bourdieu's] theory fails to recognize that a certain performative force results from the rehearsal of the conventional formulae in non-conventional ways. The possibility of a resignification of that ritual is based on the prior possibility that a formula can break with its originary context, assuming meanings and functions for which it was never intended. In making social institutions static, Bourdieu fails to grasp the logic of iterability that governs the possibility of social transformation."[4] In this dissonant theoretical context, the intent of my comparative analysis of these two philosophical approaches is twofold.

First, I take their respective materialist claims at their own words to demonstrate that whether we start with Bourdieu's socio-anthropological materialist premises or with Butler's discursive and rhetorical premises, we end up with the notion that symbolic representation participates in social practices insofar as its conditions of production and communication are material. Although Bourdieu's and Butler's claims hail from historically different philosophical traditions, the two thinkers meet more than once and reach conclusions the terms of which are occasionally synonymous. Second, the tensions that exist between Butler's and Bourdieu's different perspectives on the political and ontological effects of symbolic power allow me to maintain a precarious balance between the claim that social agents have the capacity to deviate and talk back through misappropriation of dominant norms and practices (Butler) and, on the other hand, the claim that we cannot underestimate the power of social reproduction, habit, and the desire to conform (Bourdieu). The co-presence of these two patterns accounts for cultural and political transformation but also for what is perhaps more banal: the everyday scenes of self-contradiction, incoherence, and duplicity that we exhibit.

For Bourdieu, the act of defining social reality corresponds to the act of establishing a sociodicy whose function is to legislate over social reality through the creation of principles of interpretation and division among fields of knowledge and social practices. This constitutes what I call a process of social poiesis, which consists in a formidable process of creating meaning and regulating the practices and structures of social reality through symbolic and narrative means. By extrapolating Bourdieu's point, one can suggest the following: the creation of a sociodicy as a narrative, cognitive, and affective act of interpretation constituting and legislating the social world indicates that the concept of law as the power to legitimize is not only a character of legal and institutional activities but also a foundational concept and activity defining the way each and every individual and group tells and makes sense of the world. In this sense, ontology cannot be separated from the study of concepts that are designed to legislate over the material forms of the world and the identities of social beings. To be is to be legitimized through acts of symbolic representation, and to legitimize is to constitute the social world and oneself into being.[5]

Butler's analysis of performativity constitutes a theory of the microphysics of the constitution and legitimization of the world and subjectivity through symbolic representation, and language in particular. Drawing a distinction between the psyche and the subject, Butler designates the latter "as a linguistic category, a place-holder, a structure in formation. Individuals come to occupy the site of the subject (the subject simultaneously emerges as a 'site') and they enjoy intelligibility only to the extent that they are, as it were, first established in language. The subject is the linguistic occasion for the individual to achieve and reproduce intelligibility, the linguistic condition of its existence and agency."[6] She identifies performativity as the linguistic process by which symbolic representation materializes and acts upon the social world. Examining the relation between doing and language, she focuses on J.L. Austin's distinction between illocutionary and perlocutionary acts and argues that words have an "act-like" quality. "The meaning of a performative act is to be found in this apparent coincidence of signifying and enacting."[7] This apparent coincidence underscores the process of defining social identities and ways of relating to others.

The performative power of creating and legislating over the social world and social identities is held in abeyance in the case of censorship – imposed or self-inflicted – which paradoxically asserts the non-existence of a social identity by withdrawing, although not annihilating, the right to symbolic representation. In other words, censorship enacts social non-being. This is exemplified by Butler's analysis of the lesbian's social non-being. "Lesbianism is not explicitly prohibited in part because it has not even made its way into the thinkable, the imaginable, that grid of cultural intelligibility that regulates the real and the nameable. ... To be prohibited explicitly is to occupy a discursive site from which something like a reverse-discourse can be articulated; to be implicitly proscribed is not even to qualify as an object of prohibition."[8] Butler's distinction between reverse-discourse and the ghostly presence of a proscribed object of discourse poses complex questions surrounding the emergence of legitimizing norms: in the former case, reverse-discourse counters a dominant discourse and bears the signs of the norms that it seeks to resist; in the latter, proscription creates an inheritance of loss that paradoxically makes the creation of legitimizing norms potentially more fluid because it is not overdetermined by the mere logic of counter-reaction.[9]

The critique aimed at theories of discursive performativity, which usually revolves around the presumed lack of awareness of social and material realities, is motivated by the concern for an economic basis for resistance to social domination but also a suspicion about the political role and power of language.[10] However, the notion that the act of naming a reality does not address the material aspect of this reality in fact enacts the severance between symbolic representation and material reality. For it is because we name social reality implicitly or explicitly that we may be able to act upon it, and it is because we act upon this reality that we name it. It is in this context that the significance of Butler's statement should be grasped. "The public sphere is constituted in part by what cannot be said and what cannot be shown. The limits of the sayable, the limits of what can appear, circumscribe the domain in which political speech operates and certain kinds of subjects appear as viable actors."[11] Moreover, a major responsibility of democratic political practices is to name realities so that they can be politically and economically transformed.

For instance, as long as particular forms of social exploitation are not identified, legislation and governmental policies will not be edified and implemented. This applies to social realities such as child labour, abortion, economic disparities, aboriginal land claims, and privileged access to education or health services. As long as one does not name the fact that women are subject to pay discrimination, the problem does not exist; in fact, the critique that equal pay legislation is inadequate will not be possible or even meaningful. Naming social reality does not imply that policies will be implemented without a hitch, but that such a process of identification has the power to carve out social spaces where the political terms of contestation, accountability, and policy-making will be forged. The fact that despite legislation, most women in the Western world are still paid less than men indicates that forces are at work that make the legislative word *lettre morte* and that the function of political domination in Western democracies is to enucleate the performative power of symbolic activity and prevent deeds from being enacted by transformative words.

The performative power of naming is further demonstrated when it is abdicated and left in the hands of sundry incarnations of political domination – economic, expansionist, and fundamentalist – all of which understand perfectly well the performative power of words and other media and do not hesitate to use it to achieve their ends. When, on 11 and 12 December 2006, former Iranian president Mahmoud Ahmadinejad organized a conference to test the historical veracity of the Holocaust, he and other conference participants not only used words to call into question the historical event but also strategically used the academic rhetoric of scepticism and free speech as well as the conference structure of panels and presentations to deal its blow to Israel through an erasure of Jewish history.

In a Western culture where electoral promises are habitually broken, where censorship and torture are used by governments in the name of national and international security and undercover operations, where icons of counter- and subculture sell their music to peddle toothpaste or bank products, we should heed Ariel Dorfman's reflection on intellectual resistance and survival in Chile after Pinochet's military coup of 1973. "What mattered at first," he writes, "was to survive, but survival is not enough, survival is never enough, if you wish to change the world and not merely suffer it. … At times we did nothing more than denounce and offer information, fight amnesia, tell the truth as simply as possible. Because one true word is worth ten thousand lies, we have to believe that one true word is worth more than a million lies."[12] Butler's pause on language – its performative function, its power of proscription, but also its promise of social recognition and political enactment – speaks to an ethics of worth that begins with the way in which we use words not only to relate to others but also to identify others and ourselves in the polis.

Whether it is enlisted by discourses and strategies of political domination or mobilized by discourses and strategies of political resistance, symbolic activity emerges as the interaction among three elements: first, a cognitive, material, and affective constitution of the social world that is inherited as already historically constituted; second, the use of this constituting process in order to act upon the social world through the creation of social structures and practices; and third, the legitimization of social identities through this double act of constitution and social organization. This process of constituting the social world is fundamentally political to the extent that ideological concepts of interpretation are established through symbolic activity and persist through the materialization of their meaning in social structures, relationships, and practices. Inhabiting language, the subject is at the same time mortgaged to language, and in this double bind of inclusion and exclusion lies the ambivalence of symbolic activity as political resistance and as political domination. In Butler's words,

> Bound to seek recognition of its own existence in categories, terms, and names that are not of its own making, the subject seeks the sign of its own existence at once. In other words, within subjection the price of existence is subordination. Precisely at the moment in which choice is impossible, the subject pursues subordination as the promise of existence. This pursuit is not choice, but neither is it necessity. Subjection exploits the desire for existence, where existence is always conferred from elsewhere; it marks a primary vulnerability to the Other in order to be.[13]

At the heart of this conception of individuals in their agonistic relation to language and social normativity lies a potentially tragic vision of life to the extent that the very means of fashioning an identity simultaneously functions as a means of coming undone. The tragic element derives from the existential and biological vulnerability of the individual, whereby the individual has no other option than that of being exposed to pre-existing social norms such as language that exact adherence and whose seemingly inevitable effects generate the exclusion of other ways of being and doing things. My suggestion is that Bourdieu's concept of sociodicy can be read as an anthropological and sociological elaboration of Butler's analysis of the constitution and legitimation of the social world through categories, terms, or norms.

A sociodicy operates according to the transmutation of principles and decrees organizing the social world into material, objective conditions. Included in these principles and decrees are the cognitive, artistic, scientific, economic, religious, technological, and legal concepts that we use to constitute the world.[14] In this sense, a sociodicy designates a powerful performative process of organizing social structures and practices according to a discursive and narrative vision of the world: to build a hospital, a prison, or a school is to tell a particular vision and division of the social world. Although the concept of sociodicy might lead one to think of the social world as a homogeneous entity, it actually allows for the diversification of social fields within a community. This diversification operates according to cognitive and interpretive principles specific to different disciplines and activities. Thus, the "process of differentiation of the social world which leads to the existence of autonomous fields concerns both being and knowledge. In differentiating itself, the social world produces differentiation of modes of knowledge of the world. To each of the fields there corresponds a fundamental point of view on the world which *creates* its own object and finds in itself the principle of understanding and explanation appropriate to that object."[15] It is this sociocultural phenomenon of diversity that, in literature, some of the modernist narratives strikingly embody. What was for a long time foregrounded as experimental and psychologizing pyrotechnics in texts such as Virginia Woolf's *Mrs Dalloway* (1925) and Aldous Huxley's *Point Counter Point* (1928) actually constitutes the symbolic manifestation of an increasingly heterogeneous society whose diversification was driven by economic factors, the technological development of information and communication, the emergence of new gender roles and identities, new forms of spatial and temporal perception under the goad of increasing motorized transportation, and the carving out of whole areas of cognition that were to produce the dominant lexicons presiding over the organization and legislation of Western culture in the earlier part of the twentieth century.

According to Bourdieu, social fields intensify their autonomy by establishing cognitive and evaluative presuppositions and by training its members in practices that cannot be shared with the general population, thereby creating a symbolic and cognitive capital that differentiates them from others and situates them in the social hierarchy. Drawing on game theory, Bourdieu describes social fields as domains governed by rules that the players have to acquire and that limit what can and cannot be done within a particular field. In other words, the constitution of social fields is characterized by the creation of boundaries determining what is licit and illicit within the field. "The structures of thought of the philosopher, the writer, the artist or the scientist, and therefore the limits of what presents itself as thinkable or unthinkable, are always partly dependent on the structures of their field, and therefore on the history of the positions constituting the field and of the dispositions they favour. The epistemic unconscious is the history of the field."[16] In creating the sociological concepts of fields and classificatory schemes, Bourdieu develops an analysis of the way in which a doxological context – an authoritative and unquestioned way of thinking – contributes to the congruence between symbolic representation and social practices.

It is because members of a particular field share interpretive concepts that the materialization and reproduction of principles of symbolic representation into practices obtain. The relation between words and things remains, as Saussure held, arbitrary; but adherence to a common set of values ensures the transition from word to deed and the legitimacy of the point of view on the world. Bourdieu's description of the relationship between social agents and the fields within which they live, work, and communicate also establishes congruence between modes of thinking and social structures. "This experience we shall call *doxa*, so as to distinguish it from an orthodox or heterodox belief implying awareness and recognition of the possibility of different or antagonistic beliefs."[17] The way a social agent thinks within a particular field does not result from a pure act of consciousness and rational volition; instead, consciousness and the capacity to think and act cannot be conceived outside principles of the social field that operate both as *structuring* principles of social being and thinking and as *structured* principles of social organization maintained through institutions and cultural processes.

Thus, the individual's ability to think and act is mediated by the major concepts of thought and practices, or classificatory schemes, of a given field. The hegemonic dimension of these categories derives from their explanatory power and their reproducibility. As long as they have the force of explanation and as long as they can be culturally reproduced in their different fields, they accumulate cultural capital and maintain a dominant constitution of the social world. The power of doxa and classificatory schemes is illustrated by the case of Charles Smith, a paediatrician and forensic pathologist in the 1980s and 1990s, on whose expertise Ontario courts relied to convict the parents of dead infants of murder. In January 2008, Dr Smith was tried for scientific incompetence and misleading the courts in their procedures.[18] Until then, he had maintained a doxa within the field of forensic pathology in cases of infants' deaths and had dictated the classificatory terms of this specific field, condemning parents to prison while accumulating an astonishing cultural and legal capital on the basis of a stark division between those who know and those who do not.

This case also coheres with the notion that Bourdieu's and Butler's conceptions of social and political power build upon Foucault's earlier definition of governmentality as a means of governing social fields and their agents through knowledge, policies, and expertise. When Butler defines conscience "as the psychic operation of a regulatory norm," or when she argues that the "psychic operation of the norm offers a more insidious route for regulatory power than explicit coercion,"[19] she blurs the traditional ontological boundaries between subject and object, master and slave, the public sphere and the private, and makes the psychic incorporation of regulatory norms the basis for a systemic, pervasive practice of political and other forms of domination. Giving a reluctant nod to Foucault's reflection on power, Bourdieu also analyses the dispersal of modes of power through social structures whose efficacy depends on the participation of social agents.

> Ceasing to be embodied in specialized persons or institutions, power is differentiated and dispersed (this is probably what Michel Foucault meant to suggest, no doubt in opposition to the Marxist vision of the centralized, monolithic apparatus, with his rather vague metaphor of "capillarity"). It is realized and manifested only through a whole set of fields linked by *organic solidarity*, which means that they are both different and interdependent. More precisely, it is exercised, invisibly and anonymously, through the actions and reactions, apparently anarchic but in fact structurally constrained, of agents and institutions located in fields that are at once competitive and complementary, such as the economic field and the educational field, and engaged in circuits of legitimating exchanges which are ever longer and more complex and therefore symbolically ever more effective, but which also make ever more room, potentially at least, for conflicts of power and authority.[20]

The organic solidarity Bourdieu attributes to the different social fields derives chiefly from the fact that all fields share the basic principle of legislation over social areas according to concepts endowed with legitimacy. And although they are extraneous to one another by virtue of their symbolic and cognitive specialization, they also interact by virtue of their competitive claims over the same social world.

Contributing to the legitimization of apparently autonomous social fields is the arbitrariness with which the constitution of these fields generates exclusionary principles of social definition at the expense of other possible principles. The masking of this arbitrariness facilitates congruence between principles and concepts of social organization and material practices. Arbitrariness characterizes a general sociodicy as well as the constitution of social fields, and, according to Bourdieu, it is "the basis of all fields, even the 'purest' ones, like the worlds of art or science. Each of them has its 'fundamental law,' its *nomos* (a word that is normally translated as 'law' and would be better rendered as 'constitution,' a term which better recalls the arbitrary act of institution, or as 'principle of vision and division,' which is closer to the etymology)."[21] While awareness of the historical origins of principles of social organization allows for critique and diversity of representation, rationalization and the attribution of the state of nature to these principles create the conditions for an unquestioned congruence between practices and their rationale. Similarly, Butler's conception of gender identity relies on the assumption that the creation of a social reality takes place through the imposition of arbitrary norms. "To the extent that gender norms ... establish what will and will not be intelligibly human, what will and will not be considered to be 'real,' they establish the ontological field in which bodies may be given legitimate expression."[22] In this sense, the questions of social normality, principles of knowledge, and ontological legitimacy are embroiled from the start with acts of usurpation and imposition.

In particular, Bourdieu and Butler describe practices of social power that rely on the usurpation of knowledge as the basis for authority. This topos of knowledge-based power can be traced back to Plato, for whom knowledge is the guarantor of the authority of the state and the bulwark against a world of shadows and illusions. Feeding excess and fattening up the petulance of the mind, the artist "establishes a bad system of government in people's minds by gratifying their irrational side, which can't even recognize what size things are ... by creating images, and by being far removed from truth."[23] The criterion of truth remains a determinant in Plato's conception of a legitimate structure of governance. Stephen Greenblatt argues that historically, Machiavelli's political thought upset this Platonic conception of legitimate governance based on the division between knowledge and delusion. Thus, the core of Machiavellian anthropology "posited the origin of religion in an imposition of socially coercive doctrines by an educated and sophisticated lawgiver on a simple people."[24] The sovereign's imposition constituted a trick or fraud as the basis for the exercise of political power.

In this context, Shakespearean drama can be interpreted as an appropriation of Machiavellian principles of political governance, which shared with drama the power of theatricality. In this common poetics of power and theatre, "royal power is manifested to its subjects as in a theater, and the subjects are at once absorbed by the instructive, delightful, or terrible spectacles and forbidden intervention or deep intimacy. The play of authority depends upon spectators ... but the performance is made to seem entirely beyond the control of those whose 'imaginary forces' actually confer upon it its significance and force."[25] In this genealogy revolving around governance, legitimacy, and truth, Bourdieu's and Butler's analyses offer yet another reconfiguration of these key concepts by establishing that the relationship between social practices and professional, institutional, and scholastic paradigms of knowledge is governed by the principles of subterfuge, or *illusio*, or fantasy, whereby the arbitrariness of dominant principles is hidden by a political sleight of hand.

Indeed, Butler and Bourdieu argue that the exercise of social and political power depends on the illusory yet potent and subordinating effects of symbolic representation as a normative, institutional, and authoritative constitution of the social world. Thus, for Butler, "wielded within political discourse, the real is a syntactically regulated phantasm that has enormous power and efficacy. Fantasy postures *as* the real; it establishes the real through a repeated and persistent posturing, but it also contains the possibility of suspending and interrogating the ontological claim itself, of reviewing its own productions, as it were, and contesting their claim to the real."[26] For instance, she lays bare what she identifies as the fantastic construction of gay sexuality underpinning the decision to not fund artistic projects deemed to depict obscenity, a law originally proposed by US Senator Jesse Helms and passed in September 1989. She argues that "to point at Mapplethorpe's representation as the graphic articulation of homosexuality *soi-même*, is a state-sanctioned pointing (both a referring and a restraining) which effectively produces and stabilizes the homosexual real; in other words, it is a syntactically regulated phantasmatic production which assumes and preempts the claim of the real."[27] Again, this analysis of social domination aims not to establish a distinction between truth and falsehood but to lay bare a public sphere where social claims – which all originate in a process of image making and aspire to discursive normativity – compete for legitimacy. The political process of image making is illustrated by Raphael Samuel's discussion of what could be called a political legitimization of phantasmatic nationhood. He explains that in the hall of kings at Holyrood Palace in Edinburgh,

> visitors find themselves confronted with the spectacle of no fewer than 111 Scottish kings. The pictures are arranged in chronological sequence, starting with Fergus I, the mythopoeic figure who founded the kingdom – a peripatetic warrior who allegedly landed in Scotland in 330 BC – and climaxing in a wall devoted to the later Stuarts. Commissioned by Charles II, though only completed in the reign of his successor, and painted by the Dutch artist, Jacob de Wet, the portraits purport to cover some two millennia of Scottish history, giving fleshly embodiment to those royal genealogies and origin myths in which the idea of Scottish nationality seems first to have taken shape.[28]

In this and other examples, the root of the problem is not that hegemony is false, but that it creates the real as "a syntactically regulated phantasm," which imposes a monolithic, regulatory system of norms from which social practices and governance derive.

Bourdieu's examination of legitimacy and governance revolves around the two axes of concealment and misrecognition. Strategies are mobilized to conceal the material and arbitrary origins of power and to ensure the mutation of brute force into legitimated and recognized power. This analysis of strategies of legitimacy through concealment accounts for the ways in which different legal systems have legitimized and authorized political discourses. For instance, Peter Goodrich has demonstrated that, historically, English common law defined itself against the Roman Catholic Church, papal power, and Roman law. "In dialectical terms the defense of the legal authority and sacral prerogative of the Crown instituted a particular order and specific places of public or legal reason. In one sense, it established tradition, the 'unwritten' authority of institutional sources of law, and judicially approved custom and opinion, as the ever-present mystery, the logic and truth, of an immemorial and invisible law."[29] His analysis illustrates the notion of a foundational discourse structured by and structuring a sociodicy that requires the drawing of a boundary between those who belong and those who do not.

The significance of foundational discourses such as English common law concerns not only the generation of a particular institution, its language, and authority but also of a social group that the law legitimizes and regulates within a particular territory and according to rules of belonging and extradition. According to Bourdieu, the failure to see through this subterfuge of power coincides with an act of misrecognition, whereby the social agent is oblivious to the arbitrary and hegemonic dimension of social norms.

> Force cannot assert itself as such, as brute violence, an arbitrariness that is what it is, without justification; and it is a fact of experience that it can only perpetuate itself under the colours of legitimacy, and that domination succeeds in imposing itself durably only in so far as it manages to secure recognition, which is nothing other than misrecognition of the arbitrariness of its principle ... the effect of legitimation is greatest when all real or visible relationship of material or symbolic interest between the agents or institutions concerned disappears and when the author of the act of recognition is himself recognized.[30]

Endorsing and justifying these norms and, simultaneously, deriving social recognition from these structuring norms – social agents buttress the arbitrariness of the principles of a dominant sociodicy. The principles are comprehended, but the very act of comprehension prevents genuine cognition. We have here a concentrate of Bourdieu's concept of social domination, which binds the activities of symbolic representation and knowledge with social structures and practices through conjuring and subterfuge.

Having identified principles of knowledge as means of social regulation in fields and classificatory schemes, Bourdieu has no other option than to resort to a distinction between what he calls understanding – that is to say, that which enables the grasp of the concepts governing a social field – and self-reflexive reason – in other words, that which enables the individual to see through the arbitrariness and functioning of the concepts governing a social field. Bourdieu's advocacy of self-reflexive reason engenders a critique of reason as instrument of power and means of accumulating social capital.

> Reason contains the potentiality of an abuse of power: produced in fields (legal, scientific, etc.) based on *skhole* and objectively engaged (especially through their links with the educational system) in the division of the

> labour of domination, it has a rarity which causes it always to function as (cultural or informational) capital and also, in so far as the economic and social conditions of its production remain misrecognized, as symbolic capital and therefore both a source of material and symbolic profits and as an instrument of domination and legitimation. It even offers the supreme form of legitimation, with *rationalization* (in both Freud's and Weber's senses) or, more precisely, universalization, which is the sociodicy par excellence.[31]

Through rationalization, classificatory schemes organizing thought and practices in a social field derive their cultural authority from being considered as part of the state of nature. Softly and inexorably, the self-evidence of the principles organizing society imposes itself by becoming integrated into practices and inscribed upon the world of objects and structures surrounding the individual. In this context, congruence between symbolic representation and material practices procures an illusory sense of social and ontological harmony, which is enjoyed at the cost of historical and political self-deception.

The powerful mechanism of such deliberate subscription to arbitrary principles is brought out by Butler's analysis of the imposition of gender identities through social norms. Gender, she writes, is "a construction that regularly conceals its genesis; the tacit collective agreement to perform, produce, and sustain discrete and polar genders as cultural fictions is obscured by the credibility of those productions – and the punishments that attend not agreeing to believe in them; the construction 'compels' our belief in its necessity and naturalness."[32] Butler's analysis of performativity as political power distinguishes between power as a myth of origin and the historical genesis of power. The former is crucial to strategies of concealment, while the latter results from the type of self-reflexive analysis that Bourdieu assigns to sociology and other scholastic activities. Both Bourdieu and Butler debunk the role that mythical origins play in the process of rationalizing and instituting social power.

Butler's explanation of the process of gender identification depends on a reinterpretation of mimesis beyond the Platonic imitation of the timeless and universal archetypes that function as the original forms of the social and natural world. Citing Fredric Jameson's distinction between parody as a case of mocking mimicry and postmodern pastiche as a case of blank parody without satirical effects, she argues that gender is the product of a process of parodic imitation of a constructed gender norm that does not have an archetype or origin. Social and normative power proceeds through metalepsis, whereby the effect of a process produces the illusion of an authoritative origin to this process. Concrete examples of such metaleptic processes include the account for hierarchical differences between men and women and between races in terms of biological or genetic differences, propensities, and principles of social organization that are supposed to originate in nature.[33] A historical, religious, and economic scheme of social organization produces specific social relationships, identities, and practices, which in turn are proffered as the index of a foundational and originary discourse of being.

From a legal standpoint, constitutional texts are based on this metaleptic function and typically invoke the foundational people to which they give birth on paper and from which they claim their authority, as in: "We the people of the United States, in order to form a more perfect union, establish justice, insure domestic tranquility, provide for the common defense, promote the general welfare, and secure the blessings of liberty to ourselves and our posterity, do ordain and establish this Constitution for the United States of America."[34] The circularity and redundancy of the sentence derives from its metaleptic force and objective. From the standpoint of the social subject under domination, the subject can be said to be successfully enthralled as soon as the terms of subjection are claimed by this subject. Thus, "no subject comes into being without power, but ... its coming into being involves the dissimulation of power, a metaleptic reversal in which the subject produced by power becomes heralded as the subject who *founds* power."[35] In terms of practices, the illusion of a natural origin to various social norms is sustained through daily references to custom, which is instilled with the aura of immemorial tradition and is misrecognized as the natural way of doing things.

In sum, Bourdieu's and Butler's conceptions of social domination upset the traditional boundaries among knowledge, affect, and symbolic representation upon which accounts of legitimate governance have relied. In their visions of hegemony, knowledge functions as a means of producing interpretive norms, which gain their authority and legitimacy through repetition and social reproduction. While Plato drew a line between the shadows of artistic representation and the rational organization of the state, Bourdieu and Butler turn the tables and attribute a major role to the manufacture of norms and the rationalized narratives of social identities. It is no coincidence that games should be one of Bourdieu's recurring metaphors to explain social adherence to the doxa of different fields or that Butler explains the production of gendered bodies and identities with reference to performance and rehearsal. Although these metaphors are used to describe deadly processes of social domination, they nevertheless borrow from the lexicon of art and invention, and attest to an aesthetic of politics that through symbolic activity has performative and material purchase.

The notion that politics and aesthetics share the process of configuring the sensory field of social organization reappears in Jacques Rancière's thinking. "The distribution of the sensible reveals who can have a share in what is common to the community based on what they do and on the time and space in which this activity is performed. Having a particular 'occupation' thereby determines the ability or inability to take charge of what is common to the community; it defines what is visible or not in a common space, endowed with a common language, etc. There is thus an 'aesthetics' at the core of politics."[36]

It is this conjunction between aesthetics and politics that, in "The Work of Art in the Age of Mechanical Reproduction" (1936), Walter Benjamin identifies when he reflects on the aura of the traditional art object and on the aesthetic dimension of Nazi and fascist politics. In taking a nostalgic look at the aura of traditional art and in simultaneously maintaining fascist aesthetics in his peripheral vision, Benjamin not only analyses the secularizing effects of mechanical reproduction but also reflects on the concept of aesthetics, which, far from vanishing with the death of artistic aura, actually functions as a means of naturalizing political narratives and institutional discourses.

While Bourdieu's and Butler's forays into aesthetics allow them to bring out the provisional status of political power and its rhetorical strategies of *inventio*, their demonstration that political power uses forms of representation, affect, narration, and cognition to achieve its ends indicates that the deployment of aesthetic principles on the stage of politics is not only a characteristic of totalitarian power but also a feature governing the contemporary democratic polis and institutional law in particular.[37] In their characteristically pragmatic way, Anthony G. Amsterdam and Jerome Bruner provide a fascinating account of the rhetorical tactics and feints that litigation involves.

> Law-talk, particularly the law-talk used in litigation, is always subject to shattering without warning, as one or another of its users suddenly questions assumptions that had been accepted a moment before or turns some

> previously inconspicuous component of the interpretive frame into a subject of concern or controversy. ... What a speaker says in legal discourse needs to be made only reasonably and revocably clear to the hearer; and what the speaker *means* by what is said needs to be made only reasonably, revocably, and partly clear. Some part of what is meant will almost always be concealed or ambiguous, despite the fact that the hearer will often suspect that something more is there and even suspect what it is.[38]

The strategic use of speech acts in litigation is characterized by deceit and a discrepancy between saying and meaning, a rhetorical manoeuvring goaded by intent and a hermeneutics of suspicion. In other words, held under suspicion are not only the defendant but also the language with which lawyers spar and on which judges decide. The use of narrative and legal framing is governed by an economy of linguistic tactics devoid of disinterest, charged with craft and hawking. At the same time, and as Bourdieu points out, the exercise of social domination rests on a subterfuge involving strategies that include monologism and the promotion of disinterestedness. The strategy is to transform the contingent values and beliefs of a particular field into universal ones so that the members of that field, displaying a "*particular interest in the universal*, in reason, truth, virtue, engage themselves with weapons which are nothing other than the most universal conquests of the previous struggles."[39] The principle of disinterestedness can be understood as a type of thinking masking the relationship between the accumulation of symbolic capital and the accumulation of material capital.

Inevitably, the effect of the concept of disinterestedness is to create a division between, on the one hand, the public sphere of political and economic discourse and, on the other, the individual and detached sphere of theoretical or contemplative reflection on the former sphere. However, the fact that symbolic means of constituting the world cannot claim a transcendental status of disinterested purity, and that they remain culturally, historically, and economically situated, is blatantly illustrated by Leni Riefenstahl's cinematographic achievements during the Third Reich. As several critics point out, Riefenstahl's films constitute major contributions to the development of cinematographic techniques. Yet the montage of *Triumph of the Will* (1935), its creation of chiaroscuro, its panoramic panning of soldiers organized in perfect geometric phalanxes, its picturesque crowds lined up on quaint streets in Nuremberg and swooning at the arrival of the political leader, its mechanical ballet of motorized vehicles and representatives from the different German states marching through the halls of the convention centre – all these means of symbolic representation are harnessed to communicate one and only one message – namely, that the *Führer* is the *Vaterland* and the *Vaterland* the *Führer*, thereby crystallizing the foundation of Nazi totalitarian power in aesthetic and affective terms while concealing the arbitrary nature of the political dogma.[40]

This particular historical example demonstrates art's capacity to constitute the social and political world according to powerful terms of interpretation, which Riefenstahl organized in a narrative so as to create a myth of origin for the domination of the Nazi state, all the while masking the historical origins of its political birth. Thus, despite belonging to the age of mechanical reproduction, *Triumph of the Will* is impregnated with the aura that Walter Benjamin saw reincarnated in fascist and Nazi totalitarian politics. The objective underlying the production of the film was to legitimize a political interpretation of social reality and to spell out a new vocabulary, which was intended to function as a means of reading and acting in and upon the social world.

This discussion might seem obsolete at a time when well-established schools of theory and criticism such as historicism, feminism, postcolonial studies, and cultural studies have rested their analyses on the premise that the concept of aesthetic disinterestedness is deeply flawed. Yet, in some pedagogical and institutional contexts, the boundary between the teaching of literature and the practice of literature persists and remains governed by what Bourdieu calls the doxa of *skhole*. Entrenchment of such *doxa* translates into a regressive and archaic discourse defending the purity and traditional knowledge of individual fields despite practices that for more than forty years have undermined this very conception of academic knowledge.

The renewed attempt to counter the inertia of the discourse of disinterestedness was the topic of discussion of four papers presented at the annual gathering of the Modern Language Association in 2005, one of which was prepared by Julia Kristeva. In this paper, she calls for a reconstruction of humanism in which "literature and art do not constitute an aesthetic décor any more than philosophy and psychoanalysis claim to bring salvation. But each of these experiences, in its diversity, offers itself as a laboratory of new forms of humanism."[41] As her use of words such as "experience" and "laboratory" indicates, Kristeva envisages such reconstruction from the standpoint of postmodern materialism and, like Bourdieu and Butler, participates in the philosophical movement that blurred the boundaries between traditional dualist categories of thought.

In addition, her words are historically contextualized and stem from her reflection on youth and race revolts in French suburbia as an expression of despair and nihilism through acts of violence. A new humanism would seek to address "the need to believe, constitutive of the psychic life with and for the other"[42] manifested by these acts of violence. Kristeva's materialist parti pris is conveyed in the following terms: "What matters is that from the outset the thinking subject connects [his/her] thought to [his/her] being in the world through affective, political, and ethical transference. My practice as a psychoanalyst, my novel writing, and my work in the social domain are not 'commitments'; rather these activities are an extension of a mode of thinking I look for and conceive as an *energeia* in the Aristotelian sense of thoughts as act, the actuality of intelligence."[43] In invoking Aristotelian thought, Kristeva draws on a philosophical tradition different from Butler's, but the project of anchoring thought in the body, language in matter, utterance in actuality – and correlatively, of constituting the body, matter, and actuality through symbolic activity – remains common to both thinkers.

On this basis, to indict discourse analysis, or "theory," or the humanities for their political impotence is to court the notion that symbolic communication has no social power and thereby to fall prey to the strategy of domination, which consists in simultaneously appropriating and masking the power of symbolic communication. From a discursive perspective, "there is no meaningful reference to a 'human reality' outside the terms of culture. The political program for overcoming binary restrictions ought to be concerned, then, with cultural innovations rather than myths of transcendence."[44] Therefore, a focus on discursive constructs of power does not necessarily coincide with a withdrawal from public discourse, communication, and political participation. For the problem does not lie in discourse analysis but in the dematerializing effects of a discourse analysis severed from its historical, political, and economic context. In fact, the critical analysis of the political use of symbolic representation constitutes a powerful means of contestation not only because we cannot politically act upon a phenomenon that has not been legitimized through the act of naming but also because symbolic power lies at the heart of the political organization of the social world.

Chapter Two

Social Poiesis and Symbolic Power

In the previous chapter, I considered the concept of legitimacy outside the conventional understanding of the concept with reference to a legal framework. On the basis of my comparative analysis of Butler's and Bourdieu's reflections on the symbolic and discursive constitution of the social world, I proposed to reconfigure legitimacy as a fundamentally ontological and political mode of relationship to the world. Here I pursue this analysis of legitimacy and the ways in which it rests on the deployment of symbolic power as a poietic process of making sense of the social world. The production of social meaning through material fashioning indicates that the poietic function extends beyond the field of art and literature. In their analyses of the constitution of the social world through symbolic and normative activity, Bourdieu and Butler foreground the material dimension of this activity. For Butler, the production of meaning is a process of materialization, whereby to matter means at once to materialize and to mean. If words are to achieve a performative effect, this effect has to be seen as derivative of a tension between language and materiality, the two of which can neither be merely equated nor neatly differentiated.

> It is not that one cannot get outside of language in order to grasp materiality in and of itself; rather, every effort to refer to materiality takes place through a signifying process which, in its phenomenality, is always already material. In this sense, then, language and materiality are not opposed, for language both is and refers to that which is material, and what is material never fully escapes from the process by which it is signified.
>
> But if language is not opposed to materiality, neither can materiality be summarily collapsed into an identity with language. On the one hand, the

> process of signification is always material; signs work *by appearing* (visibly, aurally), and appearing through material means, although what appears only signifies by virtue of those non-phenomenal relations, i.e., relations of differentiation, that tacitly structure and propel signification itself. … Yet what allows for a signifier to signify will never be its materiality alone; that materiality will be at once an instrumentality and deployment of a set of larger linguistic relations.[1]

For Bourdieu, social nomoi materialize through a relationship among the body, time, language, and space. If nomos is the law or that which constitutes the principles of vision and division of a social field, then the legitimation of this social organization depends on a process of materialization without which the principles of the nomos remain *lettre morte*. The self is situated in a social world of objects and structures to which it relates through affects such as anticipation and expectation and which it incorporates by acquiring practical knowledge about this world. The social agent's practical knowledge of the world is a dual sign of adaptation and unconscious adherence to the practices and structures of this world.

> *Exposed to the world*, to sensation, feeling, suffering, etc., in other words engaged in the world, in play and at stake in the world, the body (well) disposed towards the world is, to the same extent, oriented towards the world and what immediately presents itself there to be seen, felt and expected: it is capable of mastering it by providing an adequate response, having a hold on it, using it (and not decoding it) as an instrument that is "well in hand" (in the terms of Heidegger's famous analysis) and which, never considered as such, is run through, as if it were transparent, by the task that it enables the agent to perform and towards which it is oriented.[2]

On the basis of Bourdieu's and Butler's analyses, I suggest that the constitution of the social world into a nomos together with the fabrication of normative identities share fundamental features with artistic poiesis. Thus, the relationship between art as symbolic activity and its material, performative impact on the viewer/reader/audience/participant *foregrounds* the ways in which social legitimacy as a whole depends on a material process of poiesis.

To elaborate this claim, I begin with an analysis of the material processes of fashioning and producing meaning by which literature seeks to legitimize its representations and practices. The objective of this initial analysis is to show that this fashioning of meaning is not exclusive to literature but is fundamental to the general process of social poiesis and the generation of meaning in the polis. Drawing on Butler's and Bourdieu's reflections on the materiality of symbolic power, I suggest that strategies of legitimacy take hold only if they take the path of materiality. In particular, it can be argued that without technologies of mediation and social practices, and without the sensorial body – its affects, desire, and temporality – the social poiesis of normativity cannot materialize.

Like any other social process, literature constitutes the world through material supports and resorts to devices and practices of representation to legitimize its interpretation of the world. Literature exemplifies the intimate relationship between matter and the legitimizing of meaning: on the one hand, it relies on visual and auditory perception, the temporal process involved in reading, and the technological means of creating a text on a page, a CD, an iPad, or a reading tablet or in a PDF file; on the other hand, it fashions a nomos through generic conventions. Thus, the genre of poetry will draw on the materiality of sounds, visual patterns, or computer-based generation of combinations, as in the case of Erín Moure's *Pillage Laud* (1999),[3] or texting shortcuts, as in Caroline Bergvall's "Cropper" (2011). Or fictional plots will address our sense of time in either a linear or a fragmentary fashion, emphasizing relations of cause and effect, or the experience of duration and simultaneity, or the experience of memory, or the production of meaning out of random combinations. In other words, literature is a structured and structuring process displaying generic norms, while legitimizing meaning through its different media and sensorial materials. In this context, the notion of genre is understood as a constantly evolving historical process fostering hybridity. Thus, the experimental text will deconstitute, deregulate, and delegitimize generic conventions and foreground poetic narratives and narrative poems, creating generic hybrids. Drama can combine all of the above but has privileged access to body and voice as a supplementary means of constituting the world through communication.

These sentient aspects of literature cannot be separated from the poietic process of making sense. Whatever concepts and values the literary text conveys, they will appear to the reader only through the materiality of signs actualizing these concepts and values. In addition, the much vilified process of self-identification of the reader with a character, a fictitious situation, or a set of emotions – with which only first-year students are apparently stricken – should in fact be grasped as a crucial and unavoidable material process through which readers become acquainted with the textual message, just as social agents identify with norms and principles of social organization through their bodies and emotional dispositions. If readers identify with the protagonists of Sarah Waters's *The Little Stranger* (2009), Ali Smith's *The Accidental* (2005), China Miéville's *King Rat* (1998), or an airport novel, it is not so much that they are naive and lack sophistication; rather, they draw on ontological affective and sensuous processes of understanding and communication that the literary critic has been trained to analyse with more or less discrimination. The cognitive and affective experience of reading and its performative unpredictability is captured in *Between the Acts* (1941), in which Virginia Woolf describes Isa's response to a newspaper article.

> For her generation the newspaper was a book; and, as her father-in-law had dropped the *Times*, she took it and read: "A horse with a green tail ..." which was fantastic. Next, "The guard at Whitehall ..." which was romantic and then, building word upon word she read: "The troopers told her the horse had a green tail; but she found it was just an ordinary horse. And they dragged her up to the barrack room where she was thrown upon a bed. Then one of the troopers removed part of her clothing, and she screamed and hit him about the face. ..."
>
> That was real; so real that on the mahogany door panels she saw the Arch in Whitehall; through the Arch the barrack room; in the barrack room the bed, and on the bed the girl was screaming and hitting him about the face, when the door (for in fact it was a door) opened and in came Mrs Swithin carrying a hammer.[4]

Just as language and materiality are not opposed, reality and phantasm are not antinomic to the extent that, both in our apprehension of reality and in our imaginary projections, we rely on the performative effects of signs and norms of interpretation and fashion the world into being, building word upon word, gesture upon gesture, norm upon norm. This material, affective response to and constitution of the symbolic lies at the heart of litigation in courts. Laura Hanft Korobkin describes the rhetorical effect of legal narratives of affect that aim to sway the jurors' evaluative capacities for a favourable verdict.

> The "best" stories ... *always* draw juror-readers into their ambit, so that they see their verdict-vote as part of the story, and themselves as characters in it. Such stories connect jurors' private lives and values to the case

> at hand. Sometimes this takes the form of elaborate suggestions that only by vindicating the defendants' virtue and innocence can the jurors believe in the virtue and innocence of their own loved ones. At other times, lawyers invite jurors to see themselves as the defendants' saviors, capable through their verdict-rendering power (and therefore the only ones who can accomplish the task) of righting the wrongs and healing the psychic wounds of the defendant. ... By voting one way or the other, the juror can write himself into a narrative about his own life that either increases his security and self-esteem or destroys it.[5]

In doing so, the juror engages in an affective performance as a legal subject in response to another legal subject and effects the law into being through a voting that is underpinned by the terms of the cultural sociodicy in which the verdict is rendered and that legitimizes the authority of institutional law.

Like any other social field, literature has established its cultural authority as an autonomous field of activity generated by practices and principles that evolve historically and regulate those who adhere to or challenge the *doxa* of that field. In addition, academic discourse on literature, book reviewing in the media (such as newspapers, literary magazines, blogs), together with copyrights, censorship, and obscenity laws have all participated in carving out a specialized space for literature, competing in the production of cultural, critical, and theoretical legitimacy. For instance, in the last fifty years we have seen the full spectrum of generic criticism, from narratological typologies to the engendering of new hybrids such as literary non-fiction or the re-conception of genre as a fluid, metamorphic, historical concept and practice.[6] This indicates that despite the drive for social self-differentiation, the academic concept of literary genre and generic practices of writing have undergone the same type of transformation that other social fields have experienced through exposure to other symbolic norms and practices, which have unsettled the fantastic boundaries that past academic dogmas might have enforced.

The tension between the social autonomy of art and its social porosity is exemplified by the way in which literature has the capacity to affect different types of readers in powerful ways and influence the social values, practices, and mannerisms of entire groups in cultural history. In analyses of their contemporary cultures, proto-feminist critiques such as Christine de Pizan's *The Book of the City of Ladies* (1405) were keenly aware of the symbolic power of books and attributed the persistence of patriarchal constructs to the symbolic and narrative power of the Bible; nor is it any coincidence that, in *A Vindication of the Rights of Woman* (1792), Mary Wollstonecraft lingered over the interpretation of the myth of Genesis and its account of the creation of Eve out of Adam's rib to analyse eighteenth-century gender norms and practices.

In her comparative analysis of the nineteenth-century representation of woman in the realist tradition of the novel and the persistence of character assessment in the development of criminal law, Nicola Lacey argues that legal actors in the administration of criminal law were directly influenced by a fictional representation of themes such as individual responsibility and autonomy, character, and conduct. "This is because the system … was still largely administered … not by professional criminal justice officials and lawyers but by ordinary citizens in their roles as Justices of the Peace, parish constables and people bringing prosecutions or testifying about offences – many of them drawn from the middling classes who were prime consumers of the novel."[7] The point here is not so much that literature is reflected by law but that the two fields at various historical moments contributed to the circulation of social constructs and practices, while producing different performative social effects.[8]

The dislocation of one construct from one field to another field and the transformation of social meaning occasioned by this dislocation are illustrated by Lacey's analysis of the interaction between law and literature. She claims that the new code of femininity, which novels such as Samuel Richardson's *Clarissa* (1748) and Jane Austin's *Mansfield Park* (1814) elaborated, and which filtered through the legal assessment of the criminal's character, in effect "would instantly mark [women who did not meet the norms of bourgeois femininity] as unable to establish their veracity within the prevailing system of credibility, and hence as worthy of social control."[9] In transiting from fiction to the court of law, the bourgeois discourse of femininity became the ground for legal categorization and eventually the creation of the social abject – sexual and economic.

What Lacey's analysis demonstrates is that law and literature share the capacity to produce narratives with performative social effects on legal subjects and/or readers. Language is a rhetorical and constitutive means of creating a vision and division of the world and of competing for legitimacy. In other words, the rhetorical act coincides with an ontological claim in which desire and power – the suave and the compelling – combine to persuade the addressee. As a material activity of symbolic power, literature is an inherently rhetorical process with persuasive intent and effect, even when the intent and effect are to counter this rhetorical capacity (as in the case of Samuel Beckett's gutting out of meaning) or to call into question norms of social behaviour and symbolic representation (as in Gothic writing). So the problem lies not so much in whether the symbolic dimension of art prevents it from acting upon the social world as in what conditions prevail that either foster art's symbolic capacity to inflect social practices or abort it somewhere along the way, as it contends with norms of governance that are institutionally legislated as well as norms of social behaviour that are culturally and economically legitimated.

Generally speaking, it can be argued that art's capacity to inflect social practices revolves around practices of social representation and technologies of communication. For instance, there is a fundamental complicity between the reproductive rhythms of social customs and realistic conventions in literature and other media of representation, such as realist cinema. This complicity derives from mimetic techniques of language, social characterization, familiar settings, and, above all, plots that embody social and orthodox expectations about life cycles from birth to death and the organization of social time in various fields, such as the academe in David Lodge's *Nice Work* (1988) or the factory in Hugh Garner's *Cabbagetown* (1950). Shifts of power occur in the field of art whenever artists succeed in contesting orthodox representations and established media of representation. Historically, avant-garde strategies of provocation have functioned as heretical disruptions of hegemonic categories of political and technological legitimacy and, in fact, as a dismantling of the very concept of legitimacy, especially in its Dadaist forms. From a contemporary standpoint, one can think of Caroline Bergvall's fractal poetry in "Les jets de la Poupée" (2000) or Nicole Brossard's experimental texts such as *L'amèr* (1977), in which she resists conventions of realism and its ideological grip on words and plots, where gendered principles of a sociodicy and a normative conception of desire lie in wait.

Reflecting on literature as a means of normative transformation, Bruner argues that the device of peripeteia may be used to represent such transformation. "Literary narrative 'subjunctivizes' reality … making room not only for what is but what might be or might have been. A subjunctivized world, though it may not be comfortable, is provocative. It keeps the familiar and the possible cheek by jowl."[10] If peripeteia is the event that sends the terms of a sociodicy under representation off track, then through their symbolic power literary narratives may open up social possibilities. However, I suggest that this "as if" strategy – to borrow from Hans Vaihinger's famous title – is not specific to literature and that it actually underwrites symbolic activities in the entire polis.[11] The power that we ascribe to creativity assumes a hyperbolic form in the discrete field of art, which shares with social poiesis the symbolic means of constituting the social world – that is to say, historically to constitute and reconstitute norms, practices, and principles of social organization.

It can be argued that, in any social field governed by symbolic activity, the terms of social poiesis will acquire legitimacy insofar as their meaning is socially materialized and integrated into technological, economic, institutional, and other structures. Furthermore, domination – political and other – can be defined as the set of activities that aim to rob symbolic representation of its legitimacy through strategies of exclusion, abjection, and outlawing. Domination through delegitimization does not exist as a separate entity, but invests the very structures, textures, and practices of the material world. Materiality, Butler argues, "designates a certain effect of power or, rather, *is* power in its formative or constituting effects. Insofar as power operates successfully by constituting an object domain, a field of intelligibility, as a taken-for-granted ontology, its material effects are taken as material data or primary givens."[12] The centrepiece of social strategies of domination is the body, which, as in these science fiction narratives of mutants and aliens of all stripes, is the matrix for norms and principles to gestate, grow, and reproduce. For Bourdieu, the constitution of the social world is governed by a principle

> generating and unifying all practices, the system of inseparably cognitive and evaluative structures which organizes the vision of the world in accordance with the objective structures of a determinate state of the social world: this principle is nothing other than the *socially informed body*, with its tastes and distastes, its compulsions and repulsions, with, in a word, all its *senses*, that is to say, not only the traditional five senses – which never escape the structuring action of social determinisms – but also the sense of necessity and the sense of duty, the sense of direction and the sense of reality, the sense of propriety, the sense of balance and the sense of beauty, common sense and the sense of the sacred, tactical sense and the sense of responsibility, business sense and the sense of propriety, the sense of humour and the sense of absurdity, moral sense and the sense of practicality, and so on.[13]

At the basis of Bourdieu's and Butler's descriptions of power is the fundamental process that engages meaning through matter, or that actualizes the potentiality of meaning through materialization, and which takes the form of social and individual poiesis or metamorphoses into social practices and structures that demand the exclusion of others for their existence and persistence. If such is the case, then the basic principle of normative domination is to develop strategies to appropriate and retain a stranglehold on the relation between meaning and matter, whereby to acquire legitimacy and exercise authority is to control the process of materializing meaning.

In this sense, the exercise of domination is truly and etymologically aesthetic to the extent that its meaning is first and foremost generated through a material process of symbolic mediation involving the body, the senses, and affect.[14] The process of social poiesis does not rest in the forceful subjugation of the self to a set of openly tyrannical ideological and discursive principles. Instead, the force of these principles and the constitutive efficacy of social poiesis derive from lifelong incorporation based on daily practices and affective adherence. Thus, "what constitutes the fixity of the body, its contours, its movements, will be fully material, but materiality will be rethought as the effect of power, as power's most productive effect."[15] It is not so much that the norm is imposed on a pre-existing body, but that the materiality of the body is accessible only through a regulatory norm and vice versa. Butler reverses the traditional understanding of identity by switching from the subject autonomously adopting normative values to the system of normative values infiltrating and regulating the process of self-formation.

As the norm requires materialization for existence and efficacy, the embodied self is constituted. In more specific terms, gender norms exert their power through that process of materialization. "The imaginary practice of identification must itself be understood as a double movement: in citing the symbolic, an identification (re)invokes and (re) invests the symbolic law, seeks recourse to it as a constituting authority that precedes its imaginary instancing. The priority and the authority of the symbolic is, however, constituted *through* that recursive turn, such that citation, here as above, effectively brings into being the very prior authority to which it then defers."[16] Bourdieu's and Butler's conceptions of the relation between signs and matter transcend the traditional oppositions between normativity and freedom, subjectivity and objectivity, language and body, past and present. To exercise freedom is to act from within a normative framework; to be a subject is to be materialized according to norms objectified through social structures and processes; to produce meaning is to stamp matter with intelligibility; and to live in the present material world is to authorize, refashion, or depart from the norms of the past.

The exercise of domination consists not only in the usurpation of materialized and materializing discursive principles and norms of social organization but also in the occultation of such materializing processes. If the power of symbolic activity as resistance depends on processes and practices of materialization, then strategies of political domination will also resort to the dematerialization of meaning by masking the overt material basis of meaning.[17] Commenting on Luce Irigaray's analysis of Plato's chora, Butler analyses the paradoxical subterfuge that such a strategy involves. "The [Platonic] body that is reason dematerializes the bodies that may not properly stand for reason or its replicas, and yet this is a figure in crisis, for this body of reason is itself the phantasmic dematerialization of masculinity, one which requires that women and slaves, children and animals be the body, perform the bodily functions, that it will not perform."[18] This logic remains more than ever relevant to contemporary forms of social and cultural domination. Although arbitrary, the norms and principles of social organization underlying a public message will maintain hegemony as long as they paradoxically succeed in concealing their materiality and in claiming a disembodied status.[19]

But one can push Butler's argument even further and argue that, conversely, hyperbolic materialization can function as a means of exercising usurpatory power. Contemporary culture is demonstrably characterized by an obsessive preoccupation with matter and the body in such a way as to impoverish the capacity to create new meanings that matter. Marion I. Young (1989), Susan Bartky (1990), and Susan Bordo (1993) have each provided feminist analyses of this cultural obsession with the body, which affects gender identity and practices. It is not so much that such cultural phenomena as bodybuilding, home-making, dieting, and cosmetics trump the materialization of meaning as that they hijack the process and reduce its scope.

So sociodicy or the normative organization of the world can acquire legitimacy only by being manifested through public inscriptions in bodies, material structures, and social practices. If this public process of social poiesis does not take place, then the terms of social organization either suffer the fate of political muteness or become affected by historical obsolescence. Neo-Marxist conceptions of the political role of art have persisted in modern political discourse precisely because of this preoccupation with the materiality of symbolic representation. For instance, in his critique of the politics of colonialism, Frantz Fanon asserts that the anti-colonialist literature of combat "moulds the national consciousness, giving it form and contours and flinging open before it new and boundless horizons."[20] On the relation between symbolic activity and materiality depends the political efficacy of this art of combat so much so that by "carving figures and faces which are full of life, and by taking as his theme a group fixed on the same pedestal, the artist invites participation in an organized movement."[21]

In a famous passage in *Grundrisse,* Marx explores the implications of his political theorem that social being determines consciousness by providing a contrast between Greek art and the type of culture prevailing in nineteenth-century industrial England.[22] Greek art, Marx argues, relied on the mastery of nature through acts of the imagination. The prevalence of Greek mythology implicitly indicates that Greek society produced limited technological and economic means of exploiting nature. Marx posits that these social and material conditions determined the difference between Greek art and nineteenth-century art as the latter evolved in the context of an industrialized and mechanized relationship to nature. He concludes that the nineteenth century's lingering fascination with Greek art is a fascination for Greek culture as the childhood of humanity. On this Marxist basis, one could argue that, in today's cybernetic culture, Greek art does not stand a chance of appealing to a readership and that its social and performative significance is simply nil. It is quite likely that, in the 1990s, should a rhapsode have rushed into a cybercafe, declaiming the *Iliad,* the earphoned patrons would have remained oblivious and indifferent to the performance. So, taking Marx's argument at face value, we would have to conclude that, in the era of cybernetics, mythology is hackneyed and the Gutenberg Galaxy, too, crashed long ago.

But then how does one explain the popularity of movies such as *Gladiator* (2000) and *300* (2007), the latter drawing on the archetypal plot of the Battle of Thermopylae, which Frank Miller's graphic novel appropriated and which Zack Snyder digitized? Missing from Marx's argument is a reflection on the way in which technologies and symbolic activities keep evolving through a process of hybridity that renews symbolic power rather than rendering it merely obsolete or nostalgically seductive. The temporality of symbolic power is not teleological but recursive and citational. Thus, reading and writing are still nestled in hypertextuality, having undergone redefinition through new, technology-goaded practices. Similarly, it is in the wake of a box office success at theatres that publishers reissue novels and narratives – from Jane Austen's *Pride and Prejudice* (1813) through Ian Fleming's *Casino Royale* (1953) to Ian McEwan's *Atonement* (2001).

In other words, if the cultural legitimacy of these texts has been renewed, it is because their meaning has been renegotiated through the sensuous medium of cinematic and digitized images. Finally, the legitimacy of symbolic representation and communication derives from the economic ability to have access to major broadcasting tools, and this applies not only to literature but also to other zones of activity in the cultural sphere, so that political messages cannot be conceived without the funding of political campaigns, sports events cannot affect the viewing public without sponsorship, and authors can hardly decline the request to launch their books through promotional meet-the-author tours. So, if the cultural and political legitimacy of social poiesis depends on its capacity to materialize meaningfully, its social relevance and efficacy lie not solely in its material origins but also in its ability to renew historically its material and economic forms of communication.

For this material production of meaning to obtain – for nomos to maintain its legitimacy – time is of the essence: whatever principle legitimates the social world cannot have any efficacy if it is not temporalized. Principles of social and political legitimacy feed on time and, in particular, on a temporality of repetition and duration. Therefore, the materiality of meaning consists not only in the embodiment of norms though social practices and institutional structures but also in a temporal process that ensures that the materialization of meaning occurs on a continuous basis, ensuring consistency of performance and predictability without which action cannot occur.

Thus, it is no coincidence that artists of the twentieth century should have explored the dimension of duration through repetition, against which the temporality of apocalypse assumed a renewed meaning. From Henri Dutilleux to Philip Glass, from Marjan Mozetich to R. Murray Schafer, from Pierre Soulages to Jean-Paul Riopelle, from Gertrude Stein to Samuel Beckett, repetition has affected the composition of musical scores, the design of serigraphs and paintings, and the sequence of words at a time when the teleological and transcendental temporality of Christianity has long ceased to define the dominant nomos of Western society. Ravel's *Bolero* (1928) ushered in a modern world in which repetition was destined to reach the heights of aesthetic sublimity but also to incarnate the deadening effects of mechanization, the reproduction of commodities on a global scale, the systematized depletion of planetary resources, and the nightmare of the industrialized and rationalized extermination of human beings in Nazi concentration camps.

In the century of repetition – industrial, social, artistic, consumerist – Butler's theory of performativity can be partly designated as a study of the temporality of social domination or of the way in which this domination is born out of discursive reiteration, which effects social norms charged with political authority and social legitimacy. For instance, if "'sex' is assumed in the same way that a law is cited, then the 'law of sex' is repeatedly fortified and idealized as the law only to the extent that it is ideal, by the very citations it is said to command. … The law is no longer given in a fixed form *prior* to its citation, but is produced through citation as that which precedes and exceeds the mortal approximations enacted by the subject."[23] This implies that the conception of the social nomos in timeless terms indicates either a subscription to the mythic notion of transcendental concepts outside the social and temporal world or a deliberate strategy to obscure the historical and contingent origin of this nomos. Just as the body is the incarnation of principles that do not take effect until they are fleshed out, so reiteration is the process by which this social normative meaning is legitimized. Thus, "performativity is not a singular act, but a repetition and a ritual, which achieves its effects through its naturalization in the context of a body, understood, in part, as a culturally sustained temporal duration."[24] In stating that gender identity can be understood as a process whose "repetition is at once a reenactment and reexperiencing of a set of meanings already socially established … [a] mundane and ritualized form of their legitimation,"[25] Butler provides a definition of social performativity that has similarities with Bourdieu's concept of habitus. Habitus is based on the notion that principles of social organization do not acquire legitimate meaning until they are materialized through social practices and structures, which social agents experience and re-inscribe through their bodies and in time. Crucial to this process of social poiesis is a temporality of social reproduction, which characterizes the basic repetitive process attending the constitution of social agents, who shape and are shaped by different social fields.

In Bourdieu's theoretical account of the social agent, habitus plays a pivotal role and can be best described as the incarnation of specific social structures and their history. On it depends the congruence of the principles of interpretation of the social world and the social structures within which practices materialize these interpretive principles. Bourdieu defines *habitus* in the following terms: "Every field is the institutionalization of a point of view in things and in habitus. The specific habitus, which is demanded of the new entrants as a condition of entry, is nothing other than a specific mode of thought (an *eidos*), the principle of a specific construction of reality, grounded in a prereflexive belief in the undisputed value of the instruments of construction and the objects thus constructed (an *ethos*)."[26] The individual as habitus is characterized by elements such as social origin, educational principles, and qualifications, which combine to make the individual fit in a particular field and subscribe to its social doxa. Education takes place in pedagogical institutions but also begins within the site of the family. To this extent, family culture participates in the production of habitus and determines in what way children will be able to inherit and perform in the different types of social, educational, and professional habitus. But whether we are dealing with values and beliefs in family sites or in pedagogical institutions, the acquisition of these values and beliefs results from a repeated inculcation socializing and habituating the biological body through *hexis*.

> Body *hexis* speaks directly to the motor function, in the form of a pattern of postures that is both individual and systematic, because linked to a whole system of techniques involving the body and tools, and charged with a host of social meanings and values: in all societies, children are primarily attentive to gestures and postures which, in their eyes, express everything that goes to make an accomplished adult – a way of walking, a tilt of the head, facial expressions, ways of sitting and of using implements, always associated with a tone of voice, a style of speech, and (how could it be otherwise?) a certain subjective experience. ... Bodily *hexis* is political mythology realized, *em-bodied*, turned into a permanent disposition, a durable manner of standing, speaking, and thereby of *feeling* and *thinking*.[27]

In addition, the history of a particular cultural field rests on the transmission of habitus, or organizing principles of the field from the past to the future. In other words, the legitimacy of a particular social field is ensured continuity by the temporalization of its principles and practices to which the individual adheres through repeated exposure. The individual anticipates and apprehends this world in the mode of these principles and thereby ensures its social and political reproduction.

In conceptualizing the habitus as being "grounded in a prereflexive belief in the undisputed value of the instruments of construction and the objects thus constructed," Bourdieu exposes himself to the charge that his vision of human beings reduces them to puppetry and that his account of domination through social reproduction ensures that such reproduction is ineluctable.[28] At the same time, the strength of his account lies in his (perhaps self-reflexive) analysis of the relationship between desire and power. Indeed, the force of habitus derives from the role of affect in the process of social reproduction, which is predicated on the social agent's desire "to be part of," "to exercise membership in, "to be legit" – in sum, the desire for recognition. In his comparative analysis of Bourdieu's and Butler's theories of social power, Terry Lovell argues that Bourdieu's "reflexive sociology does not include any critical links between the habitual self and the unconscious, in which the psychic life of power takes root."[29] And yet, in Bourdieu's thinking, habitus is a manifestation of desire whose fulfilment is premised on a psychological process of misrecognition and *illusion*. "Habitus as a system of dispositions to be and to do is a potentiality, a desire to be which, in a certain way, seeks to create the conditions of its fulfilment, and therefore to create the conditions most favourable to what it is."[30] Habitus can therefore be grasped as a concept upon which converge three temporalities: the time of repetition, which enlists the biological body through everyday practices of life; the time of desire, which habituates the agent to social forms of recognition; and the time of history, which the social agent fashions through different types of habitus.

In other words, Bourdieu's theory of domination combines desire with a poiesis of normative reproduction through social rituals that rely on a psychosocial dependency on the other for recognition. Specifically, the legitimacy of social being requires rites of passage that confer status on the social agent. Rituals such as professional promotion, school graduation, marriage, the launching of new products, children's birthday parties, the inauguration of an institution, the institutional and economic bestowing of status on social agents in various playing fields are the sites of public performance validating the values associated with the different cultural fields to which the social subject presumably assents and with which other subjects are eager to identify.

This conjunction of ritualistic repetition, affective adherence to forms of recognition, and the historical reproduction of social norms and structures can be seen at play in the institution of the law. Legal writers such as Ngaire Naffine and Duncan Kennedy have produced various analyses of the habitus of the law.[31] According to Naffine, "only like-minded types are admitted, and dissenting, critical voices are discouraged. The result is a common intellectual outlook, a 'unity of legal thought' in which barristers and judges are actually likely to make similar decisions using similar reasoning."[32] As for Kennedy, his critique points to a paradox whereby law students' selection of their field of legal practice according to their social origins reflects a social and political consciousness, which, however, does not upset the structures, practices, and nomos of the law.[33] In other words, Naffine and Kennedy pause on the dynamic of the same to describe the way legal actors maintain cohesiveness. This logic of the same, it seems to me, speaks to a desire to make one with the law as institution and social mirror of identification.[34]

But one can detect the force of desire in the legal habitus by pausing on law's ritualistic use of language. On the one hand, law has traditionally presented itself as an exercise of impartiality and reasoning through a case with reference to established codification and past decisions. On the other, Peter Goodrich identifies two major rhetorical traits of law: one is a reliance on apology, whose function is to defend the law. As such, the legal apologist resorts to praise as a discourse of affect. "The apology is the defining discourse of community, and so its positive characteristics lie in identifying, most often in eulogistic terms, the authorities, axioms, and other unities and longevities of the tradition."[35] The other major rhetorical trait of law is antirrhesis, a combative discourse that supports the rhetoric of apology by creating the figure of the enemy threatening the values of the community.[36] In establishing a discourse that excludes outsiders, iconoclasts, and radical critics, the antirrhetic functions as the doxological discourse of Bourdieu's description, which seeks to thwart heretical discourse or at the very least to maintain orthodoxy. The force of this double discourse of eulogy and exclusion derives from its ritualistic repetition in the institution of the law, a process of legitimacy and recognition that takes the path of social desire through identification with norms of doing and saying things in the field of law.[37]

In other words, the path of social power is the path of affect whenever it is enlisted in a desire for social recognition. On this, Bourdieu's and Butler's thoughts converge to the extent that they maintain that, while the norm has to be social, institutional, linguistic, and structural, it cannot perform as long as it is not fleshed out and identified with. It is equally clear that they subscribe to the principle that the social subject fully participates in social rituals of adherence by defining themselves in complicity with social norms, discursive practices, and structures. Drawing on Foucault's principle that power is not only subordinating but also constitutive, while diverging from his critique of the Freudian repressive hypothesis, Butler argues that the child's psychic and social persistence is predicated on an inevitable process of dependency and attachment over which the child has no mastery and on whose partial denial depends the emergence of the subject.[38] The effect of this foundational process of coming into being through love of the other is to make the psychic political and politics psychic. "The situation of primary dependency conditions the political formation and regulation of subjects and becomes the means of their subjection. If there is no formation of the subject without a passionate attachment to those by whom she or he is subordinated, then subordination proves central to the becoming of the subject."[39] What Butler proposes here is an ontology whereby desire, normative subordination, and the poiesis of social identity are entangled from the start.

However, it is also the same notion of subjugation through adherence to terms of normativity that leads Butler and Bourdieu to diverge in their reflection on the relation between the exercise of power and resistance to it. While for Bourdieu social and political resistance lies in our self-reflexive ability to see through the subterfuges of dominant sociodicy, unveil the epistemic unconscious of social fields, and resist the lures of *illusio*, for Butler our ontological state of vulnerability, which is all at once political and psychic, is also a resource for social resistance and agency. Of the two, Butler provides a more operative account of desire in constituting oneself as a social subject, which does not become narrowed to the calculation of the ratio between hopes and social probabilities, *illusio* and *lusiones* – to use Bourdieu's own terms of analysis – and which, beyond the logic of non-contradiction, can equally function as a factor of agency. In other words, Butler's conception of power and agency is governed by a logic of ambivalence, which suggests that the meaning of normative utterances, social performative practices, and institutional structures is not absolute and never guaranteed; instead, their significance remains subject to sociopolitical contexts and social agents' capacity to reinterpret beliefs and principles while performing according to them.

Butler invokes the principle of citation to account for the subject's negotiations with social norms. Thus, the "forming, bearing, circulation, signification of [the] sexed body will not be a set of actions performed in compliance with the law; on the contrary, they will be a set of actions mobilized by the law, the citational accumulation and dissimulation of the law that produces material effects, the lived necessity of those effects as well as the lived contestation of that necessity."[40] While she concurs with Bourdieu on the strategies of dissimulation characterizing the institution of dominant norms, her principle of normative citation as a device of social performance allows for the conception of a *gap* between the norm and the act, between social rules and the subject's practices. When she states that the sexed body is constituted of "actions mobilized by the law," Butler reactivates the Latin etymology of the word *cite*, which means "to move, excite, summon ... to set in motion, call."[41] It is this very act of mobilization that allows us to think of the social subject as capable of countering and deviating from normative summons through a poietic process of citation, reinterpretation, and appropriation. To this extent, the citation of social norms through social practices shares with artistic and literary intertextuality a creative dimension, whereby new ways of telling the world, oneself, and our relation to others are made possible.

The linchpin in this scenario is the body, which functions like a paradox: a body that speaks but that is also in excess of language and norms while constituted through them. The occasion for resistance is located not outside cultural and discursive norms but at the hinge of normativity and the body. Resistance depends for its enactment on a dislocation of meaning and engagement with social poiesis, which are made possible by the fundamentally unstable and ambivalent nature of symbolic activity and the practices and structures deriving from it. This existential, as opposed to transcendental, logic of ambivalence and non-contradiction will be crucial to my argument in chapter 4, where I explore what I call the political uncanny as a sign of delegitimation through a comparative analysis of Butler's and Bourdieu's theories of normative abjection and symbolic violence from the standpoint of Freud's notion of the uncanny. However, my immediate concern is to explore the ways in which, in the process of social poiesis, the law as a social institution defines its own terms of legitimacy and its authority to legitimize and regularize the social world. If, as argued in this and the previous chapter, symbolic power consists in poietic processes of materialization in various social fields with a view to claiming legitimacy for the principles governing these fields, then what differentiates this type of legitimacy from the legitimacy that the law authorizes and confers?

Chapter Three

Law's Symbolic Power to Legitimize

The question of law's ability to legitimize normative configurations of the social world abuts on the broader question of what constitutes law's singularity. If, as maintained in the previous two chapters, the process of legitimizing and constituting the world ontologically characterizes the political and social organization of the polis, the naming of identities and social relations, and social governance through practices and structures, what distinguishes this process of social poiesis from law's ability to legitimize and authorize social normativity? At the centre of the problem is the specific relationship between law's prerogative to make binding decisions and the performativity of its symbolic power in the polis.

The question of law's identity is a recurrent topos in the history of jurisprudence. At stake is an exercise not so much in typology and nomenclature as in establishing the relationship between law's sovereign authority and the effects of its symbolic power on the polis, which is itself characterized by historical transformation and normative plurality. Traditionally, the authority of the law has been predicated on its self-sufficiency and its institutional separation from broader cultural and political practices. Peter Goodrich offers a critique of this definition of the law, identifying its historical origins.

> The legal institution itself has maintained a virtually uninterrupted doctrinal belief in the distinctiveness of the law, a belief in its unity and its separation from other phenomena of social control. ... [The] "essence" or unifying feature of law has been variable in its content but relatively constant in its form: the formal unity of law has traditionally been based upon its derivation from an absolute source or origin. ... The divine origin

> of law becomes the secular sovereign, the State or even the "will of the people," but as a source of law it retains its equality as an external and absolute justification for legal regulation, discipline and law. This external, non-legal, legitimation of the legal order provides the law with its ideational unity and renders the wide spectrum of substantive legal rules into a "system" of rules.[1]

The divine origin of the word functioned as a means of justification and self-containment. In secularized cultures, the removal of this divine authority from the unlimited production of texts may be conceived as something excessive and threatening, unbounded by the absence of an alpha and omega. Thus, specific to twentieth-century and contemporary exegesis is a proliferation of legal statements not securely sanctified by the mythic authority of the originary text or author. This results in a conflict between the liberating effect of a discourse no longer framed in transcendental terms and the persisting conception of the law as authoritative producer of norms and rules, between the free play of normative and cultural differences and the anthropological establishing of boundaries along stable and defined terms of meaning.

Given Goodrich's critique, is the endeavour to define the identity of the law an impertinent exercise, or are there social and political reasons for pursuing the question? Does the endeavour necessarily undermine what Nicola Lacey refers to as "a general commitment to theorizing law as a *social* phenomenon,"[2] or what Rosie Harding construes as the decentering of the law, whereby law constitutes and is constituted by everyday life practices?[3] Or does the possibility exist of pondering the question beyond the divide between analytical jurisprudence and materialist approaches, such as legal consciousness studies? Granted that the supremacy of the law does not derive from a transcendental status, how do we address the implicit or explicit expectation that the performative effect of compliance with a legal statement remains a specific attribute of the law? Granted that law's authority is metaleptic – that performing socially according to its edicts constitutes its institutional authority – does this aspect of the law preclude one from asking whether its identity as performative and binding authority is worth investigating and framing from a conceptual and practical standpoint? The problem revolves not so much around the notion of an essence that would make law a supreme means of legitimacy as around the following questions. First, what is instrumentally specific to the law that enables it to legitimize and regulate cultural norms of being, doing things, and organizing structures and relations? Second, what are the implications of such capacity in law's relationship to the symbolic process of social poiesis?

Historically, Hans Kelsen's and H.L.A. Hart's philosophical investigations of the law constituted a major departure from John Austin's conception of legal command as the manifestation of the sovereign's power. They crossed over into a semantic field by establishing the law as a system of principles and rules conceived as social signs rather than natural attributes whose essence remains to be determined. Kelsen's premise is that the law remains a coercive system but that a rational construct of the law is our best shield against political tyranny and moral contingencies. He states his normative approach as follows: "What makes ... an event a legal (or an illegal) act is not its facticity, nor its being natural, that is governed by causal laws and included in the system of nature. Rather, what makes such an event a legal act is its meaning, the objective sense that attaches to the act. The specifically legal sense of the event in question, its own peculiarly legal meaning, comes by way of a norm whose content refers to the event and legal meaning of it; the act can be interpreted, then, according to this norm. The norm functions as a scheme of interpretation."[4] His theory of a formidably self-contained legal system anchored in a foundational (*Grund*) norm has been submitted to criticism for its indifference to the social aspect of the law;[5] at the same time, however, it can be read as an attempt to sanction and justify the coercive legal power of the state and the legitimacy of the law on the basis of reason. To this extent, Kelsen's philosophy can be regarded as a strategy to deflect the usurping and arbitrary effects of a naturalized conception and practice of the law.[6]

In his rereading of Austin's attempt to establish what law is, Hart's theory inaugurates a definition of law as a means of constituting social reality according to the basic principle of compliance, with rules functioning as signs of legitimacy both for citizens and for practitioners in the legal institution. In other words, legal positivists such as Hart have enacted a constructivist turn in the history of jurisprudence even though a consideration of the historical, cultural, and political dimension of law as a construct was not their main concern.[7] This constructivist turn is signalled by the recurrence of the term *norm* in different theoretical writings, which philosophers of law use to designate the rules specific to the law as a regulating and rational system. In this context, the question of command and obedience remains a major preoccupation, but is now translated into normative terms, so that the legal specificity of these norms of compliance becomes the object of the investigation. This approach is succinctly exemplified by Tony Honoré's definitional model to regulate a social group. "[The] capacity to inflict grave sanctions or similar measures should feature in any accurate definition of law. ... One [criterion of definition] is the capacity of the group which possesses a legal system to inflict grave sanctions or similar measures on those who violate its norms, even when other groups compete with it for allegiance. The other [criterion] is effectiveness: the fact that the bulk of its members habitually conform to the legal norms."[8] Recurrent through these different analyses is the assumption that the law exercises a supreme type of power insofar as it commands obedience that is irreducible to challenge and insofar as it provides the means of establishing congruence between word and deed.

It is also clear that in devising primary rules of recognition and secondary rules regulating the modification and creation of laws, Hart is proposing a meta-legal reflection on practices of legal authority to legitimize social norms and exact compliance. For Hart, obedience to the law is not an unconscious habitual act, but an act of rational consciousness, which functions as the best insurance against law's tyranny. "Where ... a [legal] rule is accepted [the legislator] will not only in fact specify what is to be done but will have the *right* to do this; and not only will there be general obedience to his orders, but it will be generally accepted that it is *right* to obey him. [The legislator] will in fact be a legislator with the *authority* to legislate, i.e. to introduce new standards of behaviour into the life of the group, and there is no reason, since we are concerned with standards, not 'orders,' why he should not be bound by his own legislation."[9] Hart proposes a rational systematization of legal command and obedience, placing his faith in the capacity of reason to create conceptual grounds for justice, authority, and legitimacy.[10]

The constructivist implications of modern analytical legal philosophy are brought out by Joseph Raz's distinction between a normative utterance and adherence to such an utterance. In his influential *The Authority of Law*, published in 1979 and re-edited in 2009, Raz maintains that a legal theorist or a lawyer teaching students may present legal claims without necessarily agreeing with their content.[11] From an institutional standpoint, the same distinction obtains in the presence of "institutions with power to determine the normative situation of specified individuals, which are required to exercise these powers by applying existing norms, but whose decisions are binding even when wrong."[12] Where Butler points to the gaps generated by normative citation and social performativity to reveal the contingent aspect of sociocultural systems, Raz draws on the gaps between normative utterance and normative adherence to signal the authoritative character of the law.

Kelsen's, Hart's, and Raz's inquiries into what constitutes the law developed at a time when in other legal and theoretical quarters writers established a virulent critique of the traditional notion that the law is autopoietic and self-contained. A traditional critique of Hart's distinction between what law is and what law ought to be emanates from thinkers such as Lon Fuller, who in the aftermath of the Nazi regime maintained that the dream of severing law from moral principles failed to distinguish between legal order and good legal order. In addition, schools of thought such as critical legal studies, feminist legal criticism and theory, and the cultural study of the law have endeavoured to demonstrate that the claim of law's self-sufficiency and self-containment is untenable.

However, that law's identity remains a live question is illustrated by statements in which legal thinkers dissociate themselves from positivist tenets on the topic, yet propose direct or indirect analyses of the specificity of the law. For instance, J. Peter Burgess argues against the autopoietic status of the law and asserts instead a homology between law and culture, whereby the concept of nomos as naming and legitimating is common to all cultural fields.[13] He further maintains that the law can never be self-legitimizing because, far from establishing itself *ex nihilo*, it always rests on a cultural system of values. This analysis does not shun the question of law's identity; instead, it reads like a veiled definition that seeks to bring forth law's cultural and social dimensions.

Similarly, Desmond Manderson and Richard Mohr, who cannot be faulted for having a positivist conception of the law, nonetheless assume that there *is* such a thing as a law that can accommodate diversity. Their conception is ethical in that they define law in terms of legal concerns for social justice and moral responsibility, but their position is also located beyond the natural theory of law to the extent that ethical law ought to accommodate different social perspectives and practices in a social group. Their position is exemplified by the following:

> Like scholarly research, although through quite different methods, that is one of its own normative foundations. A form of legal action which could recognise a diversity of interests may be more than a means, and instead be involved in debates over worthwhile outcomes. The name we give to a practice which is understood and accordingly *limited* by reference to its

> ultimate social ends, is ethics. An ethics of law comprehends legal argument as a way of helping us to distinguish between alternative outcomes (*phronesis*, or prudence) rather than simply dictate the shortest route to a predetermined goal (*techne*).[14]

Whether we agree with this assignation to law, the point is that Manderson and Mohr's subscription to an ethical cultivation of prudence enabling legal practitioners to recognize and act upon a diversity of interests indicates that they ascribe a specific character to the law. Or consider Roberto Mangabeira Unger, who in his distinction between the law as legal formalism and the law as substantive justice assumes the existence of a procedure specific to the law that renders its decisions justified. In the former case, the law addresses the problem of the relativism of values by resorting to rules as a means of superseding conflicts of interests and values. Only rule-based decisions are held to be valid and to guarantee freedom. In the latter case, "each [legal] decision is justified because it is one best calculated to advance some accepted objective. The relation between a particular decision and the objective is that of a means to an end."[15] For Unger, it follows that the defining characteristic of the law consists in its use of pragmatic rationality to achieve social ends without presumptive resort to a pre-established set of rules or legal doctrine.

Thus, whether they seek to establish the authority of the law or criticize it as a source of political and social coercion, most modern theorists of the law address the power that the law derives from the performative effects of its utterances and procedures, which are deemed to have supreme authority over other statements.[16] As argued in chapter 1, the ability to legitimize and regulate is not unique to the law and, therefore, does not constitute its specificity, but the type of performative power the law wields does. This is why the attempt to define the identity of the law is neither an armchair exercise nor a sign of conservative thinking. Nor are the open-endedness of language and the opacity of subjectivity reasons for not considering the ways in which the law differs from other fields, particularly with regard to its specific use of language. The notion that normative and discursive systems cannot aspire to a stable and originary meaning because, as Butler argues, there exists a performative gap between norms and their social deployment does not stand in the way of an examination of law's identity and the role of its performatives in social poiesis. In fact, it is precisely because language, which is a major tool of the law, produces meaning in a historical state of transformation that the political and social question of the identity of the law and its authoritative utterances of legitimacy acquire renewed significance. The elucidation of what constitutes law's specificity in Western culture can begin with an analysis of its *jurisdiction* – that is, its capacity to say (*dicere*) the law (*juris*) by means of performatives.

Jack Balkin and Sanford Levinson address the performative function of the law by arguing that acts of interpretation, be they literary or legal, constitute performative acts of power and that institutional compliance with legal norms through such performative utterances is the norm, not the exception, of interpretive processes in general. In particular, legal, musical, and literary interpretive processes share the same relationship of command between signs and performance.

> What is a musical score but a series of directions concerning tempo, meter, pitch, rhythm, attack, and orchestration that are to be carried out over time by a group of performers? To be sure, the skilled musician can read a score like the ordinary person can read a novel, but this is not normally the way either enjoys music. Rather, one listens to the result of the commands brought to life by the performers so instructed. ... Far closer to the musical score is the play, which includes both the lines to be spoken by actors and the relevant stage directions. ... Most people would agree that the artistic expression in a play is not fully realized except through its performance on the stage. Dramatic genres thus undermine the distinction between interpretation of artistic expression and interpretation of command, for a play's artistic interpretation requires interpretation and observance of commands.[17]

This analysis of the performative power of the law strives to establish a tension between the interpellation of a score, a poem, or a play and the respondent's scope for interpretation. The objective is to provide an analogy for the tension at work in legal interpretations of established rules and decisions. However, their account remains tangential to the performative effects of legal interpretation, partly because the analogy between the audience of a play or a symphony and the addressees of the law is bound to collapse. Indeed, the major difference between such an audience and addressees of legal decisions is that, in the latter case, the act of interpretation is overdetermined by the injunction to comply and obey, which the principle of the rule of law prescribes. The specific power to make decisions binding according to the rule of law transforms a legal interpretation and decision into an exclusive normative script for social performance as compliance. This relation between the interpretation of and compliance with the text of the law determines two levels of legal performance: legal practitioners prepare and adjudicate cases by filtering social situations through various texts with a view to having their interpretation gain force of law; and the addressees of the laws – citizens and corporations – are hailed by the injunction to comply with the legal terms of interpretation of their social situations. In both cases, the objective is to prepare the ground for congruence between utterances and their performative, material, and compulsory effects.

In the case of literary reception, the reader interprets the fictional text but is not summoned to act upon the result of the interpretive process, let alone comply with the cultural norms of a narrative. In fact, some have shown a long time ago that to do so would lead one to fight Quixotic windmills. While the literary text has a performative effect on readers, it is not one of absolute command or mere compliance, even in the case of didactic literature. For this reason, Robin West rejects a mere analogy between law and literature. "Adjudication is in form interpretive, but in substance it is an exercise of power in a way that truly interpretive acts, such as literary interpretation, are not."[18] Either the reader's act of interpretation gives credit to dominant social norms mediated by the fictional text; or/and the text produces a heretic discourse, which the reader may reject or which the reader may appropriate for its subversive capacity. In this respect, the reader's response determines the authority of the text by recognizing the legitimacy of the fictional representation. This dynamic of textual authority and reader's response through performative interpretation is absent from the relation between legal texts and subjects of the law. The latter have no choice but to comply with the legal statement and thereby to acknowledge and reinforce the authority of the legal utterance, be it oral or written. If the legal subject does not comply – that is to say, if the subject acts upon a different interpretation of the normative judgment – the subject is automatically banned and relegated to an illegitimate position.

Therefore, the tasks of establishing institutional authority, justifying processes of interpretation and adjudication with performative effects through the use of words (whether we are dealing with statutory texts, precedents, legal opinions, or plea bargaining), and exacting certain outcomes can be said to be specific to the law as an institutional structure and discourse, which constitute and regulate identities, relationships, and practices in the social world. The cost of the legal word and, by implication, of the heretic stand against the doxa of the legal word, is that which distinguishes it from the literary and other words. In this context, Ronald Dworkin's attempt to justify the authority of the law by establishing an analogy between literary narration and the authorship of the law through fidelity to past decisions lacks persuasion. He argues that

> [a judge] knows that other judges have decided cases that, although not exactly like his case, deal with related problems; he must think of their decisions as part of a long story he must interpret and then continue, according to his own judgment of how to make the developing story as good as it can be. ... The judge's decision – his post interpretive conclusions – must be drawn from an interpretation that both fits and justifies what has gone before, so far as is possible. But in law as in literature the interplay between fit and justification is complex. Just as interpretation within a chain novel is for each interpreter a delicate balance among different types of literary and artistic attitudes, so in law it is a delicate balance among political convictions of different sorts; in law as in literature these must be sufficiently related yet disjoint to allow an overall judgment that trades off an interpretation's success on one type of standard against its failure on another.[19]

Although there are generic norms in literature and the arts in general, and although writers such as Aristotle, Pierre Corneille, and Samuel Johnson strove to establish the statutes of literature and playwriting, it is doubtful that literary texts have ever coincided with those statutes, and there is no doubt that a great number of literary texts have made a point of referring to generic and narrative norms in order to flout, transform, and experiment with them.

So, rather than a process of fitting and justification, the production and interpretation of literature are better understood as a process of citation, recreation through intertextual references, subversion through normative parody, and innovation through generic hybridization. Where Dworkin seeks to secure a sense of legal coherence and completeness through a normative approach to the texts of the law, actual practices of literary production point to patterns of generic displacement and strutting infidelity to tradition. In fact, his analogy – whose gender deictic speaks to a traditional conception of the author derived from a male, monotheistic culture – derives from a juridical conception of the literary process of interpretation and creativity by making the observance of generic rules a process of compliance, which is expected to have the performative effect of producing legal coherence and authority.[20]

In order to avoid the pitfalls of the analogy between law and literature, which in the above examples tends to reduce one to the other, often at the cost of legalizing literary practices, we need to reconsider the two practices in the context of a common social poiesis that configures social normativity. This common capacity for normative configuration and performative effects of legitimacy indicates that neither literature nor law is self-contained and that they are both involved with the cultural sphere as a whole through rhetorical appropriation of linguistic practices from other social fields. I propose to illustrate my point by reconsidering Carol Smart's Foucaultian critique of law's discursive power. Smart identifies what she regards as law's rhetorical strategies of appropriation through legal categorizations.

> On hearing the client's story, the solicitor sifts it through a sieve of legal knowledge and formulations. Most of the story will be chaff as far as the lawyer is concerned, no matter how significant the rejected elements are to the client. ... The legal version becomes the only valid one. The barrister and the judge may then proceed to the stages of interpreting legal texts in order to reach the correct legal decision on each individual case. Of course, most cases never go this far and many individual practitioners fall short of this 'ideal.' However, the system is constantly reproduced each time legal advice is sought.[21]

Smart's analysis of the law as an autonomous field presents similarities with Gunther Teubner's thesis that the law functions as an autopoietic system, which like any other such system is open to other means of symbolization, communication, and implementation, but which retains its specificity by translating other systems of communication into its own terms for its own purposes. However, Smart conceptualizes the relationship between law and social fields in terms of a power dynamic, whereby the law establishes its authority by absorbing discursive knowledge and practices that are external to its own field. While Teubner regards this process as common to all cultural fields, and in fact determinant of the capacity of the fields to function and persist, for Smart law's discursive translation is a sign of institutional cannibalism. Uncovering the metaleptic effect underlying the autarchic conception of law, she argues that it derives its authority not so much from an intrinsic status as from the performative effects of its practices of absorbing and regulating other social discourses.

However, the capacity to assimilate and graft on other social discourses is not unique to the law, as can be observed in literature, among other symbolic and cognitive fields. Bakhtin has shown that the dialogical imagination is apt to absorb other symbolic representations and fields of knowledge: it can absorb the Darwinian scientific field of palaeontology, as in John Fowles's *The French Lieutenant's Woman* (1969); the nineteenth-century evolving field of medicine and hygiene, as in Patricia Duncker's *James Miranda Barry* (1999); corporate culture, as in Julian Barnes's *England, England* (1998); the culture of jazz, as in Jackie Kay's *Trumpet* (1998); historiography and sociology, as in Rose Tremain's *Music and Silence* (1999); sociocultural practices and the use of language in subcultures, as in Irvine Welsh's *Trainspotting* (1993); the aesthetic and religious discourses of Renaissance Florence, as in Sarah Dunant's *The Birth of Venus* (2003) – and, in the process of representation, this dialogic imagination mines and mimics these fields, their discourses, habitus, and practices. In all cases, the symbolic power of literature functions as a means of citation and reproduction, oscillating somewhere between realism and pastiche. Like the law, literature creates a vast social process of performative interpretation operating according to social systems of normativity and communication, while filtering them through generic and rhetorical conventions specific to its field. This indicates that if both law and literature engage in various practices of discursive appropriations, law's power effects do not necessarily derive from these practices. Instead, these effects derive from discursive appropriations within an institutional context that ascribes a different kind of symbolic power to such appropriations. It is on this basis that I would like to reconsider the jurisprudential debate concerning the specificity of the law by bringing to the fore what I see as the nexus among law, its institutional singularity, and its legitimizing of social poiesis.

For Joseph Raz, law is open to social values, yet its singularity lies in its ability to use reasons for command and compliance that exclude any other reason. The specificity, or what he also names the "inherent virtue of law,"[22] lies in the fact that "courts have power to make an authoritative determination of people's legal situation. Private individuals may express their opinion on the subject but their views are not binding."[23] Justice cannot be done if the institution of the law does not have the authority to prevail over other types of reasoning and positions. Thus, "conformity to the rule of law," Raz argues, "is an inherent value of laws, indeed it is their most important inherent value. It is of the essence of law to guide behaviour through rules and courts in charge of their application. Therefore, the rule of law is the specific excellence of the law."[24] In selecting the rule of law as a defining criterion, Raz singles out the way in which through binding utterances the law legitimizes citizens and practices.[25]

If conformity to the rule of law is an inherent character of the law, it is inherent insofar as citizens – both practitioners and those affected by the law – conform with legal norms, which in themselves have no value whatsoever as long as they are not mobilized by the law and are complied with by citizens. In other words, and drawing on Butler's distinction between the psyche and the subject, the rule of law creates the legal subject "as a linguistic category, a place-holder, a structure in formation."[26] Citizens enjoy legal intelligibility and legitimacy insofar as they are established through the discursive norms of the law, whose performative effects are *specifically* ensured by the rule of law. If, as Bourdieu argues, the autonomy of social fields derives from their creation of objects according to modes of knowledge that provide principles of understanding of these objects, then law's autonomy derives from its doctrinal point of view, most conspicuous in the principle of the rule of law, which creates the citizen (or any other entity, for that matter) as the object of its knowledge, perspective, language, and regulation.

Specific to the identity of the law is the principle that its performativity will be sealed with supreme social authority. To borrow from Butler on political discourse, within legal performative discourse, the real is a syntactically regulated phantasm that has enormous power and efficacy over all other social fields. On this basis, it is tempting to jump to the conclusion that the principle that law operates according to the rule of compliance is synonymous with law's coercive effects. In fact, this constitutes Bourdieu's major charge against the law. "As the quintessential form of legitimized discourse, the law can exercise its specific power only to the extent that it attains recognition, that is, to the extent that the element of arbitrariness at the heart of its functioning (which may vary from case to case) remains unrecognized. The tacit grant of *faith* in the juridical order must be ceaselessly reproduced."[27] However, I suggest that the relationship between the sovereignty of the law and the coercive effects of its symbolic power needs to be reconsidered in light of the fact that the binding principle of the rule of law is invoked by antinomic legal discourses, be they conservative, critical, or radical.

This seems to indicate that the coercive effects of the law exceed the rule of law as that which constitutes its specificity.

That the subscription to the rule of law and the expectation it creates are not necessarily the exclusive sign of conservatism is exemplified by the discourse unfolding in the six judicial reviews produced by the Women's Court of Canada, in which academic legal thinkers responded to six cases adjudicated by the Supreme Court of Canada by generating dissenting types of decision.[28] Their endorsement of the rule of law presents a complex socio-legal phenomenon. This complexity derives from the fact that while the six reviews clearly challenge the sacrosanct principle that the judgments of the Supreme Court are without appeal and supremely binding, their challenge to the court's supreme authority nevertheless operates on the implicit assumption that justice can be rendered only as long as the rule of law is honoured.

This implicit endorsement of the rule of law is exemplified in a statement made by Gwen Brodsky et al. while reviewing *Gosselin v. Québec (Attorney General)*, in which the Supreme Court ruled that the reduction of financial assistance to unemployed youth did not constitute an infringement on their rights and liberties. To counter this judgment, the authors of the judicial review invoke section 1 of the Canadian Charter of Rights and Freedoms and make the following statement:

> A robust exploration of the idea that section 15 has an irreducible core has been rendered necessary by the propensity of courts to fail to perceive the operation of stereotypical thinking when it is systemic and applied to society's most disadvantaged groups and the license that governments believe they have to erode social programs and to respond to successful equality rights challenges by equalizing downwards. Vulnerable Canadians need the guardians of their section 15 equality rights to tell governments that there are some benefits and protections that are so essential to the inherent equality of the person that there is a constitutional obligation on governments to provide them and to ensure their adequacy. A subsistence income adequate enough to ensure access to food, clothing, and housing is such a benefit.[29]

The notions that section 15 has an irreducible core, that it functions as a guardian of equality rights, and that there is a constitutional obligation to provide social benefits that ensure equitable treatment – these three notions have no performative import unless the authors of this statement place their faith in the rule of law and its legal, material, economic, and political effects. This further implies that, in their view, the rule of law is not so much concerned with the power of the sovereign in the Austinian sense of the term as with the guarantee of certain values conceived as rights. The implicit invocation of the rule of law to protect equity rights can also be seen at work in Mary Eberts, Sharon McIvor, and Teressa Nahanee's review of *Native Women's Association of Canada v. Canada.* Their strategy is to refer to principles entrenched in case law – such as the principle of gender equality in Canada's Persons Case (the British Privy Council's affirmative decision was rendered in 1929); the principle of aboriginal representation in section 35.1 of the Constitution Act, 1982;[30] the principle of democratic representation in the final report of the Royal Commission on Electoral Reform and Party Financing, *Reforming Electoral Democracy*;[31] and the principle of the freedom of expression guaranteed in sections 2(b) and 28 of the Charter of Rights and Freedoms[32] – so as to hold these principles to the rule of law. The strategy theoretically implies that these binding principles are not only authoritative but will also have beneficial effects on the lives of aboriginal women in Canada. In this context, inviting representatives from the Native Women's Association of Canada (NWAC) to the negotiating table to participate in constitutional discussions constitutes a materialization of the performative statements by Canadian law.

> Inviting the NWAC to participate provides substantive equality for Aboriginal women, by recognizing their particular interests and experience, including over a century of systemic discrimination against them by the government of Canada. In the *Reference re Electoral Boundaries* case … the Supreme Court of Canada emphasized the need to find substantive effectiveness for the vote rather than formal mathematical parity among voters. … For all these reasons, this court rules that Canada's exclusion of the NWAC from the constitutional talks is a violation of section 15 of the Charter.[33]

According to a chiasmic relationship, the invitation would have mobilized the authority of Canadian law, while through their inclusion Canadian law would have authorized the legitimacy of aboriginal women's self-representation. On the one hand, the authors of the judicial review charge that Canadian law usurped aboriginal women's equity rights by shaving off the performative effects of legal words; on the other, their recommendation to devise remedies that will re-establish the performative effects of these legal words to address specific conditions of inequity speak to a belief in the efficacy of the rule of law.

The relationship between statements by the Women's Court and the principle of the rule of law is made even more complex when one considers that the Women's Court seeks to function within the legal institution – as exemplified by its legal rhetoric, use of precedents, and meting out of judgments – while at the same time it subverts the rule of law by calling into question judgments that are supposed to be beyond the appeal process since they emanate from the Supreme Court. In this sense, the Women's Court institutes itself as a paralegal system, taking justice seriously – to parody a famous title – seriously enough to subvert and challenge binding decisions. By the same token, and from a legal standpoint, their strategies of legitimacy are cut short as they cannot take hold and materialize within institutional law.

Nevertheless, the Women's Court's challenge to the authority of the Supreme Court of Canada raises two useful questions in the elucidation of law's specificity. First, does its rewriting of judgments imply a parody of legal writing and legal decision making? Quite possibly, but the irreverence of mimicry is also known for its transformative potential, as Luce Irigaray argued long ago.[34] Second, does the rewriting imply the dislocation of a legal decision from its supreme and institutional frame? As I stated above, the arguments unfolding in the different rewritings indicate a belief in the rule of law and its capacity to bind decisions based on what the authors deem to be socially equitable decisions. If this were the case, the authors' decision to write within the parameters of judicial writing would indicate that they conceived of their para-judgments as a representation of dissent within the law.[35] The paradoxical position of the Women's Court – in and out – reinforces Raz's jurisprudential point: through its institutional procedures, rules, and practices, the law operates by making decisions that legitimize and authorize norms with binding effects. However, by citing the rhetoric and procedures of the law, these para-judgments function as realistic counterfeits appropriating law's supremacy. In doing so, they reveal that except for the institutional power of the law, the ability to create a discourse of legitimacy that sounds and reads like the law does occur outside the law. The only reason for the law either to reject or ignore these para-judgments is its institutional authority privileging its symbolic power.

Further, with one foot in legal rhetorics and another in legal and political critique, these para-judgments demonstrate that although legal norms constitute the doxa of the separate field of the law, the challenge to legal statements is fundamentally driven by a historicized socio-legal process of resignification that endows legal rules with a meaning originating in a political vision of the social world. In particular, these para-judgments address the challenge posed by Unger when he argued that social values and legal rules are antinomic. "A system of law or rules (legal justice) can neither dispense with a consideration of values in the process of adjudication, nor be made consistent with such a consideration. Moreover, judgments about how to further general values in particular situations (substantive justice) can neither do without rules, nor be made compatible with them. This is the antinomy of rules and values."[36] The symbolic power of the Women's Court derives from its implicit demonstration that the symbolic violence of the law does not originate in its binding sovereignty, but in the nexus between the institutional power to bind and the sociodicy the law legitimizes. If this is the case, then the specificity of the law includes more than the rule of law. Thus, missing from Raz's account is a consideration that legal normativity is yoked to the cultural normativity generated through social poiesis.

While he affirms that the law "claims to provide the general framework for the conduct of all aspects of social life and sets itself up as the supreme guardian of society,"[37] for Raz law's identity and validity derive from its internal system. Thus, "while the direct (i.e. non-systemic) validity of a rule turns on the goals and values which it serves or harms, its legal, systemic validity depends on the fact that it belongs to a given legal system and that it is justified as such."[38] This implies that the social value that the law serves or harms will change, but that the individual court, judge, lawyer, and levels of legislature will expect the binding performatives of the law to remain in place by virtue of the law as system. On this basis, Raz argues that the language of statutory categories functions in a general way that speaks to the stability of the legal word without determining specific outcomes. "Legal categories are resources for legal justificatory argument; they create possibilities but will not definitely exclude any specific desired options. Legal categories will enforce a particular vocabulary and will also provide a particular way of correctly posing and arguing legal questions, but nobody could be expected to read the case reports as in any sense containing mathematically precise formulations of legal rules."[39] Although Raz is correct in pointing to the gaps between legal categories and the performative outcome of legal cases, his assertion that its categories are mere resources for legal justificatory arguments shears off the performative power that these norms carry as vehicles for specific social values and beliefs. His characterization of statutory language and common law categories is in keeping with his ontological focus on the systemic efficacy and authority of the law, but it also emphasizes a partial conception of the performative effects of the rule of law. His strategy to define law's identity occults the complexity of law's double relation to social poiesis.

While Raz focuses on the binding and performative power of the rule of law – its institutional efficacy – as the sign of law's identity, it can be argued that this identity lies more specifically in the interaction between the institutional specificity of the law and the cultural codes that it legitimizes and regulates with authority. For a legal norm is *all at once* the sign of an institutional system of regulations and the assertion of legitimized cultural and social values. Indeed, the sign of the law rests on its referential ambivalence: it functions as an intra-referential sign as it cites its own institutional texts and decisions; and it functions as an exo-referential sign as it refers to norms of being and doing things in the social world with a view to legitimizing and regulating them. It is the interaction between these two codes of reference within the framework of the rule of law that differentiates the law from other systems of legitimacy and performative normativity. In its intentional capacity to legitimize a particular social norm – that is to say, in its performative power to materialize a social norm and to bind its legitimacy, lies law's identity as symbolic power and social practice. This interaction between legal normativity and social normativity – and the historical transformation it potentially engenders – constitutes the double helix of the law in the Western world.

If law operates as a double helix, then we cannot separate the institutional specificity of law from the belief or value content that the law legitimizes through its binding effects. In other words, law's identity does not lie in its systemic form as separate from its value content.[40] The performative power of the rule of law is redoubled by the performative power of discursive beliefs and social norms embedded in social structures and legitimated through reiterated social practices. If legal regulations are contextualized by social, political, moral, or other values at the moment of legislation, then these values – which initially do not have the stamp of the law – are legitimized through institutionalization and acquire legal currency through law's performative supremacy. This means that the power of the law consists in entrenching, legitimizing, and institutionalizing a particular and historical sociodicy, whether the latter is conservative or radical.

If we consider the law as a double helix, whereby it operates to legitimize values and principles as a means of organizing a social world, then the symbolic power of the law interacts with the competition for symbolic power in the social fields that the law regulates. For philosophers of the law such as Raz, conformity and binding capacity characterize the law and provide stability, fairness, and predictability. However, it is this very capacity to enforce and bind that is the central problem because, far from functioning in a vacuum, this capacity will graft on social discourses, practices, and structures that seek to maintain their legitimacy and authority at the expense of other terms of legitimacy. So, while the law's identity is characterized by its supreme and binding authority, it is also characterized by contingency and arbitrariness through its exposure to and interference with historical principles and beliefs, which constitute the particular sociodicy of a particular social group.

In his critique of rational idealism and Hart's conception of the law, Dworkin develops a position indicating that he is aware of the dual nature of law insofar as it combines a legal code with a cultural code, the latter being, in his particular argument, moral. Rather than suppressing cultural normativity from justice as fairness, he asserts that "we cannot understand legal argument and controversy except on the assumption that the truth conditions of propositions of law include moral considerations."[41] His characterization of legal interpretation rests on a similar bifocal conception of the law by distinguishing between the two concepts of justice and law. On the one hand, justice "is a matter of the correct or best theory of moral and political rights, and anyone's conception of justice is his theory, imposed by his own personal convictions, of what these rights actually are. [On the other hand, law] is a matter of which supposed rights supply a justification for using or withholding the collective force of the state because they are included in or implied by actual political decisions of the past."[42] So, while justice is informed by the historical, contingent values to which the legal practitioner may subscribe, law refers to the institutional, autopoietic capacity to build a normative archive and to enact authoritative decisions that will be binding through the rule of law and that will ensure continuity. The truth value of a legal utterance derives from the strength of the legal argument, which must exhaust all possibilities.

In other words, Dworkin singles out instrumental reason in the adjudicative process, and although he does not reach this conclusion, he can also be interpreted as saying that only another legal argument can prove the legal claim to truth false, in which case the truth of the claim lasts as long as it has not been disproved, thereby leaving room for reconsideration, appeal, and transformation. Hercules, the judge of

Dworkin's legal imagination, remains faithful to this principle of integrity by endeavouring not

> to reach what he believes is the best substantive result, but to find the best justification he can of a past legislative event. He tries to show a piece of social history – the story of a democratically elected legislature enacting a particular text in particular circumstances – in the best light overall, and this means his account must justify the story as a whole, not just its ending. His interpretation must be sensitive, that is, not only to his convictions about justice and wise conservation policy, though these will play a part, but also to his convictions about the ideals of political integrity and fairness and procedural due process as these apply specifically to legislation in a democracy.[43]

Although the judge will filter the social phenomenon through the legal norm, taking into account the prevailing principles of political morality of the moment, the outcome of this process will be determined first and foremost by the necessity to ensure that the present decision will not contravene past legal norms and principles. This necessity is intra-referential and canonical. Its function is to buttress the doxa of the field of law and maintain doctrinal consistency and authority. The objective is to provide a mechanism to ward off excessive or tyrannical uses of the law, while offering the citizenry a stable, predictable, and fair legal institution.[44]

In contrast to Butler's analysis of the inevitable constraints of the past on the endeavour to create new means of social configuration, Dworkin is not merely acknowledging the inheritance of the past; he is also holding up the past as the guarantee of legality, legal authority, and social legitimacy. In advocating the preservation of past legal decisions, he is not making a plea for the preservation of pure, formal norms since he has already argued that legal norms are the carriers of political and moral norms. But if, as he rightly argues, legal norms are also political or moral norms, then they will be the product of historical and social constructs whose ideological import may run right up against the attempt to respond to new social phenomena. Therefore, while acknowledging the double valence of legal norms – their legal and political or moral value – Dworkin does not examine the performativity of legal norms to the full, and he occults from his theory of law the contextual implications of a value-based conception of legal norms. For, if legal norms are also cultural values, then the concept of fit cannot be exclusively applied to legal norms for the sake of legal coherence. The notion that coherence with past legal norms coincides with proper past political or moral values is no guarantee of rights protection because political and moral values will keep evolving in the cultural sphere to which the time capsule of legal archives may remain hermetically closed.[45]

This blind spot in Dworkin's reflection becomes manifest when he argues that law's instances of violence can be reduced to cases of exception. "A full political theory of law ... includes at least two main parts: it speaks both to the *grounds* of law – circumstances in which particular propositions of law should be taken to be sound or true – and to the *force* of law – the relative power of any true proposition of law to justify coercion in different sorts of exceptional circumstance."[46] A conception of legal violence as moments of exception neglects the performative, daily effects of practices governed by social norms – moral and political – that exert symbolic violence in a reiterative mode and with the force of the law. Dworkin's conception of legal violence bypasses what Shoshana Felman has analysed as the law's complicity with a history of collective and individual traumas through its forgetting of the affective circumstances surrounding the judicial decisions taken in the past and that now constitute legal precedents as a basis for future cases. Her conception of precedents as law's unconscious is diametrically opposed to the enlightening and cognitive function that Dworkin attributes to precedents.

> Legal memory is constituted ... not just by the "chain of law" and by the conscious repetition of precedents, but by a forgotten chain of cultural wounds and by compulsive or unconscious legal repetitions of traumatic, wounding legal cases. ... Historically unconscious legal repetitions inadvertently play out in the historical arena the political unconscious of the law. These traumatic repetitions illustrate, therefore, in legal history, the Freudian notion of "a return of the repressed"; in the ghost of the return of a traumatizing legal case, what compulsively, historically returns from the forgotten legal past is the repressed of the judicial institution.[47]

In effect, Felman's conception of the history of the law allows the database of case law to emerge as an archive of feelings and historical injuries that threaten to engender social reproduction and its traumatic repetitions. Although Dworkin develops theoretical principles of justice grounded in social values to address what he regards as the weaknesses of Hart's and Raz's conceptions of law, his belief in the power, integrity, and objectivity of legal argumentation leads him to neglect this collective history of traumas that the presence of social norms in legal reasoning will generate.

Insofar as institutional law *structures* and *is structured by* social practices, identities, and relations, we cannot ignore the sociopolitical tenor of legal decisions while considering law's identity. This implies that there is no clean distinction between law and justice, archival autopoiesis and practices. On the one hand, through renewed practices of social poiesis, we have the capacity to organize the social world by using legal language, which through social performativity will constitute and legitimize principles and processes of justice. On the other hand, seeking in law the signs of our legitimate existence, we expose ourselves to the symbolic violence of the social terms that the law legitimizes. We are both at home and expelled from the law and its language; we both coin and perform according to the normative language of the law.

From the legal subject's standpoint, the rule of law creates two possibilities: either we comply and shirk the price to be paid for being outlawed, or/and we demand that justice be rendered. So, while Robert Cover is right in pointing to the havoc wreaked by the law, his analysis of the violence of the legal nomos speaks implicitly to a desire for justice. A woman who has the right to an abortion will have a certain expectation concerning the legal implementation of her right; a Caribbean man who is raped with a broom by New York police officers may have enough self-respect left to expect that the law will redress this injustice;[48] an aboriginal woman now in her nineties will remember that the program of linguistic, cultural, and religious assimilation carried out by Canadian residential schools and overseen by the Department of Indian Affairs stole her culture and language, and she and her grandchildren will have an expectation about the way the law will redress this cultural genocide.

In these and other cases, the expectation will also be that once a legal decision in the form of redress has been reached, it will become the law of the land and be complied with. If we ascribe a performative role to language, if indeed language has an act-like quality, then the legal practitioner as user of legal language becomes subject to ethical responsibility and accountable to the desire for justice. In this sense, Butler's critique of the power of discursive performativity implies redress for the injustice that the performative word may commit. Her theory of discursive power can then be read as not only a critique of domination but also a desire for, if not a claim to, justice – that is to say, for the proleptic use of just words, which will not implement practices and structures of social delegitimation.

If this is the case, the legal word and its dual valence – both legally formal and socially normative – is inscribed in the agon between the potential symbolic violence of the social norms it legitimizes and the demand for justice. The process of legitimization is a competitive, normative struggle that is enacted whenever the courts and legal professionals make their cases. The rule of law is a locus of social poiesis and political competition for the authorization and legitimation of norms of social organization.[49] Law's binding decisions function as a means of establishing a normative archive of political, social, economic, and cultural governance, and this archive is kept alive and performative through legal decisions that may either transform or entrench normative principles of social organization, which, in turn, performatively endow these legal decisions with authority. The perceived authority of the law does not derive from an intrinsic and originary virtue, but from the social and performative practice of citing – that is, mobilizing – the law as an institutional and valid source of doing justice. Performing justice, citing the law, and mobilizing its authority speak to the social desire for legitimacy and recognition in response to the historical, political, and social challenges that citizens pose today.

Chapter Four

Symbolic Violence and Illegitimacy: The Political Uncanny

Relying on symbolic power, social fields compete to legitimize their norms of being and doing things, and in their attempts for political ascendency, they produce effects of symbolic violence. Symbolic violence results from strategies of naturalization and dehistoricization that usurp symbolic means of constituting the world and exclude other possible ways of constituting this world. This usurpatory process produces effects of domination, which can be analysed as the spectralization and abjection of citizens who either do not cohere with normative carvings of the social world or who do not recognize themselves in them.

For Bourdieu, symbolic violence occurs at the level of practical knowledge – that is to say, the level where the subject engages with a social field by implementing the beliefs and structuring principles of that field and by endorsing the rules of the game, according to which to adhere successfully to these beliefs and structures is to be socially rewarded and legitimized. For Butler, the very process of identity formation constitutes a process of subjugation insofar as the social subject is always engaged in self-constitution through terms that historically precede these acts of self-constitution. If social performativity is theatrical, it is not so much that the social subject is carousing with existing norms as that, in order to gain legitimacy, the subject performs in the context of a predetermined discursive and political script. The violence of the process derives from an ontological condition of vulnerability to and dependence upon the socially constituted world.

In this agonistic generation of social poiesis, the position of the law is rather unique: through its institutional practices, it is tasked with the process of legitimizing social norms, while, like any other social field, it has to maintain its own institutional legitimacy. And it is in the double process of legitimizing itself and the polis that it can also wreak havoc by delegitimizing. Thus, the relationship between law and citizens is characterized by a peculiar ambivalence. On the one hand, this relationship revolves around a utopian belief in the possibility of justice, which the binding authority of the law is expected to materialize. This utopian desire is subject to contingency and the randomness of the social performativity of legal procedures – from supreme courts and high courts to the daily administering of the law through municipal policies, the policing of a community, or the regulation of economic activities. On the other hand, through its singular conative address to the citizen, the law has the capacity to exercise symbolic violence by grafting its binding authority onto exclusionary social norms of beings, practices, and relationships. As argued in chapter 3, the symbolic violence of the law does not originate in its binding sovereignty, but in the nexus between the institutional power to bind and the sociodicy the law legitimizes. The legal word and its dual valence – both legally formal and culturally normative – is inscribed in the tension between the potential symbolic violence of the social norms it legitimizes and the demand for justice.

In the present chapter, my immediate objective is to further Bourdieu's analysis of symbolic violence and Butler's analysis of discursive exclusionary effects by using the uncanny as an analytical device to demonstrate that the effects of symbolic violence indicate the operation of a political unconscious. In analysing the deployment of Gothic tropes in their writings, I seek to re-conceptualize the Freudian unconscious in the context of the relationship between symbolic violence and its psychosocial effects. My ulterior objective is to prepare the ground for the chapters that follow. In chapter 5, I will present an analysis of the production of the political uncanny as the potential effect of law's binding utterances. In chapters 6, 7, and 8, I will focus on the family as a particular site of social poiesis in which family law and Gothic narratives engage and from which emerges an agon for legitimacy, which manifests itself through the uncanny as a sign of symbolic violence and proscription.

While not using the concept of the uncanny, Butler and Bourdieu deploy tropes of the uncanny to account for the ways in which social normativity is experienced as a conflict between that which makes the social subject at home in the world and that which renders the world unfamiliar to the subject, between that which establishes a plenipotentiary sense of identity and that which hints at an estrangement from one's psychic and historical origins. Their use of Gothic tropes begets an account of social and political repression, which takes into consideration the affective dimension of symbolic violence as well as the institutional and material shaping of the psyche. The process of subordination through symbolic activity that they describe is fundamentally grounded in a state of existential ambivalence, whereby the relationships between agency and subordination, social legitimacy and exclusion, the proscription and constitution of desire, knowledge and blindness, fantasy and social reality are not organized according to a logic of antinomy but according to the principle of non-contradiction. If their terms of analysis still generate a contrast between concealment and revelation, normative dominance and proscription, they have also undergone a transformation: Butler's reflection on social abjection and spectralization and Bourdieu's reflection on the creation of a collective and historical unconscious do not revolve around the revelation of truth, but around strategies that aim at exposing the political imposture and misrecognition of social norms as universal and incontrovertible truths.

In 1919, Freud analysed identity formation in terms of repression, repetition, and the uncanny. In its ethnological, mythological, and religious references, his essay "The Uncanny" reflects the development of anthropology in the nineteenth and early twentieth centuries, epitomized by the publication of an abbreviated version of James Frazer's *The Golden Bough* (1922).[1] Freud's essay straddles the four areas of the psychological experience of castration and intrauterine fantasies, the animistic conception of the world, the anthropological experience of death, and the writer's magus-like power to hold readers under sway by creating narratives of the uncanny.

Freud's and Frazer's analyses cannot be fully understood without recognizing the context of the colonial expansionism of the nineteenth century, which spawned a new scientific (Charles Darwin) and anthropological (Lewis Henry Morgan, Franz Boas) discourse, both in Europe and the United States. However, there is another dimension to Freud's essay, which is its publication in the wake of the First World War. Although Freud makes only two passing references to the war,[2] his analysis of the uncanny as the repressed haunting the surfaces of social and personal consciousness is itself shadowed by the trauma of the conflict.[3] Although the critical tendency has been to concentrate on Freud's concept of the uncanny at the level of the individual psyche, his musing on the uncanny in the shadow of a worldwide conflict is also the occasion for considering the political implications of the concept.[4]

There are two basic Freudian criteria signalling the presence of the uncanny: one is that the uncanny is something that is familiar to the mind, which through repression has become alienated from consciousness; the other is that the uncanny operates in the mode of recurrence. Freud's analysis of E.T.A. Hoffmann's tale "The Sand-Man" (1816) derives from his assumption that psychological development takes place according to the Oedipal complex, which he sees as the centrepiece of the psychosocial normative system governing identity and the social organization of kinship and its practices. Thus, the premise of his interpretation is that in Hoffmann's tale the uncanny represents the threat of castration, which Nathaniel has repressed and which comes back to haunt him in the recurrent manifestations of castrating figures. So the repression of the familiar – that is to say, the repression of an affect – originates in a normative system that establishes terms of social legitimacy and acceptability. It is therefore no coincidence that Freud should have selected a story in which the Oedipal figure of authority, Coppelius, should be a lawyer, a representative of legal normativity, whose respectability is lined with the violence of castrating retribution.[5]

Furthermore, the trace of the normative in uncanny manifestations is indicated by Freud's predilection for Schelling's definition of the *unheimlich*. After an exhaustive linguistic analysis of the ambivalent meaning of the terms *heimlich* and *unheimlich*, Freud pauses on Schelling's definition. "*'Unheimlich' is the name for everything that ought to have remained … secret and hidden but has come to light.*"[6] The difference between this definition – which he mentions in two other instances – and the others is that through the verb "ought to," Freud points to the normative origin of the repression. In other words, the uncanny in "The Sand-Man" can be interpreted as a site where adherence to and legitimacy in the heterosexual organization of kinship are haunted by an affect that is identified and banned by norms, functioning as a potential source of illegitimacy and exclusion. In addition, the dread that repression generates is the residue of a normative process exacting the proscription of an unavowable affect that nevertheless persistently demands recognition. Thus, Freud's conception of the uncanny rests on the double bind of exclusion and inclusion, whereby the subject's social inclusion depends on the exclusion of that which deviates from normative heterosexual kinship and which at the same time sustains the validity of these normative terms of legitimate kinship. It is this fundamental mechanism of psychological repression, and the collateral emergence of a normative, symbolic, and historical unconscious that render Freud's conception of the uncanny relevant to Bourdieu's and Butler's accounts of the struggle for legitimacy in the context of social domination.

However, the ontological implications of Bourdieu's and Butler's conceptions of social domination entail a reconsideration of Freud's distinction between psychological reality and material reality, which leads him first to differentiate between the uncanny as an experience of primitive beliefs "in real life" and the uncanny as it "proceeds from repressed infantile complexes."[7] On the basis of this problematic distinction, he states, "Where the uncanny comes from infantile complexes the question of material reality does not arise; its place is taken by psychical reality."[8] Applying a further twist, Freud goes on to suggest that since "primitive beliefs [experienced in real life] are most intimately connected with infantile complexes, and are, in fact, based on them, we shall not be greatly astonished to find that the distinction is often a hazy one."[9] In contrast, Butler's concept of the normative self as the investment of fantasy into discursive norms implies that material, social, and political reality is bound to be innervated by desire, which courses its way through social utterances and practices.

This leads Butler to call into question the traditional antithesis between reality and fantasy. Rather than supposing that the real preexists fantasy, "We can understand the 'real' as a variable construction which is always and only determined in relation to its constitutive outside: fantasy, the unthinkable, the unreal. ... Here the distinction between real and unreal contrives a boundary between the legitimate domain of the phantasmatic and the illegitimate."[10] This conception of social domination disturbs the traditional relation between knowledge and truth by positing that the truth value of a cognitive, discursive, and material constitution of the social world depends not only on its purchase on political legitimacy but also on its capacity to affect and effect.

In this respect, Bourdieu's concept of the habitus is the site where the social agent's identification with symbolic principles of social organization is charged with *illusio* – that is to say, "a way of *being in* the world, of being occupied by the world, which means that an agent can be affected by something very distant, even absent, if it participates in the game in which he is engaged. The body is linked to a place by a direct relationship of contact, which is just one way among others of relating to the world."[11] It can be argued that when Bourdieu describes the enactment of symbolic violence as an act of magic exercising mysterious, remote, and apparently inexplicable power upon the socialized body through social practices and structures, or when Butler describes the fabrication of identity through the performative power of discursive norms affecting the contours of bodies, they are reconfiguring a Freudian source of the uncanny, and that is the omnipotence of thoughts, which Freud explains as the psyche's delusional belief in the power of symbolic representation over the material world.

Freud offers a dualist and rationalist explanation of the omnipotence of thoughts along ontogenetic and phylogenetic lines. Making the assumption that the earlier phase of individual development corresponds to the "primitive" animistic stage of human development, he concludes that "everything which now strikes us as 'uncanny' fulfils the condition of touching those residues of animistic mental activity within us and bringing them to expression."[12] However, in Bourdieu's and Butler's theories, the omnipotence of thoughts is dislodged from this anthropological discourse and integrated into an ontological and political discourse, whereby categories of gender and political principles of a sociodicy exercise their omnipotence through the processes of social inculcation, usurpation, and incorporation. This is most conspicuous when Butler argues that

> acts, gestures, and desire produce the effect of an internal core or substance, but produce this *on the surface* of the body, through the play of signifying absences that suggest, but never reveal, the organizing principle of identity as a cause. Such acts, gestures, enactments, generally construed, are *performative* in the sense that the essence or identity that they otherwise purport to express are *fabrications* manufactured and sustained through corporeal signs and other discursive means. That the gendered body is performative suggests that it has no ontological status apart from the various acts which constitute its reality. This also suggests that if reality is fabricated as an interior essence, that very interiority is an effect and function of a decidedly public and social discourse, the public regulation of fantasy through the surface politics of the body, the gender border control that differentiates inner from outer, and so institutes the "integrity" of the subject.[13]

In Bourdieu's and Butler's accounts, the omnipotence of thoughts functions like a major device of fabricating social legitimacy and an index of our capacity not only for the organization of the material world through symbolic activity but also for symbolic violence, whereby adherence to beliefs and values does violence to the self in the making. When Butler envisages interiority as the effect of a public and regulatory discourse, or when Bourdieu analyses the habitus as the product of an assimilation of social principles of being and practices, they ascribe a power to thoughts originating not in the individual's wishful thinking and fantasies, but in the polis, whose organization results from the projection of discursive categories and principles of social vision and division according to which social agents perform, not always aware of their historical origins and contingent meanings. Our symbolic activity and our desire to act upon the world according to our representations participate in this animistic relation to the world.

In both theories, processes of legitimization and socialization are predicated on the twin concepts of censorship and the collateral emergence of a social unconscious. The symbolic governance of the social world and the creation of terms of social legitimacy are shadowed by divergent narratives of subjectivity and social relations precluded from participating in the constitution of a dominant sociodicy. From Butler's standpoint, normative governance exacts the abjection of potentially differing norms of identity, while from Bourdieu's standpoint, the repressive effects of such governance consist of the collective occlusion of the historical origins of the principles of social organization. The "social effects of the family *fatum*," Bourdieu writes, "in other words the set of positive or negative verdicts pronounced on the child, performative statements of the being of the child which bring about what they state, or, more subtly and insidiously, the whole set of *silent censures* imposed by the very logic of the domestic order as a moral order, would not be so powerful or so dramatic if they were not charged with desire and, through repression, buried in the deepest level of the body where they are recorded in the form of guilts, phobias, or, in a word, passion."[14] Although this violence operates at the level of signs and through rational communication, it is on the body, which has objectified the symbolic vision and divisions of the social world, that one has to look for signs of domination.

Symbolic violence also manifests itself through emotions that speak to the way in which the subject experiences and struggles with social structures and practices. The body becomes the site of an agon between the subject's recognition of dominating and censuring social norms and his/her betrayal of normative judgment. Similarly, Butler argues that the subjecting effects of symbolic governance depend on "a series of demands, taboos, sanctions, injunctions, prohibitions, impossible idealizations, and threats – performative speech acts, as it were, that wield the power to produce the field of culturally viable sexual subjects: performative acts, in other words, with the power to produce or materialize the subjectivating effects."[15] The process of identity formation within culture and language is premised on what she refers to as a vexation of desire, whereby, in order to remain socially legitimate, the subject must thwart its own desire. At the core of both theoretical analyses is the account of the ways in which the social agent is tossed in and out of normative matrices. Either the irreverent self is expropriated from the social world as a home of mythical origin (Butler) or the self is willing to inhabit the world unaware of the small print in the social contract that requires the mortgaging of historical reason in exchange for an illusory sense of domestic bliss (Bourdieu).

In distinguishing between social consciousness and the existence of a political unconscious as the side effect of censorship or proscription through sociodicies and normative regulation, Bourdieu and Butler regard the polis as a fundamentally ambivalent zone organized around boundaries between those who belong and those who live in estrangement. In their accounts, agency and subjugation, knowledge and misrecognition, discursivity and censorship, *illusio* and the social real, legitimacy and repression jostle with one another, cheek by jowl. To this extent, their analyses of the social unconscious participate in Freud's conception of the uncanny, whose logic of ambivalence defies the rationalist discourse of non-contradiction. In a Freudian universe, you can have your cake and eat it too: through repression, that which is familiar is also unfamiliar. "Thus *heimlich* is a word the meaning of which develops in the direction of ambivalence, until it finally coincides with its opposite, *unheimlich.*"[16]

In the context of Bourdieu's analysis, the social agent is at home in the world not only because s/he is biologically programmed to be predisposed towards it, but also because through exposure to the social world, s/he becomes apt to perform according to social rules that create the illusion of a natural and desirable harmony between the world and the self. This process of inscribing oneself into the material and social world procures the pleasure of recognition and shelters one from anonymity, but it is co-extensive with collusion with the terms of social domination. Symbolic violence does not operate according to the traditional binaries of constraint and consent, coercion and free will; instead, "the effect of symbolic domination (whether ethnic, gender, cultural or linguistic) is exerted not in the pure logic of knowing consciousnesses but through schemes of perception, appreciation and action that are constitutive of habitus, and which, below the level of the decisions of consciousness and the controls of the will, set up a cognitive relationship that is profoundly obscure to itself."[17] It is in the desire for harmony that the ambivalence of the concept of habitus originates.

Therefore, the concept encapsulates the ambivalence of the *heimlich* and the *unheimlich,* whereby the self inhabits the beliefs and values of a particular cultural field but is forever alienated by the recurrent effects of symbolic violence through the body. Under the spell of symbolic violence, s/he functions like a well-oiled mechanism, an automaton that because it is well disposed towards the principles of the social field, is prompted into action by its injunctions and symbolic representations. In Bourdieu's vision of the world, there are as many Olympias as there are selves willing to play the social game and being rewarded for doing so. If the social agent is at home in the world, and if the world appears in a familiar guise, it is because the arbitrariness of the nomos has been removed from sight. Thus, the "unconscious is history – the collective history that has produced our categories of thought, and the individual history through which they have been inculcated in us."[18] In other words, if the social subject has incorporated the principles of social organization and therefore feels at home, it has been at the cost of being evicted from the house of history. That which was once historically familiar has become unfamiliar and reappears at the surface of the socialized body in the form of symbolic violence.

A similar dynamic of ambivalence obtains in Butler's conception of normative identification to the extent that the desire that comes under the proscription of hegemonic norms re-emerges as the sustaining affect of those norms. At the same time, signs of abjection appear whenever patterns that are held deviant disrupt the routine of social performativity and point back to the spectres of social beings relegated to a domain of social abjection and dispossession. Endorsing Foucault's principle that power is constitutive, Butler nevertheless reinstates the mechanism of social proscription and deflection of desire in accordance with the Freudian logic of non-contradiction: the domain of unthinkable and unlivable bodies is not the opposite of the domain of intelligible bodies, "for oppositions are, after all, part of intelligibility; the latter is the excluded and illegible domain that haunts the former domain as the spectre of its own impossibility, the very limit to intelligibility, its constitutive outside."[19] The social subject inhabits the world by performing according to the dominant discursive norms governing the society in which s/he lives, oblivious to or suppressing the quotidian discrepancies that might emerge through social performance or the instances of incongruence that arise from various social scripts.

The usurpation underlying the legitimation of dominant norms of social organization can be compared to the Freudian concept of dream work, whereby unconscious material is repressed through the process of condensation, distortion, and displacement. This is exemplified by Butler's analysis of the creation of the concept of subjective interiority. "If the 'cause' of desire, gesture, and act can be localized within the 'self' of the actor, then the political regulations and disciplinary practices which produce that ostensibly coherent gender are effectively displaced from view. The displacement of a political and discursive origin of gender identity onto a psychological 'core' precludes an analysis of the political constitution of the gendered subject and its fabricated notions about the ineffable interiority of its sex or of its true identity."[20] Pursuing the analogy, we can say that the process of acquiring social, institutional, and discursive legitimacy under conditions of normative domination is a fundamentally uncanny process.

The historical and cultural origins of the norms have been occluded only to reappear in the guise of a misrecognized fabrication posturing as the real, the natural, and the legitimate. That which is unfamiliar – the signs of normative and affective deviance, which are always threatened with extradition – haunts the dominant, legitimate constitution of the social world, its social identities and practices. Clearly, Butler's politicization and socialization of the unconscious demarcates her from an established psychoanalytical discourse when she states that "the unconscious is not pre-social, but *a certain mode in which the unspeakable endures.* ... [It] *is also an ongoing psychic condition in which norms are registered in both normalizing and non-normalizing ways, the postulated site of their fortification, their undoing and their perversion.*"[21] This conception of the social unconscious results from the double bind of inclusion through exclusion to the extent that the process of undoing, perverting, deviating, which is normatively excluded, is nevertheless included through its derivation from and indebtedness to social norms.

The logic of ambivalence so typical of the uncanny, whereby boundaries are created only to be blurred or made porous, is especially relevant to Butler's and Bourdieu's argument that domination is not located outside the social subject. Instead, the subject or social agent mobilizes while drawing on the process of normative domination. Preexisting social, institutional, and discursive structures materialize dominant values and beliefs, but their persistence and reproduction can be guaranteed only by subjective adherence. In other words, the social agent or subject is the host of the dominant norms, just as our bodies are the active hosts of cancerous cells whose propagation feeds on our physiological processes. Dominant norms and values prevail not because they are true but because they derive their persuasive power from affective and phantasmatic investment.

Thus, discursive performativity provides social legitimacy while simultaneously generating symptoms of exclusion from the social world. In particular, repetition allows the self to be familiar with the world, but at the heart of this familiarity lies the unfamiliar, or that which has become unfamiliar and which symptomatically recurs between the beats of the social performance of norms. The reiterative rhythm of social identification with regulating norms is also the rhythm of that which has been excluded through the social performance of norms. This common temporality indicates that the normative self and its abject alternative constitute the uncanny double of social domination, whereby the abject haunts the social performance of the normative.

> The abject designates ... precisely those "unlivable" and "uninhabitable" zones of social life which are nevertheless densely populated by those who do not enjoy the status of the subject, but whose living under the sign of the "unlivable" is required to circumscribe the domain of the subject. This zone of uninhabitability will constitute the defining limit of the subject's domain; it will constitute that site of dreaded identification against which – and by virtue of which – the domain of the subject will circumscribe its own claim to autonomy and life. In this sense, then, the subject is constituted through the force of exclusion and abjection, one which produces a constitutive outside to the subject, an abjected outside, which is, after all, "inside" the subject as its own founding repudiation.[22]

The abjected social body lives in the uninhabitable zone of the *unheimlich* as it does not have access to representation, although it ghosts the normative self as the unwanted and concealed illegitimate progeny of social regulation. It is spirited away from the intelligible – that is to say, from the social body that has been legitimized through the reiterative and exclusionary power of performativity.[23] To account for the spectralization of modes of being, Butler borrows from Freud's theory of melancholia, which he developed in "Mourning and Melancholia" (1917). While in "The Uncanny" Freud emphasizes the mechanism of repression – "every affect belonging to an emotional impulse, whatever its kind, is transformed, if it is repressed, into anxiety"[24] – in "Mourning and Melancholia" he distinguishes between mourning, whereby the individual struggles through a process of grieving, and melancholia, whereby the individual incorporates the object of loss in an attempt to preserve it, while resisting the process of grieving. The individual not only becomes a living mausoleum – a death-in-life figure – but also internalizes the feelings of self-beratement and destruction directed at the object of loss. Butler appropriates the Freudian concept of melancholia to account for the emergence of the subject, which is all at once ontological and political.

The subject emerges as its own desire is thwarted through the incorporation of pre-existing norms. For Butler, this fundamental torsion of desire inaugurates the subject in and through language and, from a linguistic standpoint, constitutes the tropological foundation of subjectivity. "The trope [of desire turning on itself] appears to be the shadow of a body, a shadowing of that body's violence against itself, a body in spectral and linguistic form that is the signifying mark of the psyche's emergence."[25] From a cultural and social viewpoint, the performative and regulated subject is shadowed by aberrant and illegitimate modes of being, which remain unnamed as they are barred from social discourse, self-representation, and social practices and as they remain foreclosed to the very subject. This foreclosure of possible ways of being designates social legitimacy as a site of melancholia from which the subject cannot subtract itself because it remains existentially vulnerable and exposed to normative construction and governance of the social world. Butler therefore raises Freud's concept of melancholia to a cultural and ultimately political level to demonstrate the spectralizing effects of discursive performativity.

To some extent, Bourdieu shares this concept of foreclosure with Butler, although his explanatory terms do not operate in the context of a cultural and political theory of melancholia. Thus, the social agent acquires legitimacy by adhering to a nomos, a social field and its habitus under the spell of *illusio,* which does not brook analysis. Under the empire of universalized arbitrary principles and enthralled by misrecognition, the social agent acts like an automaton as long as the arbitrariness and historicity of the principles remain unconscious. This "means that once one has accepted the viewpoint that is constitutive of a field, one can no longer take an external viewpoint on it. … As a legitimate principle of division which can be applied to all the fundamental aspects of existence, defining the thinkable and the unthinkable, the prescribed and the proscribed, it must remain unthought."[26] In a spectacular reversal of Freudian typology, the social agent as automaton is symptomatic of a collective pathology, as – far from originating from an ill-fitted psyche – madness lies in the historical erasure of the mythic origins of the sociodicy organizing the social world and automating the social body.

Extrapolating from Butler's account, one can say that whenever we encounter norms of social organization, institutions, and practices that turn individuals into ab-humans, we are dealing with the double process of a cultural melancholia and political uncanny, whereby that which has been shoved back into the dark inexorably surges in full light, beyond recognition yet so close. For Butler, the foreclosure of same-sex desire constitutes a particular instance of melancholic loss, whereby the subject is forever haunted by the double stress of an unavowable identification and its unacknowledged refusal in favour of a heterosexual identity. Resorting to Gothic tropes, Butler seeks to define the refused identification with same-sex desire as "a love and a loss haunted by the specter of a certain unreality, a certain unthinkability, the double disavowal of the 'I never loved her, and I never lost her,' uttered by a woman, the 'I never loved him, and I never lost him,' uttered by a man."[27] In the latter analysis, Butler concentrates on the constitution of gender identities, but the spectralization of foreclosed social content also obtains in the general engineering of heterosexuality.

In *Antigone's Claim*, she examines the extent to which Hegel, Freud, Levi-Strauss, and Lacan both subvert and maintain normative terms of heterosexuality. She proposes to interpret Antigone as a figure of aberration, who calls into question the very social structure and discourse of heterosexuality whose hallmark remains the incest taboo. Rather than considering this taboo as an ahistorical and pre-social concept, she examines it as the epigone of a heteronormative construct of social and sexual relationships that functions in the mode of foreclosure and spectrality. Thus, to "the extent that the incest taboo contains its infraction within itself, it does not simply prohibit incest but rather sustains and cultivates incest as a necessary spectre of social dissolution, a spectre without which social bonds cannot emerge."[28] If melancholia is the term that describes the effect of normative foreclosure – silencing and barring the domain of the possible – then the uncanny designates the political effects of such foreclosure, the effects of "a primary violence"[29] to which the subject is subordinated under the social pressure to maintain legitimacy.

The political uncanny can therefore be defined as the return of that which was familiar but barred and silenced in the name of a dominant normativity and which is identified as the anomaly both haunting and maintaining the norms of the dominant nomos of a particular field. The political uncanny concerns the relation between the *anomalous* and the *nomos* constituted through performative norms. Butler's selection of the trope of catachresis as the means of misappropriating discursive norms so as to gesture to that which cannot be communicated, or that which remains illegible because it does not have access to the discursive norms of social organization and therefore cannot claim legitimacy, participates in this discourse of the political forms of the uncanny. Nor is the recurrence of the Gothic figure of the spectre in her prose a coincidence, for the trope functions in the catachrestic mode: the ghost is this entity that has no substance; shadow or invisible presence, it cannot be pinned down, yet its presence haunts the domain of signification, disturbs schemas of cognitive and affective representation, encroaches on the borders of public rationality, and leaves aberrations unexplained yet significant. Butler's conception of subjectivity as a normative process engendering melancholia in the context of a polis haunted by the living dead of social performativity indicates to what extent her philosophical discourse is governed by the tropes of the uncanny raised to a political level.

> How are we to grasp this dilemma of language that emerges when "human" takes on that doubled sense, the normative one based on radical exclusion and the one that emerges in the sphere of the excluded, not negated, not dead, perhaps slowly dying, yes, surely dying from a lack of recognition, dying, indeed, from the premature circumscription of the norms by which recognition as human can be conferred, a recognition without which the human cannot come into being but must remain on the far side of being, as what does not qualify as that which is and can be? Is this not a melancholy of the public sphere?[30]

An account of identification as the simultaneous process of normative legitimacy and dispossession and as the site of ambivalence, where to recognize is also to exclude and to name is also to silence, indicates that normative identification can be both the cause of subordination and the occasion for resistance to such subordination. In the context of a non-transcendental, historical, and material conception of the world, social transformation depends on the instability and discrepancies that will characterize the performance of social norms and on the possibilities that such gaps will generate for proscribed ways of being and doing things to have access to public manifestation and normative legitimacy.[31]

Butler's and Bourdieu's insistence that social domination be not understood as the manifestation of a raw form of hegemony outside our normative, cultural interpretation and organization of the world implies that the terms of freedom also lie in the same symbolic capacity to interpret the social world and engage in ceaseless processes of social poiesis, modifying or manufacturing new ways of being and doing things. On this basis, I suggest that we can distinguish between symbolic violence and sovereign power by identifying the latter as the political form of domination that seeks to control by depriving citizens of their symbolic capacity to organize the social world. Specifically, a distinction can be made between, on the one hand, subordination as normative adherence or the "inaugurative alienation in sociality"[32] through which the social agent is both recognized and subjected and, on the other, practices of power that seek to eliminate the condition to be within language and be constituted as a social agent endowed with symbolic power. Sovereign power seeks first and foremost to assert control by deconstituting the subject as symbolic subject and, in the process, spawns its own political uncanny effects. I propose to examine this slip from symbolic violence to sovereign power through a rereading of Giorgio Agamben's concepts of sovereign power and bare life from the standpoint of the political uncanny.

In *Homo Sacer*, Agamben reflects on the persistence of sovereign power in the midst of democratic governance. In focusing on sovereignty, his objective is to lay bare the aporia characterizing modern democracy, according to which the exercise of sovereign power underwrites institutionalized norms. Drawing on but also moving beyond Foucault's conception of power as discursive and epistemological techniques of biopower,[33] Agamben argues that forms of sovereign power have persisted throughout the twentieth century and transformed political thinking by making "bare life" – that is to say, the biological body – the main target of domination. Thus, he maintains that "the entry of *zoē* into the sphere of the *polis* – the politicization of bare life as such – constitutes the decisive event of modernity and signals a radical transformation of the political-philosophical categories of classical thought."[34] Taking the "juridico-political order" as his major example,[35] Agamben provides an anatomy of sovereign power, which underwrites normative organization while resting on the state of exception. "Since 'there is no rule that is applicable to chaos,'[36] chaos must first be included in the juridical order through the creation of a zone of indistinction between outside and inside, chaos and the normal situation – the state of exception. ... In its archetypal form, the state of exception is therefore the principle of every juridical localization, since only the state of exception opens the space in which the determination of a certain juridical order and a particular territory first becomes possible."[37] The law is a system of norms differentiating the lawful from the unlawful, the licit from the illicit, the legitimate from the illegitimate; however, shadowing the normative organization of legal categories, and elusively haunting the symbolic field of the law lies this "originary" zone of indistinction, where chaos and violence – that which exceeds the law – are constitutive of the law, not extraneous to it.[38]

In this context, sovereign power, whose violence draws on a double bind of inclusion and exclusion, is characterized by a structure that he names a relation of exception. "What is outside is included not simply by means of an interdiction or an internment, but rather by means of the suspension of the juridical order's validity – by letting the juridical order, that is, withdraw from the exception and abandon it. The exception does not subtract itself from the rule; rather, the rule, suspending itself, gives rise to the exception and, maintaining itself in relation to the exception, first constitutes itself as a rule."[39] Sovereignty derives from the power to suspend norms of regulation and legitimization so as to create an exception to these norms. By suspending itself, the norm begets the exception to which it remains kindred. So, if the exception is external to the norm, its exteriority also proceeds from the norm in suspension.

If violence is the primary fact of the law, then law as constituted power is arbitrary, while the legitimacy of law as constituting power remains grounded in violence.[40] The citizen regulated and sanctioned by sovereign law is ensnared in this state of exception, whereby s/he is all at once banned by the law and abandoned by the law. More specifically, sovereign law deprives the citizen of legitimacy, but this act of exclusion paradoxically still maintains this citizen in a relation of dependence on the law since the act of exclusion is nothing but the suspension of the norm. To be illegitimate is not to stand outside the law, but to be bereft of the recognition that the actions and utterances of the law bestow. Borrowing the concept from Jean-Luc Nancy, Agamben states that "*the originary relation of law to life is not application but*

Abandonment. The matchless potentiality of the *nomos, its originary 'force of law,'* is that it holds life in its ban by abandoning it."[41] In this sense, the abandoned citizen is maintained in a double state of indebtedness and orphancy.

Agamben's philosophy of the state of exception in the midst of our democracies is a philosophy for dark times, and it is no coincidence that some of his major thinkers of reference should be Hannah Arendt and Walter Benjamin, the philosophers of sovereign and totalitarian power. At the same time, Agamben's account of the state of exception and his, at times, ambiguous conception of bare life seem to imply a form of power beyond or below the forms of domination materialized through historical norms and practices of governance. Ernesto Laclau has criticized what he regards as the reductive dehistoricizing of cultural heterogeneity and the monological premise of state power in Agamben's account of sovereignty.[42]

While agreeing with Laclau's critique, I reconsider Agamben's concept of sovereign power from a socio-historical standpoint as the manifestation of the politics of excess in the midst of normative governance. While Agamben concentrates on the juridical order, elaborating a theory of juridical and political state power, I refer to acts of sovereign power as acts of usurpation and appropriation of the human capacity to organize the social world through symbolic activity. In other words, I read Agamben through the claim that each and every act of constitution of the world is a claim to symbolic legitimacy vulnerable to sovereign power and its strategies of abandonment. The coincidence between a sovereign use of power and the stripping of symbolic power from those under its ban constitutes the conditions for a particular form of domination, whereby not so much a particular norm as the means of materializing norms is the target. Referring to the concentration camps of Nazi Germany, Agamben states, "Whoever entered the camp moved in a zone of indistinction between outside and inside, exception and rule, licit and illicit, in which the very concepts of subjective right and juridical protection no longer made any sense. … Insofar as its inhabitants were stripped of every political status and wholly reduced to bare life, the camp was also the most absolute biopolitical space ever to have been realized, in which power confronts nothing but pure life, *without any mediation*."[43] My purpose is to draw on Agamben's reflection on sovereign power so as to examine strategies of reduction to bare life in the midst of historical and mediated forms of governance.

Sovereign power is characterized by an intent aided and abetted by identifiable techniques and strategies of control that seek to bring individuals to the brink of annihilation.[44] In this sense, my concern is with the jurisdiction over what constitutes political being and with practices that dispossess subjects of symbolic and discursive power. In my rereading of Agamben, states of exception are characterized by a disruption of access to symbolic power, whereby agents of domination monopolize means of mediation while seeking to deprive those they dominate of their symbolic agency with the political intent to reduce them to "bare life."

This rereading focuses on the ways in which acts of sovereign power rupture democratic governance and signal a shift from symbolic violence as the toxic effect of a dominant sociodicy to a violence that makes the creation of a sociodicy a unilateral and totalitarian exercise. Seeking to maintain the social subject in a double state of inclusion and exclusion, within and without language, patterns of sovereign power manifest themselves through the creation of an uncanny space to which social agents are confined and where they are deconstituted as symbolic subjects. Although Agamben considers sovereign power at the level of the state and the law, I suggest that the slide from symbolic violence to sovereign power can also occur within the practices of everyday life and through the social performance of dominant norms of social organization. In other words, although the will to sovereign power is most blatant at the state level, it can also be exercised within normative practices and outside the state apparatus.[45] As argued in the next four chapters, legal and literary strategies of symbolic legitimacy over the jurisdiction of the social nomos, its naming and unnaming, are haunted by a political uncanny that emerges from the exercise of not only symbolic violence but also sovereign power as coterminous historical forms of domination.

Chapter Five

The Symbolic Power and Violence of Legal Utterances

In the 2006 *Report of the Events Relating to Maher Arar: Analysis and Recommendations* produced by the Commission of Inquiry into the Actions of Canadian Officials in Relation to Maher Arar, Commissioner Dennis O'Connor stated, "I am able to say categorically that there is no evidence to indicate that Mr. Arar has committed any offence or that his activities constitute a threat to the security of Canada."[1] With this single statement, Commissioner O'Connor cleared Arar of terrorist affiliation. The authority of the statement derives solely from the first two clauses of the sentence, "I am able to say categorically that there is no evidence to indicate." Shorn of these two clauses, the statement could have been heard on a radio show, in a conversation in a café, or in a vigorous exchange between two individuals walking up the steps of a court of justice. The supremacy of the utterance derives from the institutional authority of these first two clauses.

Drawing on a performative conception of language, Joseph Raz provides a theoretical definition of a legal utterance by distinguishing it from a general command. This definition is illustrated by the following reasoning (with the usual gender markers): "A man, or body of men, *has authority* if it follows from his saying 'Let *X* happen,' that *X* ought to happen."[2] This definition "applies to all types of practical authority over persons and not merely to political authority. It makes clear that one can exercise authority not only by commanding but in other ways as well."[3] Next, Raz modifies the formula to establish what he sees as the authoritative specificity of legal utterances. "*X* has authority over *Y* if his saying, 'Let *Y* φ,' is a reason for *Y* to φ."[4] On this basis, he concludes that law's "authority is ability to change reasons for action."[5] In making the claim that its utterances have supreme authority, the law is making the claim that it is the authoritative source of all legitimizing processes under the rule of law.

Raz adds that the law justifies its authority to make binding statements by keeping within the boundaries of the legal system, which ensures that no extra-legal interest interferes with its procedures and doctrines. Thus, the binding mechanism applies both to its legal subjects and to the practitioners of the law: through utterances, legal practitioners are authorized to make law binding for social agents insofar as they themselves remain bound by the binding principles of the law. To do otherwise is to work outside the law. In sum, legal practitioners operate on the fundamental premise that legal utterances are endowed with the supreme authority to overrule other claims emanating from different social fields and subjects.

However, there is another way of reading or even hearing Commissioner O'Connor's statement. Charged with a rhetoric of assertion that brooks neither dissent nor doubt – "I am able to say categorically" – the utterance is deployed in the omnipotent mode typical of the rhetoric of magic. Its effect is one of a powerful and incontrovertible identification of the status and legitimacy of the person who has been indicted and threatened with delegitimation and sanction. In his analysis of law's authority, Bourdieu endows the institutional authority of legal utterances with the illocutionary power of magic utterances. "The judgment of a court, which decides conflicts or negotiations concerning persons or things by publicly proclaiming the truth about them, belongs in the final analysis to the class of *acts of naming* or of *instituting*. The judgment represents the quintessential form of authorized, public, official speech which is spoken in the name of and to everyone. These performative utterances ... are magical acts which succeed because they have the power to make themselves universally recognized."[6] I propose to expand Bourdieu's analysis of the magical power of legal utterance into an analysis of the temporality specific to the law and its symbolic power.

The potency of Commissioner O'Connor's utterance, the conclusion to a detailed and careful reasoning, also results from the use of the present tense, which has a double effect: it absolves past doing of any guilt and endows present and future doing with legitimacy. In addition, the effect of the utterance is to establish the binding validity of the legal decision according to the rule of law, which operates according to a temporality of universal recurrence. Similarly, charters of rights, universal declarations, and legal statutes are phrased to function in the mode of the eternal present. In international conventions such as the European Convention on Human Rights, the Convention on the Elimination of All Forms of Discrimination against Women, the Convention on the Rights of the Child; in covenants such as the International Covenant on Economic, Social and Cultural Rights; and in declarations and charters such as the European Social Charter, the Canadian Charter of Rights and Freedoms, and the Universal Declaration of Human Rights, legal rhetoric is deployed in the mode of the sublime, which transports the legal subject into the seductive and awesome realm of universal claims. The eternal present of the legal statute is the present of a dehistoricized act of reading, and its power derives from its claim to apply to the past, the present, and the future beyond the historical fluctuations of a given social group. In resorting to the temporality of the eternal present, legal practitioners reiteratively cite the supreme authority of legal utterances as a universal principle.

To this extent, the rhetoric and institutional practices of the law participate in the social forms of ritualistic reiteration or the reproductive rhythms of a habitus on which effects of symbolic and discursive power depend. In particular, Butler conceptualizes the role of law's authority through the judge's recursive acts of speech.

> The judge is ... installed in the midst of a signifying chain, receiving and reciting the law and, in the reciting, echoing forth the authority of the law. When the law functions as ordinance or sanction, it operates as an imperative that brings into being that which it legally enjoins and protects. The performative speaking of the law, an "utterance" that is most often within legal discourse inscribed in a book of laws, works only by reworking a set of already operative conventions. And these conventions are grounded in no other legitimating authority than the echo-chain of their own reinvocation.[7]

In focusing on the echo-chain of legal conventions that the judge reinvokes, Butler provides another account of legal practitioners' autopoietic practices to entrench the doxa and principles of knowledge constitutive of the field of law. The autopoietic process coincides with incantation. However, if we agree that the law functions as a double helix, then we need to probe beyond this temporality of sublime and incantatory reiteration. As I argued in chapter 2, the basic principle of normative ascendency is to develop strategies to appropriate the relation between meaning and matter, whereby to acquire legitimacy and exercise authority is to control the process of materializing meaning. On this basis, it can be argued that the symbolic power of the law is materially deployed through the social temporality of its utterances. This is the way in which the law participates in processes of social poiesis. Law legitimizes social norms not only through the binding effect of its performatives, but also through its regulation of social time – that is to say, the everyday practices of being and doing things. If legal utterances maintain their legitimacy through social time, then an analysis of the relation between legal time and social time is required to grasp law's intervention into social poiesis.

The time of the law is disjointed: on the one hand, in order to secure its authority, the law has recourse to detemporalizing strategies, buttressing its regulation of the real by means of a statutory syntax that addresses social agents through the legal trope of the universal legal subject; on the other hand, in generating an archive of precedents, law is both productive of and exposed to social time. The law has at its disposal three basic means of shaping social time through its utterances. To begin with, legal statutes are characterized by the rhetoric of definition, which has the intent of setting limits on the meaning of words and stabilizing the temporality of language. In so doing, the law circumscribes a field of reference while making the terms of definition flexible enough to be adjusted to different situations. In addition, through the strategy of analogy, which allows for the generation of principles stemming from authoritative utterances that act as precedents, the law draws on past utterances to create present utterances, which will shape the social future. Last, the law has the capacity to control the proliferation of social meaning and to curtail the polysemic character of language by claiming a coincidence between the facts of a case and an institutional utterance that puts an end to deliberation. In all cases, the effect of these institutional and rhetorical practices is to convert historical contingency into legal time.

However, in the very process of engaging with the practices and idiosyncrasies of the social world, the law exposes itself to and grapples with the social time of cultural norms. Social fields and normative practices are characterized by heterogeneous histories and potentialities for social reproduction but also historical ruptures. In his analysis of Maurice Blanchot's encounter with a magistrate in 1960 after he had authored the Declaration of the Right to Insubordination in the Algerian War to protest against the French colonial war in Algeria, Patrick Hanafin identifies Blanchot's resistance to the magistrate's use of power against his political engagement as the sign of destabilization of the authority of the law. Blanchot is reported to have made two points to the magistrate: outside the legal institution, the then prime minister had already indicated that the signatories of the Declaration would be severely punished, a statement that undermines the magical effect of the law by making it redundant. Second, Blanchot objected to the magistrate's decision to write Blanchot's deposition in his own legal words. Drawing on the traditional trope of space, Hanafin argues that Blanchot's "insubordinate performance points to [a] space of resistance"[8] where limits are challenged.

However, I suggest that Blanchot's insubordinate performance actually points to a temporality of resistance. His insubordination enacts a temporal rupture through which the law is seen to miss a beat in its governance of social time. While Blanchot's resistance is an act of isolated, quasi-heroic insurgency that does not upset the institutional sovereignty of the law, it nevertheless demonstrates that the law remains accountable to the social world insofar as it is able to negotiate the historical fluidity of that social world. The contest between the French magistrate and Blanchot is not only a contest revolving around the appropriation of utterances – who authors the deposition? – but also one revolving around the ability to control the time of utterances and their performative social and political effects.

In other words, the law regulates not only by assimilating the social world to its taxonomic and syntactic categories, but also by adjusting social clocks to its own procedural and doxological temporality. Time, that through which we act and plot social poiesis, is of the essence of legal power, whether the latter is reformist or conservative. A legal utterance is the occasion for the convergence of legal time and social time, and therein lies the potential mechanism for the transformation of legal authority into a manifestation of symbolic violence that hits at the very heart of social agency and historical transformation. While Robert Cover wrote about the temporal effects of the legal word in the form of devastating consequences for the subject of the law, it can also be argued that law's symbolic violence occurs whenever legal utterances mask their affiliation with contingent social norms by raising them to timeless truths. In other words, legal utterances have effects of domination whenever they dehistoricize.

To counteract dehistoricizing effects, socio-legal and feminist critique has developed a long-standing analysis of the decontextualizing effects of legal practices, which select and sift through social elements of a given case.[9] The legal presentation of facts pertaining to a case draws on what, in his analysis of historiography, Hayden White has identified as the activity of emplotment, which involves the selection of events or facts and their syntactic arrangement productive of social and political meaning.[10] In their review of *Gosselin v. Québec (Attorney General)*, Brodsky and her co-authors explicitly refer to this narrative and poietic aspect of adjudication.

> In any hearing before the courts, a particular situation, such as Louise Gosselin's, is described, usually years after the fact, through testimony and exhibits and other documentation. Choices are made. Some aspects of the situation are described in testimony or written and filed in evidence; others are not. The case takes on a life of its own. The judge chooses which of the multitude of facts that made it into evidence to report in his or her decision. This decision then becomes the official version of what happened. Inevitably, the decision distills the facts, crystallizing some while others fade away. The Supreme Court of Canada's decision has become the constructed version of Louise Gosselin's story. However, this official version was constructed through a long and convoluted judicial process that started in the gritty streets of Montreal and finished in the polished marble halls of the Supreme Court of Canada in Ottawa. It seemed important to us to tell the story differently.[11]

In fact, the whole project of the Women's Court can be seen as a sustained effort to tell the story differently through recontextualized readings of the elements of particular cases. While supporting the concept of contextualization, as in the political analysis of public culture and social structure, along with questions of substantive access to public goods,[12] Nicola Lacey also maintains that a simple contrast between the decontextualizing effects of law's formal categorizations and the recontextualizing critique of law with reference to gender, race, or class masks the fact that legal practices do engage in contextualization. "This emphasis occludes our perception of law's more pervasive – and, at least rhetorically, equally violent – disciplinary power, not to mention the material 'field of pain and death' within which law operates."[13] So the problem is not so much that law decontextualizes but that legal practitioners and the courts engage in a narrative process organizing beings and events according to criteria of categorization, with socially and politically normative consequences.

Critics of law and literature have identified the symbolic power of contextualizing processes in law, which is particularly conspicuous in the narrative elements characterizing the adjudicating process. For instance, Peter Brooks argues that "the making, transmission, and reception of stories is never innocent or unproblematic ... on the contrary it activates unacknowledged ideologies and doxa, ... [while] the formal design of narratives reflects their intention, their tendency, their construal and their outcome."[14] Adjudicating processes amount to microcosmic acts of social poiesis that either seek to reproduce the status quo or take advantage of these narrative acts to modify terms of social regulation and legitimacy. Therefore, the act of contextualizing does not guarantee a radical or reformative outcome. It is not so much that the act of contextualizing makes law reformative as that the selection of specific criteria of contextualization might.[15] This implies that acts of contextualization are characterized by intentionality: the contextualizing process, which depends on an emplotment of various social elements that will constitute the context of an analysis, presents itself as an intentional means of legitimizing the particular normative terms of a sociodicy. A manifestation of the will for symbolic power, intentionality endows legal utterances with a telos, mobilizing and stretching (which is the etymological origin of the word *intent*) performatives towards specific consequences whose significance for the legal subject or social field under its jurisdiction is binding.

How are we to understand the intentionality of legal utterances? If law's use of language is in part determined by its doxa and principles of knowledge, does the intentionality of its utterances display a specificity that distinguishes them from other intentional speech acts? What occasions for social transformation, or what effects of symbolic violence, do these specific intentional utterances create? Stanley Fish extends the function of intentionality to all human processes of communication. "One cannot read *or* reread independently of intention, independently, that is, of the assumption that one is dealing with marks or sounds produced by an intentional being, a being situated in some enterprise in relation to which he has a purpose or a point of view."[16] In contrast, in literary criticism and theoretical discussions, writers have called into question the possibility of ascertaining intentionality in a literary text.

In particular, Monroe C. Beardsley and William K. Wimsatt published an influential essay on what they called the intentional fallacy (1946), which consists in attributing thoughts and ideas to an author as if the relation between the author's mind and literary language were transparent. From a structuralist standpoint, the concept of intentionality was undermined by a shift from biographical criticism to an analysis of the role of linguistic structures in literature, which rendered the question of intentionality moot. The last straw landed on the camel's back when in 1969 Foucault discussed the literary work as "the murderer of its author"[17] and regarded the author's name as a discursive function. However, the concept of intentionality and its relation to affect persisted in analyses such as Roman Jakobson's theorizing of the six functions of communication.[18] In his analysis of these functions, Jakobson assigns a conative function to the communication of a message, which refers to the intent or desired outcome of the act of communication. Although limited in scope, Jakobson's identification of this function of communication is precious in the context of an analysis of legal language, which remains based on law's conative address to the legal subject in the mode of a binding imperative with obedience as the exclusive outcome.

It can be argued that intentionality is a fundamental characteristic of legal rhetoric and practices. In the context of the analysis of legal processes and utterances, Tony Honoré maintains that legal interpretation is a form of practical reasoning with a purpose. "It must, even if the historical evidence is inadequate, assign to the form of words or practice to be interpreted a meaning which can be applied to the facts of the case. It differs in this respect, for example, from the interpretation of a newly discovered fragment of papyrus. Moreover the legal solution must be workable. ... Legal interpretation has to be in part forward-looking."[19] The intentionality of the law can also be grasped through Raz's analysis of the ways in which courts are called upon to fill in the gaps between a legal system of rules and cases at hand. "Unregulated disputes are ... partly regulated, hence the court has to apply existing law as well as to make new law. But since, by definition, in an unregulated dispute the law contains a gap, since it fails to provide a solution to the case, the court cannot make law without changing existing law. It makes law by filling in the gaps."[20] It is by filling these gaps that law becomes law – that is to say, it is by producing meaning that the law is recognized as the law. The gap is the occasion for a new regulation, and, in filling the gap, the law releases its effect of authority and acts on its capacity to change reasons for action. In doing so, the law exhibits and exercises its intentionality, giving direction to meaning so as to meet specific objectives, reach conclusions, and make binding decisions.

The intentionality of the law and the ways in which this intentionality regulates and intervenes in practices of social poiesis are exemplified by a statement appearing in the 2003 report of the Law Commission in the United Kingdom on the role of partial defences in criminal cases.

> The debate ... [on partial defences] raises serious moral and policy questions about the proper approach of the law to standards of self-control. We have already referred to the ambiguity of the requirement that the defendant should have acted under a sudden loss of self-control, making him or her for the moment "not master of his mind." Historically, passion was recognised as something that might temporarily deprive a person of his reasoning faculties. In modern cases a person's capacity for self-control is treated as a medical or psychological matter, but it is important to recognise the limits of medicine. In provocation, we are concerned with cases where the defendant's conduct is volitional in the sense of being rationally directed. Psychiatrists can explain whether the defendant was suffering from an abnormality of mind recognised as a mental illness or from a personality disorder. Psychiatrists may also help to explain why a particular person may respond in particular circumstances in a particular way. But a doctor cannot answer medically the question whether a person *can* control himself (except in cases which would be classified legally as automatism, such as sleep walking). Where conduct is volitional in the sense of being rationally directed, the law operates under a belief of free will. All sorts of events from the moment of conception may affect someone's personality and temperament, including their propensity to anger. But, subject to limited exceptions, the criminal law sets uniform standards of behaviour for public policy reasons. The principal exceptions relate to children and young persons and to mentally abnormal offenders.[21]

Consider the rhetorical moves of the above argument. The statement begins with a historical perspective on the topic of self-control, and it clearly signals a critical distance from past conceptions by creating an ironic clash between the grammatical distinction "him"/"her" and the quoted "not master of his mind." The statement also indicates a shift in epistemic paradigms by contrasting the traditional belief in mental mastery with psychiatric evaluations of mental illnesses and disorders. What comes next is a doxological move, whereby a question is indirectly posed that medicine is shown incapable of answering. "But a doctor cannot answer medically the question whether a person *can* control himself (except in cases which would be classified legally as automatism, such as sleep walking)." The statement proceeds to provide a legal answer. "Where conduct is volitional in the sense of being rationally directed, the law operates under a belief of free will ... subject to limited exceptions, the criminal law sets uniform standards of behaviour for public policy reasons." The performative effect of the legal utterance is to reduce the scope of interpretation and explanation to the single principle of volition or free will. Predictably, the intentionality of legal utterances coincides with a reduction in semantic scope. The last sentence is added to justify the shift from an exploratory and historical mode of utterance to an imperative mode, which asserts that the law is to be governed by reasons of public policy. At this point, legal time takes the stage where localized phenomena become subject to "uniform standards of behaviour" and to the sole legal doctrine of free will. The criterion of uniformity introduces a process of predictability and controlled reiteration in the law's dealing with contingency and a multiplicity of circumstances.

This doctrinal approach to legal utterances – achieving continuity through uniformity – reveals the specificity of intentionality of these institutional utterances. If the language of the law has force, it is because its intentional utterances are loaded with the principle of the rule of law, which enhances the power of performative legal utterances. Further, while the intentional dimension of legal utterances is taken for granted in judges' reports, it also appears in naked form in documents such as parliamentary bills. On 24 April 2009, Harriet Harman presented a bill to the UK Parliament on behalf of the Government Equalities Office.[22] The intent of the bill was formulated as follows:

> Make provision to require Ministers of the Crown and others when making strategic decisions about the exercise of their functions to have regard to the desirability of reducing socio-economic inequalities; to reform and harmonise equality law and restate the greater part of the enactments relating to discrimination and harassment related to certain personal characteristics; to enable certain employers to be required to publish information about the differences in pay between male and female employees; to prohibit victimisation in certain circumstances; to require the exercise of certain functions to be with regard to the need to eliminate discrimination and other prohibited conduct; to enable duties to be imposed in relation to the exercise of public procurement functions; to increase equality of opportunity; and for connected purposes.[23]

This proto-legal utterance consists of a series of vectors mobilizing the legislative apparatus to enact social transformation. From a rhetorical standpoint, the intentional statement is organized around two devices. One concerns the anaphoric repetition of the formula based on the preposition *to* plus a verb, which creates a sense of accumulation.

The other is the creation of parallel objectives, which invoke the performative power of utterances once translated into legislative terms. This value-oriented emphasis makes full use of the potential performativity of utterances and opens up a vista of the future, when, ideally, the law will be authorized to enact these values and when social agents will be entitled to call upon the law for redress. If and when legislated in one form or another, these social terms will become legitimate terms of the general sociodicy according to which the law and social agents will keep telling and retelling the terms of their social practices and structural principles of employment and equity.

However, the intentionality of legal principles does not guarantee the outcome of the decision-making process. Interestingly, Honoré locates the derailing of legal intentionality at the point where legal rules meet cultural and historical normativity. He points out that when "norms set by society or individuals are incorporated in texts they become to some extent independent of the intentions of those who originally drafted or adopted them. ... This fact leaves room, in the process of interpretation, for arguments which are not concerned with any possible meaning of the words used, let alone the one intended by its original author."[24] The point is crucial because it reinjects a level of performative flexibility into the very terms of the law and allows for an account of the ways in which unpredictability and contingency affect law's identity, its performatives of legitimation, and its agency in the poiesis of social norms.

However, it is also in this gap between intention and outcome that, drawing on Paul de Man's analysis of discourse, Adam Thurschwell locates the force of speech acts. "All utterances possess, by virtue of the fact that they are speech acts, the certainty of producing (unknowingly and uncontrollably) effects – semantic and otherwise – that exceed the semantic entity posited by the utterance itself as its final destination."[25] So we end up with a paradox: by virtue of its mandate to regulate and legitimize the social organization of a community, the symbolic power of the law is defined by a fundamental and institutional intentionality; by virtue of its use of language, whose historical and social origins it cannot shave off, the law's intentionality grafts onto the symbolic power and prevalence of whatever social norms it seeks to regulate and legitimize. As a nexus of legal autopoietic formality and cultural normativity, the law cannot aspire to total mastery over the effects of its intentional decisions because the cultural and historical performativity of the social norms it regulates will remain beyond law's control. This is most conspicuous when one considers that the application of a particular law will have different effects on different legal subjects, who will be socially situated on account of their class, gender, and ethnic trajectories.

Conversely, the fact that social norms infiltrate the institutional language of the law implies that its intentionality will be affected by the temporality of these social norms, their social reproduction, and cultural antecedence. Legal utterances do not tap their potential for social performativity until statutory and other principles are deployed through processes of contextualizing and intentional narration that analyses of counselling and adjudication fully reveal.[26] In other words, the narrative character of legal procedures constitutes the locus and the occasion for the double helix of the law to appear in full view. While statutes present themselves as a discrete series of sections and clauses that are sequentially organized, legal contextualizing processes have the effect of establishing syntagmatic and referential connections between the legal rules stated in the discrete sections and the social circumstances of a particular case.[27]

The narrative configuration of a case is not the sole product of legal reasoning; instead, the narrative mobilization of legal codification takes place in the twin contexts of cultural normativity and legal normativity, as exemplified by precedents, evidentiary procedure, and doctrinal principles of the law. In this process, intentionality and contextualization remain the factors of normative variability concerning the potential legal outcome of a case because these factors are grounded in the cultural norms, beliefs, and principles that constitute the sociodicy of the social group in which legal decisions are made. If we agree that legal regulation is intertwined with cultural normativity, and that different groups and social agents compete for the legitimacy of their terms of existence, then case law and the narration that unfolds in this process represent a major site of normative struggle of social poiesis.[28] The adjudicating process coincides with what can be called the narrativization of legal utterances as they regulate and legitimize social normativity. In this respect, Bourdieu's concept of classificatory schemes sheds light on the interpretive process of adjudication in the grips of hegemonic social norms that turn the legal process into a mechanism of social reproduction and political reinforcement of inequity.

Thus, the symbolic violence of law is fully deployed whenever legal utterances perform as exclusionary narratives, as demonstrated by Anna Carline, who, in various analyses of courts' approaches to women who kill, draws on Butler's theory of political resignification in the process of the construction of legal subjects. In particular, she focuses on the case of Zoora Shah, who in December 1993 was found guilty of murdering Mohammed Azam after she had poisoned his food with arsenic. "Zoora, a Pakistani woman who lived in Bradford, developed a relationship with Azam after her husband left her for a younger woman. In addition to her murder conviction, Zoora was also convicted of forgery, soliciting murder and attempted murder. Zoora appealed her convictions for murder and attempted murder on the grounds that fresh evidence should be admitted under s 23 of the Criminal Appeals Act 1968. The Court of Appeal rejected her appeal and also refused to grant leave to appeal to the House of Lords."[29] According to Carline, "the identity of a woman who kills is constructed through the identity categories generated by the legislature, the courts and also academic commentary. Hence the law and the courtroom become a site of struggle over the battered woman's identity."[30] However, it can also be argued that the constitution of the battered woman is not the sole outcome of these specialized fields of knowledge and conceptualization.[31]

Indeed, at work in court are the classificatory schemes of the battered woman, which generate a gender and political discourse revolving around the legitimacy of Muslim culture in the United Kingdom in the context of immigration. In elaborating its reasons for murder conviction, the court engaged in what seems to be an implacable process of citation of normative beliefs, whose confirmation and validity Zoora Shah was assumed to embody and perform.[32] Thus, Carline's analysis can be reread to reveal how, in its practices of contextualization and intentionality, the law and its legal utterances intervene and regulate social poiesis.

On the one hand, the court seeks to construct Zoora Shah as a speaker, a mother, and a victim of domestic violence and, on the basis of this construct, to reach a verdict. On the other, this process of intentionality is derailed by Zoora Shah's passive resistance, which creates a gap between her conduct and gender- and race-based normative characterization. If the court fills this gap, it is not so much by creating a new legal argument as by seeing in it evidence of guilt.[33] In this case, practical reasoning, which Honoré considers a major characteristic of the law, plays into the classificatory schemes of race and gender and delivers a judgment on deviations from social narratives of behaviour. The law needs Shah's body to perform according to cultural norms of assessment that underwrite the court's search for evidence. But Shah's body matters to the law in selected ways, which will confirm a social narrative. Indeed,

Carline points out that, in assessing the case, the court did not take into account the marks of domestic violence on Shah's body, which might have shed light on the circumstances of the murder.

In this case, the symbolic violence of the law derives from the violence of its emplotment of the case, which is reinforced by the social nomos infiltrating its legal reasoning. The court's instrumental use of reason and language is clearly informed by orthodoxies that reappear as the bad mother, the female liar, and the Muslim woman without shame or honour, all of which are deployed in culturally determined scenarios that keep being enacted through symbolic activities and structural practices at work and in school, church, sports, the media, politics, and families.[34] Thus, the temporality of statutory criminal law grafts onto the temporality of social norms of behaviour and characterization, which are deployed according to predictable narrative plots. Out of these binding legal utterances emerges Zoora Shah as the grotesque, unrecognizable "unusual woman," who lashes out inexplicably and who therefore cannot benefit from extenuated circumstances. In other words, the performative effect of these legal utterances is the production of the legal subject as strange and uncanny. At stake is not so much whether Zoora Shah killed Mohammed Azam – this is a fact – as the rationalizing terms of conviction, which turn a deaf ear to the cultural narrative of a stranger. If anything, this is a clear demonstration of the cultural, sociopolitical origin and destination of legal performative utterances.

As argued in chapter 1, social fields exercise symbolic violence whenever their social agents usurp the capacity to make sense of the world by silencing and excluding other means of generating norms of social poiesis. Carline's analyses shed light on this usurpation of social meaning in which the law engages whenever it uses classificatory schemes to produce uniformity in decision making. The exclusionary effects of legal interpretation are also illustrated by the courts' handling of the battered woman syndrome in their assessment of homicides during domestic violence. Carline examines five different cases where the courts considered this syndrome as a criterion of assessment in their deliberations. She demonstrates that the construct of gender fluctuated among the five different cases. Two of the cases were made to fit the test of the battered woman syndrome, while three others were made to fit the criteria of depression and mental illness at the cost of ignoring signs of deliberate agency.[35] In other words, the courts applied the syndrome as a criterion to determine whether the accused women were doing their gender and domesticity right without taking into account evidence that these women were not performing according to script.[36]

Butler's analysis of the rewards and punishments that social subjects receive at the hands of legal regulation assumes a grim dimension in the context of Carline's demonstration: women who do not fit criteria such as depression or the battered woman syndrome – that is to say, women who do not do their domestic homicides for the right reasons – tend to receive harsher convictions than men and other women. "Some women receive a harsher punishment for their transgressive behaviour, for failing to be sufficiently 'exceptional.' Such transgressive behaviour can be seen to be being an alcoholic, not suffering from a sufficient mental illness, and for being aggressive. In such situations the law has found a more subtle way in which to mark their unintelligibility. As opposed to the imposition of a murder conviction, some 'unexceptional women' receive a custodial sentence. However, the perceived absence of any culturally acceptable 'exceptional circumstances' tends to lead to a murder conviction."[37] This implies that, in its intent to reach a decision, the law refuses to legitimize the terms of existence of these women – that is to say, in the name of coherence and consistency, the law sentences that which threatens to undo its terms of legitimacy through intentional contextualization.

If we accept Carline's terms of analysis, then the legal decision to sentence women who do not fit cultural expectations on the count of murder constitutes an exacerbated illustration of what Goodrich has characterized as a dual logic in law manifested through

> inheritance and possession, tradition and compliance, belonging and identification. [This logic] establishes a constitution, a public order of lawful reason that can admit only of a binary and antithetically defined classification of those that belong and those that are excluded, those that listen and those that speak back. ... Its antiportrait depicts an obverse or outside of reason in specifically denunciatory and exclusory terms; those that do not belong to reason and the institution exist in the twilight and spectral zone of idols, fantasies, and dreams: the outsider inhabits a world of the half living and of the dead; she is both a nihilist and an augur of an apocalyptic fate.[38]

In other words, the antirrhetic dynamic that characterizes law's utterances combines with the symbolic violence of the social norms that infiltrate its rhetorical practices and reasoning processes and acquire legitimacy through decisions invoking the principle of the rule of law. It is in this context that we can reconsider what, in a reference to Roman Jakobson's linguistic analysis, I described as the conative dimension of legal utterances. From the interaction between legal utterances and cultural norms emerges the fluctuating relation between legal addresser and addressee: if the law addresses citizens in the mode of an imperative, citizens address the law not only by expecting accountability but also by making their claims of legitimacy.

If the legal subject – grammatical, economic, political, and historical – is the effect of law's imperative address, the law and its authority are also the metaleptic effect of the subject's address to the law. While the law's conative address constitutes the legal subject as an obedient subject, the legal subject's conative address to the law is sustained by a desire for justice and a narrative of expectation concerning the law and the performative outcomes of its utterances. As Ravit Reichman states, we expect that law will make sense of catastrophe and "generate an understanding of its vicissitudes and a judgment of its horrors. But this *story* of expectations suggests, too, the narrative demands we bring to law: the story of our desire for a gripping encounter, one that makes sense because it takes place before an enchanted audience."[39]

That the law does not fulfil its claims to justice prompts anger and indignation, if not cynicism. In 2006, Ratna Kapur remarked, "The proliferation of measures to expand racial and gender equality and child rights has not resulted in more equality. More men, women, and children starved to death in the twentieth century – supposedly the human rights century – than at any other point in human history. And laws against violence against women or trafficking have not necessarily afforded women greater freedom or protection from harm."[40] In this assessment, Kapur is measuring the gap between law's utterances in the form of legal rights and a political scene of destruction and violence. Now consider Joanne Conaghan's assessment of feminist theoretical thinking, which she claims has made a difference and contributed to historical transformation.

> The feminist focus on women workers ... has contributed to the radical transformation of the framework and content of employment protection legislation. The experiences of women victims of male violence have gradually found their way into legal debate on criminal justice reform, resulting in changes in the attitudes, practices, and powers of criminal justice actors. Recognition of the vulnerable economic position of wives and

> homemakers has produced a series of adjustments to property and equity principles in the context of the "marital" home, encroaching even on the boundaries of surety and banking law. Finally, it has been the vocalization of women's pain that has led to the recognition of "new" legal wrongs such as sexual harassment.[41]

Common to both statements is the implicit assumption that the law is accountable to the social group it legislates and regulates and that its decisions, which always take the form of utterances, can be measured by the yardsticks of social efficacy, transformation, and equity. Either the social and political performativity of law's utterances is governed by a discrepancy between utterances and the persistence, if not worsening, of social inequity or an instrumental relation of congruity obtains between legal reform goaded by feminist discourse and acts of historical transformation. In other words, in evaluating the social impact of the law – its promise for justice and failure to deliver – we are gauging the temporal relation between legal utterances and their social performativity. Just as in *Excitable Speech* Butler's analysis of hate speech and terms of injury reveals a desire for plenipotentiary power over language and its effects, the desire for legal words to be just speaks to a belief that in the name of justice, the law *will* match words with deeds.

Expanding on Butler's conception of performative transformation within the site of regulation, one can suggest that the law as an institution represents a poietic future of social possibilities whenever it is prepared to use regulation to respond to and be accountable for the terms of a particular case instead of striving for a fit between its interpretation of the case and its past decisions. Through the legal interpretation of case law, statutes, constitutions and charters, courts have the capacity to inject new meaning into legal archives and to make them performative by establishing a relationship between intent and objective.[42]

Distinguishing between originalist and textualist interpretations of legal statements such as statutes and constitutional texts, Helen Irving introduces the third term of "purposive interpretation" to reflect on how to achieve a particular social objective given the intent and meaning of past law. "A purposive approach, bringing together the historical purpose with 'the interests, goals, values, aims, policies, and function that the constitutional text is designed to actualize in democracy,' may provide the best compromise between the historical goals or purposes that one wants to retain and current interest that one wants to promote. It is, importantly, sensitive to *context*. It brings purpose and context together, allowing the object of the former to find new expression in the latter."[43] The assumption is that, in devising a particular purpose, the legal decision will performatively endow with renewed authority and significance the legal archive, which will function as a major point of bearing but not one of sclerosis. Irving takes the example of Canada's Persons Case of 1929, in which the Judicial Committee of the British Privy Council, which functioned as the highest court of appeal in the British Empire, interpreted the British North America Act, 1867 to include women under the category of person, arguing that the Act "had planted in Canada a living tree capable of growth and expansion within its natural limits."[44] Whatever the political intent of the government of Canada for rejecting the petition and of the Privy Council for supporting it, it remains that the two parties gave the 1867 Canadian Constitution a different interpretation by attributing to it a different intent in order to achieve an objective.

In her analysis of purposive interpretation, Irving describes a major strategy available to law to shape the process of social poiesis through acts that performatively interpret and legitimize the terms of a sociodicy in the making. This refashioning of the social world is precluded whenever the narrativization of legal statutes according to dominant classificatory schemes – that is to say, hegemonic ways of telling what we do and who we are – obliterate the horizon of future possibilities. At the same time, a socio-legal critique of the symbolic violence of the law does not preclude an ethical and political critique of the factors that seek to interrupt legal performativity. The law poses a dilemma: the desire to be accommodated in the house of the law depends on one's indenture to the terms of the law. In this respect, the reiterated, down-to-earth, everyday challenge is to preserve law's claim to supremacy so as to protect civic guardianship while countering the symbolic violence lurking in legal performatives.

Chapter Six

The Legitimacy of the Family: Family Law and Gothic Fiction

In this and the next two chapters, I pursue the analysis of the agon for legitimacy through symbolic power by concentrating on the social poiesis of the family, in which English family statutory law and Gothic narratives engage. My approach to the concept of the family is not premised on a predefined cultural concept; instead, the family can be regarded as an example of the ways in which various social agents and symbolic fields generate social poiesis through symbolic power and practices. Thus, while certainly bearing imprints of historical, political, and cultural development, the meaning of the family is never stable as it operates like a constant process of family constitution vying for legitimacy in the polis. In selecting family law and Gothic narratives, I point to the fact that both the modern development of the law and the emergence of the Gothic in eighteenth-century England were characterized by attempts to establish their authority as law and literature. Further, I suggest that, in exercising their symbolic power, law and literature generated a social poiesis revolving around the usurpatory and arbitrary constitution of the family as the legitimate manifestation of state power.

My concern is to demonstrate that late twentieth- and early twenty-first-century family law and instances of Gothic narratives are still haunted by a patriarchal sociodicy that manifests itself through the political uncanny as a sign of symbolic violence and sovereign power. Thus, the major claim governing my analysis of the social poiesis of the family is that the Gothic presents itself as a site where hybrid forms of power spawned by family regulation and cultural practices are spectacularly narrated.

The historical and legal origins of the agon for the legitimacy of the family in the United Kingdom emerge from my analysis of English statutory law. As an institution, law lends its authority to family norms by issuing statutes, schedules, and case-law decisions that sustain practices of kinship through a process of cultural and legal citation. State authority constitutes the family subject through regulatory norms and processes that can be traced back to statutory law, which is interpreted not only through judiciary processes in and outside the courts, but also by governmental agencies and local authorities. With the proliferation of statutory texts, family law arose in the twentieth century as a specialized discourse both legislating the habitus and space of kinship and regulating its economic practices and relationships.[1] In constituting and legitimizing the family through statutes, family law has the capacity to exercise symbolic violence over cultural practices surrounding the family.

However, the purpose of my focus on statutory law is not to reduce law to legal statutes, lawyers, and court procedures. Mariana Valverde has demonstrated the ways in which various techniques among police officers, vice squads, and administrative personnel produce knowledge of law through everyday practices. Further, "legal facts and legal judgments are only meaningful and effective within a network, one that connects legal decisions and statutes but also includes buildings (e.g., prisons), clothes (robes, uniforms), information codes, individuals, institutions such as legislatures, law schools, and courts, professional associations, and extralegally produced texts such as psychological reports, police notes, and scene-of-crime photographs."[2] In this context, my intent is to dislodge legal texts from a method that would reinstate a dual relationship between statutory regulation and social practices. Statutory law exemplifies the double helix of the law: sociodicy through codification. Haunting this codifying and legitimizing power is another form of power, manifesting itself whenever legal and cultural norms of constituting the family become a potent means of wielding sovereign power by usurping the practice of symbolic power. This link between normative power and sovereign power points to a historical continuum between the state and the family whose historical and cultural origins I examine in this chapter.

One can distinguish between two basic approaches to the interaction between law and the Gothic in current criticism. On the one hand, critics have focused on the representation of law in Gothic narratives, as in the case of David Punter, who in *Gothic Pathologies* (1998) has analysed the four motifs of the attorney, legal language as a language of duplicity, the prison, and the trial.[3] In another instance, Avril Horner and Sue Zlosnik (*Gothic and the Comic Turn*, 2005) have analysed the legal regulation of land ownership through Protestant laws and capitalism in Ireland, described in novels such as Maria Edgeworth's *Castle Rackrent* (1800). The other approach consists in examining the philosophical and cultural implications concerning the interaction between discourses of/on the law and the Gothic. Repeatedly, critics have held that the Gothic concerns the deletion of normative boundaries, the transgression of interdicts, the manufacture of monstrosity through normative injunctions, the generation of hideous progenies and doppelgängers under the pressure of social conventions, and the grotesqueries of bodies possessed by discourses of knowledge such as psychoanalysis, as in Patrick McGrath's *Asylum* (1997).

On this basis, Punter establishes a contrast between the excesses of Gothic fiction and the law as a regime of regulation. Gothic textuality "is always ruined. And behind this thought stand the forms of obsession, compulsion. We might say that obsessive actions – Melmoth's quest for souls, Pat Bateman's serial murders – are the ruin of action; in so far as action may be designed to produce an effect, then obsession denies the possibility of that effect ever escaping from a closed circle, ever moving beyond square one."[4] Punter constructs the Gothic as the site of the production of meaning with nothingness as its haunting presence. In contrast, the law is posited as "the imposition of certainty, the rhetorical summation of absence, or the loss, of doubt."[5] While this may be true of positivist interpretations of the law, the law considered in its institutional, historical, and, above all, performative dimension presents a more complex relation with certainty. The notion that "the law can have no cognizance of ghosts"[6] is tempered by the consideration of the law as a double helix, whereby, as I argued in chapter 3, social history intertwines with legal normativity. As such, the law is actually a propitious ground for the haunting of symbolic violence and patterns of the political uncanny.

That the law is a discourse among others, and that it functions as a means of imagining social reality with the force of institutional authority, is an idea that Punter actually considers when he suggests that "*rule*, the operation of a regime ... takes its form as a defensive strategy, a type of fabulation."[7] It is this conception of law as fertile ground for Gothic fabulation that Sue Chaplin considers in her analysis of eighteenth-century law in England.[8] In her critique of the autotelic claim for the law as a self-contained, autonomous, and rational structure, Chaplin uses the Gothic mode – a mode of writing that resists categorization and does not belong to a genre – as a means of destabilizing law's claims to discursive authority and natural origins. Specifically, she argues that common to the rise of Gothic writing, as exemplified by Horace Walpole's *Castle of Otranto* (1764), and to modern law, as exemplified by William Blackstone's *Commentaries on the Laws of England* (1769), is a myth of origins, according to which there was a foundational period when England was governed by the Goths before the advent of Protestant governance, spirituality, and industriousness.[9]

As the Gothic period was also associated with the Dark Ages in the historical imaginary, this invocation of the Gothic past threatens Blackstone's project with the unruly and Walpole's project with the illegitimate. For Blackstone, in particular, the challenge was to invoke the old common law as evidence of an English lineage while countering its labyrinthine aspects by developing a rational, codified, and constitutional approach to law.[10] In her critique of the all-powerful logos and the claim for a mythical transcendental origin that would shore up law's authority, Chaplin suggests that the law is a phantasmatic narrative haunted by "socially and historically contingent rules bearing no relation to natural law but operating according to the peculiar customs of a given nation at a given time."[11] In this sense, the social and historical institution of the law functioned as a syntactically regulated phantasm, to use Butler's terms of analysis.

Although the Gothic can be enlisted to sap the law's claim to transcendental authority and origin, it is also possible to consider the Gothic as a creature of the law. While Chaplin subscribes to the notion that the Gothic defies generic identity, Michael Gamer traces connections between the Gothic as a genre and the legal category of obscene libel. Gamer identifies *R v. Curll* [1727] as a turning point in the history of English law when it identified pornography as a type or category of writing. "Curll's conviction in 1727 for publishing two obscene books ... effectively created a law against obscene libel for the first time in English history. ... [The case] created a legal classification and therefore a *category* of writing – one based on historically and geographically local definitions of obscenity and later conflated with pornography."[12] This categorization did not so much rest on textual conventions as on textual effects on the reader and citizen.

For instance, Matthew Lewis's *The Monk* (1796) and Charlotte Dacre's *Zofloya* (1806) came under attacks in the press, invoking obscene libel. According to Gamer, the legal category of obscene libel later became associated with the textual practices and readerly effects of Gothic writing and came to affect "the gothic's cultural status and trajectory for most of the nineteenth century by stigmatizing the genre legally and morally."[13] The implication of his argument is twofold: on the one hand, genre is not a purely doxological discourse of literary criticism and theory since it can also be generated by law's regulatory typology of texts; on the other, his analysis reveals that the identification of the Gothic as a subversive text is also the product of a legal speech-act. In other words, if we agree with Gamer, Gothic subversion was partly named and constituted by the law of obscene libel.[14]

Common to Punter's, Chaplin's, and Gamer's discussions of the relation between law and Gothic is the general concept of jurisdiction and how it plays out in different contexts of analysis. While the law is seen as establishing jurisdiction over various social fields, the Gothic is conceived either as a mode escaping the jurisdiction of the literary genre or as a mode spawned by the jurisdictional authority of the law.[15] Without entering the debate as to whether the Gothic is a genre and as to what the theoretical and critical implications of such a debate are, I suggest that like the discourse of institutional law, the Gothic engages in the process of social poiesis by producing narratives of social organization and normative contestation in the polis through symbolic power and social practices. If such is the case, then the Gothic as a symbolic activity will spawn its own power effects.[16] Specifically, as a formulaic mechanism of uncanny effects and as a manufacturing of affect situated between dread and laughter, the Gothic exercises power on the reader or the viewer, but the political tenor of this power will depend on historical contexts of production and interpretation. The Gothic and its uncanny machinery is a text of power within power.

This mechanical aspect of the Gothic is underlined in Eve Sedgwick's analysis of early Gothic rhetoric, in which conventions such as the oppressive ruin, the wild landscape, the Catholic or feudal society, the spatialized self, and the apocalyptic use of language recur.[17] The formulaic character of the Gothic also indicates that its rhetorical power is linked to the capacity to produce readerly and visual pleasure through recognition of familiar conventions. Peopled with "meaning machines,"[18] the Gothic seduces while undermining the Romantic cultivation of authenticity, sincerity, and spontaneity. In this context, Botting argues that "bound up with language and mechanisms (machines and mental processes), the uncanny is, in many ways, a technological phenomenon whose effects are accentuated by the shifts and disturbances of technical *innovation*."[19] Building on Terry Castle's study of the uncanny in the eighteenth century as a major symptom of modern consciousness, Botting suggests that the uncanny spectralization of consciousness and the erasure of boundaries between minds and objects, selves and machines testify to a circulation of Gothic metaphors and their contaminating effects.[20]

At the same time, these Gothic effects of symbolic power are potentially held in check by various strategies that betray the spuriousness of Gothic narratives. The Gothic text is first and foremost writing about writing, representing, symbolizing, narrating, deciphering – in sum, about producing signs that seduce into interpretation, baffling yet so obvious. As critics of the Gothic have argued, the genre is characterized by a metafictional capacity to lay bare the device or to draw attention to the over-the-top performance of its rhetoric of horror.[21] From *The Castle of Otranto*, Mary Shelley's *Frankenstein* (1818), and Emily Brontë's *Wuthering Heights* (1847) through Robert Louis Stevenson's *Dr Jekyll and Mr Hyde* (1886) and Bram Stoker's *Dracula* (1897) to Patrick McGrath's *Spider* (1990) and Julie Myerson's *Sleepwalking* (1994), Gothic narratives have been characterized by a careful elaboration of textual effects through embedded narratives, unreliable narrators, a topography of depths and surfaces (dungeons, labyrinths, burial sites, dark corridors and glens), and a sustained awareness of the power effects of media, from epistolary writing and typewriters to cinema, paintings, and hypertext. As a means of effecting dread and laughter, excess and the inexplicable, the Gothic turns out to be a highly concerted and elaborate affair.[22]

This metafictional awareness is doubled by a historical consciousness, and this combination of affect, metafiction, and history perhaps accounts for the potency and singularity of Gothic narratives. That the Gothic is profoundly historical has been underlined by several critics.[23] What both Robert Miles and Fred Botting add to this characterization of the Gothic are specific terms of historical reference that are relevant to my own analysis. Concentrating on two early writers of the Gothic, Miles brings out in two separate essays two elements on which I wish to pause. Reflecting on the historical import of the early Gothic in *The Castle of Otranto*, Miles argues that the genre was preoccupied with the legitimacy of political power. Thus, a "historical concern for the decay of models of legitimacy pervades the Gothic, not accidentally or in a general manner, which might be said of almost any text, but as an integral aspect of the Gothic's generic origins. To put it at its simplest, a concern with authenticity, legitimacy, and power follows as a matter of course from pastiche, from the self-conscious bric-a-brac with which Walpole assembled both his house and his romance."[24] In other words, techniques of pastiche and counterfeit point to a suspicion of claims to political and constitutional legitimacy.

Miles interprets *The Castle of Otranto* as a site of contestation where Walpole transforms the political claim of authority and legitimacy, shored up by the reference to the Gothic constitution, into "a parable about the contested ambiguity of all such appeals to authenticating origins. His own text, like his own house, is a self-dramatizing Gothic fake."[25] Out of Miles's interpretation emerges a political concern in the Gothic for the power of the state and its buttressing on constitutional terms of legitimacy and authority. If we now turn to Miles's interpretation of Anne Radcliffe's contribution to the early Gothic, we read that her heroines are typically endowed with middle-class sensibility and that they contest the legitimacy of patriarchal authority hailing from a dark and feudal order.[26] This critique of patriarchy, its legitimacy and authority, Botting sees as a major trope and ideological concern of the entire genre.

> Gothic fiction can be defined as a transgression of the paternal metaphor. Transgression, however, operates in a complex manner: it is not a celebratory breaking of laws and taboos considered unjust or repressive, nor a straightforward liberation from rules and conventions binding individuals within strict frameworks of duty or normative identity. Transgression, as an act that is both constructive and disruptive, forms a strangely integral process in the definition and preservations of limits. As a transgression of the paternal principle, then, Gothic fiction constitutes a game of loss and recovery, a play of forces in which it interrupts and invigorates the circulations over which it presides.[27]

In other words, the historical rise of the Gothic in England derived in part from a concern with two types of legitimacy: one is state-based, the other is family-based. I suggest that the co-presence of these two critiques in the Gothic is no historical coincidence and that the calling into question of the legitimacy of power at both levels points to a major cultural and political convergence, which I will analyse from the standpoint of symbolic violence and sovereign power as its hybrid.

Botting envisages two responses to the evacuation of the paternal metaphor: "a mourning of the father, a call for the restoration of political, religious, or family values, for instance, or a continued, even accelerating, repudiation of anything resembling a paternal institution or authority."[28] There is another possibility he does not consider, and that is the revenance of a form of sovereign power through normative, patriarchy-inflected discourses in the polis and, in particular, in institutions such as the law, which in the history of Western culture has been a repository of patriarchal principles of social vision and division. As a mode of governmentality, family statutory law has the capacity to regulate normative principles of identification and practices of the family, to disenfranchise through enlisting, to protect through normalization, but it also has the capacity to wield sovereign power. Sovereign state power manifests itself in family law whenever it grafts on the normative and constitutive statutes of domestic regulation. Strikingly, the political oscillation between governmentality and sovereign power affecting global politics in the twenty-first century reappears in the field of family law.

So, while Butler identifies the resurgence of sovereign power in the context of apocalyptic global politics in the wake of 9/11, here forms of sovereign power originate in a system of kinship – at home, so to speak. This looming of sovereign power in the regulation of kinship is not the manifestation of an ahistorical force; rather, it is grounded in a narrative of power that used to combine the figure of kinship with the legal figure of the potentate associated with religious and political power. The ghost of sovereign power in contemporary family law can be traced to the origins of English law and the early principle of *regia potestas*, which Peter Goodrich has analysed while focusing on the trope of genealogy in an earlier formative discourse of English law. Goodrich shows that through text and visual representation, the law was conceived as a family tree, with figures of power akin to paternal figures of authority.

> It is no accident that the most emblematic and significant visual illustration in the foundational work of English common law, Coke's *Institutes*, is ... of genealogical origin, a tree of consanguinity that explains the proper place, the legitimacy of the founder of modern common law, Sir Thomas Littleton. In Edward Coke's vocabulary, the degrees of consanguinity are the proper depiction of inheritance and seem to provide the most adequate visual account of the authority of the subject. Thus the tree is presented early on in the *Institutes*, precisely because it is an institutional work, because it institutes the rules of common law. What founds both inheritance of property and judicial authority is that place that is occupied upon the family tree, be it that of *patria potestas* or *regia potestas*, paternal authority or monarchical power, to borrow a phrase from an ecclesiastical author.[29]

By virtue of the institutional and religious nature of its authority, the patriarchal figure stood at the hinge of both public and private spheres, whereby state and family coincided in him and whereby the power of the Crown could be constituted as "the constitutional equivalent in natural and civil law of the absolute power of the father."[30] The historical genesis of English family law manifested itself as the fabrication of a political sociodicy sealed by a discourse of matrimonial, loyal, and obedient union between the families of the kingdom and the Crown that headed them. "In accordance with the spiritual character of any marriage, the social family is joined in a mystical union in which the relation between the elements of the union is subject to the transcendental imperative of the union as such. … Christian marriage is defined legally by *patria potestas* and socially by the subordination of women and children. The absolute dominion of the father of the social and political realm, *regia potestas*, is the logical extension and correlate of the metaphor of marriage."[31]

In other words, the national claim for the power and territorial boundaries of England rested on a legitimization of the English family as a structural and political foundation of Englishness.[32] It is no coincidence that this twinning of state and family reappears between the lines of sixteenth-century English law proscribing buggery and in Coke's comments on the violence of buggery. As Moran states, "In its close proximity to treason, buggery is an act that threatens sovereignty and State institutions."[33] There is eminent consistency in Coke's comments on *regia potestas* and buggery.

That these historical patriarchal principles underwrote the old common law is well known, and numerous are the commentators and analysts who have cited the notion that wife and children were regarded at law as the chattels of the husband and that the husband was deemed to be the lord of his castle. Undoubtedly, family law has evolved throughout the twentieth and twenty-first centuries, but this evolution has taken place in the context of the historical and foundational discourse of English common law, whose symbolic violence is manifest in the protracted constitution of women's, children's, same-sex, and transsexual rights. For at stake in these modern rights is the family as the political and national unit sealed by matrimony, which individual rights threaten to fragment. In addition, the antirrhetic dimension of family law, which is most apparent in statutes on divorce until the Family Law Act 1996, produced language that validated norms with exclusionary effects and that maintained boundaries between those who belonged and those who did not belong to the family and, therefore, the citizenry.

The emergence of modern family law actually speaks to a paradoxical development. On the one hand, in establishing principles of regulation, the law has differentiated between state and family. On the other, in devising and legitimizing techniques of family regulation, the discourse of family law has displayed symptoms of *regia potestas* through its biopolitical interventions on the bodies of families.[34] It is precisely this naturalization of the family that haunts family law whenever it grapples with the regulation of bodies, genders, and sexuality.

In my analysis of the social poiesis of the family as constituted through legal regulation, Gothic narratives, and social practices, I therefore use the term *patriarchy* to designate the relation between forms of social domination and their historical origins. Patriarchy never existed as such but, proteiform, has always morphed through beliefs, principles, social practices, and institutions. The term remains useful to describe the ways in which a sociodicy of state and family, which has lost the ubiquity and force it had in the past, nevertheless haunts social practices and principles of organization in family culture and family law. Thus, patriarchy in this study neither refers to a fortress of some sort nor invokes nostalgia for sex wars, but operates as a means of identifying social contradictions and paradoxes, which I will designate under the general term of *dyschronia*.

The persistence of patriarchal terms of social organization defeats a linear conception of historical time that would be momentarily interrupted by anachronistic elements delaying an ineluctable march towards some telos. Whether we consider Bourdieu's notion that a sociodicy secretes its own epistemic unconscious, occluding the historical and political origins of its constitution of the world, or Butler's notion that normative performativity is predicated on the relegation of deviating practices and identifications to a sepulchral zone, we are offered a conception of history that is bound to unfold in non-linear ways. In this sense, social transformation cannot be dissociated from the recursive persistence of beliefs, structures, and identifications inherited from the historical past, which are the grounds for a social and political pattern of contradiction and incoherence. I use the term *dyschronia* to elaborate the notion that this linearity is messed up by vestiges of the past and to point to recursive streaks in historical time that do not correspond to mere repetition or reproduction. Instead, dyschronia is the material sign of a social agon manifesting itself through contradictions and paradoxes, which cast a shadow on the present and on what could constitute the future.[35] Further, I will show that the terms of this vestigial form of social domination constitute the historical context for manifestations of sovereign power, which emerge in the field of family law and family culture, as historically determined by a patriarchal narrative.

The recursive haunting of a patriarchal sociodicy constitutes a feature of law's regulation of the family. Repeatedly, writers of legal criticism – Bennett, Lacey (1992), Pahl, Smart (1989) – have underlined the fact that a fundamental paradox characterizes the historical evolution of English family law.[36] While legal statutes have inscribed rights that redefine the role of men, women, and children in families, the transformative effect of these texts have remained hampered by an ideological and economic context of discrimination and inequity. In 2003, for example, Abercrombie and Warde reported that the majority of women in England remained economically inferior to men as they earned 81 per cent of men's hourly rates (59 per cent for part-timers); although women had access to the job market, the majority of female jobs were part-time jobs; the majority of women were still responsible for domestic tasks; and various economic policies accounted for the poverty of single mothers.[37] The continuing impact of patriarchal practices can be seen at work in professional gender imbalance (as in law) or the inconsistent provision of childcare programs in various countries. These economic structures and gender practices originate in a general sociodicy that characterized women as keepers of the hearth and as carers of family members (children and the elderly).

The family doxa underlying this conception of women was encouraged and disseminated by Thatcherism. In 1988, at the Conservative Women's Conference, Margaret Thatcher declared that the family "is the building block of society. … It encompasses the whole of society. It fashions our beliefs. It is a preparation for the rest of our life" and added that it "is a nursery, a school, a hospital, a leisure centre, a place of refuge and a place of rest. … And women run it."[38] The statement manufactures a family construct fostering a particular conception of women as educators, nurses, entertainers, and protectors. These multiple roles are validated insofar as they are performed within the traditional discourse of the family. However, as soon as women distance themselves from the family kernel, they lose their status and are held accountable for the collapse of family values and the emergence of social unrest.

The purchase of this family nomos during the Thatcher years is illustrated by the statement made by Tory member of Parliament Rhodes Boyson in 1989 that "the intentional one parent family is probably the most evil product of our time. Their increased numbers are the cause of violent crime, football hooliganism, mugging and inner city revolt."[39] Further, the materialization of family discursive norms is typically revealed by an analysis of the economic distribution of family benefits, which indicates that in devising economic policies, the state determines kinship structures, relationships, and identities. As Alec Samuels argues, the "very act of defining benefits, let alone prescribing the conditions for their receipt, involves choices that must be reflections of values. ... The whole of the welfare state is shot through with paradox. At the most obvious level, the more benefits the State provides the more potent becomes social control through defining the conditions for entitlement and through threats of withdrawal."[40] Thus, family members are encouraged to identify with the dominant family habitus through a system of material and economic rewards guaranteeing social recognition and approval.

In addition, the language and principles of reform have historically displayed an inconsistent, see-saw pattern within the law. For instance, Ruth Deech refers to principles of reform in the 1963 Family Charter, which states that "men and women are equal before the law; marriage is neither an insurance policy for women, designed to keep them in economic security, nor is it a conveyance of property ... parties to a marriage which has completely broken down should never find themselves irretrievably tied to each other; children are entitled to special protection and are not to be treated as pawns in a battle between their parents."[41] Further, despite its mandate to reform family culture and practices, the Law Commission, a "statutory independent body created by the Law Commissions Act 1965 to keep the law under review and to recommend reform where it is needed," was criticized for its patriarchal conception of marriage and gender identities.[42] Whether we consider the requirement of long periods of waiting before divorce could be granted, women's exposure to economic precariousness after divorce, or law's accommodation of fathers' rights, the evolution of family law as registered by the commission's reports betrays signs of contradictions and incoherence, which can be traced to an agon between the legitimization of new social practices and the persistence of principles of social organization inherited from the past.

Deech published her historical assessment of the Law Commission in 1986, and one might expect the legal scene to have undergone transformation in keeping with social transformation. However, eleven years later, Maggie Rae published an analysis of family law that clearly brings out the persistence of the patriarchal nomos in English courts and records a discrepancy between the implicit vision of the world stated through statutory law and the empirical, economic, and cultural evolution of social mores. In 2000, she stated the following: "Legislation, which governs our present system, was introduced in 1971, nearly 30 years ago. Much has changed since then. More women work; people live much longer after retirement; there are more opportunities for women in the workplace. Importantly, ideas of equality between men and women have changed. It is here most of all that I believe the law lags behind public thinking and needs to be reformed."[43] Ghosted by a patriarchal conception of gender relations and practices, twentieth-century law in the United Kingdom was forever engaged in a Zeno paradox, through which it struggled to keep pace with changing patterns in the polis.

Most important, twentieth-century family law remained haunted by patriarchal prejudices that originated in the medieval common law and acts passed over the centuries and that the institutional process of citing precedents continued to re-invoke. The contradictions engendered by the citational effect of a patriarchal nomos is illustrated by the legal decision on marital rape, upon which Katherine O'Donovan comments in the following terms: "When the House of Lords gave judgment on the R v R (1991) appeal the line of approach was similar to that in the Court of Appeal. What is noticeable is the effort to preserve the authority system of precedent and to maintain deference to Hale's views while at the same time abolishing the supposed immunity for marital rapists from the criminal law."[44] This example is particularly telling because it presents a complex and fascinating description of the problem characterizing the law. It is not so much that twentieth-century family law was evil and that all family judges were backward-looking patriarchs; rather, it is that the symbolic power of the law as an institutional tradition, procedure, habitus, and social source of distinction was such that it interfered with the very stated reformative intent of the criminalization of marital rape.

Finally, the recursive haunting of patriarchal terms and the attendant pattern of dyschronia has affected the more general narratives of the family. The signals that English society emitted in the latter part of the twentieth century are, to say the least, baffling. On the one hand, English society saw increasing economic activity and educational participation among women as well as the emergence of new forms of kinship and gender relationships. Thus, in 1995, Richard Collier pointed out that the "most cursory look at contemporary households shows that there is no 'one' single, British family form but rather a plurality of 'families.'"[45] On the other hand, during this historical period, family culture remained dominated by a traditional nomos. Thus, O'Donovan argues that

> the family is presented in the Britain of the 1990s as the bedrock of traditional values and common sense. Thus the individualism contained in economic programmes is to be countered by the reassuring image of the nation as an extended family. At the same time, a search for shared values is apparent ... in political rhetoric the family serves many purposes. It is a totem, emblem of stability, reassurance and common sense. It can be used to reject challenges to established authority and to castigate critics as "trendy." It also serves to be made guilty, to be blamed for crime rates, delinquency, illiteracy. Yet it can stand against the state as bulwark against intrusion and interference.[46]

In other words, there was a blatant disjunction between the discursive norms of family discourse and the sociologically recorded structures of kinship and gender practices, which rendered the discursive norms obsolete. In interpreting instances of Gothic fiction, I have sought to capture this pattern of historical evolution in the symbolic representation of the family, which is characterized by a complex and dyschronous interaction among political, social, and legal inconsistencies.

In the next two chapters, my argument will revolve around the notion that dyschronous manifestations of patriarchal norms of the family produce symbolic violence and agonistic relationships between family law and Gothic narratives. Patricia Duncker's *The Deadly Space Between* (2002) and Lesley Glaister's *Honour thy Father* (1990) present themselves as literary narratives of kinship contesting the legitimacy of the family as a site of normative reproduction.[47] Functioning like hideous mirror images of a family nomos gone wrong, these texts stand in chiasmic relation to the dominant discourse of the family, revealing the political uncanny of the family as regulated and legitimized by family law. With their tropes of monstrosity, states of abjection, and plots of haunting, they constitute the improper domain of the family clashing with the values of national identity, social stability, gender propriety, and welfare. As catachrestic narratives, Duncker's and Glaister's texts are located at the frontier between that which is discursively and politically proscribed and that which is publicly and politically legitimate, between that which is established as the legal status quo and that which is incipient and anticipatory of a new materialization of social norms.

What is specific to these two novels is that the patriarchal power grafted onto the norms of kinship is represented in spectral or grotesque terms. We are dealing with a dyschronous representation of an apparitional patriarchy, whose uneasy persistence characters experience in the context of a dislocated kinship system.[48] It is there and it is not; it governs and it totters; bodies assimilate it and submit to its rules; but they also dispel what turns out to have always been a political phantasm with nevertheless deadly and material effects.[49] It is therefore no coincidence that the two texts function in the pastiche mode to the extent that they cite a patriarchal discourse inherited from the past.[50] This spectral patriarchy reappears between the lines of English family statutory law and signals the presence of a political uncanny in the midst of reformative family law striving to respond to the pressure for social transformation and claims for legitimacy by social agents that in the past were not recognized by the terms of the law. In concentrating on laws dealing with civil partnership and domestic violence, I will argue that in its regulation of domestic space and same-sex desire, family law produces a normative language that betrays a potential intent to exercise sovereign power over the space of kinship and bodies that do not fit heteronormative norms of sexuality.

In the process of subverting the legitimacy of the family as a site of normative reproduction, Duncker's and Glaister's Gothic narratives produce patterns of aberration that reveal the work of sovereign power in the midst of the family as a site of social poiesis and legal regulation. The well-established Gothic trope of confinement, which is common to the two narratives, reads like a powerful device enacting the transition from the family as a normative site of symbolic violence to an uncanny space of exception.[51] This space of exception typically emerges from a scenario in which historical awareness is occulted, spatial confinement severs the subject from social processes of contestation and transformation, and characters are threatened with bare life according to a regime of power that regulates with impunity. In this context, I propose to conceptualize heterotopia as a site of social and political performativity, where instances of sovereign power jut through, turning the family habitus into the inhospitable and begetting paroxysmal scenes of dread for the subject under the threat of ban.[52]

Common to the plots of the two novels and to family law is a cultural discourse concerned with the incest interdict, a legal marker of degrees of affiliation as well as an object of transgression.[53] Incest revolves around relationships of desire and power, and it disrupts the moral and social organization of kinship. While the transgression of the interdict speaks to the trauma of physical and psychological violation, an analysis of the cultural terms of the interdict reveals its political and social function. Here my point is not to silence narratives of trauma but to track political terms of power framing the interdict.

The analysis of the political significance of the incest interdict has a long feminist history, which began in the late 1970s. For instance, Luce Irigaray established an analogy between the exchange of commodities and the exchange of women in a patriarchal organization of gender relationships. Her first point concerned the fundamentally homosocial aspect of patriarchal organization (an analysis that was to become the central thesis of Eve Kosofsky Sedgwick's work in the 1990s). "The law that orders our society is the exclusive valorization of men's needs/desires, of exchanges among men. What the anthropologist calls the passage from nature to culture thus amounts to the institution of the reign of ho(m)mo-sexuality. Not in an 'immediate' practice, but in its 'social' mediation."[54] Second, Irigaray argued that the mother as the body of reproduction threatens the patriarchal appropriation of nature and its transformation into commodities. At the same time, this reproductive body is essential to the reproduction of social and economic organization. Hence, the incest taboo in a homosocial dynamic prevents the exchange among female bodies while controlling their biological reproductivity.[55]

In her rereading of Marxist, structuralist, and psychoanalytical interpretations of the family, Gayle Rubin similarly argued that the incest interdict functions as a dual means of establishing a binary understanding of gender identities between man and woman and of consolidating heteronormativity at the expense of same-sex desire and terms of identification. "The incest taboo presupposes a prior, less articulate taboo on homosexuality. ... Gender is not only an identification with one sex; it also entails that sexual desire be directed toward the other sex."[56] The interdict operates as a social and eventually political means of engineering a specific social narrative or sociodicy in heteronormative terms whose political dominance is reinforced by a power relation between genders.[57] The link between this social engineering and the political exercise of power is explored in *Antigone's Claim*, where, in a rereading of Sophocles's play, Butler reinterprets the implications of Antigone's decision to bury her brother despite Creon's edict forbidding this act.

Antigone's disobedience, which speaks to her love and incestuous desire, has the effect of destabilizing the construct of kinship. As Creon does not recognize this desire, Antigone's claim remains irreducible to the language of kinship and state sovereignty. In this respect, the key term in the title of Butler's book is Antigone's "claim," which establishes a link between Antigone's grief and the social and performative significance of her complaint to the figure of state. "The melancholic ... registers his or her 'plaint,' levels a juridical claim, where the language becomes the event of the grievance, where, emerging from the unspeakable, language carries a violence that brings it to the limits of speakability."[58] She is a death-in-life figure in the normative discourse of kinship, which forecloses her desire and her ability to avow it. As Butler argues, "To the extent that the incest taboo contains its infraction within itself, it does not simply prohibit incest but rather sustains and cultivates incest as a necessary spectre of social dissolution, a spectre without which social bonds cannot emerge."[59] In Antigone, Butler sees a figure interrogating established and dehistoricized structures of kinship and adumbrating other possible legitimacies that are shut off by the exercise of power over the bodies of kinship. Just as the patriarchal figure of Goodrich's description stands at the historical origins of the conversion of symbolic violence into sovereign power, the incest interdict is the cultural and legal device that makes it possible for techniques of family regulation to slide into sovereign interventions on the bodies of the family by holding each and every social subject under the ban of the law, while relegating them to abandonment if they transgress it.

Chapter Seven

The Political Uncanny of the Family: Patricia Duncker's *The Deadly Space Between* and the Civil Partnership Act 2004

In this chapter, I concentrate on the symbolic violence generated by the historical transition from an exclusively matrimonial nomos of kinship in the Marriage Act 1949 to a same-sex union nomos of kinship in the Civil Partnership Act 2004 (CPA).[1] In the Marriage Act, the family nomos is carved out in terms of a heteronormative division between man and woman and, through the incest interdict, between the licit and the illicit, kin and non-kin. The cultural significance of the CPA lies in its act of interpretation and reading of same-sex partnership through the Marriage Act and its heteronormative regulation of sexuality, gender, and desire. Through a series of analogical steps, the CPA exemplifies the social way in which norms always derive from other norms and, as such, create occasions for historical transformation and contests for normative legitimacy. For, if the CPA constitutes institutional terms of legitimation for same-sex union, it also opens a potential breach of reinterpretation of heteronormativity from within the Marriage Act by transposing many of its terms to a same-sex context.

However, while the Marriage Act is protected from this potential contamination by a cordon sanitaire between heteronormative matrimony and same-sex union, the transposition of the incest interdict to the CPA re-inscribes a heteronormative regulation of gender identity and relations revolving around an Oedipal interpretation of degrees of affiliation. I will suggest that the political uncanny of the CPA derives from the Trojan Horse of a sociodicy of heteronormative reproduction, whose power effect is to silence sexual bodies that do not fit. This usurpation of symbolic power and the ensuing agon for legitimacy originate in a legislating act of reading and interpreting bodies. This twin act of reading and interpretation is central to Patricia Duncker's *The Deadly*

Space Between (2002). As a reading subject and interpreting producer of narratives of kinship, the main protagonist of the novel is exposed to their symbolic violence, but also produces an account in which the transgression of the incest interdict becomes the phantasmatic means of deregulating compulsory heterosexual norms. However, this deregulation also coincides with paroxystic bouts of sovereign power and a struggle for legitimacy in the space of kinship.

At the turn of the twenty-first century, the nomos and practices of the family in Western culture are characterized by contradictions and paradoxes. On the one hand, social practices attest to the fragmentation and diversification of the nuclear family.[2] From single-parent families and reconstituted families following divorce to same-sex and transsexual parenthood, the postmodern family has emerged from a process of implosion, which the law has sought to regulate on its own terms. On the other hand, the law, political discourse, and representations in the polis keep constituting a family sociodicy harking back to what Martha Fineman has dubbed the family metanarrative, whose cultural definition still prevails. "The pervasiveness of the sexual-family-as-natural imagery qualifies it as a 'metanarrative' – a narrative transcending disciplines and crossing social divisions to define and direct discourses. The shared assumption is that the appropriate family is founded on the heterosexual couple – a reproductive, biological pairing that is designated as divinely ordained in religion, crucial in social policy, and a normative imperative in ideology."[3] Identifying the pervasiveness of this family narrative, Davina Cooper argues that "in Britain at the turn of the twenty-first century, the reinforcing of inequality is articulated to the predominance of norms of belonging, familialism, and home, that is to private norms over the public ones, within civil and political life. ... [Thus] we can see the institutional pervasiveness of private norms in the popular discourse of social inclusion, which is largely about incorporating people within community – as belonging – the good stranger reinscribed in the familial trope of kin."[4] The persistence of this family narrative is all the more paradoxical as it coexists with the development of technology-assisted reproduction, which has effected a major historical transition from a procreative account of the family to an account that foregrounds the precedence of social relations over biological origins.

In particular, Marilyn Strathern maintains that "what gave Euro-American culture its modernist cast in this regard was that the core of the family was constituted in the procreative act of the conjugal pair in such a way that the child's biogenetic closeness to its parents endorsed the nurturing closeness of the conjugal couple. Though the parents were not born kin to each other, the child was born kin to both of them. The child they produced created a closeness, defined in the way familial and kinship relations overlapped."[5] With technology-assisted reproduction, this closeness is called into question by what Strathern calls "dispersed kinship," which includes "those who 'produce' the child with assistance as well as those who assist. ... There thus exists a field of procreators whose relationship to one another and to the product of conception is contained in the act of conception itself and not in the family as such."[6] In other words, despite the fact that an anonymous donor of semen is referred to as the biological father and a woman bearing a child as the surrogate mother, the concept of kinship exceeds the conjugal definition of family by detaching the procreative act from the way the family produces a child.

The second major norm to be disrupted is reproduction as transmission from parents to children insofar as the social origins of egg and sperm become irrelevant to the technologies of reproduction. "If finally what remains intact is the intention or desire to have a child, then that desire is what the child 'reproduces.' So in becoming a means to fulfil such a desire, procreation itself ceases to be the crucial reproductive moment. We might see that moment as instead the acting out of intention or desire."[7] In this context, having a child in a same-sex relationship becomes emblematic of the historical transformation, whereby the child is no longer a biological and legal sign of sexual consummation and reproduction, but a sign of the intention or desire to have a child. In this context, same-sex parenthood lays bare the desire for a child beyond a narrative of genealogical procreativity.

In the early days of the same-sex marriage debate, gay and lesbian writers saw in matrimony the occasion to foster cultural heterogeneity and social transformation by creating gender and sexual trouble for family culture and the institution of family law. For instance, in 1991, Nan D. Hunter argued that while the legalization of lesbian and gay marriage "has the fascinating potential for denaturalizing the gender structure of marriage law for heterosexual couples," it also "poses a threat to gender systems, not simply to antilesbian and antigay bigotry."[8] A few years later, Didi Herman also cautiously argued that "the legal recognition of lesbian and gay families does not so much approve a mimicking of the idealized 'norm' as 'trouble' the norm itself. Certainly, the vociferous opposition of conservatives to lesbian and gay familial claims might suggest this."[9] At the same time, the terms of the debate were not solely underwritten by a political belief in radical difference in that the desire to make trouble coexisted with the conviction that extending the right to marry to same-sex couples would blaze the way to social recognition.

This discourse of recognition, which still persists today, oscillates between tropes of affective recognition, whereby same-sex couples *feel* recognized, and tropes of civic recognition, whereby same-sex couples are recognized as full *citizens*.[10] For instance, in their 2007 interviews with members of the LGBTQ community who support same-sex union, Beccy Shipman and Carol Smart report that five prominent reasons emerged out of the conversations: "i) love, ii) acknowledging mutual responsibility, iii) the importance of family recognition, iv) legal rights and recognition and v) the importance of a public statement of commitment. We found very quickly that although the issue of legal rights was important (especially at certain times in the lifecourse) the significance of entering into a CP was not driven purely by instrumental reasons, nor a preoccupation with equality."[11] It is clear from these five criteria that the interviewees had appropriated the traditional, heteronormative discourse of love, marriage, and commitment to voice same-sex desire. Whether they intended to radicalize or politicize these norms, proponents are dancing around the floor of normativity, crossing and recrossing lines while refashioning practices through affective terms of recognition. This act of reinterpretation of quasi-matrimonial commitment is all the more thought-arresting as commentators have noted that the resurgence of matrimonial discourse occurred at a time when the rate of marriage in Britain had declined.[12]

So, in this instance, we have three narratives in the social web of family poiesis: one is ideological and shores up a nomos with the family as its natural foundation; another is scientific and severs sexual reproduction from conjugal family; and the third seeks to appropriate the traditional nomos of the family in a double desire for difference and sameness, radicalism and assimilation. In all cases, we see social poiesis in action, renaming and unnaming through their practices and symbolic power the norms of kinship and affiliation. The legal implications of Strathern's anthropological argument for a reformulation of legitimate kinship is articulated by William Rountree, who points out that through contractual arrangements, same-sex couples create "legal rights for the non-biologically related parent, while extinguishing some of the legal rights of the biological parent."[13] This conception of parenthood creates a tension with the biologically oriented discourse of the family. Yet, according to Fineman, the natural and heteronormative family remains the major template for legal reform and prevents alternative conceptions that, from her standpoint, would be based on the mother/child dyad and would foster caretaking as the defining criterion of the family. This master narrative prevents the legal reformulation from upsetting fundamental norms of the family template and tends to blunt the potentially disruptive effects of a new social paradigm.[14]

The pattern of contradictions and paradoxes characterizing this sociodicy of the family and its practices are testimony to the agonistic aspects of a social poiesis that unfolds through time, all at once unruly and pandering to comforting norms, disruptive of and indebted to a historical narrative. The definition of the family in matrimonial and para- or quasi-matrimonial terms becomes a ground for competition and power struggle: at stake is the social and political desire for recognition and the desire for maintaining terms of legitimacy and symbolic power in the polis. The contradictions are generated by a discursive dyschronia, whereby the conception of the family, grounded in a discourse of natural sexuality and reproduction, clashes with family and technological practices that point to other ways of telling the family. It is in this context that I propose to analyse the legitimation of same-sex union in the CPA and the contestation of a dominant heteronormative constitution of gender and sexual identities in *The Deadly Space Between*.

If the legal meaning of the CPA derives from its intertextual relation to other texts of family law, and if Duncker's novel is inscribed in a literary genealogy of representations of desire and identity, their significance is accrued when cross-examined as part of the vast social constitution of the family, desire, and gender identities. From this cultural intertextuality among various fields of knowledge, regulation, and representation emerges a performative process of social poiesis, which seeks to sustain but also prod norms of social organization and which leaves in its wake a historical narrative characterized by contradictions, dissent, and uncanny patterns, each of which marks an agon for social meaning and political legitimacy. The Marriage Act and the CPA are located at the intersection of different communities and their vying for symbolic power over the organization and legitimation of kinship.

This vying can be formulated by drawing on the writings of Leslie J. Moran and Ruthann Robson, in which they reflect on the symbolic power of legal discourse. While Moran refers to the "machinery of naming" of the Wolfenden Report,[15] Robson discusses the process of unnaming the family as "an important, if underutilized form of resistance"[16] against the coercive effects of legal categorization. Following Foucault's notion that social power is constitutive, Moran adds that the legal machinery of naming "has a great capacity not only to incite, extract, distribute, and institutionalize the discourse of (homo)sexuality, but also to put sex into a discourse that has unruly tendencies, produces unexpected meaning, and is in need of control."[17] In naming and unnaming social scripts inherited from the past, and decoding and encoding social identities and relationships through acts of interpretation and reading, the CPA and *The Deadly Space Between* generate effects of symbolic violence and sovereign power.

In *The Deadly Space Between*, we have an example of the ways in which literature engages in the semiotic process of social poiesis, as described in chapter 2. The novel presents itself as an account of illegitimacy queering the arbitrary effects of a dominant discourse of heteronormativity usurping other ways of doing and telling the family. Duncker's novel reads like a journey towards origins: the origins of Toby's existence and his family; the origins of Gothic tales of family, which share with fairy tales a fascination for the unfamiliar, the forbidden, and sexual violence; the origins of the Western, bourgeois family, whose matrimonial heteronormativity was legitimated in 1753 in English family statutory law and theorized by Freud in his writings on the Oedipal complex; and the origins of that which could be but has been spectralized by proscription and symbolic violence. A site of aberrant performativity, the novel queers the family as a cultural, psychic, and sexual legacy regulated by heteronormative principles of social organization.[18]

The novel presents itself like a Gothic disfiguration of heteronormative kinship, which gives the literary genre of the Bildungsroman renewed significance. Toby's first-person narrative builds and unbuilds the traditional sociodicy of gender identification and sexuality within a matrix where queer desire jostles with heteronormative desire. As the eighteen-year-old narrator, he seems destined to reproduce the Oedipal script to the extent that he experiences incestuous desire for his mother, Iso, and displays the normative signs of parricidal jealousy towards a mysterious father figure, who appears out of nowhere and ravishes his mother and whose identity remains enigmatic until the last page. Woven into this narrative is the naming and unnaming of this father figure, Roehm, whose name is elusive if not spurious, whose sexual identity oscillates between straight and gay, and who as a Gothic revenant straddles the past, present, and future.

In their reviews of the novel, commentators have noted the predictability of the Oedipal plot, which they have identified as a weakness of Duncker's writing.[19] I suggest that the reading, interpreting, and rehearsal of the Oedipal complex is precisely the central concern of the novel, whereby Toby's account presents itself as a performative rewriting of Western foundational texts, which, like speech-acts, have authorized and reiterated the narrative terms of the Oedipal complex as the cornerstone of heteronormative sociodicy. These include writings by Freud but also Sophocles (*Oedipus Rex*), Shakespeare (*Hamlet, Othello*), Herman Melville (*Billy Budd*), Carl Maria von Weber (his opera *Der Freischütz*, also translated as *The Marksman*), Thomas Mann (*Mario and the Magician*), and Mary Shelley (*Frankenstein*), all of which are cited in more or less explicit terms in Duncker's text, with a particular emphasis on Shelley's novel.[20]

However, the novel is not a pure exercise in intertextual virtuosity; instead, it reads as a dizzying and dangerous experiment that through the citing and reinterpretation of Oedipal scripts, engages in a contestatory poiesis of kinship that erodes binary structures of identity and relationships. David Punter argues that vestment and the ceremonial characterize Gothic narratives.[21] The novel takes this Gothic vestism one step further by developing a narrative transvestism, whereby in his narrative performance Toby dons on and off the different accounts of the Oedipal myth that have been produced throughout the centuries. Spectacles of desire and performances of gender and kinship are enhanced through intertextual references to opera, painting, hypertext, literature, psychoanalysis, and music, all of which constitute an archive of Oedipal culture. This Gothic narrative vestism is reinforced by a sartorial motif that underlines gender and sexual identifications through a poietic process of fashioning.[22] Different characters resort to dressing, fashion, cross-dressing, and other media of representation to manifest both their socialization into dominant norms of gender and their deviation from them.

Thus, Duncker draws on the ornamental texture of Gothic fiction, in which sexual excess is matched by a metamorphic narrative that queers the telling and retelling of identity and desire with fluctuation. The political uncanny of this Gothic travesty derives from Toby's struggling with a syntactically regulated phantasm of Oedipal kinship that functions as a placeholder for family subjects, who become immured in a structure of conflicting and predatory discourses inherited from the past. In this sense, the novel is profoundly Gothic: while Gothic language can be used to stage and describe social, psychological, or political situations of confinement and paranoia, Duncker's novel flips language upon itself by staging a narrative in which linguistic performatives of kinship, sexuality, and gender identification relentlessly haunt the protagonist.[23]

The novel is characterized by performatives of sexual desire that circulate from one cultural template of gender identification to another and that in the process destabilize, dislodge, and scramble dominant norms of sexual regulation. While in Oedipal logic the desiring subject is summoned to substitute an external object of desire for the originary parental object of love, in Duncker's novel this logic of substitution is superseded by one of permutation and repeated displacement beyond established gender binaries. The characters' relations revolve around triangles of desire that take their cue from the Oedipal script but that also reformulate it by unmooring it from its heteronormative origins.

The novel opens with the depiction of the queer network within which Toby grew up. What Toby calls the "Amazonian triangle" of desire consists of the fashion designer and great-aunt Luce, the lawyer Liberty as the great-aunt's lesbian partner, and the painter Iso as Luce's niece and Toby's mother. Toby's narrative participates in the poietic reconfiguration of kinship not only through his description of lesbian kinship but also through the citing and appropriation of symbolic representations from the cradle of Western culture. Thus, in an oblique reference to the dramaturgic origins of Oedipus, Toby states that "this triangle of women … was like a companionable Greek chorus."[24] The Amazonian triangle is therefore governed by a social and psychic performance entangling reproduction with deviation, sameness with difference.

Similarly, the relation between Toby and his mother derives from a process of gender fusion and exchange instead of heteronormative differentiation. Toby and Iso are said to look alike and through mimetic desire swap conventional gender characteristics: "short, straight, blonde hair, like a couple of Nordic heroes, pale freckled skins which burn easily, and the same grey-blue eyes. I looked into her face and saw the reassuring mirror of my own … my hands were smooth and untouched. I had the hands of a rich, spoilt woman. She had a man's hands."[25] The irruption of Roehm as Iso's mysterious lover establishes a contrast between the Amazonian triangle of desire and kinship and a heterosexual triangle, and it triggers the narrative of Oedipal rivalry between father and son.

The regulatory dimension of the Oedipal complex is conveyed by Toby's translation into English of a French text on geometry. This geometric representation of the triangle becomes the symbolic means of transforming Toby into an Oedipal subject both at the discursive and the affective levels. From a geometric figure, the triangle becomes the means of describing the affective space from which Toby observes his mother's meeting with the man who appears at night to pick her up in a heavy black car. "[Iso] walked past her own car, peering briefly into the back seat. Then she looked up and quickened her stride. I followed the line of her gaze. From the angle of the window I was secure at the apex of the triangle, watching her flicker across the void, converging on the obscure point, fixed, unseen. There was a slight movement, a hand descending. And my gaze came to rest on the figure in the coming dark."[26] By the end of the first chapter, Toby predictably exhibits the signs of parricidal jealousy towards the mysterious man he identifies as his unknown father. In this configuration, Roehm as the name-of-the-father is the manifestation of an Oedipal cultural script that is "thousands and thousands of years old."[27] To borrow from Bourdieu, Toby's narrative is in the grips of a social *fatum* – "the play can begin"[28] – which he apparently cannot but rehearse.

Seduced by the Oedipal narrative of kinship, Toby cites it, seeks approval from it, reinforces it metaleptically, but also deviates from it. For a third triangle of desire emerges as Toby competes for Roehm with Iso. Shadowing the Amazonian triangle and the heteronormative triangle of desire is the unfolding of the unpatterned side of things, where the object of desire is also the father, an ambivalent figure all at once irresistible and dreadful, a source of pleasure and annihilation. The formula of casino games, "*Faites vos jeux. Rien ne va plus,*"[29] captures the paradox of Toby's account, which both reproduces and deviates from the cultural patterns of telling identity and sexuality. As desire circulates through the different configurations of kinship, Toby's appearance undergoes metamorphoses, alternatively displaying masculinity at school, when he jabs a bully's hand with the sharp leg of his compass, and displaying the femininity of an "Aryan Cleopatra"[30] when he wears a crown of flowers.

This process of fluidity and resignification courses its way through the novel, whose function is to create a site of impropriety, "a deadly space between," which appears whenever Toby crosses cultural thresholds through acts and/or phantasms of sexual and gender transgression. In this sense, the novel upsets the social concept of proper place, which "works generally to legitimize and naturalize the physical and metaphorical division and segregation of identities, activities, and discourses in ways that sustain inequalities of power."[31] Duncker redraws the map of kinship by blurring the lines between the public and the private through the representation of Toby's sexual desire, which roams from one place to another, as when he desires Iso at home and later in a hotel, or as when he is attracted to Roehm on Old Compton Street and later in the privacy of the family home, where Roehm performs as the cook that Iso refuses to be.

Running through the different triangles of desire is the transgression of the incest interdict that does not differentiate between same-sex and heterosexual desire, young and old, and that in fact unlocks gender and sexual identities from the dominant heteronormative nomos of identification. In Toby's account, the infraction of the interdict is common to the three triangles of desire and migrates from one set of relations to the next. The reader is never in a position to ascertain whether actual transgression occurs or whether it is phantasmatic. The account troubles realistic premises of narration, while never affirming its possible phantasmatic origins. Incestuous desire is full-fledged in the description of the lovemaking between Iso and Toby when she is thirty-three and he eighteen. Toby accounts for their encounter in the following terms: "She accepted me back into her body, whenever I leaned against her belly, her thighs, her breasts. She was the open door. She had never pushed me away, forcing me to leave her, find someone else, grow up. The silk twist she had let down for me had never frayed or broken. It held, tight and strong."[32] It is no accident that the incestuous encounter between Iso and Toby should be heralded by an initial ritual of cross-dressing between the mother and the son. While Iso is cross-dressed as a hunter in a green costume, Toby is fantastically cross-dressed "as a lesbian boy in one of Liberty's dashing tuxedos with a lilac bow tie and a green carnation made of silk."[33] The gender trouble created by the infraction of the incest interdict coincides with a disrobing and redressing of Toby's and Iso's gender appearances while fostering a chimera of normative permutation and mobility.

Incestuous forms of desire reappear in the relation between Luce and Liberty, who is said to be even younger than Toby's mother and at least twenty-five years younger than Aunt Luce. In other words, the maternal relation between Luce and Iso establishes age as a norm for a proper relation and identifies Luce as a transgressor. Furthermore, Toby's incestuous desire for the mother does not reproduce the logic of the

Oedipal complex to the extent that the phantasm not only thwarts the displacing of desire onto another woman but is also shadowed by the equally incestuous same-sex desire for Roehm as the paternal figure.

A third incestuous triangle shadows the Amazonian and Oedipal triangles and plays out among Toby, Roehm, and Iso. Toby's incestuous desire for Roehm leads to yet another reconfiguration of the meaning of mythological figures. When he describes his first encounter with Roehm, he calls upon the Greek myth of the Minotaur but reverses its terms of gender references. "His outline suggested the Minotaur, metamorphosed completely into man, irrefutably male, yet unequivocally bestial. She dwindled into pathos behind him. ... I felt him watching me creep down the staircase, reading my body rather than my face. My mother took my arm and led me down to him as if I was a virgin bride."[34] Toby's account reveals a desire for the father through the mother and a desire for the son through the mother.

As Eve Kosofsky Sedgwick long ago argued, "Oedipal schematics to the contrary, there is no secure boundary between wanting what somebody else (e.g. Daddy) has, and wanting Daddy."[35] While Toby states that he wanted his mother's place, he ascribes a similar incestuous desire to Roehm. "I remembered all the nights lying awake, waiting for her to come home, all the sly prying which had turned me into a spy, the sexual Charybdis of triangular desire, the moment when he had offered her to me, the moment when he had made me long for him. But above all I remembered the uncanny sensation, which came and went like a flutter of a moth, that it was not the woman that he wanted but the boy, and that he had seduced the mother to possess the son."[36] Through these three triangles, terms of desire fluctuate and alternate as they are told and retold, coursing their way through an economy of metamorphosis and permutation that exceeds the historical and social terms of kinship.

The scandalous significance of the novel does not lie in Toby's phantasmal or physical enactment of incestuous desire, but in the revelation through incestuous desire of the contiguity of heteronormative regulation of kinship to queer identification. The co-presence of the three triangles of desire in Toby's narrative indicates a narrative logic of exchange through the transference, displacement, and volatility of desire. Rattling the Oedipal pattern of kinship, gender identification, and proper expressions of sexual desire, Toby's narrative inherits normative patterns from a historical sociodicy and submits them to a drag show of metamorphosis, reversing and twisting terms of symbolic representation of kinship. His poietic account creates a space for creativity and reproduction, transformation and reiteration. At the same time, his narrative remains outside the pale of normative legitimacy, not only because it infringes on social and legal norms of kinship but also because his first-person account remains invalidated, unreliable, and phantasmal. This is particularly the case when one considers that his account is characterized by a fundamental narrative absurdity as it is driven by a diabolical logic resting on the notion that, as a spectre, Roehm does not actually exist yet is the object of Toby's and Iso's desire.[37]

Indeed, in the novel representatives of the law undermine either the existence of Roehm or the validity of Iso's and Toby's reference to Roehm. When Toby confides in Liberty, the lawyer, and enlists her help to investigate Roehm's identity, she announces that Roehm is nowhere to be located and that there is no legal proof of his existence, his scientific activities, or his academic affiliation. At the end of the novel, when a frantic Iso, who thinks she has spotted Roehm walking towards her and her son on the glacier in Chamonix, tells her story to a *gendarme*, the latter tells her off, asserting that the body she has seen is in fact the frozen body of a nineteenth-century Swiss botanist, which the melting of the glacier has uncovered. In other words, twice the law intervenes to erase any evidence that would substantiate Toby's account, rendering it either erroneous or purely phantasmal. Therefore, the novel revolves around a narrative malapropism that is signified by the ghostly presence/absence of the character and that upsets the relation between the reader and the text as the reader is at the beck and call of a hermeneutics of suspicion and indeterminacy.

That Toby's account of his incestuous fantasies should occupy the public space of literature, yet be transcribed in phantasmal terms, indicates that the narrative is still governed by a logic of interdict and transgression, norm and deviance.[38] His narrative remains fundamentally spectral, the effect of normative regulation and proscription orchestrated by the oxymorons of a sociodicy: Oedipal yet natural. In other words, this heteronormative sociodicy turns on a political uncanny to the extent that its arbitrary and historical origins have evaporated to make room for a usurpatory and dyschronous narrative of the way things are.

The fact that some critics have responded negatively to the novel's indirection and unreliability highlights the notion that Toby's narrative remains beyond normative reception and recognition because it cannot be authorized. Ceaselessly shuffling the cards, Duncker has created a baffling, queering, and profoundly satisfactory Gothic narrative that begins to explore, in Butler's words, "what happens when we begin to understand Oedipus outside the exchange of women and the presumption of heterosexual exchange."[39] The impropriety of desire in Duncker's novel designates a deadly-space-between, which social discourse and practices cloister to contain what is deemed unnatural desire within kinship. And this cloistering is no more evident than in the Civil Partnership Act, whose political unconscious shadows family law's endeavour to legitimize same-sex union.

Although this act contributes to the fashioning of new rights and obligations, its textuality also resists this poiesis of historical transformation and, through statutory language, seeks to regulate excess and deviation. This ambivalence stems from the fact that the CPA is governed by an intertextual cross-reference to the Marriage Act and is thus determined by an analogical type of thinking. A comparative analysis of the way in which analogy governs the relation between the Marriage Act and the CPA indicates that legislators wavered between granting similar rights to different social agents and maintaining normative boundaries between these social agents, both liberalizing and colonizing same-sex unions.[40] The Gothic tropes of Duncker's novel speak to the ways in which an uncanny narrative of sexual phantasms and incestuous desire throws a system of kinship into disarray, turning the family into the unfamiliar and unsettling gender and sexual norms. In contrast, the statutory language of the CPA remains governed by the nomos of sexual reproduction regulated by the incest interdict, which functions as the terms of a political uncanny and creates the conditions for the spectralizing of same-sex sexuality and for the delegitimizing of same-sex terms of kinship. Rhetorically speaking, the law's containment of the transformative effects of same-sex union is enacted by the statutory use of analogical thinking relying on a trope of assimilation, which is none other than the simile.[41]

The analogical relationship between the CPA and the Marriage Act is not specific to these two acts as it has a precedent in the relationship between religious marriage and civil marriage in English family law. The Marriage Act is divided into three parts. Part 1 addresses specific restrictions on marriage, Part 2 regulates religious marriage, while Part 3 regulates civil marriage. The creation of the last two parts speaks to the cultural notion that religious marriage and civil marriage are mutually exclusive. Thus, subsection 45A(4) states that "no religious service shall be used at any marriage solemnized in the presence of a superintendent registrar."[42]

At the same time, a close reading reveals that through a process of linguistic and functional mimesis, the act establishes a series of equivalences between religious marriage and civil marriage. Broadly speaking, these equivalences include the following: a religious marriage is regulated by the Church of England, while a civil marriage is officiated by the superintendent registrar as the representative of the registrar general. On the one hand, a religious marriage can be obtained through the publication of banns in the parish of residence, a common licence (temporary residence), a special licence (not a member of the parish, or housebound because of illness), or on the authority of certificates delivered by the registrar of the district of residence. On the other hand, a civil marriage can be obtained through the delivery of a marriage certificate at a ceremony officiated by the superintendent registrar and can be conducted according to the usages of the Society of Friends or according to the usages of the Jewish religion. Finally, a civil marriage can be registered in combination with the publications of banns according to the rites of the Church of England. In all these instances, statutory language negotiates cultural difference by establishing equivalence through analogy while maintaining boundaries between a secular culture and a religious.

However, the fact that a historical process of secularization has occurred does not erase the religious origins of marriage. It is clear that the Marriage Act and its twin procedures make religious marriage the point of normative and anthropological reference. From a textual standpoint, the codification of religious marriage precedes the regulation of civil marriage, as if the textual sequence functioned as a means of recording the historical and normative precedence of this religious institution. In fact, we could go back even further by considering the intertextual links between the text of the Marriage Act and the Book of Common Prayer, which is referred to in subsection 7(2). This religious and anthropological precedence determines the sociodicy of kinship in England, as legitimated and authorized by family law. No wonder, then, that in his dismissal of Susan Wilkinson's petition to have her Canadian marriage to Celia Kitzinger recognized under English law, Mark Potter, president of the Family Division of the High Court of Justice, stated in 2006, "By withholding from same-sex partners the actual title and status of marriage, the Government declined to alter the deep-rooted and almost universal recognition of marriage as a relationship between a man and a woman, but without in any way interfering with or failing to recognise the right of same-sex couples to respect for their private or family life in the sense, or to the extent, that European jurisprudence regards them as requiring protection."[43] This statement captures the paradoxical terms in which the transition from the Marriage Act to the CPA was framed.

The CPA is based on a two-fold strategy: on the one hand, it establishes a boundary between civil partnership and civil marriage, with religious marriage as its foundation. Thus, the relation between the two acts is based on a cordon sanitaire, which ensures that same-sex individuals cannot marry and, vice-versa, that heterosexual individuals cannot enter a civil partnership. The cultural precedence of religious marriage is clearly conveyed in subsection 2(5), which states, "No religious service is to be used while the civil partnership registrar is officiating at the signing of a civil partnership document."[44] On the other hand, the statutes establish an analogical relation between civil marriage and civil partnership. So the same double relation of segregation and functional mimesis governing the relation between religious marriage and civil marriage obtains between civil partnership and marriage. Just as civil marriage is functionally like religious marriage, but the two are not the same, so civil partnership is functionally like marriage by registration, but the two are not the same.[45]

This analogy is established through the use of a terminology that allows for equivalence but not identity. Marriage becomes partnership; the superintendent registrar becomes the civil partnership registrar. The institutional, strategic use of space and time to authorize marriage also operates in the case of civil partnership. Thus, the place of registration may be a place provided by the registration authority in its own "area" or a place agreed within the "area" of the registration authority. Persons desiring to become partners must also give notice of such intention to the registration authority and have resided in England and Wales for at least seven days immediately before giving this notice. The notice of partnership corresponds to the notice of marriage under sections 27 and 28, in which the registrar records information about the persons, names, places of residence, degrees of affinity or kinship, and need for consent in the case of a person under the age of eighteen. On this basis, a partnership schedule is prepared. The "waiting period" of section 17 is the equivalent of the twenty-one-day period after the publication of the banns or the fifteen-day waiting period of civil marriage. The marriage certificate becomes a "civil partnership schedule" (s. 14), which is granted if there is no impediment to the partnership. These are some examples demonstrating the way in which legislators developed linguistic strategies that seek to neutralize the gender and sexual implications of the shift from a heteronormative to a homonormative union.

The objective seems to have been the establishing of universality and equality by de-gendering the language of the Marriage Act – despite the fact that some mind-boggling lapses occur, such as the notion that a civil partnership is voidable if, among other causes, "at the time of its formation, the respondent was pregnant by some person other than the applicant."[46] However, at the heart of the statutory language of the Marriage Act and the CPA lies a mimetic device of kinship reproduction, which indicates that English family law regulates same-sex partnership by superimposing on it a heteronormative governance of kinship and identification.[47] To this extent, family law exercises symbolic violence by legitimizing a dominant, "almost universal" sociodicy of kinship and by sealing it through acts of institutional power.

In discussing the preponderance of heteronormative principles of social organization and the effect of familialism on same-sex spousal recognition at the turn of the twenty-first century in England, Cooper argues that "hegemonic private norms, whether articulated to practices within the street or home, reflect a sensibility and form of organization based on discipline, consumption, limited responsibility, and a zero-sum conception of belonging. This has particular implications for those defined as outsiders by virtue of their ethnicity, sexuality or class; indeed the private – or what I would call 'akinship': organizing people according to their apparent similarities, consanguinity and social ties of belonging – reinforces the constitution of them as such."[48] The proscriptive effects of these heteronormative principles of social organization constitute the political uncanny of the CPA.

The unconscious effect of this mode of knowing the social world and shaping gender and sexual norms of identification does not lie in psychological repression; instead, it lies in the masking of the historical and arbitrary origins of this mode of shaping the practices of the social nomos. The paradox of the CPA derives from its intentionality to maintain heteronormative preponderance while seeking to authorize and legitimize same-sex unions in a language pruned of its heteronormative lexicon. The progeny of this paradox is a fundamentally euphemistic statute in that it creates pockets of silence and elusion about the sexual specificity of the union and its implications for kinship.[49]

The silencing of the sexual body in the CPA has been noticed by two major commentators in two separate analyses published in the same year. In 2006, Carl F. Stychin observed that consummation and adultery, historically central to the institution of marriage, are noticeably absent from the CPA under the pretext that the two concepts are irrelevant to same-sex relationships. According to Stychin, "this absence in the legislation – and the coy explanations that accompany it – provide a useful illustration of the continuing centrality of penetrative intercourse in the way in which the law constitutes heterosexual relationships."[50] To this must be added Stephen Cretney's shrewd analysis of the transition from the wording in the Marriage Act to that of the CPA.

Cretney makes two crucial points. To begin with, he remarks that, unlike the Marriage Act, the CPA does not include exchanging marriage vows, whose tradition dates back to the Marriage Act 1836 and which "involves an *exchange of spoken words* in the presence of a Registrar and witnesses. In contrast, a civil partnership can apparently be created in complete silence."[51] Only a signature on the civil partnership schedule is required. In other words, civil partnership is constituted by law through silence, whereby the sexual nature of the union is omitted.[52] In contrast, and as Cretney reminds us, "marriage is founded on the principle that (save in exceptional cases) a sexual relationship is of the essence: 'with my body, I thee worship' as the Book of Common Prayer puts it. But the same is apparently not intended, as a matter of law, to be true of civil partnership."[53]

In a second point, Cretney comments on the fact that the Human Fertilization and Embryology Act 1990 does not extend to the CPA, which allows "a married woman's husband (or indeed a man to whom she is not married but with whom she has received fertility treatment) to be treated as the father of a child conceived as the result of insemination with a third party donor's sperm. In the case of the relation between same-sex couple and child, legally (and genetically) the sperm donor will be the child's father."[54] In 2006, the only option was to seek an adoption order to establish the relation between civil partners and child. Nestled in the apparent neutrality of the CPA language are norms of sexuality and family constitution that are incompatible with the

Marriage Act and its belief in matrimony as the cornerstone of a natural conception of heterosexuality geared towards sexual reproduction. This ideological incompatibility is therefore signalled by a disruption in the intertextual network of statutory law, but also culminates in an aberrant utterance, which Cretney also identifies.

Indeed, if we re-examine section 3 ("Eligibility") of the CPA and its appended schedule 1 in light of section 1 ("Restrictions on Marriage") and schedule 1 of the Marriage Act, we discover a language that regulates degrees of affinity as a means of establishing the types of union that do not infringe upon the incest interdict. In other words, when one opens the Marriage Act and the CPA, the first items one comes across are a legitimation and codification of what Freud conceptualized as the Oedipal complex. The persistence and reproduction of these Oedipal terms of kinship are brought out in Table 7.1, which compares prohibited degrees of affinity and is appended to this chapter. Throughout the three parts of this table, the first two columns on the left stem from the Marriage Act, while the column on the right stems from the CPA. While heteronormative terms such as *mother, father, daughter*, and *son* have been replaced in the CPA with neutral terms such as *parent, child or adopted child*, and *sibling*, the same device securing the gender distinction between man and woman shadows the regulation of same-sex relationships. This shadowy presence of heteronormative gender identity is revealed by the statement that "in the list 'sibling' means a brother, sister, half-brother or half-sister."[55] Therefore, governing the CPA is a premise that maintains a heterosexual constitution of kinship.

In analysing this integration of the prohibited degrees of affinity, Cretney argues that "there is … no way (save, possibly, where a post-operative transsexual is involved) in which a same sex couple can have offspring of which they are both the *genetic* parents."[56] He goes on to conclude that the main motive for the reproduction of the prohibited degrees of marriage into civil partnerships was to devise a "check on the use of civil partnerships as a means of tax minimization within the family."[57] However, there is a possible different interpretation to which Cretney's own analysis leads yet eschews. From a rhetorical standpoint, the integration of the prohibited degrees presents itself as a non sequitur, whereby euphemized same-sex sexuality is hitched onto a lexicon of reproductive sexuality. This non sequitur is the express sign that the CPA remains fundamentally caught in the time warp of a kinship system that rests on what Strathern identified as the natural family governed by concepts of biological closeness and continuity.

The heteronormative premise of the CPA also hits at the heart of gender reconfiguration and cancels out the possibility of heterogeneity, which earlier commentators associated with same-sex marriage. The heteronormative significance of the legal schedule in the Marriage Act becomes clear when one highlights the terms *mother/father/daughter/son* as the four poles of Western kinship. The remaining terms in the first two columns of Table 7.1 result from a systematic scaffolding upon these four foundational terms of affinity. The statutory language used to interpret the schedule leaves no doubt as to the partitioning effect of matrimonial law, which traces firm boundaries between the licit and the illicit, man and woman, kin and non-kin. In transposing this social engineering of gender and family to the CPA, the law blurts out a fundamental contradiction: on the one hand, it legitimizes the deletion of binary gender differences by same-sex union; on the other, in applying an interdict that reinstates the Oedipal logic of binary relations, it undoes the acknowledgment of same-sex union. The outlandish language of the statute reveals how the incest interdict as a discursive tool to regulate practices both bans and enlists the subject of kinship, including and excluding those who do their gender and kinship right.[58] This constitutes the power effects of the political uncanny at the heart of English family law, whose mimetic reproduction of the heteronormative incest taboo betrays a rejection of what it regulates, pushing it back into the closet.[59]

The heteronormative premise of the statute points to the specificity of the law as double helix: through its intentional utterances, family law seeks to produce a biopolitical body as the performative site of its sovereign power.[60] The CPA functions as the ground on which the state through law reasserts exclusionary terms of citizenship, while appropriating the symbolic agency of queer bodies. In other words, in an act of *regia potestas*, the state through the law maintains kinship as the privileged nexus where nation, nativity, and naturalness meet and where private and public spheres collide.[61] Clearly, through the CPA the state appropriates a discourse of kinship as a site of privacy in order to regulate the public legitimation of a not very productive same-sex desire. Far from legitimizing the social poiesis of a queer culture through encounters between strangers "sharing equal regard,"[62] the CPA slips into sovereign power over bare life, reducing citizenship to reproductive biology, and civic identity to a "naturally" prescribed and gendered body.[63]

While English family law asserts its sovereignty over same-sex kinship through civil partnership, in *The Deadly Space Between* Toby presents himself as the narrative agent developing his account of family origins and destiny. While the CPA seeks to regulate same-sex desire through silence and a usurping heteronormative scheme of affiliation, Toby's account disturbs Oedipal boundaries by dislodging the name-of-the-father from its monological meaning. As argued in chapter 6, the history of sovereign power in England hinges on the figure of *regia potestas*, whereby state and family coincide in the patriarchal figure. It is this historical constitution of sovereignty that family law authorizes and legitimizes in the CPA. If this is the case, the question becomes, to what extent does Duncker's novel counter this national narrative of usurpation?

At the outset of his narrative, Toby searches for Roehm's origins by googling his name. Toby pursues his phantasm in a virtual universe, where Roehm becomes a shape-shifter, an embodiment of public and historical figures, such as a homosexual Nazi chief of staff, a French film director and interpreter of the Marquise of O, and an eighteenth-century Swiss Alpine explorer and botanist. This destabilizing of the name-of-the-father accounts for the complexity of the narrative, which in fact should be approached as a network of para-narratives defusing the claim to a central narrative of kinship. The novel is first and foremost a hologram, displaying on one and the same surface contradictory meanings, which are manifested not so much through an act of excavation as through the deployment of different discourses of kinship, what they entail and what they mask. Toby's phantasmatic identification with Roehm deregulates degrees of affiliation and throws the heteronormative family into disarray, as conveyed by his account of a dream.

> I dreamed about him that night. I saw him in the laboratory, but there were no more walls, no doors, no locked spaces. ... And in my dream I see myself as if I am two people. One is pressed, sweating, terrified, against the damp slab of heat and the other supple, erotic, a boy sure of his power to entice and possess. ... I see myself, erect and untouched, pushing towards him through the ensnaring green. Roehm does not move, but he smiles, eerie, suggestive, ambiguous, triumphant. And then I know that I love this man, that he has come back for me, that he has never forgotten me. It is my desire that you should come for me. And I am unafraid.[64]

Toby is enthralled, and it is no accident that, in an allusion to *Paradise Lost* and *Faust*, Roehm should be the satanic apologist of desire, excess, and transgression. Out of this queer economy of desire under proscription emerges a figure of demonization described as the "erotic green cadaver of the Demon Huntsman,"[65] a protagonist in Weber's *The Marksman*, which Toby, Iso, and Roehm discover on a night at the opera. The Demon Huntsman operates like a mobile trope of excess transiting from Iso to Roehm. While Roehm's physical appearance is associated with the Demon, Iso makes him the subject of her painting. "His cape swept the floor, and with a meticulous attention to detail she had drawn the giant hollowed chest and the ghostly ribcage of his living corpse."[66] The Demon Huntsman is the Gothic trope at the heart of the narrative of heteronormative kinship: excessive, incestuous, improper desire pounding in the ribcage of the living corpse.[67]

In this phantasmal demonization of desire, Toby crystallizes transgressive desire through his reading of Freud's account of the Wolf Man.[68] His identification with the Freudian script occurs at the same time as his incestuous encounter with Iso, as if the transgression of the incest interdict laid bare the violence inaugurating the emergence of the desiring son. "There in the mirror she stood, framed and fixed in red and green as if she was a nineteenth-century portrait of an aristocrat in hunting costume. She was the Wolf Man's mother, ready for the forests and the great sweep of snow. The figure in the mirror bowed low before me."[69] In identifying Iso as the mother of the Wolf Man, Toby identifies himself as the Wolf Man, Iso as the object of sexual aggression, and Roehm as the bestial copulator of the mother. Toby's narrative retells the archetype of the Freudian primal scene of desire as a nocturnal staging of sadomasochistic heterosexuality between Iso and Roehm on which, he tells the reader, he spied from the garden while raking leaves. Here is the mise en scène. "Behind them rose [Iso's] latest project, a huge canvas, six by four, representing a procession of grey and white pillars, in which the white dominates. ... She had her arms around [Roehm's] neck. It was as if he covered her completely, his darkness bearing upon her puckered flesh, the two of them framed by the almost white canvas towering behind them. They became part of her painting. ... She leans her head against his chest. I see her naked face for the first time. She is in pain. Her mouth is open, her eyes closed, her cheek a terrible unearthly shrieking white."[70] Toby's identification with the Oedipal script coincides with the narrative rehearsal of a genealogy of phantasmatic tropes of kinship.

At the same time, Toby's parasitic identification with the sexual maternal body and vicarious enjoyment of Roehm's sexual penetration queers the tableau so that the meaning of the Wolf Man functions according to a different register and context. Upon recollecting the scene, Toby's feeling of horror morphs into pleasure and desire for the father figure. "I was no longer angry, humiliated, ashamed, but strangely excited. The worm of pleasure had entered my skin and begun to burrow and turn."[71] As a configuration of desire, the trope of the Wolf Man ignores cordons sanitaires and propagates, its meanings varying exponentially with each and every different narrative context.

In this poietic reconfiguration, Toby is not master of his narrative terms, as those are steeped in textual precedents, be they psychoanalytical, literary, musical, painterly, political, and/or legal. To put it in Butler's terms, Toby remains unaccountable even as he persists in accounting for his origins. "If I try to give an account of myself, if I try to make myself recognizable and understandable, then I might begin with a narrative account of my life. But this narrative will be disoriented by what is not mine, or not mine alone. And I will, to some degree, have to make myself substitutable in order to make myself recognizable. The narrative authority of the 'I' must give way to the perspective and temporality of a set of norms that contest the singularity of my story."[72] Toby's desire therefore unfolds as a double symbolic process, whereby he gives an account while reading past narratives of identification. His narrative presents itself as a poietic project of self-constitution, which Butler associates with the process of identity formation as a tropological turn, whereby through desire the subject in formation attaches to the bearers – parental and others – of normative discourse, principles, and beliefs regulating social practices.

When Butler writes of the psychic life of power, she posits the notion that the self results from the psychic operation of social regulatory norms that feed on the desire to adhere to forms of identification procuring social recognition. This process of identification with normative terms of power coincides with what she names a tropological inauguration of the subject. "The form this power takes is relentlessly marked by a figure of turning, a turning back upon oneself or even a turning *on* oneself. This figure operates as part of the explanation of how a subject is produced, and so there is no subject, strictly speaking, who makes this turn. On the contrary, the turn appears to function as a tropological inauguration of the subject, a founding moment whose ontological status remains permanently uncertain."[73] In this scenario, that which is in the process of becoming the self attaches to social norms of being and practices by curbing its own desire. This entails that subjectivity is an ambivalent process, pivoting on a deference to and differing from norms that historically precede the subject. The poiesis of the self is a constant exercise in tightrope walking, balancing between subjugation and appropriation, ontological bankruptcy and social capital.

Just as the CPA makes queers law's subjects, past narratives of kinship author Toby's desire. Toby gets lost in a maze of textual indices of subjectivity and narratives of kinship that simultaneously illuminate and obscure the identities of the characters and their interaction. As a family subject, Toby is undone if not outdone by this maze of cultural and artistic intertextuality. Analysing the textual intricacies of *Frankenstein*, Halberstam states, "The monstrosity of [the novel] is literally built into the textuality of the novel to the point where textual production itself is responsible for generating monsters."[74] In *The Deadly Space Between*, this monstrous textuality is in the grips of the political uncanny, secreted by the normative precedents that Toby absorbs like a sponge. In particular, if his account of incestuous desire creates a phantasmatic, aberrant, and transgressive space of kinship, it also remains haunted by a spectral textuality casting a shadow on his interpretations while exposing him not only to the symbolic violence of normative injunctions of kinship but also to the excesses of sovereign power.[75] For, in tapping the archives of the Oedipal family, Toby's account also brings back from the dead the patriarchal bogeyman. Roehm as the Wolf Man also functions as a trope of historical revenance and exhibits signs of sovereign power over bare life in the space of kinship. In this sense, Duncker's novel stages the dynamics of an agon, whereby the desire for a new poiesis of gender and sexual norms clashes with and is eventually defeated by the recursive effects of a spectral form of sovereign power.

The first hint of this sovereign power is conveyed in Toby's earlier account of his visit to Roehm's scientific laboratory, located in the basement of a hospital in central London, where he apparently experiments with species and climate change. Toby describes an eerie progression through a labyrinth; like the Minotaur, Roehm leads him by unlocking a series of secret doors, descending further and further into a primeval world of vegetation and animals. In this subterraneous space, both scientific and fantastic, Toby perceives Roehm as a murderous threat as he hears "his shoes clicking like dog's claws on the polished floors"[76] and as he reads signs of panic in the animals' fretting. Roehm leads the young man to a heterotopic space of subjugation over caged animals, separated from the social world and functioning as a space of exception, where violence is deployed and where Toby deciphers in Roehm a threatening Frankenstein wielding sovereign power over all forms of life. Toby identifies this sovereign power as that which lies outside normality. "To pass from a normal nature to [Roehm] one must cross 'the deadly space between.' And we had passed that delicate snow bridge. He was in our blood, our bones. … He was always there. We had become his creatures."[77] Haunting the deregulation of heteronormative kinship is yet another narrative pattern, through which Roehm exercises power in the space of kinship. The father figure as intruder and violator is indissociable from Toby's perception of his own familial origins, which he recounts at the end of the novel.

At this point, the first-person narrative becomes an exercise in ventriloquism, through which the reader assumes to be hearing Iso's first-person account of her encounter with Roehm on a school trip to Austria when she was fifteen. Toby's account reads very much like a romance of origins, whereby the child fantasizes about its conception and invents surrogate parental figures and fabulous origins. According to this account, a Rapunzel-like Iso left her parental home the daughter of a religious couple, disciplined into a flat-shod, long-haired, and docile body. As Roehm pays for a haircut and a new wardrobe, Iso emerges as a figure of desire, while the age difference between her and Roehm identifies him as a father figure and Iso as the daughter of his incestuous desire. Iso's sexual awakening follows the path of a symbolic process that includes a reconfiguration of her body and a sartorial transformation, but the sexual initiation veers into an act of subjugation through violation, which reduces Iso to silence and bare life. "When he pushed inside me I felt as if I was being torn open with a giant iron bar. … All I could feel was his brutal weight and the unhesitating accuracy of the pain that rose into my intestines, my stomach. He intended to hurt me. I was being ripped open, laid to waste."[78] We are also led to believe that Toby was born out of this one sexual act. It took place at the Austrian *Gasthof*, which is also the place to which Iso as a mature woman and mother takes refuge after escaping Roehm and where Toby finds her.

In joining his mother at the inn, Toby not only returns to his place of origin but also, despite the name of the inn, to a space of inhospitality, where the exercise of violence upon bodies unfolds according to a contamination of sovereign power among characters. Indeed, when Toby endeavours to take care of his frightened mother and encourages her to take a bath, he reports discovering marks of violence on her back, which he ascribes to Roehm. Later on, the welts vanish as if they had been the uncanny projection of Toby's demonic fantasizing about his mother's body, his relation to it, or his fantasizing about Roehm's treatment of Iso.

Roehm as the aggressor functions as a dyschronous sign in the midst of social transformation of kinship – that is to say, as the spectral and contaminating effect of a historical form of masculine domination. From a seductive and enchanting figure showering Iso's family with Christmas gifts, the figure progressively turns into the Gothic patriarchal villain, perpetrator of violence against mothers and Little Red Riding Hoods – male or female. This switch in characterization sets in motion the archetypal plot of the villain stalking mother and son. Initially fascinated by Roehm, Iso and Toby eventually dread him and flee first to Austria, then to the ski resort of Chamonix in the French Alps.

By the end of the novel, Toby is left stranded in a spectral zone where the process of destabilizing and reinventing gender identification is frozen into stasis. In a rewriting of *Frankenstein*, Duncker chooses the icy universe of the Mer de Glace in Chamonix to create the landscape of the psychic life of power. This icy universe, which Toby discovers while on a Christmas holiday with his great-aunt, is characterized by ambivalence: both depth and surface, solid and fluid, inside and outside, masculine and feminine, perceived and fantasized, the glacier becomes the expression of Toby's estrangement from Iso – a mère de glace who spends a weekend in Paris with Roehm – but also of his identification with Roehm, who once declared, "Mountains are the most beautiful pure space I have ever known."[79] While this inner/outer scape reappears in Iso's earlier painting, it is also associated with the father figure, as Roehm's spectral body is said to be made of cold.

This ice world is fantastic and grotesque, deleting the boundaries between the animate and the inanimate, the geological and the animal. "Only in the walls of the cave, where the halogen lights penetrated the flesh of the glacier, were its muscles clearly visible. And there it seemed alive. I stood staring into the ambiguous depths of frozen cold. I stroked the wet solidity of the glacier and touched its intimate uncanny life."[80]

The significance of this wintry heterotopia lies in its ambivalence: its potential liquidity signifies transformation and flow; its solidity threatens with stasis and containment. Stepping into the virtual surroundings of the glacier, Toby wanders into a space governed by the metamorphic principle of the narrative, neither male nor female, neither static nor mobile, neither dangerous nor hospitable – but all at once. "I am wandering across the surface of the Mer de Glace. ... I am walking the dragon's spine. There are no markers in the snow. To my left and right a muscle of rock is thrown up from the white flesh of this living thing moving beneath me. The creature is carefully, surreptitiously, flexing its length, white as a dove, subtle as a serpent. Its white hood is spread out before me. The skin of the glacier moves more swiftly than the braided ice far beneath. ... I sense the yawning gulfs of ice below and the terrible fragility of my steps."[81] The uncanniness of the ice world increases when the narrative switches from Toby's sensorial perception of the glacier to his exploration of a website documenting the geological properties of a glacier. In deciphering Toby's account, the hypertextual scientific description, and the allusions to Shelley's narrative, the reader journeys into the recesses of Toby's mind and crosses the space between phantasm and perception, chaos and normative scripts, alertness and hallucination.[82]

From this point onward, the paranoid plot of Gothic tradition leaps into action, and the uncanny ice world ceases to operate as a potential site of transformation. Toby and Iso are fleeing from Roehm, whose apparitions at the casino, in the ski lift, and on the glacier vampirize their mental energy. The initial attraction for the father's body has become an object of uncanny representation, relegated to a spectral zone of homoeroticism. The construct of the father as bogeyman works at the expense of the son's queer desire, which remains crippled by cultural narratives of kinship through which sexual and gender identification have historically taken place. Toby's expeditions to Chamonix are repeated voyages towards this father figure, but the desire is foreclosed when Roehm is revealed as the Swiss botanist whose body lies frozen in the Mer de Glace: proscribed desire reappears in the form of the cryogenic body of the father. Through police intervention, the body is returned to where it belongs: the site of phantasmatic, obsessive grotesqueries – a solipsistic theatre for "a sombre gust of queer fantasies"[83] shorn of their potential for the political and historical resignification of gender, sexuality, and kinship.

Table 7.1 Comparison of Prohibited Degrees of Affinity in the Marriage Act 1949 (First Schedule) and Civil Partnership Act 2004 (Schedule 1)

Marriage Act		Civil Partnership Act	
Prohibited Degrees of Relationship		Absolute Prohibitions	
Mother Adoptive mother or former adoptive mother **Daughter** Adoptive daughter or former adoptive daughter Father's mother Mother's mother Son's daughter Daughter's daughter Sister Father's sister Mother's sister Brother's daughter Sister's daughter	**Father** Adoptive father or former adoptive father **Son** Adoptive son or former adoptive son Father's father Mother's father Son's son Daughter's son Brother Father's brother Mother's brother Brother's son Sister's son	Adoptive child Adoptive parent Child Former adoptive child Former adoptive parent Grandparent Grandchild Parent Parent's sibling Sibling Sibling's child	
Degrees of Affinity in s. 1(2) and (3)[84]		Qualified Prohibitions[85]	
Daughter of former wife Former wife of father Former wife of father's father Former wife of mother's father Daughter of son of former wife Daughter of daughter of former wife	Son of former husband Former husband of mother Former husband of father's mother Former husband of mother's mother Son of son of former husband Son of daughter of former husband	Child of former civil partner Child of former spouse Former civil partner of grandparent Former civil partner of parent Former spouse of grandparent Former spouse of parent Grandchild of former civil partner Grandchild of former spouse	
Degrees of Affinity in s. 1(4) and (5)[86]		Qualified Prohibitions[87]	
		Relationship	**Relevant deaths**
Mother of former wife	Father of former husband	Former civil partner of child	The child; the child's other parent
Former wife of son	Former husband of daughter	Former spouse of child	The child; the child's other parent
		Parent of former civil partner	The former civil partner; the former civil partner's other parent
		Parent of former spouse	The former spouse; the former spouse's other parent

Chapter Eight

Legitimizing the Subject of Domestic Violence: Lesley Glaister's *Honour Thy Father* and Laws of the Household

Consider the following four narratives, which were published in the late 1990s and the first decade of the twenty-first century. The first is from a collection of journalistic reports on domestic violence. We read of Karen Newman, whose sister lived for twenty-five years with a man who "conducted a mental reign of terror. The husband, Tommy Elden, demanded cups of tea, his dinner cooked a certain way, things to be done immediately. Then one night in 1997 he decided that he did not like his dinner and so he threw his wife out into the back garden. This time Margaret left. 'I had gone to his house with my niece Laura to pick up my sister's stuff. He asked us where Margaret was and then he locked us in,' said Ms Newman. Elden turned and Ms Newman realised that he was holding a knife. He stabbed his daughter and sister-in-law for almost half an hour, retreating only when they played dead."[1]

The second is from a manual on how school counsellors can help children who struggle with domestic violence. In it, Abigail Sterne et al. describe the worry bag activity, in which a child is invited to draw the outline of a bag and to stick onto it pieces of cards where his or her worries are named. The child talks about these individual worries with the counsellor, who may use a scale of 1 to 10 to measure the degree of anxiety associated with each worry. To exemplify the function of the worry bag, the authors provide the following account:

> Through his worry bag, a boy indicated extreme fear of and nightmares about his father breaking into the house and attacking the mother. ... He was also bedwetting. The child had devised a number of home-made solutions, such as leaving skates on the stairs in the hope he could trip his father up. The counselor related the fears to his mother, who considered them realistic and who herself was living in fear. The mother was

then supported to contact the police domestic violence unit who made the house more secure with panic button and cameras. Once these things were in place, the boy's anxiety rating for this fear was reduced and work moved on to the next anxiety – about being seen by the father on the way to school.[2]

The third narrative is from Jackie Barron's 1990 analysis of the court process through which women went when they applied for protection from domestic violence in county courts and magistrates' courts in the United Kingdom. Here is a woman's description of the turmoil she experiences as she waits all day in the waiting area before she appears before the Bristol County Court. Her husband is also present in the waiting area. "It's got a long corridor and you've got another corridor that leads onto other corridors, so every time you want to go anywhere you've got to pass each other and it's terrible. That's enough to get you really worked up. I was a total wreck before I even started, before I walked into the court room, just through (husband) being there, and the looking, the looks, and more or less he was mouthing things down the corridor and it was awful, it was terrible."[3]

The fourth narrative is provided by Marie Ashe, who, as a lawyer in a public defender's office in the United States, co-authored an article dealing with the role of women in domestic violence. In the following account, she records her observation of the effects of physical violence on children:

> It has been troubling to see a client's baby lying in a hospital nursery, his groin burned, blistered and pustulated. It has been troubling to see a young boy who has suffered a fractured skull, whose arms and legs have been broken in the first year of his life, and whose face has lost all appearance of symmetry because of neurological damage. It has been troubling to see a four-year-old girl behaving in the stylized sexual fashion which evidences that she has been a victim of sexual abuse and that she will likely continue to be such a victim. And it has been particularly troubling to know that in each of these cases, and in others, the harms and injuries appeared to have been tolerated or directly perpetrated by my "bad mother" clients.[4]

The first excerpt is an exemplar of narrative descriptions of domestic violence that one encounters in the press. Based on an archetypal plot triggered when the particular aggressor kicks into puppet-like action, they constitute terms of representation fit for a Gothic narrative of paranoia, violence, and excess. This is not to say that all accounts of domestic violence are Gothic, but that there is an element common to them that is susceptible of Gothic treatment. This is also true of the woman's account in Barron's text, which will strike a chord in readers familiar with Gothic narratives of paranoia, where, as in Ann Radcliffe's *The Mysteries of Udolpho* (1794), female protagonists are persecuted in a warren of corridors from which they cannot escape.

The story of the little boy who is stalked by an ogre-like father reveals a peculiar dynamic of domestic violence. In this excerpt, one can descry two sites and two levels of power: on the one hand, the boy and his mother are at the hands of a threatening figure that repeatedly and obsessively exercises domination over them in the home; on the other hand, social intervention to protect the mother and the son takes the form of control and, more particularly, technological surveillance of their living space. This reveals the extent to which power circulates among the spaces and time-bands of domesticity, social practices, and the law, breaking the neat boundary between outlawed power and legitimized violence in the form of surveillance. The fourth excerpt speaks to the unease and loss of composure of a lawyer who is called to bear witness not only to the effects of domestic violence but also to women's alleged participation in it. Ashe's description deals a lethal blow to conceptions of instinctual maternal love and constructs of feminine care, while calling into question the attribution of domestic violence to some innate masculinity. It is clear that domestic violence troubles assumptions, dislocates preconceptions, and makes observers and writers anxious.

These four excerpts all share the compelling desire to give an *account* of domestic violence and are indicative of a social and political trend that developed mostly in the last quarter of the twentieth century. The work of activists and feminist thinkers has been fundamental to the emergence of a modern discourse on domestic violence, which in its earlier stages coincided with the development of second-wave feminism.[5] In the United Kingdom, it is common to refer to the activism and the writings of Erin Pizzey, who in 1971 with the Chiswick Women's Aid created the Chiswick refuge, where advice, childcare, and shelter were offered to women. This social model later spread to the United States in the guise of the shelter movement.

However, the impact of feminist engagement went beyond individual contributions and resulted from the lobbying of social institutions such as the Women's Aid Federation in the United Kingdom (established in

1974) and the activities of multi-agency forums.[6] This is also the period that saw the coining of terms such as *battered woman* or *battered spouse* on both sides of the Atlantic, even though the statutory term selected by English law is *molestation*, which has been variously defined by the Law Commission and through case law.[7]

The naming of domestic violence not only affected the legal and social representation of women but also brought into the open children's experience of such violence. David Cooper and David Ball indicate that the expanding field of sociological analyses of domestic violence coincided with a renaming of the phenomenon of child battering or non-accidental injury as child abuse between 1965 and 1985, first in the United States, then in the United Kingdom.[8] Similarly, Danya Glaser and Stephen Frosh trace an evolution in responses to children's accounts of sexual abuse and how, from being dismissed as instances of fantasy or malice, they became progressively the object of attention and legal action.

The legal regulation of domestic violence is part and parcel of an overall historical evolution of family law in England, which is characterized by two major stages: one is the slowly evolving gender discourse of the law, which results in statutes and policies that take women's social situation into consideration; the other is the advent of children's perspectives and the recognition of their voices and capacity for decision. In both cases, we witness the emergence of the unheard-of concepts of women's and children's rights, which derive from the chipping-away of patriarchal conceptions upheld in the old common law.[9]

While domestic violence is not a new phenomenon, the discourse of domestic violence, which I sketched above, points to a poietic process that publicly names the practices of domestic violence and pulls the bodies of that violence from the sepulchral zone to which they have been relegated for centuries. The legal and academic naming of domestic violence and the telling of domestic violence in novels such as Angela Carter's *The Magic Toyshop* (1967), Julie Myerson's *Sleepwalking* (1990), and Stevie Davies's *Arms and the Girl* (1992) are the occasion for grasping the process of social poiesis, whereby social norms are generated to name and legitimize beings and identify practices. This process has taken place in the context of a dominant nomos in the West, which revolves around the constitution of the family in the household. In common law, the matrimonial nomos can be traced back to the archaic principle according to which wife and children were in a vassal relation to the husband as head of the household. This nomos and its vision and division of the family has evolved historically, particularly against the backcloth of the Industrial Revolution and the emergence of a middle-class family and economy, or spurred by feminist activism and radical contestation of power relationships within and without the household. However, and despite the high divorce rate in the United Kingdom and the West, the nomos of the family remains symbolically powerful and premised on the principles of cohesiveness, benevolence, and care, and it has lately been underwritten by a discourse of gender equality.

In this context, the practices and the subjects of domestic violence constitute a disavowal of the nomos of the family. This nomos is powerfully materialized by the space and time of the household, which remains the site of a familial habitus – that is to say, "a specific mode of thought (an *eidos*), the principle of a specific construction of reality, grounded in a prereflexive belief in the undisputed value of the instruments of construction and the objects thus constructed (an *ethos*)."[10] A stain on the middle-class doxa and habitus of matrimony, family dynamics, and education of children, subjects of domestic violence fail to perform according to this nomos and thereby undo it. This explains why the narratives of these subjects have been notoriously confronted with awkward silence if not censorship.

In this chapter, my analysis focuses on the agon for legitimacy that subjects of domestic violence encounter in their accounts. While all subjects of domestic violence cannot by any stretch of the imagination be regarded as political radicals striving to counter a dominant discourse through their symbolic power, they nevertheless exemplify the ways in which proscribed subjects strive for recognition and seek to become intelligible under the pressure of social exclusion. That these subjects are struggling to voice their suffering, and that they typically experience shame and evasiveness, points to the operation of a political and historical unconscious that haunts the nomos of the family.

The very act of naming domestic violence is a political and material act that poses fundamental questions about one's conception of gender identity and power relations, the premises on which one's analysis of this violence rests, and the ways in which one allocates economic resources to respond to the problem. From a legal standpoint, domestic violence has led to the institutionalization of a discourse of trauma, its effects, and remedies. The four narratives at the outset of this chapter indicate a narrative desire to come to grips with trauma, and they speak to the chiasmic relation between body and language that trauma (whose Greek etymology means "wound") exacerbates. In her analysis of trauma narratives, Shulamit Almog suggests that

> the need to tell the trauma is ... not merely to reveal the facts, or even to reveal the victim's pain. Even if victims believe they accurately remember the traumatic events, and even if it is possible to externalize these memories and make them accessible to other people, it will not suffice for many trauma victims, because it will deny them the ability to choose what to tell, in what order, what to emphasize, what to omit, and what to hide.
>
> What trauma victims seem to need is to tell what happened in *a certain way* and *a certain time*. Fulfilling this need requires the use of specific poetics that fit the idiosyncratic specifications of the literature of trauma.[11]

If the narratives of the subjects of violence reveal the absence of mastery over language, they also function in a catachrestic relation to dominant principles and beliefs of the family sociodicy through their representation of improper and incestuous desire, unconventional roles of parental figures and practices, or murderous violence in what is supposed to be a shelter from the outside world. Wounding and destructive, these indecorous narratives pose a heretical and political challenge to the nomos of the family.[12]

Central to earlier feminist analyses of domestic violence was the notion that such violence reflects sex discrimination and its grounding in economic structures and legal concepts such as matrimony and coverture. In 1990, Lee Hoff noted that "academics and human service professionals have recently taken an interest in the topic of wife abuse. But professionals began to address the issue when grassroots activists – many of them former battered women – had brought it to public attention, and demonstrated that wife abuse was one result of unequal power relations between women and men, rather than the assumed psychopathology of women who seek their own victimization."[13] Today, the analysis of domestic violence poses a challenge to the analysis of gender relationships conceived in terms of masculine domination and feminine victimization.

Thus, to those who argue in favour of domestic violence as the heterosexual manifestation of masculine domination, others will point out that such violence is not the privilege of heteronormative domesticity as it also affects same-sex relationships.[14] To those who flaunt a perverse sense of equity by pointing to women's own patterns of violence, others will recite disturbing and recalcitrant statistics that predominantly identify men as agents of domestic violence.[15] In the field of sociology,

Rebecca E. Dobash and Russell P. Dobash have consistently demonstrated that, in most cases, domestic violence is committed by men. This has led them to discredit the principle of symmetry, according to which men and women are equally capable of domestic violence and male violence is justified by women's own patterns of verbal abuse. This argument has an indiscriminate and fragmentary effect on the analysis of domestic violence and does not consider the social phenomenon as the product of what the authors call a constellation of violence, which allows one to grasp this violence in its intersectional complexity.

The act of naming domestic violence reveals a complex symbolic process, whereby various fields of knowledge generate accounts of such violence. However, rather than produce a Cartesian division between the discourse of domestic violence and the bodies of such violence – both the perpetrators' and the victims' – we need to consider domestic violence itself as an act of naming and a means of communication. This symbolic, mediating process is ignored whenever we propose hyperbolic accounts of domestic violence – or any violence, for that matter.[16] Masculine domestic violence displays discursive patterns that typically justify aggression and that derive authoritativeness from a broader social and historical discourse on gender relationships. In their comparative analysis of men's violence with other men and their violence against women in a domestic relationship, Dobash and Dobash indicate that whereas the men spontaneously emphasized pride and heroism in their conflicts with other men, they were mostly inarticulate or euphemistic about their assaults on women.

These different types of assault constitute a taxonomy of symbolic communication through the body and reflect a division of labour between men and men (the homosocial significance of violence and the status it provides among men) and between men and women.[17] From a symbolic standpoint, it can be argued that the abuser uses the other's body so as to make her comply with his vision and division of the world, betraying a belief in a perfect performative match between signifier and signified – between a slap, strangulation, or a series of lethal blows with a hammer and a message of domination, if not annihilation. In this respect, the bodies of those targeted by domestic violence also exhibit the work of domination and submission, as if the rituals and techniques of aggression had shaped the body into a hexis of domesticity under siege.

Consider the following two examples from the study by Rebecca E. Dobash and Russell P. Dobash, which they conducted during interviews with men and women whose relationships were marked by violence. The italicized statements correspond to the researchers' questions to the men. "*What do you think about her being violent to you?* Well, I think she's not got the right to do that. I'm a man, and she's a woman! (man. 008)."[18] Or "*Has [she] ever been violent to you?* No, because she's a woman, I'm a man. Basically, my wife's 98 lbs (man. 041)."[19] In this discursive context, the hits and blows are performatives of a gender division of the social world within the space of kinship. The tautology of the men's answers indicates the presence of a habitus and classificatory schemes, whose apparent evidence points to an unquestioned interpretation of gender identity and relationships.[20]

The underlying connection between patterns of domestic violence and a dyschronous regime of archaic patriarchal principles is apparent in the way domestic violence grafts onto the rhythms of living and the spatial layout of a domesticity governed by norms and practices of kinship. That we are not dealing with isolated acts but with the signs of an archaic habitus is indirectly established by sociologists, who endeavour to provide definitions of violence in the family that take into account *patterns* of violent behaviour as opposed to *acts* of violence. Among other socio-legal scholars, Deborah Lockton and Richard Ward rely on institutional definitions for their claim that domestic violence should be grasped and theorized as a social pattern. They cite the Law Commission on the meaning of domestic violence.

> In its narrower meaning it describes the use or threat of physical force against a victim in the form of assault or battery. But in the context of the family, there is also a wider meaning which extends to abuse beyond the more typical instances of physical assault to include any form of physical, sexual or psychological molestation or harassment which has a serious detrimental effect upon the health and well-being of the victim, albeit that there is no violence involved in the sense of physical force. ... The degrees of severity of such behaviour depends less upon its intrinsic nature than upon it being part of a pattern and upon its effect on the victim.[21]

In effect, the definition identifies and describes the terms of a social, spatial, temporal, and affective ecosystem, in which the practice of violence is deployed. Invariably, commentators pause on the frequency, rhythms, and habits of domestic violence. For instance, it has been established that there is a recognizable pattern in the number of assaults (35 on average) that a woman usually endures before she decides to report the violence to the police.[22] In identifying domestic violence,

Malcolm Gordon considers the "frequency, chronicity, and duration of aggressive acts"[23] to be a crucial factor of determination. Therefore, the phenomenon of domestic violence, as studied, recorded, analysed, and quantified, reveals the ways in which this exercise of power is normatively and symbolically organized and reproduces itself within the site and rhythms of kinship.

That violence in the household predominantly if not exclusively speaks to archaic patterns of masculine domination; that agents of domestic violence are often, although not always, living in a social world where cultural practices have gainsaid the patriarchal organization of labour and symbolic capital; and that the socio-economic evolution of female labour is in total contradiction to the obsolete domination of the house master over the wife – all of this points to the phenomenon of dyschronia, whereby cultural archetypes govern behaviour in contradiction to other evolving social structures, practices, and beliefs.[24] In other words, patterns of domination in the form of domestic violence committed by men exceed the social and historical transformation of gender practices in other social areas.

Because domestic violence is statistically weighed towards men, sociologists, psychologists, and social workers have concentrated their efforts on the rehabilitation of perpetrators of that violence and on the protection of the victims. However, rather than consider masculine domestic violence as the expression of a hegemonic and supra-historical patriarchal structure, individual deviance, biological predisposition, or pathological conduct under the influence of alcohol and drugs, I propose to regard these practices of violence as the manifestation of the political uncanny haunting the historical and social transformation of gender relationships and family practices in the West. At a time when the concept of fatherhood is in a state of what Richard Collier and Sally Sheldon call fragmentation,[25] masculine domestic violence not only points to persisting practices of domination among men who engage in this violence, but also indicates an undertow of power struggle shadowing the nomos of a cohesive and egalitarian family.

This political uncanny is first and foremost signified by the holes and gaps in the discourse on domestic violence. Repeatedly, researchers point to the silencing and proscription of domestic violence.[26] Elizabeth Stanko sees in this censorship a hidden form of violence: the problem is so familiar as to be normal and therefore invisible. Yet, as she argues, domestic violence is well documented through "records of social service departments in the United Kingdom, rehousing requests for those seeking safe refuge, episodes recorded by schools, medical histories, and records from prisons, residential homes." She adds that "even the police are rife with documented incidents of violence."[27] Resistance to bearing witness to this violence is exemplified by midwives' reluctance to ask questions of pregnant women as part of clinical care on the pretext that this is not part of routine work or relevant to the medical care of such women.[28]

This refusal to listen to and acknowledge domestic violence also accounts for the notorious underreporting of assaults by individuals who not only fear retaliation if they tell but also experience shame or a sense of futility at the lack of receptiveness. Commenting on the outcome of an earlier study of domestic violence in Leicestershire, Lockton and Ward underline the seriousness of the underreporting. "Our initial 1991 study ... over a six-month period, into applications to Leicester county court for a remedy in cases of domestic violence revealed 299 cases. This, however, would seem to be the tip of the iceberg, as figures from the Leicestershire police force for 1995/96 reveal 5,144 reports of domestic violence and research does not suggest a massive surge in the number of reported cases since 1991."[29] It is therefore no coincidence that when men in the context of a survey are questioned about the violent physical abuse in which they engage, a high proportion of them remain all the more silent as the abuse is more destructive and abjecting. So, although everybody knows about it, nobody speaks or wants to speak about it, while researchers, social services, lawyers, journalists, and literary writers nevertheless generate a discourse about it.

We have here a curious twist to the Foucaultian thesis concerning the repressive hypothesis: on the one hand, novels, studies, manuals, reports, surveys, medical and police records amount to a proliferation of documents on domestic violence; on the other, the very topic of domestic violence is under proscription even though or, perhaps, because the phenomenon hits close to home. This is a striking example of the way in which a collective process of proscription is manufactured. Its making requires this ingeniously perverse dynamic between abjection and recognition, estrangement and tacit knowledge, whereby the group is cognizant of a situation yet systematically and as if by telepathic accord hushes it up, thereby relegating the "victims" of abuse to silence and a forced illiteracy of pain. In this sense, the discourse of domestic violence is characterized by a political uncanny, whereby historical origins of gender domination are hushed up and reappear as blotches on the social epidermis, spared full exposure by the apparent privacy of the home.

In a world haunted by domestic violence under social censorship, the challenge becomes one of the legitimacy of telling domestic violence in a context that is hostile to such accounts or that posits criteria of legitimacy, which will encroach upon and spectralize the act of telling. The specificity of this agon for legitimacy lies in the attempt to tell a tale deemed so intolerable that one's credibility will be at stake and the narrative will remain without addressee. Quoting a pastoral manager, Abigail Sterne et al. report that rare are the children who will tell their experience of domestic violence. "'Kids don't always say. They are sworn to secrecy, frightened to tell.'"[30] In their 2002 survey of domestic violence cases processed in magistrates' courts, Elizabeth Gilchrist and Jacqueline Blissett report on a pattern of decisions based on preconceptions and stereotypes calling into question the validity of women's application for protection. "Many of the Magistrates' comments seemed to be aimed at eliciting some form of explanation for the perpetrator's behaviour on the partner assault cases. This type of discussion mirrored the type of language and explanation commonly heard in domestic violence perpetrator programmes: excusing the man, minimising the assault and blaming the victim for the perpetrator's behaviour."[31] Under this type of pressure, the teller often falls back into silence, which in legal terms will lead to an impasse for lack of evidence. Thus, in naming domestic violence, legal practitioners simultaneously authorize and prescribe the terms of a legitimate subject and narrative of domestic violence.

The underreporting of domestic violence indicates that the targets of such violence are trapped in an almost perfect vicious circle, whereby the very procedural factors and social beliefs that isolate women from the social group also prevent them from seeking out recognition and redress. Judith Lewis Herman goes as far as holding the law responsible for repeating the trauma inflicted by domestic violence. "Crimes of dominance have a ritualized element designed to isolate the victim and to degrade her in the eyes of others. The crime is intended to defile the victim, so that she will be publicly stigmatized and scorned should the crime be disclosed. ... Victims understand only too well that what awaits them in the legal system is a theater of shame."[32] Shame is the affect that signals that we are dealing with domestic violence in the form of the political uncanny to the extent that it condemns women and children to a regime of silence imposed by the community. If survivors of domestic violence experience shame, it is not in response to their abusers; rather, shame is the price to pay for letting out an account of degradation that abused individuals know will extradite them from a sociodicy revolving around the nomos of the family.

The link between domestic violence and the sociodicy of a group is brought out by Herman's reporting on her study of patients who had undertaken a judicial process to obtain redress from domestic violence. "Their vision of justice combined retributive and restorative elements in the service of healing a damaged relationship, not between the victim and the offender but between the victim and his or her community. The retributive element of the survivors' vision was most apparent in their virtually unanimous wish to see the offenders exposed and disgraced. Their aims, however, were not primarily punitive ... they sought vindication from the community as a rebuke to the offenders' display of contempt for their rights and dignity."[33] Survivors call on the community to bear witness to the violation of their dignity and invoke the justice system to reinstate their belonging to the community. In other words, they expect courts of justice to reverse the process of proscription that engenders shame and to mark their re-entry into the community by legitimizing and recognizing them.

In sum, we are faced with a paradox, whereby the naming of domestic violence by sociologists, psychologists, journalists, and educators results in the proliferation of explanations and analyses, while the very naming of the same violence engenders silence and shame in the polis. Domestic violence unties tongues but also makes one deaf. This paradox indicates that subjects of domestic violence are caught in an agon for the legitimacy of their account of an experience that jars with the social expectations created by the ways the family is told. Deployed in the household, domestic violence turns the familiar into the unfamiliar and sets up a regime of dread where harmony and protection would be culturally expected. Whenever the terms of this violence are reduced to deviance or pathology, and whenever we turn a deaf ear to those tales of violence, we obliterate the political, gender, and historical origins of a dyschronous symbolic organization of power relationships lurking around the home.

In turning to Lesley Glaister's *Honour Thy Father* (1990), I propose to analyse the narrative as an appropriation of symbolic power to lay bare the political uncanny haunting the home as site of domestic violence. As a narrative of violence in the home, the novel participates in the transformation of the discourse on domestic violence by representing that which has been held under proscription. The political uncanny characterizing the culture of domestic violence is exposed through a historicizing narrative that seeks to legitimize subjects of domestic violence and their accounts. However, from within the symbolic violence of the patriarchal household emerges a pattern of sovereign power over bare life that delegitimizes these subjects of domestic violence as they in turn become perpetrators of violence. In this intractable novel, the hushing characterizing the rituals and effects of domestic violence is exposed through an act of telling that recounts the uncanny transformation of the familiar home into an alienating site of violence and traumatic memories.

The novel tells the story of four sisters – Agatha, Milly, and the twins Ellen and Esther ("Ellenanesther") – and a boy named George, who all live in a remote area of rural England from around the beginning of the twentieth century to most probably the 1970s. The main setting is a farmhouse that the daughters inherited from their deceased father and that is now falling into decay. The historical dimension of the novel is manifested by a narrative structure that oscillates between the past and the present and that, on first reading, creates disorientation in the reader. Milly, the second daughter, performs as both the narrator and the focalizer of the events of the plot. The time of narration is either 1977 or 1978: the clue is provided when Milly mentions that her elder sister Agatha's son, George, was born 60 years earlier, after his grandfather's return from the First World War. Milly mentions that her father enlisted in 1916 or 1917, so the reader gathers that the events of the past took place mostly between the beginning of the twentieth century and the end of that war.

Although the sisters are shown to live in a marginal world of their own, as if cut off from the historical development of modernity, their destinies are shaped by historical forms of institutions that include the family, war, and an economic structure. At the same time, Glaister's treatment of the historical context is not solely in the realistic mode. In fact, history does not function as a backdrop. Instead, Gothic rhetoric in this novel constitutes a means of representing history not as an external force of domination calling for collective and political resistance, but as forms of discourse, practices, and modes of temporal and spatial organization that lock characters into patterns of behaviour and condition their subjectivity.

The father, who stands as an archetypal embodiment of what reads like a timeless script of patriarchal power, rules the house where the mother and the daughters live. As a businessman in ceramic tiles and crockery before the First World War, he is the economic head and owner of the house, micro-managing the details of domesticity.

> He would bring back groceries. We enjoyed unpacking them; tight brown bags of flour and sugar, and tea to decant in the caddy; bacon and currants and cheese; and sometimes for a treat, humbugs or toffee or, best of all, tiger nuts for us to chew. Twice a year there were clothes too, dresses made

> in the town. We chose the stuff from little square samples books which he borrowed and brought for us to see. How I longed to go into town, or at least to the village, myself, on a weekday when there was a shop or two open, to go and buy something myself. But Father had forbidden it.[34]

Even after his death, the father maintains the daughters in a state of infantile dependency by organizing a trust, which allows them to survive but not to grow and thrive autonomously. The daughters experience their only social contact with their neighbours, Mrs Howgego and her son, Isaac, with whom Milly falls in love. The terms of power in the novel revolve around a binary division between two genders, the patriarchal hierarchy deriving from it, and the contradictions undermining this hierarchy.

From various events of the plot and dialogues among the characters emerge a broader vision and division along gender lines. For instance, when Mrs Howgego advises Agatha, the eldest daughter, on how to deal with menstruation, she produces a cultural guide and instructions on how to read a woman's body. "You mustn't worry yourself. That's just the curse, your monthlies, and that shows you're a woman now. If that doesn't come one month that's when you should be worrying! That means a babe's on the way. Not that there's any prospect of that till you're married," she added hastily. "As long as you keep yourself nice."[35] As for Isaac, when his father and older brothers are away from home, he proclaims himself "the man around here for now."[36] However, this division of labour between men and women mostly unfolds between the father and the mother in a scenario of domestic violence that eventually results in the mother's suicide.

This domestic violence is characterized by the father's unpredictable and tyrannical behaviour. Drawing on the code of the fairy tale, the narrative depicts him like a wolf or some canine beast. "You never did know where you were with him. He was mild mostly and distant, but sometimes he would change suddenly, grow sharp teeth and pounce. Sometimes Mother was wary of him. Her movements would shrink when he came in, caged, cagey."[37] The targets of his aggression are the mother and, after the mother has died, the children. In telling how she first witnessed her father's violence towards her mother, Milly accounts for what could be called a scene of reproduction. In the following excerpt, the target of aggression is not only the wife but also the pregnant body as emblem of sexual and family reproduction.

> I was on my way downstairs, my head full of stories and dreams, and I stopped, unnoticed, half-way down. I stood and watched my father tread,

> with his shiny black shoe, on my mother's softly slippered foot. He trod hard, grinding his heel.
>
> I saw my mother's face, the way the tears flowed over bruises. I saw my father step back off my mother's foot. I saw my mother close her eyes, and wrap her arms tightly around herself and press back against the warmth of the stove. I saw my father strike my mother sharply on the belly with his malacca cane. "Bastard," I heard him say. "Another bastard for me to feed. You fucking whore." And then he left.[38]

After the mother's death, the children become the recipients of the violence and the inheritors of a family habitus through which the rhythms of domestic violence are reproduced. "Father's moods could change as suddenly as a snap of the fingers. Some little thing, a careless word, any evidence of a slip in our manners or politeness, could send him plummeting into a foul mood that bruised and thickened the air in the room and made me feel faint with anxiety."[39]

The relationship between the daughters and the mother is affected by their perception of her as an embodiment of both pleasure and death. On the one hand, and according to a traditional topos of maternal representation in both literature and feminist writings, the mother is *mater* and matter. The daughters have glimpses of the mother's life before marriage, when she was enjoying good food and singing at a restaurant with a man. On the other hand, the smell of the maternal body functions like a bad omen of maternal reproductivity. On the birth of the twins Ellenanesther, Milly remembers experiencing the following: "There was a funny smell about Mother, an ill, animally sort of smell that was stronger than the lavender smell of her soap."[40] The mother's suicide occurs after the father, who has forbidden the daughters to interact with the Howgegos, returns from business and discovers Milly and Isaac, the neighbour's son, playing and wading in a pond on a hot afternoon. Milly struggles with a leech on her leg, and her screams attract attention. After the mother burns the leech off her daughter's leg, the father yells at Mrs Howgego and orders her out of his home, later accusing ten-year-old Milly of acting like a slut in the pond with her young neighbour.

From this point onward, the mother's behaviour takes a turn for the worse. Estranging herself from the daughters in the house, she falls into depression and eventually vanishes. "Mother died in late October when the sky was dark by tea-time; when it had been raining for a week; when the house was cold and grimy; when Father hadn't been home for almost a month. She simply went out and never came back.

She kissed us before she left. She said she loved us and that we must forgive her. She said we must try and understand. And then she went out into the dark and the rain, and she never returned."[41] After committing suicide, the mother dominates the daughters' lives as a figure of grief and a source of fragmentation. "Mother's going splintered us somehow. ... Oh we stayed together and the walls of the house contained us, but they did not hold us safe. We rattled inside, locked in our own heads – but for the twins who grew as one."[42] As a first-person dirge grieving the loss of the mother, *Honour Thy Father* challenges the notion of the coherent and autonomous self, master of its words. As Butler argues, "What grief displays ... is the thrall in which our relations with others hold us, in ways that we cannot always recount or explain, in ways that often interrupt the self-conscious account of ourselves we might try to provide, in ways that challenge the very notion of ourselves as autonomous and in control."[43] The story of the mother's loss does not occur at a particular moment in the novel; instead, it recurs at irregular intervals, and this recurrence points to the trauma with which the daughters struggle.

The symbolic significance of the loss derives from the way in which it crystallizes a sociodicy revolving around the fracture between two genders through a contrast between the mother's death and the father's survival, her defeat and his domination. Out of this gender dynamic emerges a familiar narrative of the uncanny, which has the family home as its major stage. With its representation of confinement and its topos of the domestic castle, Gothic fiction has been a fit medium to explore narratives of violence on the site of kinship. In late twentieth-century English Gothic, the home was often been represented as this cultural space stalked by patriarchal control that in turn would be reinforced by institutional or cultural authority: the son's inheritance of a mansion as heirloom from his father and his failure to live up to the role of patriarch in Susan Hill's *I'm the King of the Castle* (1970); the father's cemented garden of Ian McEwan's *The Cement Garden* (1978); the ghost of a violent father haunting a suburban home in Clapham in Julie Myerson's *Sleepwalking* (1994); or the husband's rule over the psychiatric hospital adjacent to the family home in Patrick McGrath's *Asylum* (1997). Common to these novels and to *Honour Thy Father* is the transmogrifying of the home as space of the familiar and the familial into an estranging abode where all sense of hospitality is lost and where protagonists stumble their way through the *unheimlich*.

In *Honour Thy Father*, the fracture between the father's domination and the mother's spectralization is reinforced by a topography dividing the area of the house from the area of the dyke, where the mother committed suicide. In the daughters' personal mythology, the dyke becomes Mother's Dyke, the graveyard where lies the maternal body that was never found. The father's house is a structure of sociopolitical subjugation through a social script prescribing gender roles and practices. This patriarchal governance is of the panoptical type as it does not require the father's physical presence. In fact, until he leaves for the war, he spends long periods away from the home, first leaving it to the mother's responsibility, then to the daughters' after the mother dies. The daughters, Milly and Aggie in particular, have internalized the paternal rules and remain subjugated to his laws, which do not have to be voiced to be obeyed. "He was hardly with us and yet he was with us all the time. There was no freedom from him."[44] While the father walls them inexorably into the farmhouse that he rules and regulates, the daughters become regimented by a social script that prescribes their subjectivity through domestic tasks.

In her identification with a house under siege and in decay, Milly produces the landscape of a mind in the grip of melancholia, whose capacity to dream and enact a future is crippled by obsolete yet potent patriarchal norms inherited from an archaic way of telling the world. In a dream, Milly identifies with her singing mother, who haunts her daughter like a revenant.

> The rain is cold and merciless in my dream, it pelts needle-sharp into my face. My coat is soaked, my hat, my lovely London hat disintegrates and a paper pansy falls off and catches in the crook of my elbow before falling into the mud. I just wish I could be in London, I wish fiercely that I could be there in all the noise and warmth, the bustle and friendliness of it, for here there is nothing. … Oh that would be the thing! To run there, to run away, to run and run. … I can sing. I can sing. I *can*. … But behind me there is that other thing. Behind me is a house full of draughts, full of mouths I should be feeding, mouths I should be causing to smile. That house is a big draughty box packed with guilt. … Sometimes the wind that blows for miles, that blows round and through the house, through the doors and windows, blows through me too. Inside I billow and bloat, there is a great empty space, like the inside of a church and in the centre there is a candle. One small lighted candle, its flame flapping feebly in the wind. It has stayed alight so far, that little flame, but it cannot for ever.[45]

As the ambiguous use of the "I" conveys, Milly has incorporated the lost object of maternal love and is both daughter and mother. Her identification with the dead mother effects her spectralization, whose significance is also historical.

Milly's grieving of the battered mother sheds light on the political uncanny of domestic violence and its melancholic effects on subjects of aggression. This melancholia derives from a social relation of power taking place in the home, which is both documented and hushed up, historical and ghosted. In *Honour Thy Father*, the daughters' body hexis bears witness to violence, either in the form of injury or in the form of physical abjection. In their old age, they present themselves as the extraordinary bodies of wizened witches – dirty, unkempt, clawed, and deformed – which function as somatic graphs of a genealogy of domination. As old Aggie has slipped into her sister's bed to escape her room, which has sprung a leak, Milly describes her as an object of disgust that justifies feelings of estrangement and rejection. "Agatha is still sleeping, flat on her back in the middle of the bed so I have to squash to the edge to avoid her. Her sharp gristly nose, a crow's beak, rises out of a face that has sagged back in sleep to reveal the bones beneath the shadowy skin. She is puffing, her cheeks ballooning out, thin grey balloons, and then the air escaping through her lips like a gush."[46] The bodies of domestic violence are not meant to entice; they repel and alienate. Their smells and bruises spell out a history that is expected to be buried in silence. The bodies of Glaister's novel are the bodies of domesticity shaped on the site of the *unheimlich* and pointing to the presence of a political uncanny regulating the power relationship that affects the overall dynamic of the household.[47]

Thus, it is as a body misshapen by violence that Milly tells her tale of terror and abjection. Glaister's approach stands out in that it captures the problem characterizing the telling of domestic violence by enacting the illegitimacy of such telling through the narrative dynamic of her novel. Indeed, the narrative presents itself as a first-person account, with all of the problems of unreliability that such rhetoric presents: Milly contradicts herself, cannot ascertain dates, and is not always sure of past events concerning Agatha, who might have had a different father, or concerning the mother, who perhaps was an actress. In other words, Glaister's novel is inscribed in the metafictional tradition of Gothic narratives, which through their self-reflexive devices point to the uncertainty surrounding the narrator's credibility and authority.

At the core of Milly's slanted and proofless account lies the whole issue of using a normative language to legitimate one's account of domestic violence. In the contemporary polis, schools' provisions for responding to a child's account of domestic violence allude to the legal expectation of such a normative use of language. "If a child makes a disclosure to a member of staff, s/he should write a record of the conversation as soon as possible, distinguishing clearly between fact, observation, allegation and opinion, noting any action taken in cases of possible abuse and signing and dating the note."[48] The prescribed distinction among fact, observation, allegation, and opinion is a direct outcome of the regulating effects of family law on domestic violence, which, in proximity to standards of criminal justice, cannot prosecute an offender of domestic violence unless it can offer evidence of this violence. At the same time, and operating as a double helix intertwining social norms and procedural norms, the law feeds into the notion that subjects of domestic violence are held under suspicion until proven innocent.

In the case of the novel, the reader is not expected to mete out a judgment; rather, the reader is faced with a dilemma: either Milly's account should be treated as the product of a deranged and senile mind and should be dismissed as completely unreliable, or her first-person narration signifies something else. As stated above, the novel focuses on the Gordian knot tying subjectivity with historical structures and does not rest on a grand narrative that would redeem history politically or ideologically. In offering an account of family origins that disrupts the family nomos, Milly narrates the affective experience of domestic violence, which is redacted from the statutory language of the law.

Glaister's novel troubles the twentieth-century sociodicy of the family that led the polis to turn a deaf ear to accounts of domestic violence. Just as the four daughters live severed from modern and urban England and are socially inexistent and unintelligible, Milly's account remains without addressee apart from the potential reader of Glaister's publication. Her account does not function as a confession or an appeal; instead, it presents itself as an obsessional process of naming and renaming her experience of domestic violence. If Milly's account does not make sense, it is precisely because it is meant to convey the loss of meaning the daughters have experienced.

Coupling Homer with Samuel Beckett, Glaister uses the topos of weaving. Bickering like two old maids, Aggie and Milly taunt each other on their knitting. "'*What* is it that you're knitting?' says Agatha suddenly, spitefully. 'It doesn't signify,' I reply. I will not rise to her bait tonight. 'You've been at it long enough. How many years is it? Will it be ready for Christmas?' She cackles at her idea of a joke, but I do not laugh, nor even smile. The important thing is that I'm knitting. The important thing is the rhythm of it, the clickety clickaclicka of the needles knocking their tiny heads together over and over and over."[49] Of Agatha's own knitting, Milly says that she knits all kinds of things – doilies, antimacassars, egg cosies, tea cosies, jam pot covers, blankets for the cats. "She knits them all in bright cheap indestructible nylon. But they have no meaning."[50] While Sterne et al. refer to the child's "disclosure" of domestic violence, Milly's account of Agatha's domestic knitting both mimics and deviates from the narrative of the family nomos, struggling against proscription and shame. Aggie and Milly weave out a Penelopiad that is condemned to obscurity and absurdist repetition, but to whose historical significance our act of reading may bear witness.

The only means of hailing the reader is through the use of language, its history, and its social practices of inclusion and exclusion. In this agon for legitimacy, the teller of domestic violence has to shake the prison house of language to be heard and read. In this context, the novel offers what can be called a symbolic praxis, whereby, through a process of social poiesis, Milly incorporates terms that dislocate the syntax deriving from the symbolic violence of the family nomos and a patriarchal constitution of kinship. The desire is to reinstate the mother – that is to say, to create the conditions whereby the off-limit site of Mother Dyke will turn into a stage for acceptance and transformation. The sisters' thwarting of the gender binaries between father and mother, man and woman, abuser and victim takes the path of retrieving the maternal figure from shame and spectralization that the family nomos has exacted.

This mourning process assumes the creation of a special idiom by the apparently least promising but most fascinating siblings, the twins Ellenanesther. While Milly's narrative testifies to a curse of masculine domestic violence, Ellenanesther's idiom functions like the semiotic language of Kristevan description, refractory to the common norms of language while drawing on conventions and syntax of linguistic normativity. The twins, who always speak in unison and live in a quasi-Siamese state, have developed a private language, which Milly describes. "It could not be called speech. It was like a buzzing chant. There was a rhythm but it was not a song. It grew higher and further away and it travelled outside."[51] Their buzzing has the effect of deleting the demarcation of words as in "omotheromothero; thebloodandthemudandtheholygoat; wetollthem dead" or "and the sonantheghost ohmothero anwaterandearth omotheromothero."[52] The echolalia of

Mother Dyke, whose flux and melding overcome binaries by creating a state of undifferentiation between signifiers, is the means of reconnecting with the lost mother whose voice was "like stars and crisp apples and cool water. Oh ... it was like a smile. It made you smile inside, a warm tickle in your belly."[53] Glaister has therefore chosen the familiar and secular theme of flux as a means of legitimizing the mother while liquidating the norms of patriarchal kinship. Ellenanesther's idiom is by turns sinister and bewitching, oscillating between the *unheimlich* and the *heimlich*, the catachrestic and the soothing, dirge and spell all at once. As a semiotic code, it is associated with the maternal body, whose love it celebrates and whose loss it keens. In elaborating this improper idiom, Glaister's novel redefines the lexicon of the abused body, tapping the relation between matter and language as a resource for poietic work.

However, while Milly's first-person account resignifies kinship and redeems the profane mother, it remains caught in a Gothic narrative of iterative catastrophe.[54] This iterative pattern of catastrophe derives from the obsessional aspect of the daughters' traumatic relationship to the patriarchal past. The text displays a rhetoric of repetition through which the narrator is grabbing at bits and pieces of meaning, harassed by the obsessive return of the past, which prevents any conception of the future. Sections of Milly's narrative are characterized by a paratactic, fragmented syntax; the narrative rhythm is breathless and conveys the narrator's struggle with, for instance, the memory of the traumatic loss of Isaac, who died during the First World War. "Shot? Shot where? In the head? Did the bullet smash his darling fragile skull? In the chest? In that heart I'd felt the beating of against my own breast? In his soft, smooth belly? His long pale back? Shot? Shot dead."[55] In another instance, she thinks of her brother, George, whom she and her sisters have relegated to the cellar. "Mush he eats. White mush. I don't think it matters. I don't think he tastes it. I don't think there are any teeth left in his mouth. The rages have stopped anyway, mostly. White blubber, pale body, pale eyes blinking at the light I need to see. I think he prefers the dark. Hardly a flicker on his face. Impassive now. Pale fat lips open. Spoon in it, the white mush. Hold breath against the stench."[56] In this narrative dislocation, Glaister charges the Gothic topos of confinement with renewed significance, entangling the characters in the net of a historical *fatum* through memory and obsession.

Although the binary organization of heteronormative kinship seems to be a fait accompli, the father's status as ruler of the home is undermined by actions that render his edicts meaningless or contradictory.

On the one hand, he spells out the decrees of his moral vision of the world. "You're good girls, good children. I think of you often, and fondly, while I am away. It comforts me to know you are here, tucked away. I grew up in this house, as you know, and my childhood was exemplary. It was not until I was exposed to the world that I even knew that evil existed. People will lie and steal and cheat. Worse things become of women than you could possibly dream. That is why I want to protect you. You are mine and I will keep you pure."[57] On the other hand, in engaging in an incestuous relationship with Agatha – who may be the child born of the mother's relation to another man before her marriage, but whom the father has raised like his own daughter – the father in effect suspends these norms of purity. His incestuous relation to Agatha undoes the very division of labour and power between father and mother, husband and wife, man and woman that the incest interdict is supposed to put in place. In transgressing the interdict while upholding a sociodicy of patriarchal authority within the household, the father in effect creates a space of exception in which he keeps Agatha under his ban.

The incestuous relation unfolds as Agatha looks after the father, whose leg was injured by shrapnel during the First World War. Milly's account of the relation does not follow a simplistic pattern of domination and victimization. Aggie's desire for her father, or at least the man presumed to be her father, defies social and familial conventions not only because it falls under the rule of the incest interdict, but also because it revolves around disgust and attraction, suffering and enjoyment, abjection and self-affirmation. Confiding in Milly, Agatha recalls the initial pleasure at being touched. "At first … I don't know … something came over me, washing him, caring for him so closely. When he touched me at first I was … I was … I mean I knew it was wrong but I couldn't help it, I was almost pleased. No one touched me. You would hardly speak to me. I was lonely. And when he touched me at first, it was nice. I felt proud. He was touching me like he touched Mother."[58] It is in the context of the father's fury at having broken his own law that Agatha experiences the incest as a source of abjection and shame.

> He began to call her whore. She changed. She grew pale and nervous, her confidence all gone. I would hear her whimpering sometimes at night. And then one day, accidentally through the crack where the door had swung ajar, I saw what he was doing to her, what she was letting him do to her. Ugly old man with his rotting leg. Fucking her. That was his word. I heard that word from him. Fucking her, not making love. He was doing it like an animal. I saw his red face, red and mad, the veins in his neck

bulging. I saw her face closed as if in sleep, closed, composed. But did I catch just the hint of a smile, a look of satisfaction? She had got him.

No. No. *No*. I am wrong. Agatha was frightened. I know she was. I heard her whimpering in the dark of the night. She was frightened and devoted and confused.[59]

This is not an unambiguous account on Milly's part. Her account mixes empirical observation with memory, outrage, disgust, and the suspicion that perhaps Agatha was not all that innocent. The telling of the transgression causes a breach in moral principles and kinship organization, bringing the narrator to halts and hesitations, assertions and doubts. Eventually, the daughters kill the father. Caught in the patriarchal doxa, their act of castration and parricide as a response to domination is predictable. "It was all quiet. I got up and went downstairs. There was blood on the kitchen floor; on the blue-and-white tiles; on the table; in the sink. I turned round and Ellenanesther were there. They were holding hands. They had sweet smiles on their bloody faces. 'All better now,' they said. … They had killed him with sharp knives. They had stabbed him many times. They had cut off his fingers and his thing, and lined them up beside him, neatly."[60] If there is a sense of justice in the novel, it is one that harks back to ancient myths of revenge and sacrificial rituals and that takes the path of the Gothic macabre with a good dose of dark humour.

Further, the legacy of the father's domination consists not only of a lifetime of shame and grief but also of a form of power that outlives the father's death and haunts the four daughters. The central embodiment of the political uncanny in this genealogy of power is George, the offspring of incest and the parodic cipher of primogeniture. Born with undistinguishable sexual organs, George undoes the purpose of the incest interdict as a means of drawing clean and clear boundaries between two sexes, two genders, two worlds. Milly comments on George's ambiguous sexual appearance. "He or she. I decided upon 'he' because George was more like a boy than a girl as a baby. When he was born, we could not tell. I said it was a boy to please Agatha, but his private place was strange, not like a boy's and not like a girl's."[61] His abjection operates at two levels: on the one hand, his bodily presence manifests the abjection of Aggie's own body.

He was dull and yellowish with a big tongue, a tongue too big for his mouth, lolling and protruding. He was not lovable, but he was no trouble. … When he got to seven or eight he grew more troublesome.

> He began to hurt himself, bang his head against the wall, bite his arms until they bled. And then he began to bite us too, or lunge at us, throw his arm at us as if it was a heavy branch. And he began to get fat. … His body was even more confusing then, because his chest grew rounded as if he had breasts and his face blew up into a great pale blubbery moon. We had to put him down in the cellar for our own safety. He was violent. He was ugly and stupid. He stank because he soiled and wet himself. … We could not stand seeing him or smelling him or hearing him. Agatha, particularly, could not bear to look at this monster of her own making.[62]

On the other hand, his body becomes the grotesque object of estrangement and defilement by the daughters, who seek to protect themselves from the shame it represents by reducing it to bare life. The maternal abjection of George, the refusal of care to the child as vulnerable being, represents what Adriana Cavarero has called the "symbolic catastrophe"[63] that female acts of life desecration constitute in the Western imaginary, with Medea as its archetype.

In abjecting George, the daughters set up a boundary between the "I" and the "it" so as to evacuate that which threatens the I. "No cellar is deep enough, far enough, to allow us to forget George."[64] Milly represents George as a subhuman creature that does not experience human emotions or share human sensorial characteristics. "He's not a human really, he's a freak, a heavy, ugly, stinking, drooling freak. And tonight he's a crying freak. It's a dreadful sound; a man/woman voice. It sounds frightened."[65] He is the monster necessary to their survival. At the same time, he is the mirror image of their own monstrosity; hence, the imperative is to eliminate him. Glaister's exploration of the power struggle within this matrix is merciless: each and every character crosses the line and regularly commits acts of violence. Here, the *unheimlich* is the Gothic villain at the core of the self, inhospitable to and alienated from an ethics of care and recognition.

The wielding of sovereign power is also conveyed by the ways in which the four daughters have remapped the space of kinship and carved out a space of exception. The kitchen functions as a zone of access for all four; however, the parental bedroom remains Milly's privileged zone, from which Agatha is barred. A mother and a daughter in one, Agatha is relegated to the attic, where the playroom used to be. This mapping of the household is governed by that which is unseen and unmentionable, and that is George, whom the daughters keep hidden in the darkness of the cellar of the paternal abode, away from public exposure and reduced to an inarticulate mass of slobbering flesh in the midst of the rotting foundations of domination and concomitant shame. Omnipresent through his banging and roar, yet buried alive in the spectral and forbidden zone of the cellar as space of exception, George-in-the-cellar is the political uncanny haunting the nomos of the family as a site and a practice of benevolence, happiness, and care. If the daughters did not initiate violence, they are nevertheless acting within its orbit. From persecuted maidens, the four daughters have become persecuting old maids.[66]

Through the excesses of domestic violence and the transformation of domestic space into a space of exception, *Honour Thy Father* undermines a master narrative that has the household as a major social site of kinship. More precisely, the household participates in the symbolic power of the family to the extent that it materializes the principles of the family nomos revolving around benevolence, cohesiveness, and care. With Bourdieu, one can say that the household represents a major site of the family habitus – that is to say, the site of inhabitation, where, through habits and rituals, family members are inculcated with social and political norms inherited from the past and constituting the family.

From its beginnings, family law has played the role of regulating this foundational and constitutive master narrative, which also has national implications. Not surprisingly, the historical concept of the household overlaps with the concept of *regia potestas*, discussed in chapter 6. Stephen Cretney and Judith Masson remind us that according to the British Nationality Act 1981, "British citizens have the right of abode, that is 'the right to live in, and to come and go into and from, the United Kingdom without let or hindrance.'"[67] Therefore, the state has an interest in the constitution and regulation of the abode. As Butler argues, "Not only does the state presuppose kinship and kinship presuppose the state, but 'acts' that are performed in the name of the one principle take place in the idiom of the other, confounding the distinction between the two at a rhetorical level and thus bringing into crisis the stability of the conceptual distinction between them."[68] In particular, family law operates as a major linchpin between the state and the family through its statutory discourse and provisions regulating membership in the family and access to the household.

A survey of family law in England indicates that a historical transformation occurred in the late 1960s and in the 1970s, when new legislation was passed to address domestic violence. This body of laws focuses on the space of kinship as site of domestic violence. In the act of naming domestic violence, to what degree did these statutory provisions dismantle patriarchal principles that they had legitimated in past statutes? My suggestion is that these laws regulating domestic violence engaged in a major poietic reconfiguration of the family insofar as they legitimized members of the household – whether they be victims of domestic violence or not – beyond the rights of property that used to secure patriarchal power in the household. However, in the late twentieth century, law reasserted the family nomos by upholding the principle of matrimonial unity, which is threatened by the very presence of domestic violence. In this scenario, legitimacy switches hands from the tellers of domestic violence back to the state, which through the authority of family law exercises its sovereign power by intruding upon and controlling the space of the household in the name of safety. These claims can be demonstrated by focusing on aspects of family law's regulation of domestic space.

In regulating the site of domesticity, twentieth-century English family law has played a significant role in normalizing the modern family nomos. The building is where you dwell; the function of the dwelling-house is to make the place a home; the home accommodates married or associated parties; the type of interaction among the different parties living under the same roof determines whether there is one or several households under that same roof. Roger Bird cites the Law Commission's definition of *household*, which distinguishes *household* from *house* depending on what goes on in different parts of the house. Thus, there can be a house with several households or none. "The crucial test is the degree of community life which goes on. If the parties shut themselves up in separate rooms and cease to have anything to do with each other, they live in separate households. But if they share domestic chores and shopping, eat meals together or share the same living room, they are living in the same household, however strained their relations may be."[69] In this respect, Anne Barlow traces the fluctuating definition of family and household by analysing the evolution of different Rent Acts and the extent to which statutory language and judges' reports were attuned to social transformation affecting relationships outside matrimony in England.[70]

Barlow argues that, of housing law and family law, the former turned out to have been much more forward looking and to have led the way to acknowledging social transformation in the twentieth century. Her demonstration rests on the claim that "the concept of a shared household as a legal tool with which to identify family relationships was forged … in the housing law domain."[71] I would like to pause on the implications of her analysis and probe the links that family law and housing law establish among three components: the type of relationship; the identification of a family; and the space of kinship or, legally speaking, the household.

Barlow maintains that the major break with the legal past consists in the conception of the family in terms other than those of blood and marriage.[72] As she points out, the courts' approach was progressively shaped by a functional conception of the family, whereby the question is no longer what a family is but what it does.[73] In other words, the basis for the definition of a family became performative. Housing law and its successive amendments as well as housing case law were characterized by an evolutionary trend that overall, notwithstanding a few contradictions, unsettled the consortium-based family.[74] In this social poiesis, the legal conception of family was spurred by the analogy between marriage and cohabitation and later, in accordance with the Civil Partnership Act 2004, between heterosexual spouses and same-sex spouses. In her analysis, Barlow rightly focuses on the types of functional relationship that make up a family living in a household, which an ever-increasing list of relations beyond blood, marriage, or partnership has kept diversifying. However, here I propose to shift the terms of analysis by concentrating on the relationship between the family and *access* to the household.

I suggest that a fundamental factor of historical transformation in the law's construct of the family is not so much the analogical move from married to unmarried or same-sex partners as the statutory provisions enabling the courts through orders either to exclude the offender of domestic violence from the household or to restrict access to it. Undoubtedly, the broadening of terms of affiliation throughout the twentieth century offered major terms of legitimacy by creating rights for persons who had been discriminated against for lack of family status. However, this legitimizing process turns on an extension of rights that remain analogically modelled upon the matrimonial template or that of the extended family. On the other hand, a close reading of the Domestic Violence and Matrimonial Proceedings Act 1976 reveals that, in establishing a nexus among occupation of the space of kin, matrimonial or equivalent affiliation, and domestic violence, the legal document dismantled the traditional construct of the household as man's property and space of kinship.

Historically, this space had a dual function by entrenching the husband's economic status and by mapping out a concept of kinship that traditionally required a unity based on the subsuming of the wife to the husband's estate and identity. It is in this doctrinal context that the famous late-nineteenth-century Married Women's Property Acts introduced degrees of economic distinction between husband and wife.[75]

The erosion of the doctrine of unity as the cornerstone of the matrimonial nomos has been long and arduous.[76] Should we refresh our historical memory of the doxological discourse of marriage? Here is Patrick Bromley's commentary, which recurs in several editions of his *Family Law* between 1957 and 1971. "In English law neither a married woman nor an infant is capable of acquiring a domicile of choice, but their domicile in each case depends at all times upon that of another."[77] The process of distinguishing between husband and wife was furthered by statutes such as the Matrimonial Homes Act 1967 (now repealed), whose preamble read, "This Act amends the law relating to the rights of a husband or wife to occupy a dwelling-house which has been the matrimonial home." The purpose of the act was to give "protection against eviction or exclusion from the matrimonial home to a spouse not entitled by virtue of any estate, interest, contract or enactment to occupy it." This means that the occupation of a matrimonial home was no longer determined by property rights but by virtue of a right to that occupation. Thus, a shift occurred from an economic status to a principle of welfare that is owed to the woman by virtue of being a wife, and mostly a mother, whose children need shelter and protection from homelessness.[78] In severing occupation of the home from property rights, the law took a step that had significant economic implications, even though women still struggle today in seeking refuge at underfunded and crowded shelters and often have resort to social housing for lack of economic power.[79]

The legal consequences were momentous: there now existed the conditions of asserting women's right to home occupation or tenancy,[80] which was correlated to the restriction of the abuser's access to all or part of the home. Shifting back to the Domestic Violence and Matrimonial Proceedings Act 1976, we see that the statutory language severs the hallowed link between consortium and the matrimonial site of kinship: the first part deals with the injunction orders, which either party to a marriage can obtain regardless of whether the party has engaged in a procedure for divorce or separation;[81] the second half of the text concerns amendments to the Matrimonial Homes Act 1967, thereby crystallizing the legal distinction between property rights and conditions of occupation of the matrimonial home.

The social consequences of these legal provisions have been equally momentous. By virtue of being a spouse, cohabitant, or civil partner, the individual can occupy the dwelling regardless of his/her entitlement to the property.[82] In subsection 33(1)(a)(i) of the 1996 act, the law overrides property rights by suspending them for the duration of the occupation order or terminating them. In envisaging the eviction of a husband, spouse, or cohabitant from the household that is either rented or owned, family law effectively legitimized subjects of domestic violence in the household over and beyond their economic status and capacity for property rights. The paradox is that the concept of rights to the home and the poietic refashioning of the meaning of the household emerges in the context of a crisis – that is to say, when the law names a relation on the verge of matrimonial breakdown. It is when the family is under duress that an individual's right to the site of the family is asserted in the name of protection from homelessness and economic destitution.

At the same time, a tension has persisted among evolving social practices, transformative legal decisions in housing law, and family law whenever the latter has held matrimony as the major template for its definition of the family nomos. So, while family law has indeed dematerialized the symbolic power of the patriarchal nomos by neutralizing its economic leverage, it has also resorted to matrimonial discourse to shore up the very family nomos that tales of domestic violence threaten with discomfiture.

This tension is perhaps best illustrated by an analysis of certain features of the Family Law Act 1996. It is typical to consider domestic violence law before and after this act was passed. Beforehand, the different levels of English courts had an inconsistent, piecemeal approach to domestic violence cases. Pre-1996 legislation included the following three basic components: a molested spouse or cohabitant could apply for a non-molestation order to protect the applicant from further violence; or s/he could apply for an ouster order (also called exclusion order) to forbid the abuser access to the home; the third type of solution was the undertaking order, through which the defendant undertook to cease violence towards the applicant. This seems straightforward. However, as Michael Horton explains in the case of exclusion orders, the law turned out to be a patchwork of anomalies.

> Former cohabitants could seek an ouster under the Domestic Violence and Matrimonial Proceedings Act 1976 if the parties were cohabitating at the time of, or immediately before, the incident which gave rise to the application. ... Former spouses could not use the statutory remedies at all unless they continued to live together following decree absolute. ... However, the courts asserted an inherent jurisdiction to oust a former spouse where the interests of the children so required. ... Where there were no children, no such jurisdiction existed to oust a former spouse. ... Where the parties were former cohabitants, there was no inherent jurisdiction to oust one partner, even where the interests of the children were involved.[83]

The 1996 act was created to remove inconsistencies and synthesize the different provisions in a comprehensive and coherent statutory document. The decision to protect women from repeated violence consistently through all levels of courts had motivated the Law Commission's proposals for what became Part IV of the act.[84] In particular, the act provides that "[a] person may apply for a non-molestation order if she is 'associated' with the respondent by way of a family relationship or a relationship closely akin to one. ... In addition, a non-molestation order may be made of the court's own motion in any family proceedings, to protect any party to those proceedings, or any child whose welfare is under consideration by the court."[85]

As Barlow indicates, the language of the act includes terms that lead to yet another configuration of family. In subsection 62(3)(c), the act specifies that the list of "associated persons" who can apply for non-molestation orders includes matrimonial partners, cohabitants, former spouses and former cohabitants as well as those who "live or have lived in the same household, otherwise than merely by reason of one of them being the other's employee, tenant, lodger or boarder."[86] This list testifies to the relative fluidity of the legal construct of the family living under the same roof. However, it seems to me that Barlow's statement that family law "no longer has marriage as its undisputed epicenter"[87] needs qualifying in light of the terms of Part I of the 1996 act.

> The court and any person, in exercising functions under or in consequence of Parts II and III, shall have regard to the following general principles –
>
> (a) that the institution of marriage is to be supported;
> (b) that the parties to a marriage which may have broken down are to be encouraged to take all practicable steps, whether by marriage counselling or otherwise, to save the marriage.[88]

These two principles operate as determining conditions supporting a matrimonial discourse and sociodicy, and they are all the more paradoxical as the act deals chiefly with domestic violence and divorce, both factors of disintegration of what we might think of as a family.[89] The affirmation of marriage as an institution that must be saved at a time when divorce rates have been historically high; when families form, dissolve, and restructure themselves; when single-parent families are on the rise – all this makes for a very curious statement indeed and points to an attempt to mask social practices so as to perpetuate the terms of a sociodicy disconnected from the actual work of social poiesis in the polis.[90]

It is in this context that we can return to the symbolic power of the household and the ways in which law regulates it. Common to the historical evolution of the definition of family demonstrated by Barlow is this one steady factor, which is the reference to the household. So, while the legal defining criteria of family fluctuate, the site of the family remains constant. Clearly, the concept of family has been pluralized, in which case space seems to provide the only possible stabilizing factor in this state of social fluctuation. From a symbolic standpoint, we know how powerful and tenacious the discourse of the home has remained, be it in the form of the young couple's "first home," the child navigating between households and indirectly acting as the guarantor of family sites through his or her contact with the dispersed members of the family, the conception of the home as shelter from the hectic or ruthless pace of modern life and labour relations, popular television programs on home search or home renovation, or the mere desire to own a home one cannot afford except through sub-prime mortgages. From the standpoint of the political terms of a sociodicy, the discourse surrounding the home remains primordial, and, I suggest, with it re-emerge spectres of legal narratives of sovereign power over the family or, at the very least, its site. What is most thought-arresting is that the family is never so present as when the law regulates domestic violence within the confines of the home. It is as if law's regulation of the household under siege offered the surest means of materializing a family nomos that is in practice in a state of disintegration.

The emergence of state sovereignty over the family is best grasped when one considers the ways in which statutory language establishes control over the space of the household. In their decision to grant an order that excludes a person from the family home, the courts have the duty to take into account the "balance of harm" test, according to which they weigh the potential harm to the applicant and children if the abuser remains in the family home against the consequences of evicting the abuser. By virtue of section 43, children also have the right to apply for occupation orders.[91] It is under these conditions that, according to section 33 of the Family Law Act 1996, a person who occupies a dwelling-house by virtue of a beneficial estate or interest or contract, or who benefits from matrimonial rights in relation to a dwelling-house, is entitled to apply for a court order that may:

(a) enforce the applicant's entitlement to remain in occupation as against the other person ("the respondent");
(b) require the respondent to permit the applicant to enter and remain in the dwelling-house or part of the dwelling-house;
(c) regulate the occupation of the dwelling-house by either or both parties;
(d) if the respondent is entitled as mentioned in subsection (1)(a)(i), prohibit, suspend or restrict the exercise by him of his right to occupy the dwelling-house;
(e) if the respondent has home rights in relation to the dwelling-house and the applicant is the other spouse [or civil partner], restrict or terminate those rights;
(f) require the respondent to leave the dwelling-house or part of the dwelling-house; or
(g) exclude the respondent from a defined area in which the dwelling-house is included.[92]

The above discourse of statutory law has created a paradox: on the one hand, it has contributed to the evacuation of patriarchal power from the domestic castle; on the other, the language of the law has the performative effect of relaying power from archaic patriarchal structures and practices to the state's exercise of *regia potestas* within the household. Indeed, in granting rights of occupation, the state is simultaneously exercising power by controlling access to the household: the capacity to oust has switched hands from the sovereign husband acting arbitrarily and violently asserting his ownership of territory to the law having the authority to expel the abuser from the home territory on behalf of an individual who makes an application for an occupation order.

Under this order, the household or family space becomes regulated by means of a cartography of borders and boundaries between the home and surrounding areas, zones of exclusion within the house, as in access to the kitchen but not the bedroom. Indeed, Horton indicates that "an order under s 33(3)(c) regulating the occupation of the home allows for the home to be split between the parties and for certain rooms to be used by each party only at set times."[93] This cartography controls and classifies individuals who are authorized or forbidden to cross over to the family space. To violence, the state responds with strategies of territorialization, exclusion, and penalization, the very terms that govern violence within the territory of the patriarchal family. The difference is that the law's strategies are sanctioned by its institutional authority and that the express purpose is to protect women and children from significant harm, to use statutory language.

Without any doubt, this is a significant and crucial difference, and not interfering would amount to going back to a discourse of freedom in the name of privacy, or self-righteous outrage at the passivity of law and the police when confronted with domestic violence.[94] However, the paradox is that through the legal regulation of domestic violence that destroys beings and relations, the home becomes a space haunted by the family as constructed, legitimated, and defended by the state, whose brute force has mutated into the use of legitimate and authoritative power buttressed by the principle of the rule of law. Therein lies the political uncanny of domestic violence law, which in the name of safety produces effects of sovereign power through institutional strategies of territorial control over a space of kinship under duress.

We have here an extraordinary demonstration of the relation among the law, family, and social poiesis: by naming domestic violence and devising means of interference and protection, family law has engaged in a process of recognition of the historical transformation of what used to be a sociodicy dominated by patriarchal principles. At the same time, this process of recognition has birthed a new configuration of power, whereby through the law the state fills the vacuum created by the vacillations of masculine domination and encroaches, once again, upon family space. The legal response to domestic violence has created a set of social performatives that reauthorize the concept of the family through a cartography of domestic space, which against all odds upholds a spectral token of family formation. This analysis of the relation among space, the state, and kinship constitutes a major reason for preserving the appellation "domestic violence": the terminology designates a social space that is up for grabs, while enabling us to consider the space of kinship – domiciles – as a crucial space of social and legal normativity to which we relate physically and affectively.

In *Honour Thy Father*, Milly's narrative calls for the wiping out of the household and its patriarchal legacy. If the space of kinship turns into a stage of violence, loss, and melancholia, and if the mind is the spatialized landscape of such catastrophic affects, then the superseding of such space and mental state can require only the destruction of the paternal house. While family law persists in saving the shell of a home in which terror reigns, the daughters proceed to let it go to ruins. "We haven't done the things you're meant to do: painting and papering and plastering. It would mean cleaning first. Those things come after cleaning. When things drop we leave them where they fall. When things break we leave them broken. The house is older than us. We will die: the house will fall down. And that will be a finish."[95] Instead of taking care of the home and keeping it clean, old Agatha obsessively dismantles the house and its contents. "Aggie *is* moving up there, but not sleepwalking. She is moving the furniture. Yes she is! The bitch. There she goes … a heavy thing – her bed? Where she gets the strength from I don't know. *One of these days you'll come through the floor, Agatha.* No, the house will not stand much more of it. Surely, the house cannot stand it, this constant movement."[96] The derelict and disgusting aspect of the house could be interpreted as the reflection of the daughters' abjected selves and self-destruction. However, their neglect of the house speaks equally to their rebellious agency and, to this extent, is a measure of their desire to erase the material signs of order, property, and propriety established by the father.

The household, or space of kin, recurs therefore as a constant factor and preoccupation from one discursive field to another. Whether we consider economic analyses of women's homelessness and lack of access to affordable housing, sociological analyses of the constellation of violence grafted onto the rhythms and sites of the family, statutory discourse on the protection of domesticity through surveillance, or Glaister's representation of the paternal house as a psychosocial structure of hushed-up violence, the household looms as a site of power struggle, where the political uncanny of domestic violence is enacted. This implies that our naming of and relationship to domestic space is fundamental to our understanding and engendering of family, the violence that may erupt in it, and its legal regulation.

Chapter Nine

Resistance and Legitimacy

In my analysis of the symbolic violence characterizing English family law and Gothic narratives, I have considered the role and effects of psychic power through affective adherence to norms of sociopolitical and subjective formation. Central to the two Gothic narratives is a deconstitution of being and practices, which typically materialize through affective attachment to the family as normative matrix and legislated sociodicy. Whether we are dealing with the grieving of the absent mother in the first-person dirge of *Honour Thy Father* or the intertextual labyrinth of filial identification in *The Deadly Space Between*, we are faced with aberrations and grotesqueries manifesting the presence of a political uncanny that introduces a dissonance in the regulated and regulating family nomos. In their excessive and hyperbolic mode, these two fictional pieces act like a magnifying glass on affective processes, generating a crisis of orthodoxy that throws dominant social norms of family into disarray. Clearly, Gothic texts of this kind are more concerned with rupture than with normative reconfiguration. This is the reason why they leave the reader without conclusion.

In this chapter, I examine the transition from the political uncanny as sign of proscription to the political uncanny as sign of productive crisis by developing a comparative critique of the grounds for social and political transformation in Butler's and Bourdieu's analyses, paying particular attention to the node where the social and the psychic converge. While both thinkers identify the social subject's experience of normative discordance through gaps between normative injunction and social performance, or between normative expectations and disappointment, I argue that Butler's politicization of the abject as a resource for a renewed process of legitimization presents advantages over Bourdieu's call for a forced congruence between self-reflexive reason and political transformation. According to Butler, figures of proscription threaten normative reality with disruption through the return of the repressed, which exceeds dominant norms of social self-identification. It is on this normative disruption that the shift from the political uncanny as proscription to the political uncanny as productive crisis occurs. On this basis, I suggest that the social subject's ability to defeat normative domination lies partly in the capacity to practise symbolic agency across different fields of social organization. In other words, social resistance begins with normative border crossing.

If social poiesis – the constituting of the social world as a constant and agonistic process – depends on the naming and unnaming of norms and practices, then in seeking legitimacy, how does the subject experience the detachment from hegemonic principles of social regulation? Butler frames the problem in the following terms: "What do we make of a resistance that can only undermine, but which appears to have no power to rearticulate the terms, the symbolic terms – to use Lacanian parlance – by which subjects are constituted, by which subjection is installed in the very formation of the subject? This resistance establishes the incomplete character of any effort to produce a subject by disciplinary means, but it remains unable to rearticulate the dominant terms of productive power."[1] Butler's terms of analysis imply that the account of transformative practices begins with an analysis of the node where the social and the psychic converge.

If subjection as both subordination and subjectivity derives from an attachment to social norms – if the psychic is social – then psychic resistance to subordination cannot but be social in character. Thus, the capacity for political agency and resistance to forms of symbolic violence is predicated on the symbolic power involved in the generation of social norms, relations, and practices.[2] This implies that the difference between reproductive agency and transformative agency lies in the ability to configure and reconfigure terms and practices of social legitimacy beyond the logic of penalization and proscription for deviating from the ways things are done. On the one hand, without access to and appropriation of symbolic activities, social agents cannot establish their claims to legitimacy. On the other, there is no *state* of legitimacy, only a constant, vigilant process of formulating, guaranteeing, and contesting social terms of legitimacy.

Central to Bourdieu's and Butler's analyses of social domination are the effects of the occultation of history upon the social subject. The gist of Bourdieu's argument is that the best way of interrupting social reproduction and its pernicious effects of domination is to resort to self-reflexive reason as a means of getting access to the historical foundations of the norms of social organization. The use of self-reflexive reason is to address the following problem: "The primordial political belief is a particular viewpoint, that of the dominant, which presents and imposes itself as a universal viewpoint. ... What today presents itself as self-evident, established, settled once and for all, beyond discussion, has not always been so and only gradually imposed itself as such. It is historical evolution which tends to abolish history, in particular by relegating to the past, to the unconscious, all the 'lateral possibles' which have been excluded."[3] From her standpoint, Butler argues that the transformation of social norms derives from a reinterpretation of the social nomos through the advent and legitimization of norms excluded by the dominant discourse: potential norms of being and doing things that were proscribed in the normative constitution of the subject return to visibility in the midst of normative reality.

Butler shares Bourdieu's historical outlook when she defines social performativity as a reiteration that does not belong to the domain of blind fate, but that has a historical specificity. Performativity "is not primarily theatrical; indeed, its apparent theatricality is produced to the extent that its historicity remains dissimulated (and, conversely, its theatricality gains a certain inevitability given the impossibility of a full disclosure of its historicity)."[4] In both theoretical reflections, political resistance to domination takes the form of an immanent process whose purpose is to bring to light what historically underwrites the constitution of dominant principles of social organization.

Bourdieu's analysis of the self as an agent constrained by and enacting structural principles of social organization implies that any isolated act of rebellion against dominant terms of social organization is meaningless because it remains contained within institutional and material structures of which the self is the cipher. "Revolt, when it is expressed, stops short at the limits of the immediate universe and, failing to go beyond insubordination, bravado in the face of authority or insults, it targets persons rather than structures."[5] Paradoxically but logically enough, the social agent has the best chances of changing social structures if s/he has experienced and been granted legitimacy in these structures. "Only when the heritage has taken over the inheritor can the inheritor take over the heritage."[6] The paradox stems from the notion that it is the assimilation of a set of beliefs and principles that makes the individual a social agent. Change to material conditions and practices, which the social agent has comprehended and incorporated as a habitus, is conditional on the experience of contradictions and divisions affecting these conditions and practices. Only then can the social agent become aware of the symbolic violence of social practices and their structuring principles.

Similarly, there is no apocalyptic destruction of the old for the emergence of the new in Butler's conception of social transformation. Performative power depends on the existence of an entire social framework of iteration and citation, which gives utterances their social efficacy. As in Bourdieu's case, Butler's social subject is not defined in passive terms but contributes to this production of discursive norms. For instance, the gendered self is the embodiment and enabling agent of these repeated acts of interpretation and cultural citation. Most important, it is only from within this iterative form of power that the social subject can inflect the discursive norms with new meaning. The "paradox of subjectivation (*assujettissement*) is precisely that the subject who would resist such norms is itself enabled, if not produced, by such norms. Although this constitutive constraint does not foreclose the possibility of agency, it does locate agency as a reiterative or rearticulatory practice, immanent to power, and not a relation of external opposition to power."[7] Thus, it is repeated and sustained participation in social discursive production that enables the subject to work through and alter existing terms of social legitimacy governing the material forms of the world and the embodiment of gendered selves.

Correlatively, it is only through the process of reiterated practices – "a practice of *re*signification"[8] – that renewed forms of symbolic representation will receive social legitimacy. If this mode of validation is missing, the performative act will remain a bravado – to use Bourdieu's term – or will remain an illegitimate phantasm gesturing on the margins of the social world. Butler's analysis also indicates that reiterative, performative acts have no valence in themselves. Depending on the context, normative reiteration may be responsible for social reproduction of the most coercive kind, but it can also aid and abet the introduction of new or reformed normative practices.

If the temporality of social domination is reiterative and customary, what will throw a spanner in the works of social reproduction and its coercive effects? Although their terms of explanation are different, common to Bourdieu's and Butler's accounts is the notion that a gap, a discrepancy, an incongruence, a discordance, an interval in the process of social repetition will have a disruptive and potentially subversive effect on the social agent. According to Bourdieu, habitus is the site of both the status quo and social transformation. "If it is accepted that the principle of the transformation of habitus lies in the gap, experienced as a positive or negative surprise, between expectations and experience, one must suppose that the extent of this gap and the significance attributed to it depend on habitus: one person's disappointment may be another's unexpected satisfaction, with the corresponding effects of reinforcement or inhibition."[9] The gap and the disappointment may lead to a reflection over and critique of one's social environment and a rejection of customary understanding. The experience of social destabilization is one of social malaise and ill-adjustment. It is not so much that time stops, but that the individual becomes uncomfortably aware of the contingency of social time. The fracture affects the individual both at the institutional level – family, workplace, school – and the affective level. This social and affective awakening generates a rational process towards enlightenment in response to one's experience of social contradictions and incongruities.

Similarly, Butler argues that the factor of social destabilization lies in the discrepancy between the expectations that norms of identification create and the subject's actual performance of these norms of identification. "The abiding gendered self will … be shown to be structured by repeated acts that seek to approximate the ideal of a substantial ground of identity, but which, in their occasional *dis*continuity, reveal the temporal and contingent groundlessness of this 'ground.' The possibilities of gender transformation are to be found precisely in the arbitrary relation between such acts, in the possibility of a failure to repeat, a de-formity, or a parodic repetition that exposes the phantasmatic effect of abiding identity as a politically tenuous construction."[10] The effect of the reiterated performance of a social script is to conceal the arbitrary relation between norms of social identity and the body that performs them. However, the failure to repeat, or the parody of such repetition, undermines the illusory stability of norms of self-identification and constitutes what Butler calls the occasion for a potentially productive crisis.

This normative crisis does not derive from a distinction between failed performance and successful performance; rather, as the phantasmatic staging of social identification, the act of performing never coincides with the social norm of fixed identity. The self is always an approximation and a perpetual event in the making that chases its normative shadow, "always displaced by the very repetition that sustains it."[11] In other words, there is no point where the "I" can be stabilized, and therein lies the possibility of social change. It is not so much that change cannot take place, but that the desire to adhere to norms masks the fact that as temporal creatures, we are enacting change all the time. The individual's awareness of and reaction to this discrepancy between performance and norms determines whether discursive norms succeed in maintaining their political spell, but the response to potential deviation from norms is also psychic and affective.

> The anguish and terror of leaving a prescribed gender or of trespassing upon another gender territory testifies to the social constraints upon gender interpretations as well as to the necessity *that there be* an interpretation, i.e., to the essential freedom at the origin of gender. ... [The questioning of gender norms] often engenders vertigo and terror over the possibility of losing social sanctions, of leaving a solid social station and place. That this terror is so well known gives the most credence to the notion that gender identity rests on the unstable bedrock of human invention.[12]

So, at first sight, it appears that Bourdieu's and Butler's accounts of the short-circuiting of social norms are so close as to be eerily similar. However, a closer examination of the rhetoric of their accounts and the conclusions they draw from their examination of the experience of social discordance reveals a major divergence, which creates two conceptions of what constitutes the resources of social resistance to normative domination.

While Bourdieu and Butler both address the process of social destabilization in terms of affect, their characterization of affect is notably different. Bourdieu talks about disappointment, surprise, and malaise, while Butler describes a state of existential crisis, where the subject is racked by terror and anxiety. In so doing, she borrows from the Gothic tropes of excess and terror. This semantic difference indicates a fundamental divergence, which emerges in Bourdieu's and Butler's conclusions and on which I will draw to elaborate the productive resources of the political uncanny. Where he conceives the work of social resistance in terms of a rational and historicizing critique of the social nomos, she derives a principle of sociopolitical resistance from the unconscious antibodies that the social subject has grown while being exposed to different discursive norms. In his resort to a rationalist discourse, Bourdieu places himself within a long tradition that makes him an inheritor of the Enlightenment, but also of philosophers of the neoclassical tradition, such as Pascal, and political thinkers such as Marx and Althusser, who both subscribed to the possibility of a historical science of social phenomena.

On this basis, Bourdieu distinguishes between practical knowledge stemming from comprehension and the knowledge deriving from the use of reflexive reason. While the former enables the individual to acquire legitimacy by participating in the social world and its practices, the latter is a means of denaturalizing the dogmas underwriting the terms of practical knowledge and of revealing their historical origins. On the level of comprehension, the social agent has the capacity to assimilate and implement practical knowledge. S/he acts according to dispositions that determine whether s/he is capable and desirous of adapting to a particular field. However, this participation in the world does not result from a process of rational deliberation. Practical knowledge lacks self-reflexivity but is terribly efficient in producing social automatisms that make the individual well adjusted. "The agent is never completely the subject of his practices: through the dispositions and the belief which are the basis of engagement in the game, all the presuppositions constituting the practical axiomatics of the field (the epistemic *doxa*, for example) find their way into the seemingly most lucid intentions."[13] In other words, processes of cognition and affect are hijacked by social and economic interests and are dehistoricized, the better to persist and reproduce themselves.

In contrast, social and political transformation occurs if reason is historicized – that is to say, if from functioning as a means of comprehending and implementing social dictates it becomes a means of revealing their historical and arbitrary dimension. So the use of self-reflexive reason is that which validates and legitimizes the process of social transformation and prevents its derailment into yet another set of usurpatory, dehistoricized dogmas. Thus, "one can arm oneself with a historical science of the historical conditions of [reason's] emergence to try to strengthen everything that, in each of the different fields, tends to favour the undivided rule of its specific logic, in other words independence from any kind of extrinsic power or authority – tradition, religion, the State, market forces."[14] To counteract the reifying effects of habitus and practical reason, the social agent must engage in a historical critique, which, as "*the major weapon of reflexiveness, can free thought from the constraints exerted on it* when, surrendering to the routines of the automaton, it treats reified historical constructs as things."[15] The strength of Bourdieu's explanation lies in its conception of a rational historical interpretation as a springboard towards a social agency of transformation.

In promoting reason as a self-regulating device of political legitimacy and social organization, Bourdieu seems successful in warding off an idealistic conception of thought since reason is considered a tool of historical knowledge to implement political change. However, his description of a social utopia governed by reflexive reason is disappointing and falls back on a discourse of sublimation that carries authoritarian overtones.

> One might then, in this spirit, treat the realistic description of the scientific field as a kind of reasonable utopia of what a political field conforming to democratic reason might be like; or, more precisely, as a model which, by comparison with the observed reality, would indicate the principles of action aimed at promoting the equivalent, within the political field, of what is observed in the scientific field in its most autonomous forms, that is to say, a regulated competition, which would control itself, not through the intervention of a deontology ... but by its own immanent logic, through social mechanisms capable of forcing agents to behave "rationally" and to sublimate their drives.[16]

Bourdieu seems to have fallen into the trap which he describes so well. The notion that one should use reason through social mechanisms to *force* individuals to behave rationally and sublimate their drives is almost a textbook definition of symbolic violence, which, as he so insightfully writes, is a "soft violence, imperceptible, invisible to its victims, which is essentially exerted through the purely symbolic channels of communication and of knowledge or, more precisely, through miscognition, or at the boundary of emotion."[17] His misstep reveals to what extent symbolic violence is pernicious and how, by insinuating itself through cognitive practices, it undoes the legitimacy of theoretical elaborations. It is this faith in rational and historicized consciousness that leads Bourdieu's thought to regress to a Platonic and hierarchical conception of the relationship between sociopolitical leadership and knowledge.

> The symbolic work needed in order to break out of the silent self-evidence of *doxa* and to state and denounce the arbitrariness that it conceals presupposes instruments of expression and criticism which, like the other

> forms of capital, are unequally distributed. As a consequence, there is every reason to think that it would not be possible without the intervention of professional practitioners of the work of making explicit, who, in certain historical conjunctures, may make themselves the *spokespersons* of the dominated on the base of partial solidarities.[18]

One might have been entitled to expect Bourdieu to conclude that the true work of democracy is to bring people to the stage where, armed with an awareness of the historical origins of their social and political surroundings, they can configure their views of these surroundings and act upon them. George Orwell, who in *Animal Farm* warned that "ALL ANIMALS ARE EQUAL BUT SOME ANIMALS ARE MORE EQUAL THAN OTHERS," knew that.[19] In a stupefying act of rationalist imposition, Bourdieu demands that social agents stop acting like marionettes and start behaving. What can only be called an unreasonable expectation coincides with a theoretical act of abjection: after tracing the social creation of individuals acting like automata under the spell of dehistoricized principles of social organization, Bourdieu ends up drawing a line between those who can use reason reflexively and those who are incapable of sublimating their drives. Emerging from this characterization are binary oppositions between mind and body, reason and the unconscious, order and chaos that all look terribly familiar. Thus, Bourdieu has managed to paint himself into a Gothic corner, whereby the proscription of recalcitrant and intolerable forms of desire coincides with the uncanny return of hegemonic reason in the midst of theoretical consciousness.

The blind spot in Bourdieu's theory of social practices is his conception of desire in the assimilation of habitus. Insightfully, he analyses the relationship among dominant systems of arbitrary values and the affects with which they are charged. "We learn bodily ... social order inscribes itself in bodies through this permanent confrontation, which may be more or less dramatic but is always largely marked by affectivity and, more precisely, by affective transactions with the environment."[20] However, the validity of this analysis is brought to naught because his solution to social domination does not address the embedding of symbolic violence through affect. Instead, a breach gapes between the advocacy of historicizing reason and the description of the social agent as a body that has incorporated principles of social organization through emotional and sensorial stimuli. In this scenario, desire is reduced to the concept of *illusio* and functions as but the Platonic reverse of the belief in the power of reason to see through illusions.

When Bourdieu does consider ways of countering effects of domination, he discards cognitive and discursive processes in favour of a physically based approach. Thus, "while making things explicit can help, only a thoroughgoing process of countertraining, involving repeated exercises, can, like an athlete's training, durably transform habitus."[21] This solution is based on the assumption that the transformation of the social agent requires the primary transformation of material and physical practices. But this is to make omission of the consideration that what ties the subject to these practices is the *desire* to embody and materialize the principles governing practices.

If to be a social automaton is to charge with desire the material and objective structures of society and to reproduce these structures in the mode of routine and customary practices – if, as Bourdieu himself writes, the "most serious social injunctions are addressed not to the intellect but to the body, treated as a 'memory pad'"[22] – then something must happen that will enable the social automaton to come alive and redirect desire towards other social configurations. If the social automaton is this body that has been inculcated with beliefs and principles through the affective process of symbolic violence, then the embodied self can only neutralize these beliefs at the affective level through the withdrawal of desire. Butler argues that the source of this process lies in the unconscious, which shadows the normative self and has the ability to interfere with the reiterative rhythm of performativity and the discursive production of social identities.

> If every performance repeats itself to institute the effect of identity, then every repetition requires an interval between the acts, as it were, in which risk and excess threaten to disrupt the identity being constituted. The unconscious is that excess that enables and contests every performance, and which never fully appears within the performance itself. The psyche is not "in" the body, but in the very signifying process through which that body comes to appear; it is the lapse in repetition as well as its compulsion, precisely what the performance seeks to deny, and that which compels it from the start.[23]

What Butler describes here is a normative world haunted by shadows of abjection charged with repressed desire and threatening normative reality with disruption through the return of the repressed, which exceeds dominant norms of social self-identification. Her analysis offers terms to elucidate the relationship between the political uncanny and the work of resistance to dominant norms. I suggest that the return of these abjected forms of representation and practices is the political return of that which was once familiar – that is to say, familiar because belonging to symbolic representation and constitutive of the subject – and that became unfamiliar, scandalously disruptive of normative rhythms. Thus, the political uncanny is all at once the sign of normative proscription and productive crisis.

In true Foucaultian fashion, the political uncanny is *constitutive* insofar as regulation and prohibition are not only normatively constraining but also potentially productive of social contestation. This Foucaultian principle inflects Butler's approach, as in the following: "The juridical law, the regulative law, seeks to confine, limit, or prohibit some set of acts, practices, subjects, but in the process of articulating and elaborating that prohibition, the law provides *the discursive* occasion for a resistance, a resignification, and potential self-subversion of that law."[24] It is because these inchoate forms of subversion ghost the repetitive performance of the regulated self that they have the capacity to disrupt the social rhythm of norms and to initiate a normative transformation. However, the "task will be to consider this threat and disruption not as a permanent contestation of social norms condemned to the pathos of perpetual failure, but rather as a critical resource in the struggle to rearticulate the very terms of symbolic legitimacy and intelligibility."[25] This politicization of abjection is predicated on the conception of the unconscious as socially regulated through normative exclusion. If the unconscious or the abjected irrupts on the social stage, it is not to skip and romp in some kind of pre-social kindergarten, but to actualize forms of intelligibility and symbolic representation, which are the side effects of a dominant normative discourse. Butler's concept of abjection is this excess of illegitimate meaning that social norms create: that which manifested itself as uncanny, inexplicable, and alienated reclaims public and political significance, social legitimacy, and recognition through the process of what Butler calls discursive production.

The key to transformative agency is to create material and symbolic conditions enabling the political uncanny produced by foreclosure to call into question the legitimacy of its normative double and to link up with the domain of intelligibility and social poiesis, whereby public terms of social legitimacy can be rewritten or reformulated. Butler argues that "in the case of foreclosure, where certain possibilities are ruled out so that cultural intelligibility can be instituted, giving discursive form to the foreclosure can be an inaugurating moment of destabilization. The unspeakable speaks, or the speakable speaks the unspeakable into silence, but these speech acts are recorded in speech, and speech becomes something else by virtue of having been broken open by the unspeakable."[26]

What is the process that fosters the questioning of dominant norms and the poietic process of social reconfiguration? If certain possibilities are *ruled out*, what is the process that will unlock this foreclosure? How do *foreclosed* figures of the political uncanny transit into the public symbolic domain? What will allow the emergence of foreclosed meaning to be more than unintended meaning irrupting on the stage of dominant norms of social organization? Butler states that it is not that "a subject disavows its identifications, but, rather, that certain exclusions and foreclosures institute the subject and persist as the permanent or constitutive spectre of its own destabilization."[27] But what is the process that will enable this revenant to materialize as a publicly legitimized social identity?

While the abject is said to participate in the constitution of the world and social subjects by haunting the structures of dominant norms, the term *foreclosure* seems to preclude the notion that the abject can function as a source or "modality" of reconfigured social agency. When Butler refers to the abject as the unspeakable or that which is ruled out, the implication seems to be that the abject remains excommunicated. Yet we also know that in the orthodox discourse of matrimony, the concepts of heterosexuality, sexual reproduction, and primogeniture have all produced unintended and illegitimate social practices, which were or have been under the ban of the law under the regulatory names of adultery, buggery, abortion, and the bastard or illegitimate child. At the same time (and again, depending on which culture one lives in), these historically proscribed practices have in turn led to the possibility of reorganizing the world differently – from proscribed homosexuality to same-sex union, from adultery to the creation of new relationships such as cohabitation and the elaboration of new concepts such as no-fault divorce, from clandestine abortion to legislated abortion, from illegitimacy to redefined kinship – however unsatisfactory the law might be in each and every case. So, perhaps more to the point, the abject is despicable but always speakable, if not institutionally legitimized; otherwise, we would not be able to explain how it can subvert the social map of discourse by claiming the symbolic power and social legitimacy of its practices.

The problem is not only that social forms of abjection are illegitimate, but that they are also identified in censorious and exclusionary terms. But it is precisely because the abject operates in relation to the symbolic mode of regulatory proscription that it retains its material power to spawn in the midst of social dominant norms unintentionally or strategically. In her analysis of the historical and political significance of trauma, Ann Cvetkovich argues that "affect, including the affects associated with trauma, serves as the foundation for the formation of public cultures."[28] Her conception of trauma as "the social and cultural discourse that emerges in response to the demands of grappling with the psychic consequences of historical events"[29] can be read as an instance of the psychic life of power both in its regulatory, everyday manifestations and in its potential as critical resource for social transformation. She traces the signs of trauma in lesbian and queer performance art, literature, photography, and activism, suggesting that the experience of traumas such as homophobia and incest can perform as the basis of an archive of feelings that may lead to new configurations of sexual, gender, and political norms beyond institutional and heteronormative norms of discourse.

> Because trauma can be unspeakable and unrepresentable and because it is marked by forgetting and dissociation, it often seems to leave behind no records at all. Trauma puts pressure on conventional forms of documentation, representation, and commemoration, giving rise to new genres of expression, such as testimony, and new forms of monuments, rituals, and performances that can call into being collective witnesses and publics. It thus demands an unusual archive, whose materials, in pointing to trauma's ephemerality, are themselves frequently ephemeral.[30]

The key to Cvetkovich's argument is her aesthetic conception of history, which in her account is embedded in sensorial and affective experience, which is crucial to the processes of social poiesis in the polis.[31] It seems to me that her analysis and creation of a lesbian and queer archive of feelings constitute yet another major testimony to what it means to challenge the effects of a dominant system of symbolic violence, expose its usurpatory origins, and turn the performative exclusions of the political uncanny into claims for and practices of social legitimacy.

So, if we assume that there is continuity between the proscribed symbolic forms of the political uncanny and the dominant symbolic forms of representation and social practices, the next question is, What comes first, the emergence of new social practices that lead to a symbolic, legitimate reconfiguration of social organization or the emergence of a deviating discourse that leads to the performance of different social practices? Butler's reflection on social transformation oscillates between the two poles of the symbolic return of abjected figures of social desire and the emergence of social practices. On the one hand, the return of uncanny figures of abjection brings about a reconfiguration of symbolic representations that govern social practices. "If the figures of homosexual abjection *must* be repudiated for sexed positions to be assumed, then the return of those figures as sites of erotic cathexis will refigure the domain of contested positionalities within the symbolic. Insofar as any *position* is secured through differentiation, none of these positions would exist in simple opposition to normative heterosexuality. On the contrary, they would refigure, redistribute, and resignify the constituents of that symbolic and, in this sense, constitute a subversive rearticulation of that symbolic."[32]

Thus, abjected forms of desire have found their way to social poiesis, and this results in the creation of a new gender discourse across the social spectrum, whose effect produces new normative claims of being and social practices through the performance of this new discourse. On the other hand, Butler evokes a reverse process, whereby social practices flout the dominant norms and structures of social identification. Thus, "It may be ... through practices which underscore disidentification with those regulatory norms by which sexual difference is materialized that both feminist and queer politics are mobilized. Such collective disidentification can facilitate a reconceptualization of which bodies matter, and which bodies are yet to emerge as critical matters of concern."[33] But if the gendered body is to be understood as the effect of discursive norms, how do we account for the emergence of practices of disidentification without resorting to the creation of new norms of symbolic representation in the first place?

New social practices, I suggest, emerge *as if* orphaned from a symbolic reorganization of the world whenever their performers are debarred from gaining access to socio-economic means of legitimating and disseminating their divergent conception of the social world. As Bourdieu argues, "to observe that symbolic power can only operate to the extent that the conditions of its efficacy are inscribed in the very structures that it seeks to conserve or to transform is not to deny it all independence with respect to these structures. By bringing diffuse experiences to the full existence of 'publication' and consequent officialization, this power of expression and manifestation intervenes in that uncertain site of social existence where practice is converted into signs, symbols, discourses, and it introduces a margin of freedom between the objective chances, or the implicit dispositions that are tacitly adjusted to them, and *explicit aspirations*, people's representations and manifestations."[34] Historically, new symbolic norms of organizing the social nomos have emerged outside the cultural mainstream in the form of small magazines, demonstrations and parades, associations and clubs, publishing houses and bookstores, zines, blogs, and online publishing – all of which have sought to broadcast renewed or resignified symbolic configurations.[35] To this extent, these different discursive norms and social practices have carved out for themselves public validation and legitimacy.

The sclerosis of this social poietic broadcasting occurs whenever boundaries between social fields are established, with the effect of reinforcing disciplinary, professional, and institutional autarchy. The lack of communication among different social fields creates social inertia, if not regression, and decreases the possibility of claims to new norms of legitimacy. A tension exists between new norms of social practices and established practices of specialized fields, whose axiomatic definitions of the world will either be transformed by heretical discourse or whose axiomatic tradition will resist this discourse. This phenomenon is illustrated by the intensification of a psychological and social discourse concerning mental disabilities, which in the United Kingdom created new norms of understanding the phenomenon in the 1990s and which attempted to legitimize individuals affected with these disabilities as social agents in their own right. This constituted a new configuration of the social subject, which called into question the emphasis on self-determining, rational consciousness as a condition of citizenship. This symbolic reconstitution of the world, social identity, relationships, and practices then slid over to governmental agencies such as the Disability Rights Commission, which took upon itself to disseminate this new discourse by displaying posters in the tunnels of the London Underground with a view to changing citizens' possible discriminatory perceptions of individuals affected by such disabilities. The objective was to translate these new social representations into a new symbolic understanding and new practices.

However, in January 2007, the Healthcare Commission released a report, *A Life Like No Other*, underlining factors and conditions of neglect and ill-treatment of individuals affected by learning disabilities who were confined to long-term care hospitals.[36] As a remedy, decentralization was invoked to establish a system that would provide better care for these individuals. Yet it can be argued that the core of the problem lies not solely in the institution but also in the axioms governing practices within the institution. A gap exists between the evolving psychological discourse, the didactic and legitimizing discourse of the government, and institutional practices underwritten by the notion that an individual with learning disabilities is less than human. Thus, the transition from psychological norms to governmental policies to institutional practices is hampered by the breakdown of communication between normative innovation and institutional implementation. Yet, although the psychological, governmental, and institutional fields are separate and autonomous, they are connected through a subterranean network of concepts revolving around the basic question, What constitutes the worth and legitimacy of a human being? Such basic questions as this create the major elements of a fluctuating process of social poiesis that has no settled form or shape but registers the constant and historical transformation of a polis through the ceaseless production and counter-production of social narratives and ways of constituting the social world.

In this context, I suggest that on the interaction between social fields and their attendant norms and practices depend the claims for normative legitimacy and social transformation. Social reproduction rests on normative autarchy, while transformative social poiesis thrives on normative border crossing. The polis is precisely a matrix in the making – a public-building process, as Davina Cooper argues – where major concepts and narratives of social organization are the objects of interpretation and reinterpretation engendering conflicts of meaning and contradictory social practices, which all derive from the multiplicity and simultaneity of fields constituting the social fabric. A conception of social agency must take into account the existence of a polis where principles of knowledge and interpretation characterizing fields such as kinship, work, religion, education, and law circulate from one social field to another and are in a constant state of fluctuation. Although each field constitutes itself as an authoritative discourse that has the capacity to grant social legitimacy, together they constitute the basis for a praxis of performative and intercommunicative transformation of norms and practices. On this basis, transformative social agency is the ability to appropriate symbolic activity and performative communication so as to establish one's legitimacy in discrete social fields, while defeating the hegemonic and orthodox effects of these discrete fields – their discourse, material structures, and social practices – by navigating from one field to the next.

If, as Bourdieu and Butler argue, symbolic violence and discursive domination succeed in establishing a monological experience of time that masks the fact that social performance is characterized by discordance, interruptions, and tactics of deviance and digression but also by the differences engendered through the very process of interpretation and appropriation of meaning,[37] then it is by translating from one system of symbolization to another that the subject not only reinforces the process of interruption and discordance but also actually appropriates this process so that, instead of being accidental and haphazard, it becomes a mode of living and being. Butler argues that "understanding performativity as renewable action without clear origin or end suggests that speech is finally constrained neither by its specific speaker nor its originating context. Not only defined by social context, such speech is also marked by its capacity to break with context. Thus, performativity has its own social temporality in which it remains enabled precisely by the contexts from which it breaks."[38] To this extent, social resistance means to be able to "break with context" and to translate from one field to the next in affective, cognitive, linguistic, and spatial terms. And it is this process of translation that contributes to the temporality of social poiesis. This model allows one to deflect the hegemonic and dehistoricized effect of congruence between the nomos of a particular field and its practices while preserving the ability to shape and condition social practices through performative norms and concepts of social organization. In sum, this conception of agency through normative translation allows for the creation of a polis where the disruption and reformulation of normative systems become the rhythm of social being. The fundamental desire is to make one's home in different locations without becoming indentured to a particular host.

To pursue the spatial metaphor, the objective is to multiply the spaces and locations of social agency and legitimacy so that the place of origin becomes one reference among others instead of functioning as the normative characteristic that makes emigrants aliens, or that associates social identity with territorial boundaries and national language, or that makes gender non-conformity a case of deviance. My rereading of Agamben's concept of sovereign power in chapter 4 suggests that symbolic violence will transit to sovereign power by resorting to a totalitarian nomos, strategies of confinement to compartmentalized space, and the attempt to annihilate the social agent's capacity to mediate the social world through symbolic representation and activities. This implies that resistance to sovereign power lies in mediation – that is to say, the power of plural representation not severed from the body and not confined to a single social space. If the state of exception obtains whenever the subject's capacity for mediation through symbolic activity has been mangled, then the ethical imperative is not only to regenerate mediation, but also to foster mediation of and translation across fields of knowledge and representation. Butler's claim that to mean is to matter points to the locus of social agency and encourages us to think of meaning as the mediation of and through matter, the body, and social structures.

This process of symbolic mediation of the material world affects not only the constitution of general principles of sociodicy but also practices of everyday life. The reinterpretation of the social space within which we live is exemplified by Shauna Van Praagh's argument that conflicts between the religious community of the Chasidic Jews of Outremont in Montreal and non-Chasidic residents, conflicts that were addressed by the courts from the angle of freedom of religion, can be profitably reinterpreted from the standpoint of the private law of *troubles de voisinage*, or the tort of nuisance. In particular, Van Praagh focuses on the "*eruvin* case," legally known as *Rosenberg v. Outremont*, to demonstrate that a reading of the case with reference to the concept of *voisinage* allows one to understand the conflict as an example of community members learning to live together by accommodating cultural and religious differences.

Van Praagh describes the circumstances as follows: "Chasidic communities erected wires and strings throughout Outremont. They marked *eruvin* or, in other words, public space as 'domestic' or 'private.' For religious Jewish residents, *eruvin* that extend the domestic sphere down the street allow carrying to be done in the neighbourhood on religious holidays when such carrying would be prohibited in external or public space. When the City of Outremont began to take down the wires, a complaint was brought by Chasidic community members against the municipality."[39] Van Praagh goes on to report that the court found that the dismantling of the *eruvin* constituted a failure to offer reasonable accommodation for religious practices and violated freedom of religion. However, moving the terms of analysis from an assessment of religious freedom to the framework of *voisinage*, Van Praagh suggests that "no individual can simply say that her understanding of the neighbourhood is excessively interfered with by the neighbour's understanding and use."[40] Van Praagh's insights into the symbolic function of the social agon for recognition and legitimacy are summarized in her concluding remarks.

> Each conflict that goes to the town hall, the neighbourhood paper, or the Superior Court carries with it the potential to contribute to the constant retransformation of Outremont. Each decision, whether rendered in the language of respect for administrative zoning discretion or in the language of respect for individual rights and freedoms, brings different narratives together. These are the narratives of daily life, of what it means to live in Outremont, of the ways in which identity is inscribed on every street corner. And as the narratives are told and retold and given new shape, residents continually learn how to be neighbours, and the meaning and nature of Outremont itself shifts.[41]

What is fascinating about this case is the way in which the different members of the Outremont community are seen to compete for the configuration of their urban space, one group deleting the boundaries between the public and private through barely visible lines, the other learning how to live within this new configuration, which the court argued did not prevent non-Chasidic community members from enjoying the public and secular nature of their neighbourhood. In effect, the same space is given over to different secular and religious mappings, and, through this process of trans-cultural symbolic mediation of the material surroundings, the meaning of space becomes heterogeneous and pluralized.

Finally, if we agree that our relationship to social norms is psychosocial – in other words, if there is such a thing as the psychic life of power – then a conception of legitimacy as ground for social resistance must take into account the psychological processes governing a community. In her account of the shift from forms of abjection and melancholia to the social mediation and legitimizing of divergent norms of identity and practices, Butler is describing the shift from a polis haunted on its borders by spectres to a polis where those who have been abjected and buried alive are brought back from the dead. Drawing on Levinas's ethical concept of the face, she argues that those "who remain faceless or whose faces are presented to us as so many symbols of evil, authorize us to become senseless before those lives we have eradicated, and whose grievability is infinitely postponed. Certain faces must be admitted into public view, must be seen and heard for some keener sense of the value of life, all life, to take hold. So, it is not that mourning is the goal of politics, but that without the capacity to mourn, we lose that keener sense of life we need in order to oppose violence."[42] Just as Butler redirects collective self-destructive energies of melancholia towards the reconfiguration of norms, she converts wilful adherence to dominant norms to a potential enactment of agency diverging from these very norms. The social subject cannot become manifest except through normative performativity, and it is on the basis of this allegiance that resources of resistance can be tapped.

The challenge, I suggest, is not to counter the desire to adhere, but to acknowledge the force of this desire and enlist it to cultivate the translation between and navigation across different normative discourses and discursive practices so as to defeat what Butler calls "the disciplinary cultivation of *an attachment to subjection*."[43] There is no guarantee that the social subject will transform terms and practices of adherence, and everything – including habitual practices, the fear of social alienation and isolation, social and material rewards for psychological adherence, social structures of political reproduction such as education – will conspire against such a transformation. Above all, there is no *tabula rasa* act as resistance to social norms is always bounded by the initial and historical terms of domination.

That spectral identities can reclaim public legitimacy depends on social reiteration, which can be harnessed to regenerative and transformative processes characterizing social poiesis. Social poiesis revolves around the desire for symbolic power: it is because desire is nestled in social utterances, practices, and structures that we experience the social world in the iterative mode, which is also the temporal mode of desire and its insistent beats. Through social reiteration, we may become tethered to normative practices, but our ability to make our mark on the world also derives from our desire for symbolic power, which stubbornly persists through our social interactions and practices.

Chapter Ten

Making the Law

In 2008, the Museum of Modern Art in New York presented to the public an exhibition entitled *Design and the Elastic Mind*, curated by Paola Antonelli.[1] The exhibition evolved in tandem with salons organized by Antonelli and Adam Bly from *Seed* magazine, gathering members from the scientific and design communities.[2] The philosophy underlying the exhibition drew in part on the concept of "thinkering," which the exhibition website formulated in the following terms: "Many designers, scientists, and artists have turned to design to give method to their productive tinkering, or what John Seely Brown has called 'thinkering.' They all belong to a new culture in which experimentation is guided by engagement with the world and open, constructive collaboration with colleagues and other specialists. Whether in the form of origami, nanofacture, or growth and aggregation, thinkering gives shape to the embryonic dialogue between design and science."[3] The exhibition exemplified the ways in which heterogeneous artistic, sociological, and economic fields converged through the design of objects. For instance, the iPod was regarded as the product of interaction among normative fields as diverse as information and interface technology, marketing, design, and demographic analysis.

Clearly, the project constituted the tip of a social iceberg, but it manifested the emergence of normative alliances that broke down the walls among specialized fields of knowledge, economic practices, and symbolic governance of the world. The exhibition also offered a means of gauging not only the historical transformation of normative activities but also the discourse on these activities. In 1951, Hannah Arendt expressed her faith in the human capacity to generate meaning through the process of fabrication. "Man insofar as he is *homo faber* tends to isolate himself with his work, that is to leave temporarily the realm of politics. Fabrication (poiesis, the making of things), as distinguished from action (praxis) on the one hand and sheer labor on the other, is always performed in a certain isolation from common concerns, no matter whether the result is a piece of craftsmanship or of art."[4] Arendt's constructivist and individualist claim constituted an antidote to the dehumanization of mass movements, mass production, and mass consumerism, whose ravages she had observed.

In contrast, the social vision organizing the *Design and the Elastic Mind* exhibition is one in which fabrication, or the making of things, derives from the deletion of boundaries among social fields so as to allow for normative exchange and border crossing. This inter-symbolic and inter-paradigmatic translation among fields and practices characterizes a predominantly post-industrial world, where access to symbolic activities in multiple normative fields is key to social agency and constitutes the terms of the symbolic democracy that is developing under our eyes.

To argue that the polis is a site of constitution through the poiesis of social norms – a new nomos, a reformulated social telling – is to envisage the polis not as a zone to be partitioned and haunted by shadows or walking allegories of social categories, but as the reservoir of re-imagining through renewed acts of interpretation and social practices claiming legitimacy. The question is this: In a polis characterized by patterns of migration, intensified exchanges through trade and travelling, jurisdictional redesigning of political and economic entities such as the European Community, and the multiplication of internet communities across the planet, what is the place and function of law? If the subjects of the law are increasingly undergoing social and economic transformation in a world characterized by the proliferation and dispersal of symbolic power, what are the implications for law, its conception of the legal subject, and its capacity to legitimize competing and clashing claims of symbolic power over the terms, structures, and practices of different fields?

In this concluding chapter, I first consider critiques that demonstrate that, in several instances, the law and its doxa thwart postmodern practices of social border crossing and political agency. As argued in chapter 2, strategies of political domination will succeed by masking the overt material basis of social meaning and practices. Drawing on Marx's theory of fetishism, according to which the transaction of commodities masks the human labour that produced them in the first place,[5] I will argue that the law has the capacity to effect social fetishism. To do so, I will briefly consider well-established critical analyses of three legal topics: the division between the public and the private spheres, the rights of the foetus, and the concept of contract. In each case, the law resorts to a doctrine that has the effect of fetishizing legal subjects by masking their material, social, and historical origins. Yet, as a double helix, the law has the capacity to defeat this social fetishism by responding to the increasing and challenging heterogeneity characterizing postmodern politics and culture. I will conclude this book-long reflection on social poiesis, symbolic power, and legitimacy by analysing the implications of such heterogeneity for the law and current signs of transformation in the polis affecting its conception and practices.

The economic, gender, and political critique of the division between the public and private spheres has a long history and now constitutes a traditional topos of feminist theory and legal analysis.[6] Common to these different feminist critiques of the public/private division has been the notion that such a binary approach has the effect of containing the private field by separating it from the public sphere, jamming the channels of communication between the two, and masking the material performative effects of legal decisions and governmental policies. In her 1992 analysis of the division between the private and the public in the context of legal theory and governmental policy, Nicola Lacey scrutinizes the argument as to whether the state should intervene in the private lives of citizens for the sake of social justice. Her chief strategy is to destabilize the traditional liberal and communitarian theories of justice by demonstrating that the division between the private and the public is not as watertight as theorized. While the former theory rejects state intervention to protect individual rights, the latter considers collective values such as benevolence, altruism, and collective welfare as the justification for state intervention.

Lacey argues that, in leaving the public/private sphere division intact, neither the liberal nor the communitarian conceptions analyse the effects of inequity that this division has on their conception of society. In particular, her analysis of the principles and beliefs underlying the historical institution of the welfare state in the United Kingdom reveals a ubiquitous pattern in the field of law as, more often than not, theoretical doctrine stands in blatant contradiction to social practice. For instance, the patriarchal conception of the family, with the man as head and wage earner and the woman as the stay-at-home mother, lay at the heart of Sir William Beveridge's organization of the welfare system when, on the eve of the 1950s and by sheer economic necessity, women were to join the job market in droves. So, on the one hand, the liberal conception of the individual confines the family to the private sphere, which justifies practices and a discourse of non-intervention. On the other hand, and as Lacey points out, the family is the object of heavy-handed state intervention as it is governed by statutes of family law and economic policies.[7]

Building on Lacey's critique, one can argue that the law and, through it, different levels of governmentality fetishize the family whenever they disseminate a discourse of familialism – as in the case of Margaret Thatcher's discourse on women as guardians of the hearth and the nation or as in the case of New Labour and its discourse on parental responsibility. In each case, the signs of the family nomos mask the economic constitution of the family. Today, a significant number of women in the Western world are still caught in the double bind of their economic and domestic roles, whereby they are expected to look after children, aging relatives, and domestic space while working full-time or at several part-time jobs.

Strategies of dematerialization and fetishization are also conspicuous in the law's approach to the body, when it either subsumes the female body under a predefined male body or maintains a gender binary at the expense of other gender configurations. Various feminist critiques have shown that, historically, the legal conception of the body has been based on the notion of the masculine, autonomous, and bounded body. In this context, the discourse and the decisions of the law tend to construe the body in proprietary terms: the legal subject exercises rights over its body, and those rights are infringed upon whenever the legal subject's capacity to consent is flouted. The paradoxes and contradictions that legal feminists have identified in their analyses of the doctrinal division of the public and private spheres reappear in legal conceptualizations of the body and are exacerbated in the case of the relation between the foetus and legal rights.

The legal account of the relation between the foetus and its progenitor is based on the Gordian knot of foetal rights, as distinguished from maternal rights, and on the woman's right to privacy, as distinguished from the state's intervention in the woman's experience of pregnancy. The legal nomos of the autonomous, bounded, embodied subject has the effect of proscribing the bodies of those who do not perform according to its criteria. According to Kristin Savell, "The development of advanced visualization technologies (like ultrasound and fetoscopy) and the practices to which they have given rise, enable law to 'know' and to 'see' the foetus (whole) inside the body of its mother as a distinct and separable individual. But although the foetus is seen as whole, the mother is not. She is deconstructed, opaque, her physical boundaries indeterminate."[8] The pregnant body becomes not only the object of medico-legal discourse but also an abject, both literally – as it is cropped off the visualization – and ontologically – as other possible figures of identification of the pregnant body and its relationship to the foetus are evicted from the domain of symbolization and the socio-legal imaginary.

However, symbolic violence to the pregnant body is not limited to a fuzzy image on a monitor or to the first family picture of the unborn. While the pregnant body is spirited away, it is also the uncanny site on the basis of which the autonomy of the foetus is established: it is as if the foetus could make its legal home only on condition of denying the host from whom it derives its existence or of transforming the host into a source of the *unheimlich*, or inhospitable. For instance, in court cases, the notion of bounded and separate bodies leads to an adversarial legal relation between the mother and the foetus. Rather strikingly, the paradox of the public/private sphere, according to which the state does not intervene in the private sphere – although it regulates it economically and otherwise – is reproduced in the relation between mother and foetus, whereby the foetus is considered to achieve legal personhood upon birth, while for the foetus's sake, a pregnant woman is denied her status as a separate and autonomous legal subject. Thus, the mother's "capacity to choose and to act receive[s] considerably less emphasis in law than her contribution as the 'body' from which the child separates to achieve legal personhood. That said, the law is very concerned with the choices that pregnant women make particularly when the health-care choices she makes are thought to be detrimental to the health or life of the foetus."[9] The pregnant body as object of legal codification functions, therefore, as a symptom of a fetishizing severance between the sociodicy of sexual reproduction that the law seeks to maintain and the social and economic experience of a physical reality that is refractory to the nomos as legitimated by the law.

In these instances, the law not only impounds the legal body but also regulates it according to a logic of ownership. Either the legal subject is a self-owning subject who exercises property rights over its body – and given Savell's analysis, this subject is construed as masculine – or the legal subject loses this right to self-ownership, in which case the law assumes the right. In other words, the law islands and territorializes the body the way Robinson Crusoe owns and legislates over his island, and this is one of the reasons why the legal discourse about the body hinges on the economic discourse of property through the concept of contract. It is no coincidence that Carole Pateman's critique of the legal, economic, and political doctrine of contract should overlap with Savell's analysis of the way in which the law exercises symbolic violence upon bodies through strategies of self-alienation and fetishization.

Pateman's analysis concerns the relationship among property, contract, and self-ownership. She argues that the concept of property in the person is a powerful political and regulatory fiction, which she traces to Locke's definition of freedom as based on the right to own and dispose of one's property. According to Pateman, Locke established "political standing and rights for the person who owns the property. Only the owner has the right to dispose of his property, for instance, to alienate all or part of it."[10] Correlatively, Locke held that "an owner temporarily relinquishes ownership when he alienates part of the property in his person. Thus he has no right to a claim on anything that may be produced through its use by another."[11] Thus, the concept of contract implies the construct of the person as self-ownership.

For it is the relationship to oneself in the mode of property that makes possible the doctrine that one contracts out a part of one's self, such as skills, abilities, or talents, for the purpose of employment. Pateman argues that "the fiction of separability is maintained and property in the person is treated *as if* it were alienable, and so can become the subject of contract and marketed as 'services.' … The significant aspect of contracts that constitute such relationships is not an exchange, but the alienation of a particular piece of property in the person; namely, the right of self-government."[12] The objective of Pateman's critique of the doctrine of contract is to lay bare the political and economic implications of the employment contract in the workplace. Her fundamental claim is that the notion that "capacities can be treated as separable from the person"[13] supports a political organization of the workplace and employment as a place and mode of subordination. Thus, the fiction of self-ownership and discourse of the citizen exercising autonomy in contracting out parts of its person can be said to turn the employee into a fetish of the autonomous subject since, in fact, the doctrine implies the loss of the democratic right to self-government in the workplace.[14]

The above legal conceptions of the family home, the pregnant body, and the self-sufficient, bounded, proprietary, and contractual subject enact a fetishizing of the social agent that truncates material contexts of political subordination. The legal subject is in the law's orbit insofar as s/he performs as a partial subject, whereby the part functions as the representation of the whole – that is to say, whereby the subject is discursively reduced to a synecdoche: a family cell standing for the private sphere as state of nature, a uterus caught on a medical screen, or a skill contracted out to an employer. The recurrence of this pattern of fetishizing speaks to the usurpatory use of symbolic power to shore up a sociodicy that the law legitimizes and distributes over the various fields under its jurisdiction. Bourdieu analyses this type of domination through structural consistency in terms of "organic solidarity," which allows dominant principles of social organization to be distributed and linked across different fields and habitus. Power, he argues,

> is exercised, invisibly and anonymously, through the actions and reactions, apparently anarchic but in fact structurally constrained, of agents and institutions located in fields that are at once competitive and complementary, such as the economic field and the educational field, and engaged in circuits of legitimating exchanges which are ever longer and more complex and therefore symbolically ever more effective, but which also make ever more room, potentially at least, for conflicts of power and authority.[15]

Through the performative effects of intentional and legally binding utterances and through the exercise of its institutional authority, the law maintains this organic solidarity. In the above instances, the structural consistency of social norms across the fields of family law, foetal rights, and contractual practices depends on a recurrent strategy of regulation at the cost of dematerialization and fetishization, with palpable political effects.

This strategy of regulation testifies to a process of symbolic violence, whereby, in asserting its legitimizing authority, the law hijacks the competition for social meaning and normativity through recurrent patterns of fragmentation and partitioning. In contrast, one can envisage the integration of law's authority into a model of social interaction in which communication, translation, and nomadic exposure to heterogeneous norms of being and social relations are predominant. Arendt predicates freedom on "the capacity of motion which cannot exist without space."[16] In this context, she envisages a conception of law that operates on the basis of what could be called the law's capacity to move in social space. "Laws hedge in each new beginning and at the same time assure its freedom of movement, the potentiality of something entirely new and unpredictable; the boundaries of positive laws are for the political existence of man what memory is for his historical existence: they guarantee the pre-existence of a common world, the reality of some continuity which transcends the individual span of each generation, absorbs all new origins and is nourished by them."[17] On this basis, it can be argued that the responsibility of the law as an institution endowed with binding authority is to respond to the material signs that the community emits through a multiplicity of symbolic and normative practices from within its own fields.

Conversely, the responsibility of the community is to govern its practices and relationships in accordance with the law in the name of equity and justice, but also to participate in a democratic poiesis that makes legal normativity an object of constant reappraisal. Ideally, the authority of the law derives not so much from an act of institutionalization that sets it apart from the polis as from its responsibility to codify and regulate the community's normative interests by coordinating and accommodating them according to the democratic principles of equity, fairness, and freedom. Although fundamental, this authority is never a given; instead, it is the effect of a sustained process that draws on the normative principles, practices, and structures of the law as an institution and that remains inseparable from its capacity to be set in motion by a heterogeneously and historically evolving community whose norms it legitimizes.[18]

This conception of the relation between the law and social agents in the community makes it possible to think of the law as an institution whose authoritative effects are not primarily or necessarily coercive and of a citizenry that is not condemned to bend under the yoke of law's symbolic violence. According to Nicola Lacey, difference-based feminism has encouraged a shift "from the instrumental aspects of law to its symbolic aspects. The messages about women and men transmitted by law; the role of law as a discursive practice into which the material realities of women's and men's embodied lives are inserted, and in which the assumptions underlying law's conceptualization of subjecthood are constructed as (T)ruths; the subtle role of law in categorizing and disciplining its subjects: all these became the stuff of critical legal analysis, accompanying and sometimes displacing the more materialist focus of earlier critical traditions informed by Marxism."[19] If this is the case, difference-based feminism has also provided terms of analysis that enable us to proceed beyond the mere taking stock of symbolic violence so as to reassess the way social and political reform can enlist the law as an institution drawing its authority from its responsibility for and accountability to the community. Specifically, critics have considered ways in which the inherited monolithic institution of the law can be called into question.[20] For instance, in an American context, Jack Balkin and Sanford Levinson support their concept of legal historicism by referring to Mark Tushnet's *Taking the Constitution Away from the Courts*, where

> he explicitly argues that the development of constitutional norms should largely be left to politics and not to internal legal development of doctrine. Americans should pledge faith in the aims of the "thin Constitution" whose principles are outlined in the American Declaration of Independence and the Preamble to the Constitution. However, they should work out the meaning of the Constitutional text not through the processes of judicial review but through political debate, social movements, and the institutions of representative government.[21]

The notion that the authoring of constitutional meaning is equally shared by the law and the community has the effect of multiplying the sites where these processes occur and of integrating the concepts of legal authority and legitimacy into a framework of social multiplicity and heterogeneity.[22] Such a conception of the relation between law and the community results in new concepts, such as the recognition of voices and knowledge in legal subjects previously deprived of such agency.

In addition, postmodern forms of migration have destabilized doctrinal notions of sovereignty so that the legislating of a general sociodicy that would speak to a national and self-contained identity never ceases to betray its fantastic origins. From the standpoint of the evolution of human rights, international law has already begun to effect a process of social heterogeneity and multiplicity, which calls for a rethinking of notions of citizenship and hospitality or, in other words, of what it means to be at home. Seyla Benhabib analyses the problem by invoking Kant's concept of hospitality as "a right that belongs to all human beings insofar as we view them as potential participants in a world republic."[23] This outlines a utopian scenario for the future, which leads to the questioning of national sovereignty and the loosening between civic constitution and territorial borders. In being subjected to international norms through a proliferation of human rights treaties and conventions, "the state is both sublated and reinforced in its authority. Throughout the international system, as long as territorially bounded states are recognized as the sole legitimate units of negotiation and representation, a tension, and at times even a fatal contradiction, is palpable: the modern state system is caught between *sovereignty* and *hospitality*, between the prerogative to choose to be a party to cosmopolitan norms and human rights treaties, and the obligation to extend recognition of these human rights to all."[24] In other words, the subscription to human rights puts nations under pressure, if not legal obligation, to legislate and govern according to these rights within their own jurisdictional boundaries.[25]

Benhabib envisages a mode of democratic governance goaded by what she calls "jurisgenerative processes," whereby "a democratic people, which considers itself bound by certain guiding norms and principles, engages in iterative acts by reappropriating and reinterpreting these, thereby showing itself to be not only the subject but also the author of the laws."[26] While Benhabib focuses on state sovereignty, it can be argued that this process of normative legitimacy is at work in everyday life practices in different communities, such as universities in the United Kingdom, which several years ago transformed their menus by making halal meat available to both students of Islamic faith and non-practising students.[27] Social practices of everyday life are thus reformulated and legitimated through a continuous process of vision and division of the social world.

This example may be regarded as a drop in a political sea marred by bigotry and racist practices. However, the poietic dynamic at work in this example is the crucial point. In integrating such items into their menus according to food regulations in the United Kingdom, and in drawing on its institutional authority, the university legitimizes an aspect of the religious and social nomos of sharia law within its own cultural perimeter. It is not so much that the university authorizes sharia law, since the latter already has authority in Islamic culture; rather, it is that the university recognizes the legitimacy of sharia law outside its cultural site of origins, sluicing the flow of communication between heterogeneous symbolic practices.

Thus, the problem concerning law's authority becomes one of its authority in relation to normative diversity and the dispersal of the power of symbolic representation and codification. In recognizing such social heterogeneity, the law acknowledges the community as a site of social poiesis in the making and exposes its use of language to a heterogeneity of conflictual meanings, which is part and parcel of the symbolic activities of any social field. The fluctuations of meaning attached to major terms of ontological and social definition are the object of discussion in Lacey's analysis of the meaning of responsibility in the context of criminal law. She points out that the concept of responsibility has acquired heterogeneous meanings in the context of criminal law discourse and moral philosophy. On this basis, "in each of these social practices, it would be safer to start out by making merely the modest assumption that ascriptions of and ideas about responsibility are performing distinctive practical/normative roles in relation to various structural problems. ... This is not to say that there will not turn out to be important links, at any one time, between conceptions of responsibility in, say, criminal law and moral discourse. But these links should be the object of investigation and not *a priori* assumptions."[28] From this perspective, the social world can be conceived as a political tessellation of social fields buzzing away with their symbolic activities of social poiesis yet connected and overlapping through the movement of social agents, who rarely live and act in one single field or social perimeter. It is through our physical, cultural, and cognitive displacements from one field to another that we expose ourselves to and mobilize different modes of symbolic power and practical norms.

In the twenty-first century, the citizen is a nomad not so much because s/he is homeless than because s/he is at home in different locations, apt to slip into different cultural idioms and to acquire multiple sets of skills. This type of nomadism refers to the movement of citizens across symbolic, cultural, and professional foyers, which proliferate in the political and economic contexts of class, gender, and ethnic disparities.

The nomads of modern and contemporary democracies have the potential and capacity to disturb the boundaries among the different fields across which terms of sovereignty and constitution of legitimacy seek to spread. In his analysis of Livy's *History of Rome*, Steven DeCaroli reports on how the limits of the city of Rome were marked by a *pomoerium*, a space-in-between where ploughing and building were forbidden. "It was a symbolical wall, and the path of the *pomoerium* was marked by termini, or boundary stones, which served to demarcate the limit, that is, the *limen*, within which all things were under the authority of Rome and an object of roman law (in effect, the sovereign field)."[29] Reflecting on the disruption of the sovereign field through the crossing of limits, DeCaroli suggests that "the moving of boundaries represents a very literal disruption of the relation between authority and territory – a point made clear when we understand the role these stones played in the very earliest narratives of the founding of Rome."[30]

Through their displacements and criss-crossings of social thresholds, social agents in the postmodern world connect the different fields of knowing and doing and establish productive lines of communication.

In this sense, the citizen is the symbolic nomad who acquires different social languages and learns different ways of doing things and who, through acts of practical and cognitive translation, ensures the flow of communication throughout the polis. The more diverse the social group, the more heterogeneous the flow of information and the more complex and agonistic the normative processes. The effect of such displacements is not to dematerialize historical origins but to expose the norms and practices of social fields to others so that they retain flexibility, remain open to critique, and ensure freedom from the hegemonic dangers that always attend the constitution of a particular field and its institutional principles, structures, and habitus. Exposure to and practice in these different symbolic fields will certify the citizen as a translator and participant in a performative democracy, while normative segregation will be a measure of social and historical sclerosis.[31]

The exposure of the law to nomadic tactics of the citizen as legal subject is strikingly prefigured by Rebecca West's response to the Nuremberg trials, on which she had been assigned to report by the *New Yorker*. Taking as her point of departure the discrepancy between the sublime discourse about the Allies' endeavour to respond to barbarity in rational and historical terms of justice and West's report on tedious and anticlimactic judicial procedure in the courtroom, Ravit Reichman analyses the way in which West moved out of the courtroom and engaged in a modernist *flânerie*, exploring the surroundings of the courtroom, encountering German people, and discovering a greenhouse where a one-legged man grew flowers and sold them to the foreigners attending and participating in the trial. "She undertook, in other words, not only the task of reporting the present but also of creating a complex map of memory. In supplying the trial with a context, giving it a sense of place, West's report suggests that memory demands a location, a *lieu de mémoire*. … [Her journalistic piece] 'Greenhouse with Cyclamens' … recasts this sense of memory. Rather than anchoring it in one particular location, most prominently the Palace of Justice, West lays out an unanchored series of places, a collection of sites that bear no resemblance to monuments, memorials, or other consecrated 'spaces of memory.'"[32]

Stravaiging from the courtroom and shirking the monumentalizing of a historical event, West bears witness to the trial and the horror of the Holocaust by shifting grounds and languages: from the space of the law, where justice is expected to be done, to the greenhouse of cyclamens, where boundaries between good and evil, racist totalitarianism, and subjection of the German people blur; from law's procedural, document-based utterances to a narrative voice floating in the free zone of non-fiction between fiction and journalism, where West talks about pink and purple petunias that "were bright like lamps"[33] and about her encounter with a French doctor holding in his hands a lampshade made of tattooed human skin. Reichman concludes by regarding the Nuremberg trials and West's nomadic writing as two modes of justice that exist not in isolation but in terms of "legal *and* social justice as part of a larger cultural, historical imaginary in which official and unofficial judgments occur simultaneously. … One form of justice bears on the other, exposing the other's capacities and failures."[34]

This centrifugal process of symbolic constitution takes place in a polis conceived as a site of contestation, where different groups compete for social and political recognition, exposing themselves to social acts and performatives of sovereignty and political exclusion. The agon for the legitimacy of norms generated through symbolic power characterizes social poiesis with its dangers and its opportunities, its patterns of domination and resources for political resistance. This political striving for symbolic power is not adequately taken into account by concepts of deliberative processes of justice.[35]

Consider Rawls's conception of justice as fairness, which rests on a deliberative use of democratic and ethical principles of justice. Rawls assumes that the ethical self has the capacity to devise rational principles of fairness transcending the sociopolitical factors that have conditioned his or her understanding of the social world. The dematerialization of the law is perhaps most strikingly exemplified by his famous theory of the veil of ignorance in his account of justice as fairness. In a dramatization of the allegorical representation of justice wearing a blindfold on her eyes, he imagines a group of persons gathered to devise principles of legal fairness without knowing whether their personal interests will be protected. They are therefore put in a position of ensuring that each and every interest will be protected by principles of fairness without discrimination. Consequently, "it is clear that since the differences among the parties are unknown to them, and everyone is equally rational and similarly situated, each is convinced by the same arguments. … If anyone after due reflection prefers a conception of justice to another, then they all do, and a unanimous agreement can be reached."[36] Rawls's approach is based on an instrumental conception of reason to create an original position that prepares the ground for the unanimous and homogeneous implementation of universal principles of justice. For the major impediment to justice as fairness lies in individuals' rapacious use of cunning to promote particular interests and take advantage of hierarchical positions that support these interests at the expense of other members of society. So his move is to sideswipe competitive interests on the basis that "without these limitations on knowledge the bargaining problem of the original position would be hopelessly complicated."[37] Aware of the competitive dynamic animating communities, Rawls proceeds to occult it and in effect to dematerialize the social agent.[38]

However, the polis is characterized not only by fluctuation because of its continuous practices of social poiesis but also by potential conflict and competition between antinomic ways of materializing the social nomos, its fields, practices, and governance. Rancière refers to this process as *dissensus*, which he identifies as the essence of democratic politics. "Politics ... has no proper place nor any natural subjects. A demonstration is political not because it occurs in a particular place and bears upon a particular object but rather because its form is that of a clash between two partitions of the sensible."[39] The social fields and their adherents strive to endow their norms with legal, political, and economic purchase, and this normative struggle for recognition does not take place in a social vacuum as laws and practices pre-exist and may constrain the emergence of new normative patterns. Such a struggle for symbolic power and political recognition is erased or, perhaps more precisely, made invisible by Rawls's dematerializing conception of a communal basis for consensus, which prepares the ground for the return of forms of the political uncanny that such an act of erasure generates.

In contrast, Pateman proposes to start with the assumption that there can be "no expectation that analysis begins from agreement on shared interpretations, or that the task is to justify these interpretations. Instead, since every approach embodies specific interpretations, the usual starting point is disagreement."[40] In proposing to redefine democracy along the lines of a struggle for social recognition and legitimacy, one can envisage a political process enacting a social transformation from the proscription of undesirables to a multicultural polis animated by social agents, who, through contestation, are endowed with the capacity to fashion and refashion social blueprints to be legitimized by the law.

As a double helix through which legal and cultural norms of social organization intertwine, the law cannot but engage in this struggle for social meaning. In fact, its role is to ascribe legitimacy and authority to the process of social poiesis through both judicial adjudication and legislation. The norms of a social field and its practices may not be legally protected and may necessitate new forms of legitimacy; or the norms of the field may blatantly ignore or break existing legal rules and be perceived as beyond the pale of legitimacy; or the infraction of legalized norms may be an indication that they no longer fulfil their social role, or perhaps never did, and need reforming. However, for a new or reforming set of principles and practices to attract the eyes and the ears of the law, there needs to be a social process whereby the beliefs and the practices attached to them either have acquired social legitimacy or are involved in strategies aimed at the acquisition of such legitimacy. And this is where the role of performative social poiesis comes in, for if we wish to see as democratic and productive a process as possible obtain, then we must refrain from regarding the law as the sole mechanism whereby solutions can be unilaterally created and implemented.

It is essential that practices of social poiesis remain interactive and historical, never achieving a point of rest. One can envisage this process as a praxis, a term Elizabeth Schneider uses in her discussion of human rights discourse. "The rights claim," she argues, "can emerge from a political vision and can itself be a form of political statement. Further, rights discourse can be a form of praxis – a form of legal practice that can define and reshape the articulation of theory."[41] I would go even further and argue that rights discourse *ought to be* a form of social and political praxis because rights do not solely originate with the law, even though the law seems to be the privileged means of legitimizing rights. In fact, historically, all the great claims for human rights – from the French Revolution discourse of universal rights (however limited the notion of universality was) to the abolition of slavery and child labour (however flouted these rights are), from the promotion of women's property rights to same-sex rights (however compromising these rights may be) – originated in the polis in the form of political contestation, demonstration and sedition, the actions of pressure groups and non-governmental organizations, publications, petitions, philosophical treatises, and artistic performances that set the law in motion.[42] This is the reason why maintaining a contestatory democracy is crucial to the functioning and well-being of the law, which cannot perform its legitimizing role without the promptings and mobilization of the polis. Lisa C. Bower argues that redefining identities and relations through practices in the community leads to a reconfiguration of the relationship between the law and the community.

> First, the location of what counts as political practice is shifted to the enactment of social practices and cultural codes that become vehicles for

> affirming the identities of marginalized groups. Second … the creation of [the] subject's identity and agency is contingent on forms of identification that emerge from contesting differences without necessarily asserting similarity. … Third, community is reconceived … as a historically contingent phenomenon enacted within, and limited by, the historical realm of discourses and institutions.[43]

This implies that the interpretation of normative deviation as potentially subversive is best configured by considering the dynamic between the law and practices in the polis. In this respect, and diverging from Dworkin's concept of the legal community led by Hercules, the legal interpreter, Lacey describes the way in which extra-legal interpretive communities emerge in relation to the legal community and include academic, pedagogic, critical, and contestatory communities. The counter-discourse produced by these extra-legal communities has the potential to filter through legal discourse and practices. In addition, she demonstrates that extra-legal frameworks also work in the shadow of the law, importing regulatory principles from the law.[44]

The polis of the twenty-first century will be evaluated by its capacity to foster the development of the multitasking, vocal, and contestatory social agent, translating from one social field to another; or it will be examined for its tendencies to design hierarchies in which, ominously, those at the bottom do not have access to fields of knowledge and communication, let alone to interaction among these fields, and where those at the top have control over a panoply of conceptualizations of the professional, economic, and social world. In this context, the law has the institutional authority to codify the principles and norms that the polis keeps issuing for legitimacy. These principles are contingent to the extent that they are historically specific and have no transcendental characteristic. However, in codifying these principles, the law lifts them from the stream of historical time and transforms them into authoritative norms of identity, relations, and practices that it re-injects into the social tissue. This represents its singular capacity and social function, but also its capacity to generate and authorize symbolic violence. The responsibility of social agents in the polis conceived as a contestatory democracy is to thwart this danger by exposing legal norms to historical awareness and political accountability. The law's mandate to render justice will be authoritative as long as its utterances and practices derive from and respond to this democratic and historical process of social poiesis.

Notes

Introduction

1 For a critical, comparative analysis of Butler's and Bourdieu's theories of agency, see Terry Lovell, "Resisting with Authority: Historical Specificity, Agency and the Performative Self," *Theory, Culture & Society* 20, no. 1 (2003): 1–17.
2 Pierre Bourdieu, *Pascalian Meditations*, trans. Richard Nice (London: Polity Press, 2000), 186.
3 Anne Barron, "Feminism, Aestheticism and the Limits of Law," Feminist Legal Studies 8 (2000): 275–317, quoted in ibid., 278–9.
4 Ngũgĩ wa Thiong'o, "For Peace, Justice, and Culture: The Intellectual in the Twenty-First Century," in *Profession*, ed. Rosemary G. Feal (New York: Modern Language Association, 2006), 39.
5 Kathleen O'Grady, "*Guardian of Language*: An Interview with Hélène Cixous," *Women's Education des femmes* 12, no. 4 (Winter 1996–97): 6–10, reprinted at http://bailiwick.lib.uiowa.edu/wstudies/cixous/.
6 See Julie Stone Peters, "Law, Literature, and the Vanishing Real: On the Future of an Interdisciplinary Illusion," *PMLA* 120, no. 1 (March 2005): 442–53. She delineates a historical and critical narrative of the field revolving around the three movements of humanism, hermeneutics, and narrative. For a sceptical assessment of topoi of analysis in law and literature, see Jane B. Baron, "Interdisciplinary Legal Scholarship as Guilty Pleasure: The Case of Law and Literature," in *Law and Literature: Current Legal Issues*, ed. Michael D.A. Freeman and Andrew Lewis, vol. 2 (Oxford: Oxford University Press, 1999), 21–45; and Jane B. Baron, "Law, Literature, and the Problems of Interdisciplinarity," *Yale Law Journal* 108, no. 5 (1999): 1059–85. For a genealogy of the relations among law, the humanities,

and the social sciences, see Brook Thomas, "Reflections on the Law and Literature Revival," *Critical Inquiry* 17, no. 3 (Spring 1991): 510–39.

7 Ian Ward, *Law and Literature: Possibilities and Perspectives* (Cambridge: Cambridge University Press, 1995), 38. For a critique of the romantic fallacy in law and literature as exemplified by Ward's approach, see Desmond Manderson, *Kangaroo Courts and the Rule of Law: The Legacy of Modernism* (Abingdon, UK: Routledge, 2012), 9, 11–17.

8 Ward, *Law and Literature*, 38.

9 Martha Nussbaum, *Poetic Justice: The Literary Imagination and Public Life* (Boston: Beacon Press, 1995), xvi.

10 Ibid., 10. For Robin West, "we should criticize not only law … but also the commonly shared moral beliefs with which we typically criticize law (partly themselves a product of law), by reference to some set of criteria culled from a description of our shared human nature; we should derive that description of our nature, in turn, from what is loosely called the humanities: the careful, systematic study of the narratives and critiques of narratives that we tell each other about the substance of our lives." *Narrative, Authority, and Law* (Ann Arbor: University of Michigan Press, 1993), 6. François Ost asserts that "whereas the law codifies reality, instituting it in a narrow network of agreed-upon qualifications and marking it out by a whole system of constraints and prohibitions, literature, on the other hand, liberates the possibilities in its heart, suspends our certainties, arousing in itself slumbering energies, shaking up identities and conventions and bringing us to those crossroads where everything can begin anew." "The Law as Mirrored in Literature," *SubStance* 35, no. 1 (2006): 4. See also Paul J. Heald, "The Death of Law and Literature: An Optimistic Eulogy," *Comparatist* 33 (May 2009): 20–8. In contrast, Austin Sarat asserts that "we need to find ways of thinking about law and the humanities that do not canonize the humanities. We must move from rescue and recuperation to critique." "Traditions and Trajectories in Law and Humanities Scholarship," *Yale Journal of Law & the Humanities* 10, no. 2 (1998): 404. Robert Weisberg and Guyora Binder maintain that "to recognize the constitutively literary dimension of law is not to commend law as inevitably humane or redemptive … laws, legal judgments, legal arguments, and legal transactions all have expressive meaning, and to miss law's meaning is to miss a part of what needs criticism. … To say that law is literary is also to admit that literature is, like law, an arena of strategic conflict." *Literary Criticisms of Law* (Princeton, NJ: Princeton University Press, 2000), 19. Finally, there are in-between positions that attempt to differentiate law from literature by ascribing a

transformative potential or propensity to literature while acknowledging its limitations. For instance, Maria Aristodemou suggests that "literature contains its own ideology and expresses its own values and prejudices, but it is also more likely than law to challenge received ideologies, values, and prejudices." *Law and Literature: Journeys from Here to Eternity* (Oxford: Oxford University Press, 2000), 9.

11 Shoshana Felman, *The Juridical Unconscious: Trials and Traumas in the Twentieth Century* (Cambridge, MA: Harvard University Press, 2002), 30.

12 Ibid., 153.

13 As Peter Brooks writes, "narrative is morally a chameleon that can be used to support the worse as well as the better cause." "Narrativity of the Law," *Law and Literature* 14, no. 1 (Spring 2002): 2. See also his "The Law as Narrative and Rhetoric," in *Law's Stories: Narrative and Rhetoric in the Law*, ed. Peter Brooks and Paul Gewirtz (New Haven, CT: Yale University Press, 1999), 16.

14 In *Minding the Law: How Courts Rely on Storytelling, and How Their Stories Change the Ways We Understand the Law – and Ourselves* (Cambridge, MA: Harvard University Press, 2000), Anthony G. Amsterdam and Jerome Bruner's cross-disciplinary approach and methodology seek to avoid this binary by focusing on the cultural interaction among the processes of categorizing, storytelling, and persuading. David Kennedy goes further by suggesting that "law as literature might well unravel – and literature might find in law a narrative of desire, returning to literature a consciousness of its power." "Law's Literature," in *Field Work: Sites in Literary and Cultural Studies*, ed. Marjorie Garber, Paul B. Franklin, and Rebecca L. Walkowitz (New York: Routledge, 1996), 207. Bradin Cormack bypasses the contrast between law as site of coercion and literature as site of freedom by considering law as a set of jurisdictional practices constitutive (in the Foucaultian sense of the word) of "a free national and civic identity" in the earlier development of English jurisdiction. Drawing on Jacques Rancière's notion that the aesthetic concerns the distribution of the sensible in the polis, Cormack regards law and literature "as pertaining to a single order and practice of imaginative thought." *A Power to Do Justice: Jurisdiction, English Literature, and the Rise of Common Law, 1509–1625* (Chicago: University of Chicago Press, 2007), 2, 39.

15 For James Boyd White, "the law can be seen as the culture that we remake whenever we speak as lawyers." *Heracles' Bow: Essays in the Rhetoric and Poetics of the Law* (Madison: University of Wisconsin Press, 1985), 40. Robin West extends this claim to jurisprudence, which "is part history, part vision, and part method, as is literary narrative. As such it has

aesthetic components, including plot, that can and should be understood separately." "Jurisprudence as Narrative: An Aesthetic Analysis of Modern Legal Theory," *New York University Law Review* 60, no. 2 (1985): 203. For Richard H. Weisberg, law "is utterly dependent on language; better, it *is*, utterly, language. ... Language may be used elegantly or carelessly, but it *is* the judge's medium." *Poethics and Other Strategies of Law and Literature* (New York: Columbia University Press, 1992), 11. Guyora Binder argues that "the literary must be seen to be intrinsic to law in so far as law necessarily involves the construction of the characters, personas, sensibilities, identities, myths, and traditions that compose our social world ... legal forms and legal processes play a compositional role in modern culture." "The Law-as-Literature Trope," in *Law and Literature: Current Legal Issues*, ed. Michael D.A. Freeman and Andrew Lewis, vol. 2 (Oxford: Oxford University Press, 1999), 68, 88. The aesthetic dimension of law has also been a major preoccupation in the analyses of Ronnie Warrington and Costas Douzinas. "If the law works through the creation and projection of ordered worlds, attention to style, detail and form will help understand the hidden vision of law and develop alternative worlds and visions which would derive their legitimacy from law's text, history and tradition." "The Trials of Law and Literature," *Law and Critique* 1, no. 6 (1995): 141. Peter Goodrich is, of course, another major proponent of law as a rhetorical and aesthetic practice. "The social being of law depends in large measure upon poetic, dramatic, fictional, and other imaginary forms of social presence. ... The literary imagination offers, among other things, a series of depictions of virtue and of narrative ethics, stories of the good life and of just conclusions, that both mirror and project the practice of law into the shared domains of ethics and aesthetics." "Law by Other Means," *Cardozo Studies in Law and Literature* 10, no. 2 (Winter 1998): 114. For Julie Stone Peters, "The law's performative statements – when a sovereign says 'I command' or a judge says 'I sentence you' – might be thought of as super-performatives: performatives backed by force. On the other hand, law is the ultimate institution of twice-behaved behavior: its performances represent and replay social conflict and violence, turning history into dramatic narrative, fictionalizing social trauma, transforming it into the system of social representations, exchanges, surrogacies that make up the law ... law's conjoint performativity and theatricality – are both problem and power." "Legal Performance Good and Bad," *Law, Culture and the Humanities* 4, no. 2 (2008): 185 (footnote omitted). For an analysis of the "narrative foundation" of law and for a social and cultural understanding of narrative beyond literary practices, see Randy D. Gordon, *Rehumanizing*

Law: A Theory of Law and Democracy (Toronto: Toronto University Press, 2011), 3. For a dialogical conception of law, see Manderson, who argues that in law "we must decide, but those answers will always be partial, provisional and incomplete. There can be no final resolution, no synthesis, and no balance. Instead, judgment is an endless cycle which is capable of turning the ineluctable tensions, oppositions and disagreements that make up the law into a productive and indeed constitutive dialogue" (*Kangaroo Courts*, 159).

16 Thus, Nicola Lacey argues that "one of the distinguishing features of disciplinary power is its subtly normalizing effect, and as soon as we look beyond a narrow stereotype of law as a system of rules backed up by sanctions, we begin to see that one of law's functions is precisely to distribute its subjects with disciplinary precision around a mean or norm … feminist (like other critical) analyses are interested here not just in legal doctrine but also in legal discourse, i.e. how differently sexed legal subjects are constituted by and inserted within legal categories via the mediation of judicial, police or lawyers' discourse." *Unspeakable Subjects: Feminist Essays in Legal and Social Theory* (Oxford: Hart Publishing, 1998), 9–10.

17 See Thomas on the performative character of literature and the "conflicting deployments of rhetoric within particular societies" ("Reflections on the Law," 537).

18 This is the point where my argument diverges from that of James Boyd White. *Heracles' Bow* will remain a landmark in the reflection on law, literature, and culture. As mentioned above, White ascribes a poietic and performative function to law as language. Further, this conception of the law is predicated on an ontological uncertainty concerning language. "The rhetorician, like the lawyer, is … engaged in a process of meaning-making and community-building of which he or she is in part the subject. To do this requires him or her to face and accept the condition of radical uncertainty in which we live: uncertainty as to the meanings of words, uncertainty as to their effects on others, uncertainty even as to our own motivations" (*Heracles' Bow*, 40). However, his conception of literary criticism as "the formation of taste and judgment" and of the reader's experience – "he is educated, for reading is a process in which the reader himself, through a process of assimilation and rejection, response and judgement, becomes more fully one set of the things that it is possible for him to be" – prepares the ground for a potentially exclusionary humanism. White tempers the symbolic violence of the law by invoking the principle of ethical recognition of the other within the limits and failures of language: the question is how to recognize "while we compose

our text, its inadequacy as the representation of another, and [how to find] a way to express that recognition in what we say. ... [This] means the perpetual acknowledgement of the limits of our minds and languages, the sense that they are bounded by the minds and languages of others. It is in these ways that the activity I call 'translation' – making texts in response to others while recognizing the impossibility of full comprehension or reproduction – becomes a set of practices that can serve as an ethical and political model for the law and, beyond it, as a standard of justice." James Boyd White, *Justice as Translation: An Essay in Cultural and Legal Criticism* (Chicago: University of Chicago Press, 1990), 98, 94, 258.

19 The legal concepts of partiality, cultural multiplicity, and competing realities that feminist thinkers have advocated are prefigured in modernist experiments in narratives conducted by a multiplicity of voices and from different narrative angles. See Martha Minow, "Foreword: The Supreme Court, 1986 Term – Justice Engendered," *Harvard Law Review* 110 (1987): 10–95; Sandra Fredman, *Women and the Law* (Oxford: Clarendon Press, 1997); and Lacey, *Unspeakable Subjects*.

20 Naomi Mezey designates culture as "any set of shared, signifying practices – practices by which meaning is produced, performed, contested, or transformed." "Law as Culture," in *Cultural Analysis, Cultural Studies, and the Law: Moving beyond Legal Realism*, ed. Austin Sarat and Jonathan Simon (Durham, NC: Duke University Press, 2003), 42. On discursive rupture between law and culture, see Peter Brooks, "A Slightly Polemical Comment on Austin Sarat," *Yale Journal of Law & the Humanities* 10, no. 2 (1998): 411; and Rosemary J. Coombe, "Contingent Articulations: A Critical Cultural Studies of Law," in *Law in the Domains of Culture*, ed. Austin Sarat and Thomas R. Kearns (Ann Arbor: University of Michigan Press, 1998), 21. Robert Weisberg argues that "truly interdisciplinary study, or at least fertile interdisciplinary study, entails discomfiture." "The Law-Literature Enterprise," *Yale Journal of Law & the Humanities* 1, no. 1 (1989): 4. For Peter Goodrich, "the interdisciplinary study of law is aimed rather at breaking down the closure of legal discourse and at critically articulating the internal relationships it constructs with other discourses." *Legal Discourse: Studies in Linguistics, Rhetoric, and Legal Analysis* (London: Palgrave Macmillan, 1987), 212.

21 Stuart Hall argues that "'civil society' is no ideal realm of pure freedom. Its micro-worlds include the multiplication of points of power and conflict – and thus exploitation, oppression and marginalization. More and more of our everyday lives are caught up in these forms of power, and their lines of intersection. Far from there being no resistance to the system, there has

been a proliferation of new points of antagonism, new social movements of resistance organized around them – and, consequently, a generalization of 'politics' to spheres which hitherto the left assumed to be apolitical: a politics of the family, of health, of food, of sexuality, of the body. … Perhaps there isn't, in that sense, one 'power game' at all, more a network of strategies and powers and their articulations – and thus a politics which is always positional." "The Meaning of New Times," in *Stuart Hall*, ed. Kuan-Hsing Chen and David Morley (Abingdon, UK: Taylor & Francis, 1996), 234. At http://lib.myilibrary.com?ID=24019.

22 Butler has written not only about the suspension of the rule of law but also about legal decisions in cases dealing with pornography, the artwork of Robert Mapplethorpe, and sexual education manuals in the United States.

23 Judith Butler, *Excitable Speech: A Politics of the Performative* (New York: Routledge, 1997), 32.

24 Pierre Bourdieu, *Outline of a Theory of Practice*, trans. Richard Nice (Cambridge: Cambridge University Press, 2009), 188.

25 For instance, drawing on Jacques Donzelot's *The Policing of Families*, John Eekelaar identified the ways in which family law exercises social control through normativity; see "Family and Social Control," in *Oxford Essays in Jurisprudence*, ed. John Eekelaar and John Bell (Oxford: Clarendon Press, 1987), 125–44.

26 Bourdieu, *Pascalian Meditations*, 115.

27 Nicholas Royle discusses what could be called the ubiquity of the discourse of the uncanny and this across cognitive disciplines and artistic media. "The uncanny calls for a different thinking of genre and text, and of the distinctions between the literary and non-literary, academic and non-academic writing." *The Uncanny* (New York: Routledge, 2003), 18. For Gothic tropes in Marx's writings, see Chris Baldick, *Frankenstein's Shadow: Myth, Monstrosity, Nineteenth-Century Writing* (Oxford: Clarendon Press, 1987). For Gothic tropes in queer and lesbian analyses of heteronormativity, see Paulina Palmer, *Lesbian Gothic: Transgressive Fictions* (London: Cassell, 1999); and Mair Rigby, "Uncanny Recognition: Queer Theory's Debt to the Gothic," *Gothic Studies* 11, no. 1 (May 2009): 46–57. For Gothic rhetoric in Derrida's philosophy, see Jodey Castricano, "Cryptomimesis: The Gothic and Jacques Derrida's Ghost Writing," *Gothic Studies* 2, no. 1 (April 2000): 8–22. David Punter refers to "the curious way in which current critical discourse seems to be forming itself round a certain terminology that owes much to the Gothic tradition." "Scottish and Irish Gothic," in *The Cambridge Companion to Gothic Fiction*, ed. Jerrold E. Hogle (Cambridge: Cambridge University Press, 2002), 105. Julian

Wolfreys discusses the role of Gothic tropes and thinking in Heidegger's and Derrida's writings in *Victorian Hauntings: Spectrality, Gothic, the Uncanny and Literature* (New York: Palgrave, 2002). Marshall Brown traces the ways in which Gothic tropes are filtered through philosophical discourse by Kant, Fichte, Freud, Foucault, Derrida, and Lyotard in "Philosophy and the Gothic Novel"; see *Approaches to Teaching Gothic Fiction: The British and American Traditions*, ed. Diane Long Hoeveler and Tamar Heller (New York: Modern Language Association, 2003), 46–57. Diana Wallace argues that Gothic tropes of the spectre and burial have appeared in the feminist discourse from Mary Wollstonecraft to Diana Russ as well as in queer theory; see "'The Haunting Idea': Female Gothic Metaphors and Feminist Theory," in *The Female Gothic: New Directions*, ed. Diana Wallace and Andrew Smith (Basingstoke, UK: Palgrave Macmillan, 2009), 26–41.

28 The recurrence of excess, the abject, and the sublime in the Gothic has inevitably engendered Freudian analyses of numerous Gothic texts but also discussion of the epistemological kinship between psychoanalysis and the Gothic. Dale Townshend argues that "Gothicism and psychoanalysis, though temporally separated from one another by at least one hundred years, are cognate with, or similar to, each other because they circulate within the same modern epistemic space … [and] are inflected with the same set of modern discursive assumptions." *The Orders of Gothic: Foucault, Lacan, and the Subject of Gothic Writing, 1764–1820* (New York: AMS Press, 2007), 19. Fred Botting proposes to broaden the analysis of the uncanny in postmodern culture. "As a register of social and political transformations, the uncanny, with its psychological focus, its manifestation of shifting boundaries, is an effect of the physical and ideological disturbances attendant on a move to commercial and industrial economic organization, middle-class society, democratic politics and bourgeois individualism." *Limits of Horror: Technology, Bodies, Gothic* (Manchester: Manchester University Press, 2008), 7. He associates the uncanny less with a return of the past and more with disturbances and spectres engendered by the present, "giving form to the disturbing locus of otherness" (ibid., 8).

29 The invocation of a Lacanian framework does not necessitate an ahistorical reading of the uncanny and the unconscious. In Robert Miles's analysis of the nationalist abject in Hugh Walpole's *The Castle of Otranto*, the discourse of the Real leads into an allegorical interpretation whereby the unspecified Thing is made to stand for a political allegory through which the Whig myth of nationalism is delegitimized and compromised; see "Abjection, Nationalism and the Gothic," in *The Gothic*, ed. Fred Botting (Cambridge:

D.S. Brewer, 2001), 47–70. In his analyses of the American Gothic, Eric Savoy uses psychoanalytical categories such as the uncanny, melancholia, and the Real to identify narratives of historical traumas that come back to haunt the sunny surfaces of American collective consciousness; see "The Rise of American Gothic," in *The Cambridge Companion to Gothic Fiction*, ed. Jerrold E. Hogle (Cambridge: Cambridge University Press, 2002), 167–88.

30 Avery F. Gordon, *Ghostly Matters: Haunting and the Sociological Imagination* (Minneapolis: University of Minnesota Press, 1997), 8. Gordon regards the uncanny as ghostly manifestations that appear in the gaps between social structures and everyday experiences and that require a different reading from the social agent.

31 As Judith Halberstam argues, psychoanalytic concepts can help show how social mechanisms are internalized and experienced as interiority. In fact, the transformation of the outside into the inside constitutes the basis for Halberstam's chief claim concerning the Gothic. "Skin houses the body and it is figured in Gothic as the ultimate boundary, the material that divides the inside from the outside. The vampire will puncture and mark the skin with his fangs, Mr. Hyde will covet white skin, Dorian Gray will desire his own canvas, Buffalo Bill will covet female skin, Leatherface will wear his victim's skin as a trophy and recycle his flesh as food. Slowly but surely the outside becomes the inside and the hide no longer conceals or contains, it offers itself as text, as body, as monster. The Gothic text, whether novel or film, plays out an elaborate skin show." *Skin Shows: Gothic Horror and the Technology of Monsters* (Durham, NC: Duke University Press, 1995), 7.

32 Judith Butler, *Precarious Life: The Powers of Mourning and Violence* (London: Verso Books, 2004), 66. Wendy Brown analyses the relation between governmentality and sovereign power. "Although the state may be a minor apparatus of governmentality, although it is itself governmentalized, the state remains the fulcrum of political legitimacy in late modern nations. … A full account of governmentality … would attend not only to the production, organization, and mobilization of subjects by a variety of powers but also the problem of legitimizing these operations by the singularly accountable object in the field of political power: the state." *Regulating Aversion: Tolerance in the Age of Identity and Empire* (Princeton, NJ: Princeton University Press, 2008), 83. For a detailed comparative analysis of sovereign power and governmentality in the writings of Foucault, Agamben, and Butler, see Elena Loizidou, *Judith Butler: Ethics, Law, Politics* (Abingdon, UK: Routledge-Cavendish, 2007). The implosion of the concept of power is also exemplified by recent analyses such as Adriana Cavarero's analysis of

violence in the form of horrorism, which she distinguishes from terrorism and state violence by focusing on the vulnerability of civil populations exposed to types of aggression that escape the logic of military combat and international warfare; see *Horrorism: Naming Contemporary Violence*, trans. William McCuaig (New York: Columbia University Press, 2011).

33 Kelly Hurley, *The Gothic Body: Sexuality, Materialism, and Degeneration at the Fin de Siècle* (Cambridge: Cambridge University Press, 1996). As Royle argues, "The uncanny is a crisis of the proper: it entails a critical disturbance of what is proper (from the Latin *proprius*, 'own'), a disturbance of the very idea of personal or private property including the properness of proper names, one's so-called 'own' name, but also the names of others, of places, institutions and events. It is a crisis of the natural, touching upon everything that one might have thought was 'part of nature': one's own nature, human nature, the nature of reality and the world" (*Uncanny*, 1). Cavarero describes *The Scream* as a "howl of all human howls where violence is extreme, where it consummates itself on a being that, dehumanizing itself in the phantasm now stripped of its features, freezes the sonic untranslatability of the outrage on its wide-open mouth" (*Horrorism*, 18).

34 Fred Botting describes the Gothic as an "originary print, a fabricated history, a fantasy of cultural and familial origins that belatedly – supplementarily – inscribes itself with morality and significance." "The Gothic Production of the Unconscious," in *Spectral Readings: Towards a Gothic Geography*, ed. Glennis Byron and David Punter (Houndmills, UK: Macmillan, 1990), 21. He thus identifies a particular symbolic dynamic of the Gothic, which obsessively and excessively keeps rehearsing the codes and discourses spawned by centuries of symbolic organization inflected by the law and name of the father. However, the name of the father is not written in stone, or rather, it will remain monumentalized as long as the domain of the symbolic remains predicated on this infernal scenario of the rise of the phallic law and the loss of the mother as its sidekick. As Sue-Ellen Case puts it, "If, for Lacan, sexuality is dominated by the phallus in a trench coat, for Kristeva and her ilk, it is the masked mother." "Tracking the Vampire," in *Differences: A Journal of Feminist Cultural Studies* 3, no. 2 (1991): 14.

35 Julia Kristeva's analysis of the abject is well known. "A massive and sudden emergence of uncanniness, which, familiar as it might have been in an opaque and forgotten life, now harries me radically as separate, loathsome. Not me. Not that. But not nothing, either … on the edge of non-existence and hallucination, of a reality that, if I acknowledge it,

annihilates me. There, abject and abjection are my safeguards. The primers (amorce) of my culture." *Power of Horrors: An Essay in Abjection* (New York: Columbia University Press, 1982), 2.

36 In considering laughter as "Gothic's own *doppelgänger*" and in underlining Gothic's metafictional tendency to lay bare the device, thereby creating a "ludicrous excess of further layers of fakery in the form of parody," Avril Horner and Sue Zlosnik reinforce the Freudian insight into the fundamental ambivalence of the uncanny and its capacity to turn meaning, including its own, awry. In laying bare the narrative device of the rhetoric of horror, Gothic laughter punctures the naturalizing and sanctimonious tricks of normative codification of social reality. See *Gothic and the Comic Turn* (Houndmills, UK: Palgrave Macmillan, 2005), 4, 11.

37 Rosemary J. Coombe suggests that social agents are not only structured by but also agents of structuring norms. "If we are subjects mediated *by* [normative] discourses, we are also subjects who mediate ourselves *through* discourses in incredibly diverse and creative ways." "Room for Manoeuver: Toward a Theory of Practice in Critical Legal Studies," *Law and Social Inquiry* 14, no. 1 (Winter 1989): 82.

38 Judith Butler, *The Psychic Life of Power* (Stanford, CA: Stanford University Press, 1997), 17–18.

39 Judith Butler, "Imitation and Gender Insubordination," in *The Judith Butler Reader*, ed. Sara Salih and Judith Butler (Malden, MA: Blackwell, 2004), 134.

1. Symbolic Power and Legitimacy

1 Sara Crangle, "You Touch Mine, I'll Touch Yours," *Globe and Mail*, 1 March 2000, http://www.walnet.org/csis/news/halifax_2000/gandm-000301.html.

2 Giorgio Agamben, *Homo Sacer: Sovereign Power and Bare Life*, trans. Daniel Heller-Roazen (Stanford, CA: Stanford University Press, 1998), 153.

3 Pierre Bourdieu, *Pascalian Meditations*, trans. Richard Nice (London: Polity Press, 2000), 108.

4 Judith Butler, *Excitable Speech: A Politics of the Performative* (New York: Routledge, 1997), 147.

5 François Ewald proposes a conception of norm production, or normalization, outside the pale of legislation and legal regulation. "Normalization produces not objects but procedures that will lead to some general consensus regarding the choice of norms and standards." In this context, the "norm is a means of producing social law, a law constituted

with reference to the particular society it claims to regulate and not with respect to a set of universal principles. More precisely, when the normative order comes to constitute the modernity of societies, law can be nothing other than the social." "Norms, Discipline, and the Law," in *Law and the Order of Culture*, ed. Robert Post, trans. Marjorie Beale (Berkeley: University of California Press, 1991), 148, 154–5. In the tradition of legal consciousness studies, Patricia Ewick and Susan Silbey propose a social understanding of the law and legality. "Through repeated invocations of the law and legal concepts and terminology, as well as through imaginative and unusual associations between legality and other social structures, legality is constituted through everyday actions and practices." *The Common Place of Law: Stories from Everyday Life* (Chicago: University of Chicago Press, 1998), 43. Drawing on the theory of legal pluralism, Rosie Harding further argues that "language and narrative not only reflect the social world, but also the ways in which what people say or write are, in part, constitutive of or embedded in the fabric of the social world." *Regulating Sexuality: Legal Consciousness in Lesbian and Gay Lives* (London: Routledge, 2011), 11.

6 Judith Butler, *The Psychic Life of Power* (Stanford, CA: Stanford University Press, 1997), 10–11.

7 Butler, *Excitable Speech*, 215.

8 Judith Butler, "Imitation and Gender Insubordination," in *The Judith Butler Reader*, ed. Sara Salih and Judith Butler (Malden, MA: Blackwell, 2004), 127.

9 Social agents' awareness of proscription typically generates coded representations of cultural practices, as exemplified by research into early twentieth-century lesbian practices; see Cameron Duder, *Awfully Devoted Women: Lesbian Lives in Canada, 1900–65* (Vancouver: University of British Columbia Press, 2010).

10 For instance, in her analysis of the relations among family, law, and sexuality, Susan Boyd offers a materialist feminist response to Judith Butler's discursive and normative resistance, which, she argues, lacks an understanding of the material role of the family in the context of globalization, privatization, and economic privation; see "Family, Law and Sexuality: Feminist Engagements," *Social and Legal Studies* 8, no. 3 (1999): 369–90.

11 Judith Butler, *Precarious Life: The Powers of Mourning and Violence* (London: Verso Books, 2004), xvii.

12 Ariel Dorfman, "The Lost Speech," in *Profession*, ed. Rosemary G. Feal (New York: Modern Language Association, 2006), 45.

13 Butler, *Psychic Life of Power*, 20–1.

14 Paul W. Kahn's cultural analysis of the rule of law in the United States can be read as the analysis of a powerful sociodicy of the state revolving around the foundational principles of reason and the will of the people. "The terms reason and will are themselves empty of substantive content (i.e., they do not provide a specific program). Instead, they structure the debate within the polity by establishing the larger conceptual order within which we deliberate about our political life." *The Cultural Study of Law: Reconstructing Legal Scholarship* (Chicago: University of Chicago Press, 1999), 17.
15 Bourdieu, *Pascalian Meditations*, 99.
16 Ibid.
17 Pierre Bourdieu, *Outline of a Theory of Practice*, trans. Richard Nice (Cambridge: Cambridge University Press, 2009), 164.
18 See the report by Commissioner Stephen T. Goudge on the Inquiry into Pediatric Forensic Pathology in Ontario, 1 October 2008, at http://www.attorneygeneral.jus.gov.on.ca/inquiries/goudge/index.html.
19 Butler, *Psychic Life of Power*, 5, 21.
20 Bourdieu, *Pascalian Meditations*, 102-3.
21 Ibid., 96.
22 Judith Butler, *Gender Trouble: Feminism and the Subversion of Identity* (New York: Routledge, 1999), xxiii.
23 Plato, *Republic*, trans. Robin Waterfield (Oxford: Oxford University Press, 1994), 359.
24 Stephen Greenblatt, "Invisible Bullets," chap. 2 in *Shakespearean Negotiations: The Circulation of Social Energy in Renaissance England* (Berkeley: University of California Press, 1988), 27.
25 Ibid., 65. "Imaginary forces" is quoted from the Prologue of *Henry V* by William Shakespeare.
26 Judith Butler, "The Force of Fantasy: Mapplethorpe, Feminism, and Discursive Excess," in *The Judith Butler Reader*, ed. Sara Salih and Judith Butler (Malden, MA: Blackwell, 2004), 187.
27 Ibid., 196.
28 Raphael Samuel, *Island Stories: Unravelling Britain*, vol. 2 of *Theatres of Memory* (London: Verso Books, 1999), 11.
29 Peter Goodrich, *Oedipus Lex: Psychoanalysis, History, Law* (Berkeley: University of California Press, 1995), 78–9 (footnotes omitted).
30 Bourdieu, *Pascalian Meditations*, 104–5.
31 Ibid., 78.
32 Butler, *Gender Trouble*, 178.
33 In 1988, Colette Guillaumin presciently reflected on this metaleptic function when she analysed the ways in which, from the eighteenth

century, black people were constructed as a group according to a system of marks supposedly originating in nature. She asserts that "to speak of a specificity of races or sexes, to speak of a natural specificity of social groups is to say in a sophisticated way that a particular 'nature' is directly productive of a social practice and to bypass the social relationship that this practice brings into being." "Race and Nature: The System of Marks," trans. Mary Jo Lakeland, *Gender Issues* 8, no. 2 (1988): 35.

34 U.S. Const. Preamble, accessed 16 July 2014, http://www.law.cornell.edu/constitution/preamble.

35 Butler, *Psychic Life of Power*, 16.

36 Jacques Rancière, *The Politics of Aesthetics*, trans. Gabriel Rockhill (London: Continuum, 2004), 12–13.

37 Peter Goodrich demonstrates how, in books of emblems, the law is conveyed through a secularizing rhetoric of the epideictic and the ceremonial. Characterized by playfulness and eroticism, these images produced the legal subject through instruction and pleasure; see "A Theory of the Nomogram," in *Law, Text, Terror*, ed. Peter Goodrich, Lior Barshack, and Anton Schütz (Abingdon, UK: Routledge-Cavendish, 2006), 13–33. See also Stephanie Lysyk, who explores the cultural rituals of the Basoche in France's legal culture of the fifteenth century, whose function was to ease the subject's adherence to law. These rituals included law clerks' parades, the performance of moot cases, mock trials, and the production of theatrical spectacles; see "Love of the Censor: Legendre, Censorship and the Basoche," in *Law, Text, Terror*, ed. Peter Goodrich, Lior Barshack, and Anton Schütz (Abingdon, UK: Routledge-Cavendish, 2006), 119–29.

38 Anthony G. Amsterdam and Jerome Bruner, *Minding the Law: How Courts Rely on Storytelling, and How Their Stories Change the Ways We Understand the Law – and Ourselves* (Cambridge, MA: Harvard University Press, 2000), 174, 175–6.

39 Bourdieu, *Pascalian Meditations*, 123.

40 For Riefenstahl's use of tableaux vivants, a technique overlapping with other artistic genres such as baroque tragic drama, sculpture, dance, and photography, see Brigitte Peucker, "The Fascist Choreography: Riefenstahl's Tableaux," *Modernism/Modernity* 11, no. 2 (2004): 279–97.

41 Julia Kristeva, "Thinking in Dark Times," in *Profession*, ed. Rosemary G. Feal (New York: Modern Language Association, 2006), 17.

42 Ibid., 20.

43 Ibid., 15.

44 Judith Butler, "Variations on Sex and Gender: Beauvoir, Wittig, Foucault," in *The Judith Butler Reader*, ed. Sara Salih and Judith Butler (Malden, MA: Blackwell, 2004), 32.

2. Social Poiesis and Symbolic Power

1 Judith Butler, *Bodies That Matter: On the Discursive Limits of "Sex"* (New York: Routledge, 1993), 68.

2 Pierre Bourdieu, *Pascalian Meditations*, trans. Richard Nice (London: Polity Press, 2000), 142.

3 For an analysis of materiality and intentionality in Erín Moure's use of computer-generated poetry, see Lori Emerson, "Materiality, Intentionality, and the Computer-Generated Poem: Reading Walter Benn Michaels with Erín Moure's *Pillage Laud*," *English Studies in Canada* 34, no. 4 (December 2008): 45–69.

4 Virginia Woolf, *Between the Acts* (St Albans, UK: Granada Publishing, 1978), 19.

5 Laura Hanft Korobkin, "Narrative Battles in the Courtroom," in *Field Work: Sites in Literary and Cultural Studies*, ed. Marjorie Garber, Paul B. Franklin, and Rebecca L. Walkowitz (New York: Routledge, 1996), 231.

6 For a conception of genre as a constantly evolving database, see Wai Chee Dimock, "Introduction: Genres as Fields of Knowledge," *PMLA* 122, no. 5 (October 2007): 1377–88.

7 Nicola Lacey, *Unspeakable Subjects*: *Feminist Essays in Legal and Social Theory* (Oxford: Hart Publishing, 1998), 43.

8 Jerome Bruner establishes such discursive relations among culture, literature, and law when he maintains that the publication of Afro-American literature by writers such as Langston Hughes and Richard Wright affected Jim Crow laws; see *Making Stories: Law, Literature, Life* (Cambridge, MA: Harvard University Press, 2002). Randy D. Gordon also argues that literature may have effects on legislation, and he discusses the effect of Upton Sinclair's 1906 novel *The Jungle* about the meat-packing industry in Chicago on the adoption of the 1906 Federal Meat Inspection Act and Pure Food and Drugs Act in the United States; see *Rehumanizing Law: A Theory of Law and Democracy* (Toronto: Toronto University Press, 2011). Gordon's other major example is Rachel Carson's *Silent Spring* and the emergence of the American (and international) legal discourse on pesticides, the ban on DDT, as well as the eventual creation of the Environmental Protection Agency in the United States. While Gordon's demonstration underscores the dynamic among law, culture, and literature in terms of causality, he does not consider law and literature in terms of performativity and its contingencies.

9 Lacey, *Unspeakable Subjects*, 91.

10 Bruner, *Making Stories*, 51. However, Bruner betrays a Platonic suspicion of the power of narratives when he states, "Narrative requires buffers that

guard the hearer or reader against the terrors of unlimited possibility" (ibid., 52).

11 Hans Vaihinger, *The Philosophy of "As If": A System of the Theoretical, Practical and Religious Fictions of Mankind*, trans. C.K. Ogden (London: Kegan Paul, Trench, Trubner, 1924).

12 Butler, *Bodies That Matter*, 34–5.

13 Pierre Bourdieu, *Outline of a Theory of Practice*, trans. Richard Nice (Cambridge: Cambridge University Press, 2009), 124.

14 As Jacques Rancière argues, "Political statements and literary locutions produce effects of reality. They define models of speech or action but also regimes of sensible intensity. They draft maps of the visible, trajectories between the visible and the sayable, relationships between modes of being, modes of saying, and modes of doing and making things." *The Politics of Aesthetics*, trans. Gabriel Rockhill (London: Continuum, 2004), 39. In identifying the role of aesthetics in democracy as the distribution of the sensible according to the contradictory principle of dissent, Rancière reflects on the ways in which artistic practices intervene in the configuration of the sensible. In what he calls the aesthetic regime of critical art, artistic practices create the conditions for "the autonomy of a form of sensory experience ... which appears as the germ of a new humanity, of a new form of individual and collective life." *Aesthetics and Its Discontents*, trans. Steven Corcoran (Cambridge: Polity Press, 2009), 32. Both autonomous and participating in or fulfilling new forms of life, critical art is located at the hinge of aesthetics and politics.

15 Butler, *Bodies That Matter*, 2.

16 Ibid., 108–9.

17 Commenting on Goodrich's analysis of law in aesthetic and rhetorical terms, Martin A. Kayman writes, "It is ... through the concealment of its aesthetic qualities – the rhetoric of its imagery and sensual practices, its passion, and its circumstantiality and singularity – that law constructs its authority. ... By repressing its literary qualities, the law thus denies the plurality of possible legal jurisdictions, disciplines, languages, and narratives – and thus, most of all, the law denies that there might be other regimes of legality." "Law-and-Literature: Questions of Jurisdiction," in *Law and Literature*, ed. Brook Thomas, vol. 18 of *REAL: Yearbook of Research in English and American Literature* (2002), 11.

18 Butler, *Bodies That Matter*, 49.

19 Analysing the use of the word *buggery* in English law, Lesley J. Moran argues that "in law textual prohibitions do not so much demand the absence of the thing prohibited as point to the need to represent that which is prohibited in accordance with the demands of a particular

textual style set out in the law and the rituals of their performance. Furthermore my earlier analysis of 'sodomy' also suggests that the prohibition may proscribe the individuals who might utter the name and write the forbidden with impunity." "Dangerous Words and Dead Letters: Encounters with Law and *The Love That Dares to Speak Its Name*," *Liverpool Law Review* 23 (2001): 158.

20 Frantz Fanon, *The Wretched of the Earth*, trans. Constance Farrington (London: MacGibbon and Kee, 1965), 193.
21 Ibid., 194.
22 David McLellan indicates, "The *Grundrisse* is a very long manuscript written by Marx in the years 1857–8, which remained unpublished until 1941 and even then was virtually inaccessible until 1953." Karl Marx, *Selected Writings*, ed. David McLellan (Oxford: Oxford University Press, 1977), 345.
23 Butler, *Bodies That Matter*, 14.
24 Judith Butler, *Gender Trouble: Feminism and the Subversion of Identity* (New York: Routledge, 1999), xiv–xv.
25 Ibid., 178.
26 Bourdieu, *Pascalian Meditations*, 99–100.
27 Bourdieu, *Outline of a Theory of Practice*, 87, 93–4.
28 In his early critique of Bourdieu's theoretical strategies, Michel de Certeau wrote, "Bourdieu's texts are fascinating in their analyses and aggressive in their theory. ... Scrupulously examining practices and their logic – in a way that surely has had no equivalent since Mauss – the texts finally reduce them to a mystical reality, the *habitus*, which is to bring them under the law of reproduction. The subtle descriptions of Béarnian or Kabylian tactics suddenly give way to violently imposed truths, as if the complexity so lucidly examined required the brutal counterpoint of a dogmatic reason." *The Practice of Everyday Life*, trans. Steven Rendall (Berkeley: University of California Press, 1988), 59.
29 Terry Lovell, "Resisting with Authority: Historical Specificity, Agency and the Performative Self," *Theory, Culture & Society* 20, no. 1 (2003): 5.
30 Bourdieu, *Pascalian Meditations*, 150.
31 For a Bourdieu-based analysis of the habitus in law, see Rosemary J. Coombe, "Room for Manoeuver: Toward a Theory of Practice in Critical Legal Studies," *Law and Social Inquiry* 14, no. 1 (Winter 1989): 69–121.
32 Ngaire Naffine, *Law and the Sexes: Explorations in Feminist Jurisprudence* (Sydney: Unwin and Allen, 1990), 40.
33 Duncan Kennedy, *Legal Education and the Reproduction of Hierarchy: A Polemic against the System* (New York: New York University Press, 2007), 7.

34 This logic of the same reappears in Hilary Sommerlad's more recent sociological analysis of postgraduate students as legal trainees in a city in the north of England. She argues that persistent patterns of gender, class, and race inequality undermine the potential for the transformation of the legal profession and the outcome of equality projects. "By endorsing individual equality projects on the part of minority entrants as a means of overcoming collective subordination, the situation is created where in order to achieve equality, the cultural and linguistic attributes of collective identities must be abandoned. Diversity in this form becomes a merely somatic issue, the profession's absorption of different bodily forms, but not of their experience and biography." "That Obscure Object of Desire: Sex Equality and the Legal Profession," in *Rethinking Equality Projects in Law: Feminist Challenges*, ed. Rosemary Hunter, Oñati International Series in Law and Society (Oxford: Hart Publishing, 2008), 193–4.

35 Peter Goodrich, *Oedipus Lex: Psychoanalysis, History, Law* (Berkeley: University of California Press, 1995), 46.

36 Ibid., 49.

37 Drawing on Pierre Legendre, Goodrich argues that the image is the point of transition between the subjective and the institutional. "Aesthetics teaches us that the institution of the subject requires the inscription of an image of the social as an object of love … the subject must love the signs of power, the emblems of an authority which cannot be physically present everywhere and so must appear most usually in fantasmatic and imagistic forms." See Peter Goodrich, ed., *Law and the Unconscious: A Legendre Reader* (Basingstoke, UK: Palgrave Macmillan, 1997), 17.

38 Bourdieu analyses the child as "a being-perceived, condemned to be defined as it 'really' is by the perception of others" (*Pascalian Meditations*, 166).

39 Judith Butler, *The Psychic Life of Power* (Stanford, CA: Stanford University Press, 1997), 7.

40 Butler, *Bodies That Matter*, 12.

41 *Oxford English Dictionary* Online, s.v. "cite," accessed 30 January 2014, http://www.oed.com/view/Entry/33491?rskey=MX8Egv&result=2&isAdvanced=false-eid.

3. Law's Symbolic Power to Legitimize

1 Peter Goodrich, *Reading the Law: A Critical Introduction to Legal Method and Techniques* (Oxford: Basil Blackwell, 1986), 4–5.

2 Nicola Lacey, "Analytical Jurisprudence versus Descriptive Sociology Revisited," *Texas Law Review* 84, no. 4 (2006): 980.

3 Rosie Harding, *Regulating Sexuality: Legal Consciousness in Lesbian and Gay Lives* (London: Routledge, 2011), 9.

4 Hans Kelsen, *Introduction to the Problems of Legal Theory*, trans. Bonnie Litschewski Paulson and Stanley L. Paulson (Oxford: Clarendon Press, 1992), 10.

5 Carl Schmitt criticized what he called the "sociology/jurisprudence" disjunction in Kelsen's theory; see *Political Theology: Four Chapters in the Concept of Sovereignty*, trans. George Schwab (Cambridge, MA: MIT Press, 1985), 18–21. In his critique, Lon Fuller argues that "the notion of the basic norm is admittedly a symbol, not a fact. It is a symbol that embodies the positivist quest for some clear and unambiguous test of law, for some clean, sharp line that will divide the rules which owe their validity to their source and those which owe their validity to acceptance and intrinsic appeal. The difficulties Austin avoided by sticking with the command theory, Kelsen avoids by a fiction which simplifies reality into a form that can be absorbed by positivism." "Positivism and Fidelity to Law – A Reply to Professor Hart," *Harvard Law Review* 71, no. 4 (1958): 641.

6 Etienne Balibar indicates that as part of the Vienna Circle, Kelsen and Freud engaged in a dialogue on the subject of mass psychology and state coercion. Balibar suggests that, in his elaboration of the superego, Freud sought to counter Kelsen's notion that the state's authority through law as coercion preceded the psychological formation of guilt and punishment. According to Balibar, for Kelsen, "to belong to a 'tribunal' or to a State that defines itself principally as a tribunal incarnating and monopolizing the judicial functions … is to fall within its sanction, to come under its 'jurisdiction,' and therefore, to have been *positioned there* in a manner that does not allow the individual to escape or ignore it, to challenge it." "The Invention of the Super-Ego: Freud and Kelsen 1922" (unpublished essay, n.d.), Microsoft Word file, 21, http://www.soundandsignifier.com/files/Balibar_The_Invention_of_the_Superego.doc.

7 In examining Hart's theory, Lacey considers Hart's claim that he offered a sociological description of analytical jurisprudence as "descriptive sociology." "Hart wanted to maintain the claim to universality as well as descriptiveness. In doing so, he ended up with the worst of both worlds. On the one hand, he produced a theory whose commitment to a social fact dimension meant it did indeed reflect certain specific features of institutionalization – a fact that already compromised its universality. His theory, after all, fits most comfortably with a centralized state legal order. On the other hand, in the grip of the ambition for universality, he failed to deliver any rich paradigm of law's institutional form" ("Analytical Jurisprudence," 957–8). For a comparative analysis of Noam Chomsky's

theory of linguistics and Hart's positivist jurisprudence, see Rémi Samson, who traces a Cartesian and universalist aspiration common to both endeavours in "Language and Law as Objects of Scientific Study," in *Law, Mystery, and the Humanities: Collected Essays*, ed. Logan Atkinson and Diana Majury (Toronto: University of Toronto Press, 2008), 121–42.

8 Tony Honoré, *Making Law Bind: Essays Legal and Philosophical* (Oxford: Clarendon Press, 1987), 17.

9 H.L.A. Hart, *The Concept of Law* (Oxford: Clarendon Press, 1961), 56–7.

10 Hart's invocation of reason is inscribed in a long genealogy. For instance, Mark C. Murphy quotes Thomas of Aquinas's succinct definition of law in his *Treatise on Law*. "Law is a sort of rule and measure of acts, according to which one is induced to act or restrained from acting, for *lex* (law) is said to be from *ligare* (to bind) because *obligat* (it binds) one to act. But the rule and measure of human act is reason, which is the first principle of human acts, ... for it belongs to reason to order things to the end, which is the first principle in practical matters, according to [Aristotle]." "Natural Law Theory," in *The Blackwell Guide to the Philosophy of Law and Legal Theory*, ed. Martin P. Golding and William A. Edmundson (Malden, MA: Blackwell, 2005), 16.

11 Joseph Raz, *The Authority of Law: Essays on Law and Morality* (Oxford: Clarendon Press, 1979), 156–7.

12 Ibid., 109–10.

13 J. Peter Burgess, "Law and Cultural Identity," ARENA Working Papers Series, WP 97/14 (Oslo: ARENA Centre for European Studies, 1997), 1–32, http://jpeterburgess.com/wp-content/uploads/publications/1997/Law_and_Cultural_Identity.pdf.

14 Desmond Manderson and Richard Mohr, "From Oxymoron to Intersection: An Epidemiology of Legal Research," *Law Text Culture* 6 (2003): 170.

15 Roberto Mangabeira Unger, "Liberal Political Theory," in *Critical Legal Studies*, ed. Allan Hutchinson (Totowa, NJ: Rowman and Littlefield, 1989), 28–9.

16 To this extent, their various positions illustrate Paul W. Kahn's principle that "to live under the rule of law is to maintain a set of beliefs about the self and community, time and space, authority and representation." *The Cultural Study of Law: Reconstructing Legal Scholarship* (Chicago: University of Chicago Press, 1999), 36.

17 Jack M. Balkin and Sanford Levinson, "Law, Music, and Other Performing Arts," *University of Pennsylvania Law Review* 139, no. 6 (1991): 1608–9.

18 Robin West, *Narrative, Authority, and Law* (Ann Arbor: University of Michigan Press, 1993), 93.

19 Ronald Dworkin, *Law's Empire* (Cambridge, MA: Harvard University Press, 1986), 239.

20 Carolyn Heilbrun and Judith Resnik question this claim to legal coherence and authority. "Learning what happens beyond the highest courts and the legislatures not only informs the reading of those speakers' output; such reading also enables an understanding that the most officially powerful are not necessarily the only powerful actors. Law 'texts' are generated by many people; appellate judges have no monopoly on the genre. Lower court opinions speak more directly than do the higher courts to the people whose lives give rise to the lawsuit and who may be deeply affected by it. The tone and sounds of 'the judicial voice' vary with the audience." "Convergences: Law, Literature, and Feminism," *Yale Law Journal* 99, no. 8 (1990): 1940. Ironically, through copyright law, the law upholds a concept of authorship based on singularity and originality, while in its own practices it produces multi-authored court decisions. On law and the historical evolution of the concepts of authorship, originality, singularity, and ownership, see Anne Jamison, "Collaboration v. Imitation: Authorship and the Law," *Law and Literature* 18, no. 2 (Summer 2006): 199–224. See also Martin Kayman, who argues that under the Statute of Anne (passed in Great Britain in 1710), authorship became a sign of private ownership to be regulated and protected by a statutory law that itself exhibits written properties. Out of this process emerged the historical distinction between law and literature, with the legal statute regularizing the literary imagination and preserving private ownership and public interests. "Lawful Writing: Common Law, Statute and the Properties of Literature," *New Literary History* 27, no. 4 (Autumn 1996): 761–83.

21 Carol Smart, *Law, Crime, and Sexuality: Essays in Feminism* (London: Sage Publications, 1995), 74–5. Pierre Bourdieu identifies the use of specialized language as a political means of constituting law's power. The difference between the layperson and the legal expert "is essential to a power relation upon which two systems of presuppositions, two systems of expressive intention – two world-views – are grounded. This difference, which is the basis for excluding the non-specialist, results from the establishment of a system of injunctions through the structure of the field and of the system of principles of vision and of division which are written into its fundamental law, into its *constitution*." "The Force of Law: Toward a Sociology of the Juridical Field," *Hastings Law Journal* 38, no. 5 (1987): 828–9. To counter this doxological and systemic constitution of the world, Ronnie Warrington and Costas Douzinas call for a Levinasian ethics of justice beyond law as calculation and systematization; see *Justice*

Miscarried: Ethics, Aesthetics and the Law (Hemel Hempstead, UK: Harvester Wheatsheaf, 1994), 171.

22 Raz, *Authority of Law*, 226.

23 Ibid., 108.

24 Ibid., 225.

25 Brian Z. Tamanaha distinguishes between formal and substantive theories of the rule of law. "Formal theories focus on the proper sources and form of legality, while substantive theories also include requirements about the content of the law (usually that it must comport with justice or moral principle). While the distinction is informative, it should not be taken as strict – the formal versions have substantive implications and the substantive versions incorporate formal requirements." *On the Rule of Law: History, Politics, Theory* (Cambridge: Cambridge University Press, 2004), 92. Tamanaha establishes a spectrum that comprises various conceptualizations of the rule of law as an instrument of government action; formal legality as general, prospective, clear, certain, democracy with consent determining content of law; individual rights, including property, contract, privacy, autonomy; right of dignity and/or justice; and social welfare based on concepts of substantive equality, welfare, and preservation of community. These different shades of meaning all derive from the historical, cultural, and sociopolitical evolution of the rule of law as a bulwark against forms of dictatorship and tyranny. From this perspective, the law consists in a system that provides predictability, publishes clear laws to all, and is administered by an independent judiciary in the context of "open and fair hearings without bias and review of legislative and administrative officials and limitations on the discretion of police to insure conformity to the requirements of the rule of law" (ibid., 93). Paul W. Kahn refers to the rule of law as "a kind of shorthand way of referring to a matrix of beliefs and practices within which the citizen acknowledges the possibility that the state will make a demand on his or her life and that, regardless of personal interests, the legitimacy of that claim will have to be acknowledged." "Freedom, Autonomy, and the Cultural Study of Law," in *Cultural Analysis, Cultural Studies, and the Law: Moving beyond Legal Realism*, ed. Austin Sarat and Jonathon Simon (Durham, NC: Duke University Press, 2003), 170.

26 Judith Butler, *The Psychic Life of Power* (Stanford, CA: Stanford University Press, 1997), 10.

27 Bourdieu, "Force of Law," 844.

28 In the United Kingdom, a similar initiative led to the Feminist Judgments Project; see Rosemary Hunter, Clare McGlynn, and Erika Rackley, eds., *Feminist Judgments: From Theory to Practice* (Oxford: Hart Publishing, 2010).

29 Gwen Brodsky et al., "*Gosselin v. Québec (Attorney General)*," *Canadian Journal of Women and the Law* 18, no. 1 (2006): 191.

30 Section 35.1 of the Constitution Act, 1982 provides, "The government of Canada and the provincial governments are committed to the principle that, before any amendment is made to Class 24 of section 91 of the *Constitution Act, 1867*, to section 25 of this Act or to this Part,

(*a*) a constitutional conference that includes in its agenda an item relating to the proposed amendment, composed of the Prime Minister of Canada and the first ministers of the provinces, will be convened by the Prime Minister of Canada; and

(*b*) the Prime Minister of Canada will invite representatives of the aboriginal peoples of Canada to participate in the discussions on that item. At http://laws-lois.justice.gc.ca/eng/Const/page-16.html#h-52.

31 Canada, Royal Commission on Electoral Reform and Party Financing, *Reforming Electoral Democracy: Final Report*. Ottawa: Minister of Supply and Services Canada, 1991.

32 Section 2(b) of the Charter states that everyone has "freedom of thought, belief, opinion and expression, including freedom of the press and other media of communication"; section 28 states, "Notwithstanding anything in this Charter, the rights and freedoms referred to in it are guaranteed equally to male and female persons." At http://laws-lois.justice.gc.ca/eng/Const/page-15.html#h-40.

33 Mary Eberts, Sharon McIvor, and Teressa Nahanee, "*Native Women's Association of Canada v. Canada*," *Canadian Journal of Women and the Law* 18, no. 1 (2006): 115.

34 Luce Irigaray, "The Power of Discourse and the Subordination of the Feminine," in *This Sex Which Is Not One*, trans. Catherine Porter with Carolyn Burke (Ithaca, NY: Cornell University Press, 1985), 76. Hunter, McGlynn, and Rackley describe the Feminist Judgments Project as a "form of critical scholarship" and "a form of parodic – and hence subversive – performance" (*Feminist Judgments*, 5, 8).

35 There is a precedent to the Women's Court in the French seventeenth-century activities and writings of the *précieuses*. Peter Goodrich provides a fascinating analysis of the significance of their practices. "The feminine Republic of the *précieuses* was a species of outlaw public sphere. It was also explicitly an imaginary domain, an impossible politics, a utopian assertion of a women's law within the context of a constitution governed by an antique Salic law which denied women all political and legal rights. … As an experimental and loosely heretical movement, the *précieuses* were free

to rewrite the law and to choose whatever mechanism or doctrine best suited their political enterprise. They chose the love letter. The love letter established the public space of amorous relationship, the space between lovers, that of intimacy and of affectivity, with which the Republic of the *précieuses* and their *carte du tendre* were concerned. The epistolary art was the means used to institute and express a separate jurisdiction appropriate to relationships, a justice and judgment that attended to the space between lovers." "Epistolary Justice: The Love Letter as Law," *Yale Journal of Law & the Humanities* 9, no. 2 (1997): 251. It can be argued that the *précieuses'* strategy constituted a catachrestic appropriation of the law – that is to say, a practice of misappropriation of the concept and a poetic rewriting and re/deconstitution of the law.

36 Unger, "Liberal Political Theory," 29.

37 Raz, *Authority of Law*, 121.

38 Ibid., 152.

39 Ibid., 150.

40 See Jack M. Balkin and Sanford Levinson, who have developed the concept of legal historicism as the analysis of legal decision-making deriving from political, social, and historical forces, in "Legal Historicism and Legal Academics: The Roles of Law Professors in the Wake of *Bush v. Gore*," *Georgetown Law Journal* 90, no. 1 (2001): 173–97.

41 Ronald Dworkin, *Justice in Robes* (Cambridge, MA: Harvard University Press, 2006), 234.

42 Dworkin, *Law's Empire*, 97.

43 Ibid., 338.

44 Dworkin's theory in *Law's Empire* can be seen as an elaboration of the doctrine of precedent. In this respect, Goodrich explains that "the crucial period for the modern development of the concept of a system of precedent, as a rational body of case-law rules stating in advance the law applicable to any given instance of dispute or accusation, is that between 1758, when the first lectures on the common law were delivered by Blackstone at Oxford, and 1861, when the House of Lords, sitting as a purely legal body, first clearly elaborated the doctrine of binding precedent in Beamish v Beamish [1861] 9 HLC, 274" (*Reading the Law*, 129).

45 Stanley Fish argues that Dworkin's theory of legal historical fit and integrity yields the following paradox: "One can be faithful to legal history only by revising it, by redescribing it in such a way as to accommodate and render manageably the issues raised by the present. This is a function of law's conservatism, which will not allow a case to remain unrelated to the past, and so assures that the past, in the form of the history of decisions, will be continually rewritten." *Doing What Comes Naturally* (Durham, NC:

Duke University Press, 1989), 94. In contrast to Dworkin's conception, Wai Chee Dimock argues that "law is a linguistic artifact, dependent on words and haunted by that dependency. Such an artifact is susceptible to time; it can easily be altered out of recognition. As words change their meaning, so too do laws whose wording might remain superficially the same. To enforce the letter of the law is paradoxically to depart from its original meaning, changing its scope, its mode of operation, getting it tangled up in complications entirely unforeseen. In this way, jurisprudence is plagued by all the hazards and all the treacheries of text-based knowledge." "Rules of Law, Laws of Science," *Yale Journal of Law & the Humanities* 13, no. 1 (2001): 224.

46 Dworkin, *Law's Empire*, 110.

47 Shoshana Felman, "Forms of Judicial Blindness: Traumatic Narratives and Legal Repetitions," in *History, Memory, and the Law*, ed. Austin Sarat and Thomas R. Kearns (Ann Arbor: University of Michigan Press, 2002), 30.

48 See Katherine Franke on the transmission of ideologies of gendered power in the context of Abner Louima's rape in 1997, which she contrasts with ritualized practices of fellatio in the Highlands of Papua New Guinea, where young boys are masculinized by ingesting semen, in "Law," in *A Companion to Gender Studies*, ed. Philomena Essed, David Theo Goldberg, and Audrey Kobayashi (Malden, MA: Blackwell, 2005), 160–80.

49 For an argument in favour of a substantive conception of the rule of law as well as a critique of the absence of cultural and localized practices of the rule of law in the context of foreign policy, human rights, and international development, see Rosa Ehrenreich Brooks, "The New Imperialism: Violence, Norms, and the 'Rule of Law,'" *Michigan Law Review* 101, no. 7 (June 2003): 2275–340.

4. Symbolic Violence and Illegitimacy: The Political Uncanny

1 *The Golden Bough: A Study in Comparative Religion* was first published in 1890 (retitled *The Golden Bough: A Study in Magic and Religion* in its second edition) and reissued in a twelve-volume edition between 1906 and 1915 before being published in an abridged edition in 1922.

2 Sigmund Freud, "The Uncanny," trans. James Strachey, in *The Complete Psychological Works of Sigmund Freud*, vol. 17 (London: Hogarth Press, 1955), 219–20, 244.

3 However, in the spring of 1919, Freud also wrote the introduction to "Psycho-Analysis and the War Neuroses," which preceded three papers by Sándor Ferenczi, Karl Abraham, and Ernst Simmel on the same topic.

4 Sue-Ellen Case draws attention to Freud's use of the concept of home and the *heimlich* in the context of the history of anti-Semitism and the Nazis' ideology of *Heimat*. Thus, Freud's text is "haunted by the outsider position of a myth of 'race' that violently denied the pleasure of 'home.'" "Tracking the Vampire," *Differences: A Journal of Feminist Cultural Studies* 3, no. 2 (1991): 15.

5 Freud refers to Oedipus as "the mythical criminal" whose punishment of castration symbolized by self-blinding was "the only punishment that was adequate for him by the *lex talionis*" ("Uncanny," 231).

6 Ibid., 224.

7 Ibid., 248.

8 Ibid., 248–9.

9 Ibid., 249.

10 Judith Butler, "The Force of Fantasy: Mapplethorpe, Feminism, and Discursive Excess," in *The Judith Butler Reader*, ed. Sara Salih and Judith Butler (Malden, MA: Blackwell, 2004), 186.

11 Pierre Bourdieu, *Pascalian Meditations*, trans. Richard Nice (London: Polity Press, 2000), 135.

12 Freud, "Uncanny," 241.

13 Judith Butler, *Gender Trouble: Feminism and the Subversion of Identity* (New York: Routledge, 1999), 173.

14 Bourdieu, *Pascalian Meditations*, 167.

15 Judith Butler, *Bodies That Matter: On the Discursive Limits of "Sex"* (New York: Routledge, 1993), 106.

16 Freud, "Uncanny," 226.

17 Pierre Bourdieu, *Masculine Domination*, trans. Richard Nice (Stanford, CA: Stanford University Press, 2001), 37.

18 Bourdieu, *Pascalian Meditations*, 9.

19 Butler, *Bodies That Matter*, xi.

20 Butler, *Gender Trouble*, 174–5.

21 Judith Butler, "Competing Universalities," in *Contingency, Hegemony, Universality: Contemporary Dialogues on the Left*, ed. Judith Butler, Ernesto Laclau, and Slavoj Zižek (London: Verso Books, 2000), 153.

22 Butler, *Bodies That Matter*, 3.

23 For a demonstration of the exclusionary effects of legal conceptions of subjectivity, see Sheryl Hamilton, who concentrates on liminal beings whose modes of being call into question law's ontological certainties about what constitutes a person. These include corporations, women, clones, computers, and celebrities. Exceeding normative definitions of subjectivity, liminal beings reveal that "the various symbolic processes

through which we then negotiate, legitimate, and sanction those beings as persons or not reveal the fundamental instability of a notion in whose name much is done – the person. … What is revealed in the personality debates of these liminal subjects is not, in fact, the instability of the liminal beings themselves, but of the concept by which they are measured." *Impersonations: Troubling the Person in Law and Culture* (Toronto: University of Toronto Press, 2009), 23.

24 Freud, "Uncanny," 241.

25 Judith Butler, *The Psychic Life of Power* (Stanford, CA: Stanford University Press, 1997), 68.

26 Bourdieu, *Pascalian Meditations*, 97.

27 Butler, *Psychic Life of Power*, 138.

28 Judith Butler, *Antigone's Claim: Kinship between Life and Death* (New York: Columbia University Press, 2000), 66–7.

29 Butler, *Psychic Life of Power*, 28.

30 Ibid., 81.

31 Judith Butler analyses the normative frame of ethical encounters as follows: "Though I might think of the ethical relation as dyadic or, indeed, as prosocial, I am caught up not only in the sphere of normativity but in the problematic of power when I pose the ethical question in its directness and simplicity: 'How ought I to treat you?' If the 'I' and the 'you' must first come into being, and if a normative frame is necessary for this emergence and encounter then norms work not only to direct my conduct but to condition the possible emergence of an encounter between myself and the other." *Giving an Account of Oneself* (New York: Fordham University Press, 2005), 25.

32 Butler, *Psychic Life of Power*, 28.

33 For a comparative analysis of Foucault's and Agamben's reflections on sovereignty and normativity, see Catherine Mill, "Biopolitics, Liberal Eugenics, and Nihilism," in *Giorgio Agamben: Sovereignty and Life*, ed. Matthew Calarco and Steven DeCaroli (Stanford, CA: Stanford University Press, 2007), 180–202. For a discussion of the temporality of sovereign power in the iterative and apocalyptic mode, see Charles Barbour, "Sovereign Time: Acts of Creation," *Law, Culture and the Humanities* 6, no. 2 (2010): 143–52. For a political theology of sovereignty and exception in the cultural context of the United States, see Paul W. Kahn, who, after Carl Schmitt, argues, "The exceptional turn to violence against the enemy will always be understood as the defense of sovereign existence. This includes, but is not exhausted by, the defense of the order of law that the sovereign put in place: to defend the state is not just to defend

the border, but to defend a way of life. For Americans, the rule of law is not that which eliminates the need for the violent defense of the nation, but that for the sake of which violence is deployed. Paradigmatic of this synthesis for Americans was the Civil War, in which defense of sovereignty was inseparable from defense of the Constitution. The current war on terror shows us the continued vitality of these themes of law, exception, sovereignty, and the imagined existential crisis of the state." *Political Theology: Four New Chapters on the Concept of Sovereignty* (New York: Columbia University Press, 2011), 11.

34 Giorgio Agamben, *Homo Sacer: Sovereign Power and Bare Life*, trans. Daniel Heller-Roazen (Stanford, CA: Stanford University Press, 1998), 4.

35 Ibid., 19.

36 This is a statement from Carl Schmitt, *Political Theology: Four Chapters in the Concept of Sovereignty*, trans. George Schwab (Cambridge, MA: MIT Press, 1985), 13. Note that while Schwab translated the famous statement by using the word "norm" ("there is no norm that is applicable to chaos"), Daniel Heller-Roazen uses the word "rule."

37 Agamben, *Homo Sacer*, 19.

38 In this sense, Agamben's reflection belongs to a genealogy of thinking that brings out the coupling of authority and violence, obedience and transgression. In his analysis of Hans Kelsen's reflection on law as coercion, Etienne Balibar argues that "crime, which does not contradict but rather affirms law as obligatory norm, is practically necessary to its existence. One can also consider the individuals' 'membership' to the juridical order, always already given and constantly verified by it (at least as long as this order is perpetuated), as the *effect of subjectivity* proper to the sanction." "The Invention of the Super-Ego: Freud and Kelsen 1922" (unpublished essay, n.d.), Microsoft Word file, 23, http://www.soundandsignifier.com/files/Balibar_The_Invention_of_the_Superego.doc. This, it seems to me, exemplifies Butler's use of metalepsis, whereby the effect is taken as the sign of an authoritative origin: as a performative, crime justifies law as coercion and punishment. This leads Balibar to conclude that contra Kelsen's *Grund* norm, for Freud, "*there is only transgression* and for this reason, *it is possible* to belong to this 'impersonal' order – that is the juridical order" (ibid., 24).

39 Agamben, *Homo Sacer*, 18.

40 Paul W. Kahn equally sees law as the locus of originary violence. "A cultural account of the rule of law approaches violence from the standpoint of the sacrificial demand that the state places upon the individual. … Sacrifice is the primal act of violence within the legal order. It remains the

paradigm through which other forms of violence gain their meaning." *The Cultural Study of Law: Reconstructing Legal Scholarship* (Chicago: University of Chicago Press, 1999), 95.

41 Agamben, *Homo Sacer*, 28–9.

42 Ernesto Laclau, "Bare Life or Social Indeterminacy," in *Giorgio Agamben: Sovereignty and Life*, ed. Matthew Calarco and Steven DeCaroli (Stanford, CA: Stanford University Press, 2007), 22. That Agamben does not consider the historical and therefore productive and transformational aspect of political power is a recurrent point of debate and critique among readers of his texts. Antonio Negri argues that "Agamben begins to define [the concept of biopolitics] by excluding all productive qualities and flattening it onto the ontological dimension. In other words, biopolitics is turned into a permanent *dispositive* of metaphysics." Instead, Negri argues, when "one alludes to the ontological experience of Spinozism as the great alternative within modernity (and which prefigures the postmodern), one is speaking of productive being, of a being as the indefinite singularization, reproduction, and, therefore, construction of new being." "The Discreet Taste of the Dialectic," in *Giorgio Agamben: Sovereignty and Life*, ed. Matthew Calarco and Steven DeCaroli (Stanford, CA: Stanford University Press, 2007), 122, 123. Elena Loizidou points out that although Butler and Agamben share a post-Foucaultian concern for the persistence of sovereign power in the midst of governmentality, "for Butler … it is precisely the utterance of a state of exception that creates a sovereign governmental power." *Judith Butler: Ethics, Law, Politics* (Abingdon, UK: Routledge-Cavendish, 2007), 98. For a critique of Agamben's conception of sovereign power as pure and unmediated violence, see David Pan, "Against Biopolitics: Walter Benjamin, Carl Schmitt, and Giorgio Agamben on Political Sovereignty and Symbolic Order," *German Quarterly* 82, no. 1 (Winter 2009): 42–62.

43 Agamben, *Homo Sacer*, 171 (italics mine).

44 The extreme and modern form of such power assumes the form of horrorism, which Adriana Cavarero conceptualizes as follows: "Grasping the helpless victim by the hair and standing at just the right angle to the television camera (and thus to the international media audience), the modern executioner slices off the head with a knife. More than simply being carried out, the crime is staged as an intentional offense to the ontological dignity of the victim. Evidently it is not so much the killing that is in question here but rather dehumanizing and savaging the body as body, destroying it in its figural unity, sullying it." *Horrorism: Naming Contemporary Violence*, trans. William McCuaig (New York: Columbia University Press, 2011), 9.

45 For a gendering of *homo sacer*, ban, and state of exception, see Josephine L. Savarese's analysis of sex-trade workers in "'Doing No Violence to the Sentence Imposed': Racialized Sex Worker Complainants, Racialized Offenders, and the Feminization of the *Homo Sacer* in Two Sexual Assault Cases," *Canadian Journal of Women and the Law* 22, no. 2 (2010): 365–96.

5. The Symbolic Power and Violence of Legal Utterances

1 Canada, Commission of Inquiry into the Actions of Canadian Officials in Relation to Maher Arar, *Report of the Events Relating to Maher Arar: Analysis and Recommendations*, Cat. No. CP32-88/1-2006E (Ottawa: Minister of Public Works and Government Services, 2006), 59, http://www.sirc-csars.gc.ca/pdfs/cm_arar_rec-eng.pdf.
2 Joseph Raz, *The Authority of Law: Essays on Law and Morality* (Oxford: Clarendon Press, 1979), 11.
3 Ibid., 12.
4 Ibid.
5 Ibid., 16.
6 Pierre Bourdieu, "The Force of Law: Toward a Sociology of the Juridical Field," *Hastings Law Journal* 38, no. 5 (1987): 838 (footnote omitted).
7 Judith Butler, *Bodies That Matter: On the Discursive Limits of "Sex"* (New York: Routledge, 1993), 108.
8 Patrick Hanafin, "The Writer's Refusal and Law's Malady," in *Law and Literature*, ed. Patrick Hanafin, Adam Gearey, and Joseph Brooker (Oxford: Blackwell, 2004), 8.
9 For the role of multi-disciplinary contextualization in feminist judging, see Rosemary Hunter, "An Account of Feminist Judging," in *Feminist Judgments: From Theory to Practice*, ed. Rosemary Hunter, Clare McGlynn, and Erika Rackley (Oxford: Hart Publishing, 2010), 30–43.
10 Hayden White, "The Historical Text as Literary Artifact," in *Tropics of Discourse: Essays in Cultural Criticism* (Baltimore: Johns Hopkins University Press, 1978), 84–5. From an anthropological standpoint, Clifford Geertz has famously posited that the law is an exercise in representation. "The rendering of fact so that lawyers can plead it, judges can hear it, and juries can settle it is just that, a rendering: as any other trade, science, cult, or art, law, which is a bit of all of these, propounds the world in which its description make sense." "Local Knowledge: Fact and Law in Comparative Perspective," in *Local Knowledge: Further Essays in Interpretive Anthropology* (New York: Basic Books, 1983), 173.

11 Gwen Brodsky et al., "*Gosselin v. Québec (Attorney General),*" *Canadian Journal of Women and the Law* 18, no. 1 (2006): 189–90.
12 Nicola Lacey, *Unspeakable Subjects: Feminist Essays in Legal and Social Theory* (Oxford: Hart Publishing, 1998), 60–8.
13 Nicola Lacey, "Violence, Ethics and Law: Feminist Reflections on a Familiar Dilemma," in *Visible Women*, ed. Susan James and Stephanie Palmer (Oxford: Hart Publishing, 2002), 133.
14 Peter Brooks, "Narrativity of the Law," *Law and Literature* 14, no. 1 (Spring 2002): 6.
15 Lacey argues that contextualization should be understood "not as a reformist strategy but rather as critique: in other words, the development of a critical analysis which unearths the logic, the substantive assumptions, underlying law's current contextualization of its subjects, and which can hence illuminate the interests and relationships which these arrangements privilege" (*Unspeakable Subjects*, 6–7).
16 Stanley Fish, *Doing What Comes Naturally* (Durham, NC: Duke University Press, 1989), 99–100.
17 Michel Foucault, "*What Is an Author?" in Language, Counter-Memory, Practice*, ed. Donald F. Bouchard and Sherry Simon (Ithaca, NY: Cornell University Press, 1977), 117.
18 See Roman Jakobson, "Linguistics and Poetics," in *Style in Language*, ed. Thomas A. Sebeok (Cambridge, MA: MIT Press, 1960), 355, 357.
19 Tony Honoré, *Making Law Bind: Essays Legal and Philosophical* (Oxford: Clarendon Press, 1987), 27.
20 Raz, *Authority of Law*, 182.
21 United Kingdom, Law Commission, "Partial Defences to Murder: Consultation," Consultation Paper No. 173 (31 October 2003), 10–11.
22 The website is accessible at https://www.gov.uk/government/organisations/government-equalities-office.
23 The record of the first reading is accessible at http://www.publications.parliament.uk/pa/cm200809/cmvote/90424v01.htm. The Equality Act became law on 1 October 2010.
24 Honoré, *Making Law Bind*, 26. Kate McLoughlin and Carl Gardner argue that lawyers and judges are not so much involved in ascribing authorial intention as engaging in a close reading of the legal texts according to established procedures of interpretation to determine textual meaning. "Despite avowed aims, the forensic project of ascertaining meaning seems systematically to avoid historical intentionalism in favour of a constructivist, more purely textual approach." "When Is Authorial

Intention Not Authorial Intention?," *European Journal of English Studies* 11, no. 1 (April 2007): 94.

25 Adam Thurschwell, "Reading the Law," in *The Fate of the Law*, ed. Austin Sarat and Thomas R. Kearns (Ann Arbor: University of Michigan Press, 1991), 305.

26 For an analysis of the role of intentionality in testators' creation of wills and for a reflection on the power dynamic inherent in the production of posthumous statements of commands, see Jane B. Baron, "Intention, Interpretation and Stories," *Duke Law Journal* 42, no. 3 (December 1992): 630–78.

27 In his analysis of the process of narrative selection involved in legal adjudication, Patrick Colm Hogan argues that the "difficult point for law is determining in any given case whether the selection of details is accurate and adequate; difficulty comes not in deciding that selection has taken place, but in deciding what actually occurred and what elements – what events and circumstances from the welter of factual detail – are relevant to laws governing the case at hand. The problem of selectiveness is profound in legal adjudication. However, it is crucial in precisely the areas in which it does not enter into literary study – referential validity and completeness relative to a governing precept." "On Reading Law as Literature," *College Literature* 25, no. 1 (Winter 1998): 231–2.

28 Kim Lane Scheppele underlines this normative struggle. "In law, both at trial and on appeal, all courts have is stories. Judges and jurors are not witnesses to the events at issue; they are witnesses to stories about the events. And when litigants come to court with different stories, some are accepted and become 'the facts of the case' and others are rejected and cast aside. Some of what is cast aside may indeed be false (and some of what is accepted may be too). But some of the rejected stories may be accurate versions of events that grow from experiences different from the experiences of those who are doing the choosing." "Foreword: Telling Stories," *Michigan Law Review* 87, no. 8 (1989): 2082–3 (footnote omitted).

29 Anna Carline, "Zoora Shah: 'An Unusual Woman,'" *Social and Legal Studies* 14, no. 2 (2005): 215–6.

30 Anna Carline, "Women Who Kill Their Abusive Partners: From Sameness to Gender Construction," *Liverpool Law Review* 26, no. 1 (2005): 36.

31 Analysing the ethics of criminal law, Wai Chee Dimock states that her chief concern is with "the range of symbolic inscriptions brought into play by a particular act of judgment, the wealth of referents encoded in a seemingly discrete offense. … By emphasizing the figurative in the assignment of blame – by studying the punitive, the proscriptive, and the prescriptive

as a series of symbolic relations – I mean to suggest that, in law as in literature, the ethics of punishment might not be so readily distinguishable from its aesthetics." "Criminal Law, Female Virtue, and the Rise of Liberalism," *Yale Journal of Law & the Humanities* 4, no. 2 (1992): 225.

32 For an analytical and critical survey of the evolution of the legal approach to battered women who kill, see Heather Douglas's critique, which reveals to what extent the law remains entangled in and reproduces gender categorization. "The Provocation Defence and Equality," in *Rethinking Equality Projects in Law: Feminist Challenges*, ed. Rosemary Hunter, Oñati International Series in Law and Society (Oxford: Hart Publishing, 2008), 41–57.

33 Peter Brooks identifies this process as one of legal exclusion and domestication, a tendency "particularly marked when the law has to deal with complex issues of human agency, motivation, and behavior in actors brought within the sphere of criminal procedure, since the need to assign guilt and punishment makes short shrift of all that we know – from the great novelists as well as from psychoanalysis – about these murky depths." "Law, Therapy, Culture," *Yale Journal of Law & the Humanities* 13, no. 1 (2001): 232.

34 Daniel A. Farber and Suzanna Sherry argue that "the conscious process of legal reasoning is not really what accounts for the results in cases, nor is it truly capable of changing the beliefs and values of actors. Rather, beliefs are formed at a deeper level involving unarticulated social values and mindsets – values and mindsets that are inarticulate not only in the sense of being not yet stated but also in the stronger sense of being irreducible to any finite set of propositions or rules. … These tacit understandings are communicated through images, stories, and other symbols." "Legal Storytelling and Constitutional Law," in *Law's Stories: Narrative and Rhetoric in the Law*, ed. Peter Brooks and Paul Gewirtz (New Haven, CT: Yale University Press, 1999), 49. Miranda Fricker provides a Bourdieu-like analysis of the sources of what could be called legal capital. "Testimonial injustice occurs when prejudice causes a hearer to give a deflated level of credibility to a speaker's word; hermeneutical injustice occurs at a prior stage, when a gap in collective interpretive resources puts someone at an unfair disadvantage when it comes to making sense of their social experiences. … You might say that testimonial injustice is caused by prejudice in the economy of credibility; and that hermeneutical injustice is caused by structural prejudice in the economy of collective hermeneutical resources." *Epistemic Injustice, Power and the Ethics of Knowing* (Oxford: Oxford University Press, 2007), 1. For an interpretation of the cultural,

gender, and economic context within which Zoora Shah was led to kill Mohammed Azam, see Samia Bano and Pragna Patel, "*R v Zoora (Ghulam) Shah* – Judgment," in *Feminist Judgments: From Theory to Practice*, ed. Rosemary Hunter, Clare McGlynn, and Erika Rackley (Oxford: Hart Publishing, 2010), 278–91.

35 However, according to Bano and Patel, the situation is more complex as clinical depression does not preclude agency ("*R v Zoora (Ghulam) Shah*," 286–7).

36 Anna Carline, "Resignifications and Subversive Transformations: Judith Butler's Queer Theory and Women Who Kill," *Liverpool Law Review* 27, no. 3 (2006): 323.

37 Carline, "Women Who Kill Their Abusive Partners," 39 (endnotes omitted).

38 Peter Goodrich, "Antirrhesis," *The Fate of the Law*, ed. Austin Sarat and Thomas R. Kearns (Ann Arbor: University of Michigan Press, 1991), 87.

39 Ravit Reichman, "Committed to Memory: Rebecca West's Nuremberg," in *Law and Catastrophe*, ed. Austin Sarat, Lawrence Douglas, and Martha Merrill Umphrey (Stanford, CA: Stanford University Press, 2007), 91.

40 Ratna Kapur, "Dark Times for Liberal Intellectual Thought," in *Profession*, ed. Rosemary G. Feal (New York: Modern Language Association, 2006), 23–4.

41 Joanne Conaghan, "Reassessing the Feminist Theoretical Project in Law," *Journal of Law and Society* 27, no. 3 (2000): 365–6.

42 Bourdieu ascribes this flexibility to law in the following: "Interpretation causes a *historicization of the norm* by adapting sources to new circumstances, by discovering new possibilities within them, and by eliminating what has been superseded or become obsolete. Given the extraordinary elasticity of texts, which can go as far as complete indeterminacy or ambiguity, the hermeneutic operation of the *declaration* (judgment) benefits from considerable freedom. It is not rare for the law, as a docile, adaptable, supple instrument, to be obliged to the *ex post facto* rationalization of decisions in which it had no part. To varying degrees, jurists and judges have at their disposal the power to exploit the polysemy or the ambiguity of legal formulas by appealing to such rhetorical devices as *restrictio* (narrowing), a procedure necessary to avoid applying a law which, literally understood, ought to be applied; *extensio* (broadening), a procedure which allows application of a law which, taken literally, ought not to be applied; and a whole series of techniques like analogy and the distinction of letter and spirit, which tend to maximize the law's elasticity, and even its contradictions, ambiguities, and lacunae" ("Force of Law, 827).

43 Helen Irving, *Gender and the Constitution: Equity and Agency in Comparative Constitutional Design* (Cambridge: Cambridge University Press, 2008), 60. The internal quote is taken from Aharon Barak, *Purposive Interpretation in Law* (Princeton, NJ: Princeton University Press, 2005), 377.
44 *Edwards v. Canada (Attorney General)* (1928) SCR 276.

6. The Legitimacy of the Family: Family Law and Gothic Fiction

1 Historical landmarks include acts about marriage, civil partnership, property, artificial insemination, children's rights, adoption, divorce, incest, guardianship, and domestic violence.
2 Mariana Valverde, *Law's Dream of a Common Knowledge* (Princeton, NJ: Princeton University Press, 2003), 6.
3 On law, testimonials, evidence, and truth in Gothic narratives, see Leslie J. Moran, "Gothic Law," *Griffith Law Review* 10, no. 2 (2001): 75–100; and Leslie J. Moran, "Law and the Gothic Imagination," in *The Gothic*, ed. Fred Botting (Woodbridge, UK: D.S. Brewer, 2001), 87–109. For an analysis of the representation of the law in eighteenth- and nineteenth-century Gothic pulp literature, see Diane Long Hoeveler and James D. Jenkins, "Where the Evidence Leads: Gothic Narratives and Legal Technologies," *European Romantic Review* 18, no. 3 (July 2007): 317–37. For an analysis of the representation and critique of law in Charles Dickens's writings, see Gill Ballinger, "Haunting the Law: Aspects of Gothic in Dickens's Fiction," *Gothic Studies* 10, no. 2 (November 2008): 35–50. For an analysis of the construct of black subjectivity according to white moral standards of morality in US slavery law and Gothic fiction, see Jeanne Elders DeWaard, "'The Shadow of Law': Sentimental Interiority, Gothic Terror, and the Legal Subject," *Arizona Quarterly: A Journal of American Literature, Culture, and Theory* 62, no. 4 (Winter 2006): 1–30.
4 David Punter, *Gothic Pathologies: The Text, the Body and the Law* (Houndmills, UK: Macmillan Press, 1998), 12.
5 Ibid., 2.
6 Ibid., 3.
7 Ibid., 8.
8 Sue Chaplin, *The Gothic and the Rule of Law, 1764–1820* (Houndmills, UK: Palgrave Macmillan, 2007). See also Andrew N. Sharpe, who analyses the transformation of the legal category of the monster in the shift from medieval and Renaissance English law to William Blackstone's legal commentaries in the eighteenth century in "England's Legal Monsters," *Law, Culture and the Humanities* 5, no. 1 (2009): 100–30.

9 Chaplin, *Gothic and the Rule of Law*, 40-44. Referring to Coke's *Institutes of the Laws of England* (1628) and Blackstone's *Commentaries*, Moran argues that "the Common Law, as unwritten law, is represented as a nascent wisdom revealed in precedent. A repetition and a return locates the wisdom and truth of the legal order in an archaic past, a time immemorial, a medieval time made present" ("Law and the Gothic Imagination," 89).
10 Chaplin, *Gothic and the Rule of* Law, 45.
11 Ibid.
12 Michael Gamer, "Genres for the Prosecution: Pornography and the Gothic," *PMLA* 114, no. 5 (October 1999): 1046.
13 Ibid., 1051.
14 Gamer's analysis reinforces what Michel Foucault identified as a historical relation between law and literature emerging in the aftermath of copyrights laws. "It is as if the author, at the moment he was accepted into the social order of property which governs our culture, was compensating for his new status by reviving the older bipolar field of discourse in a systematic practice of transgression and by restoring the danger of writing which, on another side, had been conferred the benefits of property." "What Is an Author?" in *Language, Counter-Memory, Practice: Selected Essays and Interviews*, ed. Donald F. Bouchard and Sherry Simon, trans. Donald F. Bouchard and Sherry Simon (Ithaca, NY: Cornell University Press, 1977), 125.
15 Fred Botting refers to eighteenth-century aesthetic judgment and how "taste and refinement rigorously police aesthetic boundaries and defend the citadel of culture from debasement: the Gothic is definitely cast out into the realms of popular, low culture, useless, indulgent, fanciful, monstrous and unedifying." See Fred Botting, ed., Preface to *The Gothic* (Woodbridge, UK: D.S. Brewer, 2001), 2.
16 Peter F. Garrett states that "what Gothic most often reflects on is the sense of narrative *force*, the force of the desire to disturb and to be disturbed that joins tellers and their audiences and the counterforces that seek to control disturbance, the force of destiny that overwhelms characters, the force of repetition that generates multiplying versions." *Gothic Reflections: Narrative Force in Nineteenth-Century Fiction* (Ithaca, NY: Cornell University Press, 2003), 10.
17 Eve Kosofsky Sedgwick, *The Coherence of Gothic Conventions* (New York: Methuen, 1986). Fred Botting also underlines "the formulaic, repetitive and sensational patterns of Gothic writing throughout the period." *Limits of Horror: Technology, Bodies, Gothic* (Manchester: Manchester University Press, 2008), 102.
18 Judith Halberstam, *Skin Shows: Gothic Horror and the Technology of Monsters* (Durham, NC: Duke University Press, 1995), 22.

19 Botting, *Limits of Horror*, 108.

20 On the Romantic emergence of a new consciousness and the perception of the other as a mental picture, a spectre, or a haunting image, see Terry Castle, *The Female Thermometer: 18th-Century Culture and the Invention of the Uncanny* (Oxford: Oxford University Press, 1987).

21 As David Punter indicates, Gothic rhetoric is "given to ornateness, hyperbole, violent exclamation." *The Literature of Terror: A History of Gothic Fictions from 1765 to the Present Day* (London: Longman, 1980), 10. According to Chris Baldick, *Frankenstein* is characterized by "an abundant excess of meanings which [it] cannot … accommodate [with stability], a surplus of significance which overruns the enclosure of the novel's form to attract new and competing mythic revisions." *In Frankenstein's Shadow: Myth, Monstrosity, and Nineteenth-Century Writing* (Oxford: Clarendon Press, 1987), 33.

22 Jerrold E. Hogle historicizes the recurrent motif of the counterfeit in Gothic writing by associating the concept with a historical, cultural, and technological evolution of representation of truth towards simulacra and simulations fuelled by modern technology: the political rise of the middle class coincides with a collective and political definition of identity, which requires the abjection of undesirables for the sake of a social norm. This process of abjection is signified by the Gothic, whose emergence coincides with the rise of mercantilism and capitalistic industrialization, with counterfeits as the mobile, evolving, and proliferating signifiers of various political ideologies; see "The Gothic Ghost of the Counterfeit and the Progress of Abjection," in *A Companion to the Gothic*, ed. David Punter (Oxford: Blackwell, 2000), 293–304.

23 Chris Baldick and Robert Mighall, "Gothic Criticism," in *A Companion to the Gothic*, ed. David Punter (Oxford: Blackwell, 2000), 209–28; and Jerrold E. Hogle, "Introduction: The Gothic in Western Culture," in *The Cambridge Companion to Gothic Fiction* (Cambridge: Cambridge University Press, 2002). Emma J. Clery has argued that in Walpole's *Castle of Otranto*, "the quasi-feudal prophecy that hangs over the Castle of Otranto resonates with the very topical assumptions concerning the correspondence of estate and natural hierarchy, far from new but driven into aggressive articulacy by the growth in economic importance of the bourgeois, commercial sections of society." *The Rise of Supernatural Fiction 1762–1800* (Cambridge: Cambridge University Press, 1995), 73. Robert Miles maintains that the Gothic "deals in subjects no longer bound by traditional forms of authority. Beginning in a crisis of legitimacy, it is from the beginning ideologically self-aware." "The Gothic and Ideology," in *Approaches to Teaching Gothic Fiction: The British and American Traditions*, ed. Diane Long Hoeveler and Tamar Heller

(New York: Modern Language Association, 2003), 59. Following Foucault's notion that a historical awareness marks the advent of modernity, Dale Townshend argues that the genre's concern with history signals its modernity; see *The Orders of Gothic: Foucault, Lacan, and the Subject of Gothic Writing, 1764–1820* (New York: AMS Press, 2007). Teresa A. Goddu argues that American Gothic narratives disrupt national and foundational self-mythologizations by resurrecting what was politically repressed; see *Gothic America: Narrative, History, and Nation* (New York: Columbia University Press, 1997).

24 Miles, "Gothic and Ideology," 65.

25 Ibid., 61–2.

26 Robert Miles, "'Mother Radcliff': Radcliffe and the Female Gothic," in *The Female Gothic: New Directions*, ed. Diana Wallace and Andrew Smith (Basingstoke, UK: Palgrave Macmillan, 2009), 46. Miles also argues that earlier Gothic texts revolved around a family secret and a female figure haunted by the buried secrets of a father; see *Gothic Writing 1750–1820: A Genealogy* (London: Routledge, 1993), 131.

27 Botting, *Limits of Horror*, 29–30. Critics such as Sandra Gilbert and Susan Gubar, Kate F. Ellis, Alison Milbank, Maggie Kilgour, and Susanne Becker have all argued that the family is a major preoccupation throughout the Gothic tradition, one that emerged in *The Castle of Otranto* (1764). Townshend regards the Gothic novel as a family romance gone somewhat wrong and as a narrative of "Gothic paternity" (*Orders of Gothic*, 148). This preoccupation with kinship and the gender implications of the family as institution led to the rise of the critical category of the "female Gothic," coined by Ellen Moers, which produced a historical rereading of Gothic texts by women writers in the landmark publication *The Female Gothic*, ed. Juliann E. Fleenor (Montreal: Eden Press, 1983). Lauren Fitzgerald argues that common to the early female Gothic and to second-wave feminists' analyses of the Gothic is the trope of property: while the heroines of Radcliffe's novels made property claims on the paternal estate, feminist critics made property claims on the authorship and origins of the Gothic genre; see "Female Gothic and the Institutionalization of Gothic Studies," in *The Female Gothic: New Directions*, ed. Diana Wallace and Andrew Smith (Basingstoke, UK: Palgrave Macmillan, 2009), 13–25. However, one should also remember that Fleenor took into consideration both the popular and the "serious" Gothic, underlined the "formless" aspect of the Gothic (a current trope of Gothic studies), and historicized the (Female) Gothic; see her introduction to *Female Gothic*, 16. Whether we are dealing with Anne Williams's claim that "the mythos or structure informing [the]

Gothic category ... is the patriarchal family," Robert Miles's interpretation of the Female and Male Gothic as manifestations of a "gender-political 'unconscious' ... constraining and shaping the narrative imagination," Avril Horner and Sue Zlosnik's suggestion that "[the] threat of obliteration of the female self – whether through psychological abuse, physical incarceration, or actual murder – is something which informs all works we might describe as Female Gothic and is a particular dimension of the fear we recognize as Gothic in its origins," Laura Mulvey-Roberts's celebration of the demonic stigmatic or monstrous woman, or Stéphanie Genz's claim that the post-feminist Gothic is the site where "femininity is an actively pursued subject position that becomes available for a potentially subversive resignification that reinterprets the female body as an emblem of agency and empowerment" – in all cases, we come across critical tendencies that seek to find terms that will describe the protagonists' relation to social power from within and without heteronormativity. For above quotations, see Anne Williams, *Art of Darkness: A Poetics of Gothic* (Chicago: University of Chicago Press, 1995), 22; Miles, "'Mother Radcliff,'" 56; Avril Horner and Sue Zlosnik, "Female Gothic," in *Teaching the Gothic*, ed. Anna Powell and Andrew Smith (Houndmills, UK: Palgrave Macmillan, 2006), 114; Laura Mulvey-Roberts, "From Bluebeard's Bloody Chamber to Demonic Stigmatic," in *The Female Gothic: New Directions*, ed. Diana Wallace and Andrew Smith (Basingstoke, UK: Palgrave Macmillan, 2009), 98–114; Stéphanie Genz, "(Re)making the Body Beautiful: Postfeminist Cinderellas and Gothic Tales of Transformation," in *Postfeminist Gothic: Critical Interventions in Contemporary Culture*, ed. Benjamin A. Brabon and Stéphanie Genz (Houndmills, UK: Palgrave Macmillan, 2007), 74.

28 Botting, *Limits of Horror*, 25.

29 Peter Goodrich, "Visive Powers: Colours, Trees and Genres of Jurisdiction," *Law and Humanities* 2, no. 2 (2008): 218.

30 Peter Goodrich, *Oedipus Lex: Psychoanalysis, History, Law* (Berkeley: University of California Press, 1995), 83.

31 Ibid., 90.

32 The persistence of this fusion between state and family is indicated by Carol Pateman's 1988 analysis of the link between sex right and patriarchal power in both contract theory and *Patriarcha*, which Robert Filmer wrote in 1680, seven decades before the passing of the Marriage Act by Parliament in 1753; see *The Sexual Contract* (London: Polity Press, 1988). See also Donna Heiland's analysis of Manfred in *The Castle of Otranto* in light of Filmer's conception of monarchy as fatherhood, in *Gothic and Gender: An*

Introduction (Malden, MA: Blackwell, 2004). Townshend analyses the father of Filmer's description as a sovereign whose power of death and life over the child turns the child into bare life (*Orders of Gothic*, 107).

33 Moran, "Law and the Gothic Imagination," 93.

34 Etienne Balibar brings out the Freudian significance of *regia potestas* when he says that "genealogical [family] coercion is in excess of institutional coercion, which it charges with instinctual energy, but the logic of the apparatuses of power is also that which renders the father or the "parent" a sovereign despot, or the absolute master in the home." "The Invention of the Super-Ego: Freud and Kelsen 1922" (unpublished essay, n.d.), Microsoft Word file, 30, http://www.soundandsignifier.com/files/Balibar_The_Invention_of_the_Superego.doc.

35 The concept is also useful in avoiding homogeneous analyses of the past. On the one hand, Hannah Barker and Elaine Chalus question second-wave feminist assumptions about the effects of industrialization and the division of the public and private spheres. They distinguish between a patriarchal discourse and practices and trajectories that contradict this discourse. For instance, they argue that women participated in the development of literacy, commercialization of leisure, and expansion of consumer society, and Gothic female authors are certainly a case in point; see *Gender in Eighteenth-Century England: Roles, Representations and Responsibilities* (London: Addison Wesley Longman, 1997). On the other hand, in her comparative analysis of earlier Gothic narratives and of English law's invocation of a constitutional past as the guarantee of rights and justice, Marie Hockenhull Smith points out that "the women who were subject to the two particular areas of remedial law dealing with adultery and child custody suffered the law as a form of violence." "The Children Will Be 'Subject to the Infamy of Their Deluded and Unfortunate Mother': Rhetoric of the Courtroom, a Gothic Fantasy and a Plain Letter to the Lord Chancellor," *Law and Literature* 18, no. 3 (2006): 408.

36 Analysts share a common view of the historical evolution of the family and regard the 1970s as a major turning point, which saw the rise of divorce rates, the increased use of contraception, the increasing number of single mothers, and the birth of children outside marriage, but also the drop in baby adoption (as the child born out of wedlock is no longer banned as illegitimate), the rise of premarital sexual experience, and the emergence of widespread cohabitation (to which can be added today sexual partners' independent households). On this basis, one sees a transformation from marriage-based policy to parenthood-based policy; see Jane Lewis, "Family Policy in the Post-War Period," in *Cross Currents: Family Law and*

Policy in the United States and England, ed. Sanford N. Katz, John Eekelaar, and Mavis Maclean (Oxford: Oxford University Press, 2000), 81–110. At the same time, the pattern of control and regulation does not disappear but is displaced onto accommodating models; see Carol Smart, "Divorce in England 1950–2000: A Moral Tale?" in *Cross Currents: Family Law and Policy in the United States and England*, ed. Sanford N. Katz, John Eekelaar, and Mavis Maclean (Oxford: Oxford University Press, 2000), 363–86; and John Eekelaar, "The End of an Era?" in *Cross Currents: Family Law and Policy in the United States and England*, ed. Sanford N. Katz, John Eekelaar, and Mavis Maclean (Oxford: Oxford University Press, 2000), 637–55. In addition, this transformation took place in the context of renewed calls for family values during both the Margaret Thatcher and Tony Blair eras. So we are dealing with a see-saw pattern, betraying contradictions and tensions – in sum, a pattern of competing ways of telling and regulating the family. Similarly, John Dewar and Stephen Parker identify a major shift away from matrimony as the means to legitimize family ties to parenthood, fulfilling the same function in the context of divorce and multi-household families; see "English Family Law since World War II: From Status to Chaos," in *Cross Currents: Family Law and Policy in the United States and England*, ed. Sanford N. Katz, John Eekelaar, and Mavis Maclean (Oxford: Oxford University Press, 2000), 123–40.

37 Nicholas Abercrombie and Alan Warde, *Contemporary British Society* (Cambridge: Polity Press, 2003), 195.

38 Margaret Thatcher, quoted in Vivien Seal, *Whose Choice: Working Class Women and the Control of Fertility* (London: Fortress Books, 1991), 7, 8. Thatcher's family doxology has historical precedents. Quoting from seventeenth century texts by authors such as William Perkins, Goodrich describes the archetypal norms of the organization or economy of the household. "A woman is defined not intrinsically but extrinsically; she is a place, she is the *gynaeceum*, the mother, the inner household. To this the law adds a second and correlative duty: 'the woman is not to take liberty of wanderings and straying abroad from her owne house,' she is to stay rather at home 'in the mans knowledge' and within his walls. … She is … to tend the immortality of the husband, the continuance of the word, through the nurture of the children to a comparable obedience to the father. … The law states her place as ancillary or secondary; the woman waits, she remains, gestates or otherwise registers an external imperative. The worst of all feminine crimes, a kind of madness, is that of the woman who takes off or leaves the home, and whether adulterous or singular, such departure from her place, her guardian or lord, deprives a woman of all rights and

benefits, or dower and inheritance. To leave would be to abandon her place, to forsake her authorities, to think for herself, to think for oneself" (*Oedipus Lex*, 135). Raphael Samuel argues that "Mrs Thatcher used 'Victorian values' as a way of conjuring up lost innocence. Against a background of inner-city disturbances, such as those which swept the streets of Toxteth and Brixton in 1981, she pictures an older Britain where parents were strict, children good-mannered, hooliganism (she erroneously believed) unknown. … By a process of selective amnesia the past becomes a historical equivalent of the dream of primal bliss, or of the enchanted space which memory accords to childhood." *Island Stories: Unravelling Britain*, vol. 2 of *Theatres of Memory* (London: Verso Books, 1999), 337, 338.

39 Rhodes Boyson, quoted in Seal, *Whose Choice*, 7.

40 Alec Samuels, ed., Introduction to *Social Security and Family Law with Special Reference to the One-Parent Family: A Comparative Survey*, United Kingdom Comparative Law Series, vol. 4 (London: British Institute of International and Comparative Law, 1979), 7.

41 Ruth Deech, "The Work of the Law Commission in Family Law," in *Essays in Family Law*, ed. Michael D.A. Freeman (London: Stevens and Sons, 1986), 59.

42 See http://lawcommission.justice.gov.uk/index.htm.

43 Maggie Rae, "Fair, Just and Reasonable?" in *Family Law: Essays for the New Millennium*, ed. Stephen Cretney (Bristol: Family Law, 2000), 168. Legal commentaries on this recurrent discrepancy are too numerous to be quoted. With regard to planned parenthood in the late twentieth century, see John M. Paxman, who stated that "the law has not kept pace with the rapid developments in family planning technology and delivery systems over the past few years." *Law and Planned Parenthood* (London: International Planned Parenthood Federation, 1980), 10.

44 Katherine O'Donovan, "A New Settlement between the Sexes? Constitutional Law and the Citizenship of Women," in *Feminist Perspectives on the Foundational Subjects of Law*, ed. Anne Bottomley (London: Cavendish Publishing, 1996), 8.

45 Richard Collier, *Masculinity, Law and the Family* (London: Routledge, 1995), 52. In his statistical analysis of the historical evolution of family and household trends in the United Kingdom, Colin Gibson reports that "the proportion of households comprising a couple with children has been steadily falling in Britain since 1960. The period has seen the percentage of all households formed by single-family households with dependent children living in the home decline by 61% between 1961 (38 per cent) and 1998 (23 per cent). The same period has experienced a

noticeable move towards people living alone; the proportion formed by such single households has increased from 11 percent to 28 per cent." In addition, the "number of cohabitating couples is forecast to double, rising from 1.56 million in 1996 to nearly 3 million by 2021." "Changing Family Patterns in England and Wales over the Last Fifty Years," in *Cross Currents: Family Law and Policy in the United States and England*, ed. Sanford N. Katz, John Eekelaar, and Mavis Maclean (Oxford: Oxford University Press, 2000), 31, 33 (footnote omitted).

46 Katherine O'Donovan, *Family Matters* (London: Pluto Press, 1933), 39–40. Smart also argues that family discourse in the 1980s and 1990s rested on the notion of stability shored up by governmental policies and feeding into national stability. This discourse is common to the Thatcher era and New Labour government, both of which viewed divorce as a sign of social crisis. See "Divorce in England 1950–2000," 364–5.

47 This disruption of the family discourse recurs in twentieth-century Gothic texts such as Susan Hill's *I'm the King of the Castle* (1970), Ian McEwan's *The Cement Garden* (1978), Iain Banks's *The Wasp Factory* (1984), Ruth Rendell's *Heartstones* (1987), Doris Lessing's *The Fifth Child* (1988), Tobias Hill's *Underground* (1990), Elspeth Barker's *O Caledonia* (1991), Julie Myerson's *Sleepwalking* (1994), and Patrick McGrath's *Asylum* (1997).

48 Benjamin A. Brabon refers to the spectral phallus as "the signifier of the paradoxical shape of masculinity in contemporary society" and adds that 'the ghostly form of the spectral phallus is a symbol of presence and absence – the manifestation of an aggressive masculine identity and a lack thereof." "The Spectral Phallus: Re-Membering the Postfeminist Man," in *Postfeminist Gothic: Critical Interventions in Contemporary Culture*, ed. Benjamin A. Brabon and Stéphanie Genz (Houndmills, UK: Palgrave Macmillan, 2007), 58.

49 Drawing on Butler's concept of resignification through repetition of norms considered as sites of contestation and revision, Genz argues for a gap between the identification with models of femininity that are threatened with "phallocentricity, the spectre of heterosexism" and the contestation of the latter from within the process of identification. In doing so, the subject is situated between agency and subjectification, autonomy and vulnerability to the ghost of patriarchal history; see "(Re)making the Body Beautiful," 71, 74.

50 On the citational practices of the Gothic, see Jacqueline Howard, *Reading Gothic Fiction: A Bakhtinian Approach* (Oxford: Clarendon Press, 1994); Maggie Kilgour, *The Rise of the Gothic Novel* (London: Routledge, 1995); and Punter, *Gothic Pathologies*.

51 As critics of Gothic studies have repeatedly demonstrated, the treatment of space is key to Gothic narratives. See Nina Auerbach on the tyrannical homely settings in Jane Austen's novels in "Jane Austen and Romantic Imprisonment," in *Jane Austen in a Social Context*, ed. David Monaghan (London: Macmillan, 1981), 9–27. Kate Ferguson Ellis suggests that "what is radical in the Gothic solution is that the terms 'home' and 'world' are inverted: evil is thus enclosed in the home and freedom lies in the world beyond it, however dangerous." *The Contested Castle: Gothic Novels and the Subversion of Domestic Ideology* (Urbana: University of Illinois Press, 1989), 50. Williams states that "the nightmarish haunted house as Gothic setting puts into play the anxieties, tensions, and imbalances inherent in family structures" (*Art of Darkness*, 46). For Diane Long Hoeveler, the challenge for the Gothic heroine of the female Gothic text is to create "a social reality that goes beyond merely internalizing the prison, the asylum, the confessional; she must redeem those institutions and mark them as female controlled and female identified." *Gothic Feminism: The Professionalization of Gender from Charlotte Smith to the Brontës* (University Park: Pennsylvania State University Press, 1998), 22.

52 Michel Foucault elaborates on the notion of heterotopia in "Des espaces autres," originally a conference paper he presented in 1967 in Tunisia and then a journal article published in 1984; see *Dits et écrits: 1954–1988, vol. II: 1976–1988*, ed. Daniel Defert and François Ewald (Paris: Éditions Gallimard, 2001), 1571–81. He distinguishes between heterotopias of crisis and those of deviance, the latter characterized by six characteristics. The main idea I borrow from his text is the notion of spaces of deviance, or what I prefer to call "aberration." For Botting's specific use of the concept of heterotopia, see Fred Botting, "In Gothic Darkly: Heterotopia, History, Culture," in *A Companion to the Gothic*, ed. David Punter (Oxford: Blackwell, 2000), 3–14.

53 The transgression of the incest interdict constitutes a topos of Gothic literature. In her analysis of Horace Walpole's *The Mysterious Mother* (1768), Emma J. Clery identifies the character of the mother as not only a sexual but also a social troublemaker: on her husband's death, she inherits his estate, trumping her son's right to it, a dislocation redoubled by her sexual desire for her son and her wilful transgression of the incest taboo; see "Horace Walpole's *The Mysterious Mother* and the Impossibility of Female Desire," in *The Gothic*, ed. Fred Botting (Woodbridge, UK: D.S. Brewer, 2001), 23–46. For a Lacanian interpretation of the incest motif from *The Castle of Otranto* to Eliza Parson's *The Castle of Wolfenbach*, *The Monk*, and *Matilda*, see Townshend, *Orders of Gothic*. For an analysis of the

rhetoric of the sublime in the representation of incestuous desire in *The Castle of Otranto*, see Heiland, *Gothic and Gender*. For a close reading of Daphne du Maurier's and Iris Murdoch's use of incest in their writings, see Avril Horner and Sue Zlosnik, "Keeping It in the Family: Incest and the Female Gothic Plot in du Maurier and Murdoch," in *The Female Gothic: New Directions*, ed. Diana Wallace and Andrew Smith (Basingstoke, UK: Palgrave Macmillan, 2009), 115–32.

54 Luce Irigaray, "Women on the Market," in *This Sex Which Is Not One*, trans. Catherine Porter with Carolyn Burke (Ithaca, NY: Cornell University Press, 1985), 171.

55 Pierre Bourdieu provides a similar analysis when he accounts for the education of Kabyle children and their inculcation with a particular habitus through exposure to relatives. "At a deeper level, there are the relationships with the mother and the father, which, by their dissymmetry in antagonistic complementarity, constitute one of the opportunities to internalize, inseparably, the schemes of the sexual division of labour and of the division of sexual labour." *Outline of a Theory of Practice*, trans. Richard Nice (Cambridge: Cambridge University Press, 2009), 89.

56 Gayle Rubin, "The Traffic among Women: Notes on the 'Political Economy' of Sex," in *Toward an Anthropology of Women*, ed. R.R. Reiter (New York: Monthly Review, 1975), 279. Judith Butler reinforces this analysis. "The mother is disallowed because she belongs to the father, so if this prohibition is fundamental, and it is understood, then the father and the mother exist as logically necessary features of the prohibition itself." "Is Kinship Always Already Heterosexual?" in *Undoing Gender* (New York: Routledge, 2004), 119. See also Judith Butler, "Quandaries of the Incest Taboo," in *Undoing Gender* (New York: Routledge, 2004), 152–3.

57 The archival recording of this heteronormative construct is exemplified by the statutory language of the Sexual Offences Act 1956. Subs. 10(1) states, "It is an offence for a man to have sexual intercourse with a woman whom he knows to be his grand-daughter, daughter, sister or mother"; subs. 11(1) states, "It is an offence for a woman of the age of sixteen or over to permit a man whom she knows to be her grandfather, father, brother or son to have sexual intercourse with her by her consent." While the male legal subject is under an interdict, the female subject is suspected to knowingly aggravate the transgressing act by giving her consent.

58 Judith Butler, *Antigone's Claim: Kinship between Life and Death* (New York: Columbia University Press, 2000), 80.

59 Ibid., 66–7.

7. The Political Uncanny of the Family: Patricia Duncker's *The Deadly Space Between* and the Civil Partnership Act 2004

1 As Carl F. Stychin states, "The key changes brought about by the Civil Partnership Act, which transplant much of the laws of marriage, have been categorised by commentators as follows: creation and dissolution; recognition of foreign civil partnerships and foreign dissolution orders; financial relief in the High Court, county court and magistrates' court; wills, intestacy, family provision and fatal accident claims; succession to and transfer of tenancies; residence, contact orders, and application for parental responsibility in relation to children; domestic violence related orders; social security benefits and tax credits; and pension provision." "Not (Quite) a Horse and Carriage: The Civil Partnership Act 2004," *Feminist Legal Studies* 14, no. 1 (2006): 82. Because the name of the act is used so frequently in this chapter, I have used the acronym CPA.

2 On the fragmentation of the family, see Richard Collier, *Masculinity, Law and the Family* (London: Routledge, 1995); Fatemeh Ebtehaj, Bridget Lindley, and Martin Richards, eds., *Kinship Matters* (Oxford: Hart Publishing, 2006); Richard Collier and Sally Sheldon, *Fragmenting Fatherhood: A Socio-Legal Study* (Oxford: Hart Publishing, 2008); and Julie McCandless, "Recognising Family Diversity: The 'Boundaries' of Re G," *Feminist Legal Studies* 13, no. 3 (2005): 323–36.

3 Martha Albertson Fineman, *The Neutered Mother, the Sexual Family and Other Twentieth Century Tragedies* (New York: Routledge, 1995), 145.

4 Davina Cooper, "Like Counting Stars? Equality and the Socio-Legal Space of Same-Sex Marriage," in *Legal Recognition of Same-Sex Partnerships: A Study of National, European and International Law*, ed. Robert Wintemute and Mads Andenaes (Oxford: Hart Publishing, 2001), 85.

5 Marilyn Strathern, "Displacing Knowledge: Technology and the Consequences for Kinship," in *Conceiving the New World Order: The Global Politics of Reproduction*, ed. Faye D. Ginsburg and Rayna Rapp (Berkeley: University of California Press, 1995), 351.

6 Ibid., 352.

7 Ibid., 355.

8 Nan D. Hunter, "Marriage, Law, and Gender: A Feminist Inquiry," *Lesbian and Gay Legal Issues* 1 no. 9 (1991): 17, 18.

9 Didi Herman, *Rights of Passage: Struggles for Gay and Lesbian Legal Equality* (Toronto: University of Toronto Press, 1994), 145.

10 Herman argues that "from the perspective of many lesbians and gay men, human rights struggles were … not about rights *per se*, but about what rights were thought to signify – public/official recognition,

social citizenship, and identification. In this sense, then, the demand for lesbian and gay rights is a struggle for membership in the human community" (ibid., 19). William N. Eskridge maintains that "without the right to marry, gay Americans are second-class citizens." *The Case for Same-Sex Marriage: From Sexual Liberty to Civilized Commitment* (New York: Free Press, 1996), 62. For Cheshire Calhoun, "being fit for marriage is intimately bound up with our cultural conception of what it means to be a citizen. ... Only those who are fit to enter marital and family life deserve full civic status." *Feminism, the Family, and the Politics of the Closet: Lesbian and Gay Displacement* (Oxford: Oxford University Press, 2000), 108. Several critics have argued that same-sex marriage provides same-sex couples equal access to social status, recognition, and economic benefits and obligations; see Celia Kitzinger and Sue Wilkinson, "The Re-branding of Marriage: Why We Got Married Instead of Registering a Civil Partnership," *Feminism & Psychology* 14, no. 1 (2004): 127–50; Maria Bevacqua, "Feminist Theory and the Question of Lesbian and Gay Marriage," *Feminism & Psychology* 14, no. 1 (2004): 36–40; and Kevin Bourassa, "Love and the Lexicon of Marriage," *Feminism & Psychology* 14, no. 1 (2004): 57–62. However, for a critique of the ways in which the recognition and constitution of sexual citizenship incur disciplinary and domesticating costs, such as the legitimation of gays and lesbians through matrimony and the border patrolling of sexual discourse in hip hop and pornographic productions, see Brenda Cossman, *Sexual Citizens: The Legal and Cultural Regulation of Sex and Belonging* (Palo Alto, CA: Stanford University Press, 2007). In 2002, Michael Warner stated, "In the modern era, marriage has become the central legitimating institution by which the state regulates and permeates people's most intimate lives; it is the zone of privacy outside of which sex is unprotected. ... The language of the love-couple ... wants recognition. It wants to rule." "Beyond Gay Marriage," in *Left Legalism / Left Critique*, ed. Wendy Brown and Janet Halley (Durham, NC: Duke University Press, 2002), 267, 272.

11 Beccy Shipman and Carol Smart, "'It's Made a Huge Difference': Recognition, Rights and the Personal Significance of Civil Partnership," *Sociological Research Online* 12, no. 1 (2007): n.p., http://www.socresonline.org.uk/12/1/shipman.html.

12 Discussing the relative unimportance of marriage, Rosemary Auchmuty reports the following figures: "Only 250,000 marriages took place in England and Wales in 2001, the lowest number for more than a century. The past 30 years in particular have seen a rapid decrease (40 percent) in the national rate. ... Cohabitation has become so common as to seem

completely normal, and two out of every five children are born out of wedlock." "Same-Sex Marriage Revived: Feminist Critique and Legal Strategy," *Feminism & Psychology* 14, no. 1 (2004): 116.

13 William Rountree, "Contract and the Legal Mooring of Same-Sex Intimacy," in *Regulating Sex: The Politics of Intimacy and Identity*, ed. Elizabeth Bernstein and Laurie Schaffner (New York: Routledge, 2005), 22.

14 Ruthann Robson develops a similar critique of the predominance of a liberal approach within law, which pluralizes the concept of the family rather than re-examine its foundations; see *Sappho Goes to Law School: Fragments in Lesbian Legal Theory* (New York: Columbia University Press, 1998), 158.

15 Leslie J. Moran, "The Homosexualization of English Law," in *Legal Inversions: Lesbians, Gay Men, and the Politics of Law*, ed. Didi Herman and Carl F. Stychin (Philadelphia: Temple University Press, 1995), 15.

16 Robson, *Sappho Goes to Law School*, 170.

17 Moran, "Homosexualization of English Law," 15.

18 Thus, Duncker's novel is inscribed in a Gothic tradition that according to Steven Bruhm, offers narratives contesting constructs of sexuality and the power that derives from these constructs; see "Gothic Sexualities," in *Teaching the Gothic*, ed. Anna Powell and Andrew Smith (Houndmills, UK: Palgrave Macmillan, 2006), 93–106. In her analysis of early Gothic, Eve Kosofsky Sedgwick argues, "Notoriously … the Gothic seems to offer a privileged view of individual and family psychology. Certain features of the Oedipal family are insistently foregrounded there: absolutes of license and prohibition, for instance; a preoccupation with possibilities of incest; a fascinated proscription of sexual activity; an atmosphere dominated by the threat of violence between generations." *The Coherence of Gothic Conventions* (New York: Methuen, 1986), 91. William Hughes argues that Poppy Z. Brite's *Lost Souls* can be read as the construct of a gay community that does not reproduce the heteronormative family based on blood ties, inheritance, and property and that aggressively asserts its difference; see "'The Taste of Blood Meant the End of Aloneness': Vampires and Gay Men in Poppy Z. Brite's *Lost Souls*," in *Queering the Gothic*, ed. William Hughes and Andrew Smith (Manchester: Manchester University Press, 2009), 142–56.

19 The few analyses of Duncker's novel range from perplexity to incomprehension. Laura Fraser argues that "the characters are going through the motions of what seem to be the historical and mythological consequences of the actions of a long string of psychological archetypes, but we don't fully understand them as people." "Frankenstein as a Modern Monster: Secrets, Incest and Intrigue Enter a Boy's Life with a

Mysterious Stranger," review of *The Deadly Space Between*, by Patricia Duncker, *SF Gate*, 7 July 2002, http://articles.sfgate.com/2002-07-07/books/17555065_1_patricia-duncker-roehm-tobias. Helen Stevenson maintains that Duncker was unable to provide a clear distinction between fantasy and narrative facts; see "*The Deadly Space Between* by Patricia Duncker: This Oedipus Is Too Complex." *Independent* (UK), 2002, accessed 23 March 2007, http://www.independent.co.uk/arts-entertainment/books/reviews/the-deadly-space-between-by-patricia-duncker-657411.html.

20 Interpretations such as Laura Mulvey-Roberts's analysis of *Frankenstein* as a palimpsest of exhumation, purification, rebirth, and reunion have turned Shelley's text into an archetype of Gothic genesis and kinship; see "The Corpse in the Corpus: Frankenstein, Rewriting Wollstonecraft and the Abject," in *Mary Shelley's Fictions: From Frankenstein to Falkner*, ed. Michael Eberle-Sinatra and Nora Crook (Houndmills, UK: Macmillan, 2000), 197–210. Duncker's novel belongs to this literary genealogy.

21 David Punter, *Gothic Pathologies: The Text, the Body and the Law* (Houndmills, UK: Macmillan Press, 1998), 11.

22 In this sense, Duncker's novel is inscribed in a Gothic tradition going back to *The Castle of Otranto* (1764). Kathy Justice Gentile has argued that "we reconceive Walpole's flagrant breaches of rhetorical and literary decorum as constituting the first fully tricked-out Gothic drag show … the grossly inflated supernatural imagery, hyperbolic passions of the characters, fantastic plot turns, and excessive accretions of terror-evoking details in *Otranto* constitute an assemblage of rhetorical effects that coalesce into the granddaddy of Gothic drag." "Sublime Drag: Supernatural Masculinity in Gothic Fiction," *Gothic Studies* 11, no. 1 (May 2009): 17, 18.

23 The comparison between Duncker's novel and the critical position she expressed in her critique of Angela Carter's rewriting of fairy tales is almost inevitable. In "Re-imagining the Fairy Tales: Angela Carter's Bloody Chambers," *Literature and History* 10, no. 1 (Spring 1984): 3–14, Patricia Duncker's critique rests on the claim that Carter was unable to dismantle the ideology of masculine domination and the gender binaries underlying the transmission of fairy tales during the rise of the bourgeoisie in the seventeenth and eighteenth centuries. Without establishing a simplistic correlation between Duncker's critical discourse and her fictional writing, it is nevertheless clear that, in her novel, she seeks to dismantle those binaries. At the same time, the representation of domination takes an unpredictable turn and reflects a higher degree of complexity and ambivalence than occurs in her critical statements. In

this sense, Duncker's novel can be read in light of Sue-Ellen Case's claim that "the queer, unlike the rather polite categories of gay and lesbian, revels in the discourse of the loathsome, the outcast, the idiomatically-proscribed position of same-sex desire. … The queer is the taboo-breaker, the monstrous, the uncanny." "Tracking the Vampire," *Differences: A Journal of Feminist Cultural Studies* 3, no. 2 (1991): 3.

24 Patricia Duncker, *The Deadly Space Between* (New York: Harper Collins, 2002), 9.

25 Ibid., 11.

26 Ibid., 25.

27 Ibid., 107.

28 Ibid., 34.

29 Ibid., 218.

30 Ibid., 7.

31 Cooper, "Like Counting Stars?," 82.

32 Duncker, *Deadly Space Between*, 116.

33 Ibid., 111–12.

34 Ibid., 33–4.

35 Eve Kosofsky Sedgwick, *Between Men: English Literature and Male Homosocial Desire* (New York: Columbia University Press, 1985), 106. For the centrality of incestuous transgression in queer Gothic fiction and its challenge to the taboo as a means of organizing patriarchal heteronormativity, see George E. Haggerty, *Queer Gothic* (Urbana: University of Illinois Press, 2006), 19. Ellis Hanson takes Sedgwick's analysis one step further. "However haunted it may be by the spectre of Freud, queer theory's main contribution to criticism on the Gothic has been a historicizing, Foucaultian challenge to the pathologizing topologies of psychoanalysis. It has also taken the Gothic as a paradigm for modern moral panics about sexuality and a paradigm even for literary criticism itself insofar as it has been preoccupied with a 'hermeneutics of suspicion.' It has further offered a richly historical and political language for valorizing those disreputable sexualities that the Gothic has traditionally rendered monstrous, not so much to purge them as to invest them with a sublime narrative energy." "Queer Gothic," in *The Routledge Companion to Gothic*, ed. Catherine Spooner and Emma McEvoy (London: Routledge, 2007), 176.

36 Duncker, *Deadly Space Between*, 179.

37 Eric Savoy considers the ghost and the trope of haunting in terms of prosopopoeia by which "the other is named, imag(in)ed, embodied: governed by the desire to make the absent, the dead, the abstract

present and palpable, its Gothic potential is always latent." "Spectres of Abjection: The Queer Subject of James's 'The Jolly Corner,'" in *Spectral Readings: Towards a Gothic Geography*, ed. Glennis Byron and David Punter (Houndmills, UK: Macmillan, 1990), 162. I suggest that both prosopopoeia and catachresis rhetorically convey the paradox of the ghost.

38 In a different context, Terry Castle has explored the significance of the phantasmal in the representation of lesbian desire. Focusing on the apparitional figure as a metaphor for "recognition through negation," she argues that the metaphor functions as a resource for making the body visible and recognizable – an "uncanny return to the flesh." *The Apparitional Lesbian: Female Homosexuality and Modern Culture* (New York: Columbia University Press, 1993), 60, 63.

39 Judith Butler, "Is Kinship Always Already Heterosexual?," *in Undoing Gender* (New York: Routledge, 2004), 128.

40 In 1999, Michael D.A. Freeman projected the next twenty years of family legislation in prescient terms. "Cohabitation will become more and more like marriage, or marriage more and more like cohabitation. … Same-sex marriages, though barely on the agenda in this country, will be allowed. So, of course, will the marriage of transsexuals. These concessions to pluralism will liberalize, but will also colonize – the state gaining control of a wider range of relationships." "Family Values and Family Justice," in *Family, State, and Law*, vol. 1, ed. Michael D.A. Freeman (Dartmouth, UK: Ashgate Publishing, 1999), 551.

41 The pitfalls of legal analogical reasoning in the context of family law have been analysed by several legal thinkers. See Mary Eaton's critique of the use of analogy in *Williamson v. A.G. Edwards and Sons Inc.* and *Watkins v. U.S. Army* in "Homosexual Unmodified," in *Legal Inversions: Lesbians, Gay Men, and the Politics of Law*, ed. Didi Herman and Carl F. Stychin (Philadelphia: Temple University Press, 1995), 46–73. For the claim that analogical thinking has the capacity to erase history through a process of abstraction, see Siobhan Somerville, "Queer Loving," *GLQ: A Journal of Gay and Lesbian Studies* 11, no. 3 (2005): 335–70. More recently, Reg Graycar and Jenny Morgan refer to the discussion paper published in Australia by the Gay and Lesbian Rights Lobby, *The Bride Wore Pink*, in which the community "raised questions about issues such as why certain rights and obligations automatically flow from marriage … and why marriage is always presumed to be the benchmark or standard against which other relationships are compared." "Equality Rights: What's Wrong?" in *Rethinking Equality Projects in Law: Feminist Challenges*, ed. Rosemary Hunter (Oxford: Hart Publishing, 2008), 117.

42 Marriage Act, subs. 45A(4), http://www.legislation.gov.uk/ukpga/Geo6/12-13-14/76/section/45A.

43 Mark Potter's decision can be read in *Wilkinson v. Kitzinger* [2006] EWHC 2022 (Fam), para. 88, http://www.bailii.org/ew/cases/EWHC/Fam/2006/2022.html. In para. 11, the president of the Family Division cites Penzance's definition of marriage in *Hyde v. Hyde* (1866) as "the voluntary union for life of one man and one woman, to the exclusion of all others."

44 CPA, subs. 2(5), http://www.legislation.gov.uk/ukpga/2004/33/section/2.

45 For Andrew Bainham, "The new status of civil partnership has been deliberately constructed to resemble marriage closely, but without extending marriage as such to same-sex couples, principally because of the religious connotations of holy matrimony. The government seems to have been determined to strike a balance between its steadfast refusal to accept same-sex marriage and its anxiety to comply with human rights obligations." "Status Anxiety? The Rush for Family Recognition," in *Kinship Matters*, ed. Fatemeh Ebtehaj, Bridget Lindley, and Martin Richards (Oxford: Hart Publishing, 2006), 52.

46 CPA, subs. 50(1)(c), http://www.legislation.gov.uk/ukpga/2004/33/section/50. On the awkwardness of the provision in the case of same-sex partnership, see also Rosie Harding and Elizabeth Peele, "'We Do'? International Perspectives on Equality, Legality and Same-Sex Relationships," *Lesbian & Gay Psychology Review* 7, no. 2 (2006): 135.

47 Adopting a Foucaultian approach, Rosie Harding argues that "the 'disciplining' of lesbians, gay men and others into heteronormative ways of living highlights the methods by which power continues to be exercised as domination, and that disciplinary mechanisms of power have not completely colonised or dislodged juridical power." *Regulating Sexuality: Legal Consciousness in Lesbian and Gay Lives* (London: Routledge, 2011), 42.

48 Cooper, "Like Counting Stars?," 85.

49 Nancy D. Polikoff argues that what began as a movement for pluralism got bogged down in a civil rights victory for formal equality that left both same-sex and different-sex people living in non-married and caregiving domestic arrangements ousted from a system that rewards matrimony with rights and benefits; see *Beyond (Straight and Gay) Marriage: Valuing All Families under the Law* (Boston, MA: Beacon Press, 2008). Polikoff's argument reflects a larger movement in the evolution of LGBTQ political activism in the United States, which through internal dissent and contestation has created a fascinating platform not only questioning formal

equality but also dismantling the binary between same-sex "lifestyles" and heteronormativity. In "Beyond Same-Sex Marriage: A New Strategic Vision for All Our Families & Relationships July 26, 2006," the signatories call for *strategies* to support a pluralist conception of families in the name of a vision of social and economic justice for all, http://www.beyondmarriage.org/full_statement.html.

50 Stychin, "Not (Quite) a Horse and Carriage," 83. For a critique of the CPA as a manifestation of the government's legal conservatism and a piece of legislation aimed at instituting a sense of sexual and social responsibility among gays and lesbians, see also Carl F. Stychin, "Family Friendly? Rights, Responsibilities and Relationship Recognition," in *Feminist Perspectives on Family Law*, ed. Alison Diduck and Katherine O'Donovan (Abingdon, UK: Routledge-Cavendish, 2006), 21–37. Harding suggests that "the absence of a legal requirement for consummation and the absence of 'adultery' as a ground for dissolution could be read as an exercise in creating a legal framework more suited to the realities of same-sex relationships, giving legal 'support' to the differences between same- and difference-sex relationships and recognising that monogamy can be less salient in same-sex relationships" (*Regulating Sexuality*, 5). I have my doubts about such a generous interpretation, which may speak more to an appropriation of the regulation of sexuality for resistance's sake than to far-seeing legislation.

51 Stephen M. Cretney, *Same Sex Relationships: From "Odious Crime" to "Gay Marriage"* (Oxford: Oxford University Press, 2006), 23.

52 Leslie J. Moran develops an analysis of the Gothic in law by focusing on the interplay between silence and language and its proscribing and spectralizing effects in former laws on sodomy, in which the act was supposed to be referred to as "not to be named amongst Christians," a formula Coke used in his *Of Buggery or Sodomy* (1628); see "Law and the Gothic Imagination," in *The Gothic*, ed. Fred Botting (Woodbridge, UK: D.S. Brewer, 2001), 87–109.

53 Cretney, *Same Sex Relationships*, 33–4.

54 Ibid., 33; also noted by Bainham in "Status Anxiety?," 56.

55 CPA, Schedule 1, Part 1, subs. 1(2), http://www.legislation.gov.uk/ukpga/2004/33/schedule/1.

56 Cretney, *Same Sex Relationships*, 36.

57 Ibid., 37.

58 On Dorothy Allison's writing about incest in *Bastard out of Carolina* and *Two or Three Things I Know for Sure*, Ann Cvetkovich writes, "Allison opens up a terrain of the unsaid that goes beyond the act of incest itself to the

psychic complexity of an aftermath that includes flashbacks along with the commingling of 'desire and hatred.' Amid a proliferation of confessional stories and a culture that consumes them voyeuristically, Allison suggests that there are stories that have not yet been told or heard because they are too disturbing." *An Archive of Feelings: Trauma, Sexuality, and Lesbian Public Cultures* (Durham, NC: Duke University Press, 2003), 108.

59 Analysing *Ulane v. Eastern Airlines, Inc.*, 742 F.2d 1081 (7th Cir. 1984), in which Kenneth Ulane, a pilot for Eastern Airlines, was fired after having sex-reassignment surgery, Lisa C. Bower refers to the "moments in which the law recognizes nonidentity as well as the legal tendency to contain the insights such moments might afford." "Queer Acts and the 'Politics of Direct Address': Rethinking Law, Culture, and Community," *Law & Society Review* 28, no. 5 (1994): 1014.

60 While analysing sovereignty in the context of colonial history, and being critical of Agamben's thesis, Megan Wachspress posits a crucial link between the regulation of difference and the exercise of sovereignty through law. In the cases she considers, "sovereignty as a legal concept … was grounded in anxieties about culturally or biologically constituted difference *and* a felt need to impose order across those differences." "Rethinking Sovereignty with Reference to History and Anthropology," *International Journal of Law in Context* 5, no. 3 (2009): 326.

61 On the nexus among nationalism, power, and sexual normativity, see Sally Munt's analysis of the conflict between Queer Nation and American Irish nationalism in *Queer Attachments: The Cultural Politics of Shame* (Aldershot, UK: Ashgate Publishing, 2007). On nationalism, discourses of kinship, and social recognition in France, see Butler's "Is Kinship Always Already Heterosexual?" On the recentring of the family in the communitarian, pluralistic approach of New Labour in a modernized and civil national space, see Carl F. Stychin, *Governing Sexuality: The Changing Politics of Citizenship and Law Reform* (Oxford: Hart Publishing, 2003), 25–47. On the sexual politics of national identity and the conflict over gays in the military, see Steven Seidman, "From Outsider to Citizen," in *Regulating Sex: The Politics of Intimacy and Identity*, ed. Elizabeth Bernstein and Laurie Schaffner (New York: Routledge, 2005), 225–45. Other authors on the topic include Shane Phelan, *Sexual Strangers: Gays, Lesbians, and Dilemmas of Citizenship* (Philadelphia: Temple University Press, 2001); Maro Pantelidou Maloutas, *The Gender of Democracy: Citizenship and Gendered Subjectivity* (London: Routledge, 2006); Davina Cooper, *Sexing the City: Lesbian and Gay Politics within the Activist State* (London: Rivers Oram Press, 1994); Lauren Berlant, *The Queen of America Goes to Washington City: Essays on Sex and*

Citizenship (Durham, NC: Duke University Press, 1997); and Martha A. Ackelsberg, *Resisting Citizenship: Feminist Essays on Politics, Community, and Democracy* (New York: Routledge, 2010).

62 Cooper, "Like Counting Stars?," 83.

63 Andrew N. Sharpe argues that "in the context of the Gender Recognition Act, it is through the legislative provision rendering non-disclosure of gender history a ground for annulment of marriage that we witness the return of sex. Thus while recognising a male to female transgender woman as female for the purposes of law, ostensibly on account of her gender, it is clear that in the event of nondisclosure it is her sex, in the sense of her biological past, around which law constructs the 'truth.' For when faced with the ever-present possibility of inadvertent communion with the homosexual, law's commitment to incorporating transgender people within the gender order becomes more suspect." "Endless Sex: The Gender Recognition Act 2004 and the Persistence of a Legal Category," *Feminist Legal Studies* 15, no. 1 (2007): 82. For other analyses of the same act, see Sharon Cowan, "'Gender Is No Substitute for Sex': A Comparative Human Rights Analysis of the Legal Regulation of Sexual Identity," *Feminist Legal Studies* 13, no. 1 (2005): 67–96; and Ralph Sandland, "Feminism and the Gender Recognition Act 2004," *Feminist Legal Studies* 13, no. 1 (2005): 43–66.

64 Duncker, *Deadly Space Between*, 69–70.

65 Ibid., 125.

66 Ibid.

67 Mair Rigby's analysis of the queer Gothic sheds light on the psychic power at play in Toby's narrative. "Uncanny, potentially erotic, overwhelming and paranoia-inducing, one consistent quality of the condition I would like to call 'queer Gothic recognition' is a sense of enthrallment to a more powerful, more knowing figure, one who wields an inexplicable and dangerous power to arrest and dominate." "'Do You Share My Madness?' Frankenstein's Queer Gothic," in *Queering the Gothic*, ed. William Hughes and Andrew Smith (Manchester: Manchester University Press, 2009), 41.

68 Duncker's novel itself is caught in a web of novelistic as well as psychoanalytical and critical texts. For instance, Peter Brooks refers to the recurrence of primal scenes in Shelley's novel and suggests an anticipation of Freud's narrative of the Wolf Man in the scene that describes Frankenstein witnessing the birth of the Monster; see "What Is a Monster? (According to Frankenstein)," chap. 7 in *Body Work: Objects of Desire in Modern Narrative* (Cambridge, MA: Harvard University Press, 1993), 216. This proliferation of Freudian and Oedipal tropes can be read in the context of Judith Halberstam's analysis. "The cannibalism of the

Gothic form, its consumption of its own sources, allows for the infinitude of interpretations because each fear, each literary source, each desire, each historical event, each social structure that the text preys upon becomes fuel for the manufacture of meaning." *Skin Shows: Gothic Horror and the Technology of Monsters* (Durham, NC: Duke University Press, 1995), 34.

69 Duncker, *Deadly Space Between*, 116.

70 Ibid., 89–91.

71 Ibid., 100. For an analysis of the discourse of lycanthropy as sexual deviance, see Gina Wisker, "Devouring Desires: Lesbian Gothic Horror," in *Queering the Gothic*, ed. William Hughes and Andrew Smith (Manchester: Manchester University Press, 2009), 128.

72 Judith Butler, *Giving an Account of Oneself* (New York: Fordham University Press, 2005), 37.

73 Judith Butler, *The Psychic Life of Power* (Stanford, CA: Stanford University Press, 1997), 3–4.

74 Halberstam, *Skin Shows*, 31.

75 Punter interprets this hauntology as central to Gothic writing; see *Gothic Pathologies*, 14.

76 Duncker, *Deadly Space Between*, 62.

77 Ibid., 246.

78 Ibid., 204.

79 Ibid., 60.

80 Ibid., 139.

81 Ibid., 147–8.

82 Analysing the ice world in Shelley's *Frankenstein*, Rigby discusses the "production of certain spaces as queer and queer desires as marginal, strange, deathly and even 'Gothic' conditions." "'Do You Share My Madness?,'" 46. For a queer reading of *Frankenstein*, see Sedgwick, *Coherence of Gothic Conventions*; Brooks, "What Is a Monster?"; Halberstam, *Skin Shows*; and Michael Eberle-Sinatra, "Readings of Homosexuality in Mary Shelley's *Frankenstein* and Four Film Adaptations," *Gothic Studies* 7, no. 2 (2005): 185–202.

83 Duncker, *Deadly Space Between*, 70.

84 The law qualifies prohibited degrees of relationship as follows: "Any such marriage as is mentioned in subsection (2) of this section shall not be void by reason only of affinity if both the parties to the marriage have attained the age of twenty-one at the time of the marriage and the younger party has not at any time before attaining the age of eighteen been a child of the family in relation to the other party"; see Marriage Act, subs. 2(3), http://www.legislation.gov.uk/ukpga/1986/16.

85 The law qualifies prohibitions as follows: "Two people are within prohibited degrees of relationship if one of them falls within the list below in relation to the other, unless –

(a) both of them have reached 21 at the time when they register as civil partners of each other, and
(b) the younger has not at any time before reaching 18 been a child of the family in relation to the other"; see CPA, Schedule 1, Part 1, subs. 2 (1), http://www.legislation.gov.uk/ukpga/2004/33/pdfs/ukpga_20040033_en.pdf.

86 The law further qualifies prohibited degrees of relationship as follows: "Any such marriage as is mentioned in subsection (4) of this section shall not be void by reason only of affinity if both the parties to the marriage have attained the age of twenty-one at the time of the marriage and the marriage is solemnized – (a) in the case of a marriage between a man and the mother of a former wife of his, after the death of both the former wife and the father of the former wife; (b) in the case of a marriage between a man and the former wife of his son, after the death of both his son and the mother of his son; (c) in the case of a marriage between a woman and the father of a former husband of hers, after the death of both the former husband and the mother of the former husband; (d) in the case of a marriage between a woman and a former husband of her daughter, after the death of both her daughter and the father of her daughter"; see Marriage Act, subs. 1(5), http://www.legislation.gov.uk/ukpga/Geo6/12-13-14/76. Incidentally, the qualification borders on the fantastic, if not the Gothic, and would require an article in itself on the relation among law, desire, and death. Death becomes the means of erasing the bonds of kinship.

87 The law further qualifies prohibitions as follows: "Two people are within prohibited degrees of relationship if one falls within column 1 of the table below in relation to the other, unless –

(a) both of them have reached 21 at the time when they register as civil partners of each other, and
(b) the persons who fall within column 2 are dead"; see CPA, Schedule 1, Part 1, s. 3, http://www.legislation.gov.uk/ukpga/2004/33/pdfs/ukpga_20040033_en.pdf.

8. Legitimizing the Subject of Domestic Violence: Lesley Glaister's *Honour Thy Father* and Laws of the Household

1 Craig Donnellan, ed. *Dealing with Domestic Violence* (Cambridge: Independence Educational Publishers, 1999), 13.
2 Abigail Sterne et al., *Domestic Violence and Children: A Handbook for Schools and Early Years Settings* (London: Routledge, 2010), 82–3.
3 Jacqueline Barron, *Not Worth the Paper? The Effectiveness of Legal Protection for Women and Children Experiencing Domestic Violence* (Bristol: Women's Aid Federation England, 1990), 45–6. For an analysis of affect in the courtroom, see Leif Dahlberg, "Emotional Tropes in the Courtroom: On Representation of Affect and Emotion in Legal Court Proceedings," *Law and Humanities* 3, no. 2 (Winter 2009): 175–205.
4 Marie Ashe and Naomi R. Cahn, "Child Abuse: A Problem for Feminist Theory," in *The Public Nature of Private Violence*, ed. Martha A. Fineman and Roxanne Mykitiuk (London: Routledge, 1994), 169.
5 See Margi Laird McCue for her analysis of major feminist contributions to the development of laws, policies, and educational and social services programs; the creation of shelters; and involvement in education and child development in *Domestic Violence: A Reference Handbook* (Santa Barbara, CA: ABC-CLIO, 2008), 16.
6 On the history of these organizations and the political tensions among them, see Lyn Shipway, *Domestic Violence: A Handbook for Professionals* (London: Routledge, 2004), 151.
7 Michael Horton, *Family Homes and Domestic Violence: The New Legislation* (London: FT Law & Tax, 1996), 53–4. Isabel Marcus mentions that the categories of *battered woman* and *battered spouse* were not coined until 1979 in the United States and that they were added to the International Classification of Diseases Clinical Modification Scheme compiled by the US National Center for Health Statistics; see "Terrorism in the Home," in *The Public Nature of Private Violence*, ed. Martha A. Fineman and Roxanne Mykitiuk (London: Routledge, 1994), 24.
8 They refer to the deaths of Maria Colwell (1974) and Jasmine Beckford (1985) as major turning points in cultural, social, and legal awareness.
9 The law's earlier response to domestic violence can be traced back to the Aggravated Assaults Act 1853 and the Offences Against the Person Act 1861. John Eekelaar indicates that domestic violence was regarded as a cause for divorce and separation in the civil courts, dissolving marriages according to the Matrimonial Causes Act 1857. However, while a husband could apply for a divorce if he could prove adultery, the wife could apply if she could prove cruelty combined with her husband's act of adultery.

"Not until the Matrimonial Causes Act 1878 was passed, after a campaign against 'wife torture' by Frances Power Cobbe, could a wife in her own right bring a complaint before justices that she might be formally released from her obligation to live with her husband." *Family Law and Social Policy* (London: Weidenfeld and Nicolson, 1984), 158. Rebecca E. Dobash and Russell P. Dobash report that few cases were prosecuted in the lower magistrates' courts. The Matrimonial Causes Act 1878 "allowed a woman to seek a separation and financial support if her husband was convicted of an 'aggravated assault' against her. ... While these legal developments were theoretically innovative for their time, the evidence suggests that, in practice, they provided little or no relief to the vast majority of women experiencing violence in the home." "Violence against Women in the Family," in *Cross Currents: Family Law and Policy in the United States and England*, ed. Sanford N. Katz, John Eekelaar, and Mavis Maclean (Oxford: Oxford University Press, 2000), 501.

10 Pierre Bourdieu, *Pascalian Meditations*, trans. Richard Nice (London: Polity Press, 2000), 99–100.

11 Shulamit Almog, "Healing Stories in Law and literature," in *Trauma and Memory: Reading, Healing, and Making Law*, ed. Austin Sarat, Nadav Davidovitch, and Michal Alberstein (Stanford, CA: Stanford University Press, 2007), 293.

12 See Avril Horner and Sue Zlosnik's analysis of Barbara Comyns's novels, which "explore the cruelties perpetrated within the middle-class family which, far from being a sanctuary of emotional warmth and protection, is frequently revealed to be a site of exploitative manipulation" in "Skin Chairs and Other Domestic Horrors: Barbara Comyns and the Female Gothic Tradition," *Gothic Studies* 6, no. 1 (May 2004): 91.

13 Lee Ann Hoff, *Battered Women as Survivors* (London: Routledge, 1990), 4. In 1987, Michael D.A. Freeman considered the usual myths surrounding domestic violence as well as medical theories, and he concluded in favour of a structural and ideological cause of masculine violence towards women. "The ideology [of subordination and control of women] remains imbricated in the legal system, even if one of its grosser manifestations has virtually disappeared. Wife battering is one of its legacies." *Dealing with Domestic Violence* (Bicester, UK: Commerce Clearing House, 1987), 4.

14 Mary Eaton claims that such violence has its own specificity as it is contextualized by the double stigma of violence and betrayal of same-sex – in particular, lesbian – idealized relations; see "Abuse by Any Other Name," in *The Public Nature of Private Violence*, ed. Martha A. Fineman and Roxanne Mykitiuk (London: Routledge, 1994), 195–223.

15 These statistics recur with dreadful regularity in sociological analyses of domestic violence from the seventies to the present, and they show no sign of decrease. Russell P. Dobash and Rebecca E. Dobash state that 90 per cent of cases of domestic violence are attributed to men; see "Women's Violence to Men in Intimate Relationships: Working on a Puzzle," in *Domestic Violence*, ed. Michael D.A. Freeman (Aldershot, UK: Ashgate Publishing, 2008), 41–66. In 2005, Richard Ward and Roger Bird reported, "Observing the rates of domestic violence, the [Government] Consultation Paper [2003] reported that domestic violence has the highest rate of repeat victimization of any crime, and that an incident of domestic violence is reported to the police every three minutes. On average, two women per week are killed by a male partner or former partner, with almost 50% of all female murders being committed by a partner or ex-partner. By contrast some 8% of murders of males are as a result of the act of a female partner or ex-partner. Whether resulting in fatal consequences or not, domestic violence crosses all boundaries in terms of age, gender, or social class, but is predominantly violence by men against women. It is also significantly under-reported, by both the official crime statistics, and the British Crime Survey." *Domestic Violence, Crime and Victims Act 2004: A Practitioner's Guide* (Bristol: Jordan Publishing, 2005), 3. Citing sources from the Council of Europe (2002) and the Department of Health (2005), Sterne et al. report that "one in nine women are thought to experience domestic violence annually," while on average, "two women a week are killed by a partner of former partner" (*Domestic Violence and Children*, 10).

16 The relation between body and language is cryptic and interstitial. It could be said that torture, pain, and trauma hold the symbolic activity in abeyance or that it affects it through disruption, incoherence, or withdrawal. The trend to consider violence at the level of an unmediated body that would exist in some pre-symbolic state is exemplified by Robin West's analysis of violence. In countering James Boyd White's concept of community formed through a production and criticism of texts, she states that "white masters and black slaves … without the benefit of shared texts, coexist in an interactive community of violence, neither formed, evidenced, nor 'constituted' through texts. Rather, they are formed through violations into and upon the physical body of the violated. It is not 'texts,' but rather whips, bits, gags, rapes, scars, and hanging that effectuate these communities of violence." "Communities, Texts, and Law: Reflections on the Law and Literature Movement," *Yale Journal of Law & the Humanities* 1, no. 1 (1989): 147. Wariness about such hyperbolic discourse, a modern form of the sublime, reappears in Jonathan Elmer's critique

of the hyperbolic discourse on torture. "It seems especially important at this moment, when the discursive absoluteness of the repudiation of torture has eroded to such an extent, that we attend closely to the relation between the symbolic dimension of our ideas about human life – its dignity or its disposability, the meaning of its mortality or immortality – and the practices undertaken that confirm or deny those ideas. Torture is a symbolically extreme practice; it manipulates bodies as a way of manipulating symbols." "Torture and Hyperbole," *Law, Culture and the Humanities* 3, no. 1 (2007): 24–5. In his critique of what he regards as Robert Cover's dehistoricizing analysis of the violence of the law, Jonathan Simon argues that, in practice, "a gap exists and repeats itself between utterance and action so that the judicial sentence will circulate and disperse throughout the judiciary hierarchy from the court all the way down to prisons where prisoners are not passive recipients of court decisions but members in a community revolving around the social performance of norms of behaviour, thought, and agency within the carceral universe." "The Vicissitudes of Law's Violence," in *Law, Violence, and the Possibility of Justice*, ed. Austin Sarat (Princeton, NJ: Princeton University Press, 2001), 30. For a more general critique of the bypassing of law's discursive and linguistic constitution of the world, see Florence Dore, "Law's Literature, Law's Body: The Aversion to Linguistic Ambiguity in Law and Literature," *Law, Culture and the Humanities* 2, no. 1 (2006): 17–28.

17 Rebecca E. Dobash and Russell P. Dobash, "Violent Men and Violent Contexts," in *Rethinking Violence against Women*, ed. Rebecca E. Dobash and Russell P. Dobash (Thousand Oaks, CA: Sage Publications, 1999), 168.

18 Dobash and Dobash, "Women's Violence to Men," 57.

19 Ibid.

20 In his brief analysis of the "historical roots of domestic violence," Eekelaar reports that according to Blackstone's *Commentaries on the Laws of England* (1765), "by the old law a husband might give his wife 'moderate correction' and that, although 'in the politer reign of Charles II, this power of correction began to be doubted: and a wife may have security of the peace against her husband,' nevertheless, 'the lower rank of people, who were always fond of the old common law, still claim and exert their ancient privilege: and the courts still permit a husband to restrain a wife on her liberty, in case of gross misbehaviour'" (*Family Law and Social Policy*, 156).

21 United Kingdom, Law Commission, *Family Law: Domestic Violence and Occupation of the Family Home*, Law Com. No. 207, London: HMSO, 1992, 4, para. 2.3, quoted in Deborah Lockton and Richard Ward, *Domestic Violence* (London: Cavendish, 1997), 1–2. The Home Office definition of

domestic violence in 2005 differs from that of the Law Commission by predictably underscoring the act of violence in its use of the term *incident*: "any incident of threatening behaviour, violence or abuse (physical, sexual, financial or emotional) between adults who are or have been in a relationship together, or between family members, regardless of gender or sexuality." United Kingdom, Home Office, "Domestic Violence: A National Report" (London: Home Office, 2005), quoted in Sterne et al., *Domestic Violence and Children*, 7.

22 Sterne et al., *Domestic Violence and Children*, 10.

23 Malcolm Gordon, "Definitional Issues in Violence against Women: Surveillance and Research from a Violence Research Perspective," in *Domestic Violence*, ed. Michael D.A. Freeman (Aldershot, UK: Ashgate Publishing, 2008), 7.

24 This leads Marcus to argue that although the legal concept of coverture was eliminated from family law in the United States, it is re-enacted by patterns of domestic violence, which deny women mental and physical autonomy; see "Terrorism in the Home." Hoff's argument that abused women may be caught in patriarchal constructs and social structures through which they filter their experience still holds: "(1) cultural values regarding women, marriage, and the family, and how these values and beliefs influence the action of individual women entrapped in a violent relationship; (2) the social and economic realities women face when they leave a violent relationship and find themselves a single parent, homeless, and often forced to return to the parental home after carrying out the adult responsibilities of wife and mother; (3) the interaction of these factors with the reality of physical threat and danger faced by the woman who threatens or attempts to leave." *Battered Women as Survivors*, 47.

25 Richard Collier and Sally Sheldon, *Fragmenting Fatherhood: A Socio-Legal Study* (Oxford: Hart Publishing, 2008).

26 In part, the power dynamic of violent and incestuous relations within families rests on a culture of secrecy in the form of self-censorship induced by shame or guilt. As Judith Lewis Herman reports, the desire to tell may be postponed by decades of silence; see "Justice from the Victim's Perspective," *Violence against Women* 11, no. 5 (2005): 199–230.

27 Elizabeth A. Stanko, "Theorizing about Violence: Observations from the Economic and Social Research Council's Violence Research Program," *Violence against Women* 12, no. 6 (2006): 109.

28 Barbara Fawcett reports on a research project at the University of Sydney by Irwin and colleagues with regard to the link between mental health and domestic violence. "They are discovering that women who have

experienced domestic violence and who then become involved with mental health services are finding themselves subject to three main types of responses. The first is about 'silencing,' with mental health service personnel not enquiring about or appearing to want to know about domestic violence. The second is linked to the first and refers to a mental health 'diagnosis' not taking domestic violence into account and the third shows how a mental health diagnosis can be used to discredit a woman's claims about domestic violence." "Women and Violence," in *Addressing Violence, Abuse and Oppression: Debates and Challenges*, ed. Barbara Fawcett and Fran Waugh (London: Routledge, 2008), 12.

29 Lockton and Ward, *Domestic Violence*, 4.

30 Sterne et al., *Domestic Violence and Children*, 12.

31 Elizabeth Gilchrist and Jacqueline Blissett, "Magistrates' Attitudes to Domestic Violence and Sentencing Options," *Howard Journal of Criminal Justice* 41, no. 4 (2002): 360.

32 Herman, "Justice from the Victim's Perspective," 200–1.

33 Ibid., 225.

34 Lesley Glaister, *Honour Thy Father* (London: Bloomsbury, 1999), 14.

35 Ibid., 19.

36 Ibid., 20.

37 Ibid., 12.

38 Ibid., 53. In this scene, the character witnesses a mother being beaten. Michelle A. Massé points out that such a scenario transforms the following Freudian syntagms of Oedipal fantasy of women's masochism and exhibitionism: "My father is beating a child"; "My father is beating me"; "A child is being beaten." Instead, Massé proposes to read Gothic narratives of violence as follows: "(1) My father is hurting a woman; (2) My father (or husband) is hurting me; (3) A woman is being hurt." *In the Name of Love: Women, Masochism and the Gothic* (Ithaca, NY: Cornell University Press, 1992), 61. Massé counters the traditional binary of female sadomasochism as follows: "By casting herself as the spectator of sado/masochistic fantasy, she ambiguously signals her distance from the story and characters she so tenaciously represents. In both cases, however, she has no doubt but that someone must suffer, and there is an admixture of pleasure in the spectacle. … Furthermore, even the figure whose position is most troublingly passive, the beaten, is recognized and perhaps even valued by dint of her very suffering. She too achieves her own form of agency and object relations via pain: her passivity may control others; her conspicuous and silent suffering can shout an accusation at her tormentors; her abuse may even be used to justify her

own later abusing of others" (ibid., 47–8). Diane Long Hoeveler proposes a different interpretation of the traditional female passive heroine: the script of the docile, passive, suffering female protagonist betrays a middle-class ideology that rewards the poor soul with the paternal estate. She identifies these narrative patterns as signs of feminine professionalization taking place at a time when the patriarchal, middle-class family was in the process of being codified and commercialized; see *Gothic Feminism: The Professionalization of Gender from Charlotte Smith to the Brontës* (University Park: Pennsylvania State University Press, 1998).

39 Glaister, *Honour Thy Father*, 89.

40 Ibid., 57.

41 Ibid., 70–1.

42 Ibid., 22.

43 Judith Butler, *Precarious Life: The Powers of Mourning and Violence* (London: Verso Books, 2004), 23.

44 Glaister, *Honour Thy Father*, 77.

45 Ibid., 71–2.

46 Ibid., 120.

47 For critical analyses of abjection in the Gothic, see Kelly Hurley, *The Gothic Body: Sexuality, Materialism, and Degeneration at the Fin de Siècle* (Cambridge: Cambridge University Press, 1996). Jerrold E. Hogle draws on Baudrillard's concepts of simulacrum and simulation to designate modes of representing abjection; see "The Gothic Ghost of the Counterfeit and the Progress of Abjection," in *A Companion to the Gothic*, ed. David Punter (Oxford: Blackwell, 2000), 293–304. For Sue Chaplin, the abject marks the absence of ontological origin and coherence in the law; see *The Gothic and the Rule of Law, 1764–1820* (Houndmills, UK: Palgrave Macmillan, 2007), 22.

48 Sterne et al., *Domestic Violence and Children*, 88.

49 Glaister, *Honour Thy Father*, 23.

50 Ibid., 25.

51 Ibid., 123.

52 Ibid., 3, 38.

53 Ibid., 41.

54 Linda Ross Meyer argues that "catastrophes … are not just bad luck, harmful events in the world, expected losses, or injustices but events that call into question our normative ground and cause radical normative disorientation. They are events that cause us to feel 'unheimlich' – not at home in the world. Everything we took for granted is open to questions. Everything we counted on is missing." "Plowing Up the Ground of Reason," in *Law and Catastrophe*, ed. Austin Sarat, Lawrence Douglas, and Martha Merrill Umphrey (Stanford, CA: Stanford University Press, 2007), 21.

55 Glaister, *Honour Thy Father*, 115.
56 Ibid., 11–12.
57 Ibid., 90.
58 Ibid., 133.
59 Ibid., 122.
60 Ibid., 123–4.
61 Ibid., 98.
62 Ibid., 98, 99.
63 Adriana Cavarero, *Horrorism: Naming Contemporary Violence*, trans. William McCuaig (New York: Columbia University Press, 2011), 112.
64 Glaister, *Honour Thy Father*, 42.
65 Ibid., 100.
66 Maria Vara traces an intertextual exchange between Ann Radcliffe's and the Marquis de Sade's representations of the persecuted maiden. While Radcliffe's heroines are rewarded with virtue at the end of their tribulations, in de Sade's *Juliette* the female protagonist is used to demonstrate the naiveté of the young woman's persistent adherence to a narrative of innocence in the face of power; see "Gothic Permutations from the 1790s to the 1970s: Rethinking the Marquis de Sade's Legacy," in *Le Gothic: Influences and Appropriations in Europe and America*, ed. Avril Horner and Sue Zloşnik (Houndmills, UK: Palgrave Macmillan, 2008), 100–15. David Gurnham argues that, traditionally, the archetypal female of Little Red Riding Hood, Sleeping Beauty, and Snow White is characterized by innocence deriving from her passivity and unknowingness. "'An innocent' is someone who *does* nothing to harm others; to be innocent is not really to be one who achieves their aims through endeavour, but one who is passive. ... The innocent, in contrast to the experienced, is one who stays at home and does not go adventuring." *Memory, Imagination, Justice: Intersections of Law and Literature* (Farnham, UK: Ashgate Publishing, 2009), 95. Interestingly, the narrative of *Honour Thy Father* reverses this convention in that while the daughters are confined to the home, they become monstrously active and retributive.
67 Stephen M. Cretney and Judith M. Masson, *Principles of Family Law*, 6th ed. (London: Sweet and Maxwell, 1997), 105.
68 Judith Butler, *Antigone's Claim: Kinship between Life and Death* (New York: Columbia University Press, 2000), 11–12.
69 United Kingdom, Law Commission, *Family Law*, para. 3.21, quoted in Roger Bird, *Domestic Violence: Law and Practice* (Bristol: Family Law, 2006), 86.
70 For an earlier discussion of the significance of the Matrimonial Homes Act 1967, Matrimonial Proceedings and Property Act 1970, and Matrimonial Homes and Property Act 1981, see W.T. Murphy and Hilary Clark, *The Family Home* (London: Sweet and Maxwell, 1983).

71 Anne Barlow, "Family Law and Housing Law: A Symbiotic Relationship?" in *Family Life and the Law: Under One Roof*, ed. Rebecca Probert (Aldershot, UK: Ashgate Publishing, 2007), 11.

72 Ibid., 11, 12.

73 On "doing family" and how this affects the relation among family, kinship, and personal communities, see Janet Finch, "Kinship as 'Family' in Contemporary Britain," in *Kinship Matters*, ed. Fatemeh Ebtehaj, Bridget Lindley, and Martin Richards (Oxford: Hart Publishing, 2006), 293–306.

74 In particular, Barlow analyses *Brock v. Wollams* [1949] 2 KB 3888, a case involving an adopted daughter and her ability to succeed to the tenancy on her adoptive father's death despite the absence of a formal adoption according to the Adoption of Children Act 1926; see "Family Law and Housing Law," 13–14. However, one has to wait until 1976 to see a similar kind of decision applying to an unmarried partnership. Barlow cites *Dyson Holdings v. Fox* [1976] QB 503, in which "a cohabitant without children was found to be a member of her deceased partner's family. Ms Fox had lived with the tenant for 21 years until his death" (ibid., 15).

75 The Matrimonial Causes Act 1857 was also a breakthrough for married women, who upon judicial separation could acquire and dispose of property as *feme sole*, without the husband being able to claim the property.

76 For an analysis of the economic difficulty women have had in establishing either beneficial ownership or trust in a home owned by their husbands, see Alison Diduck and Felicity Kaganas, "Household Economics, " chap. 6 in *Family Law, Gender and the State: Text, Cases and Materials* (Oxford: Hart Publishing, 2006).

77 Patrick Bromley, *Family Law* (London: Butterworth, 1957), 13. Jack Hamawi provides an additional useful piece of information for all parties concerned. "It has been held unreasonable for the husband to expect his wife to live with him and his mistress or with his mother when his wife found this intolerable." *Family Law* (London: Stevens and Sons, 1953), 112. For some mysterious reason, an analogical relation is established between mistress and mother-in-law. Jennifer Levin indicates that, in accordance with the Domicile and Matrimonial Proceedings Act 1973, the wife's dependent domicile was abolished. However, in 1982, she still mentions that "the domicile of origin of a legitimate child born during his father's lifetime is that of its father at the time of the child's birth. The domicile of a child born after its father's death, or of an illegitimate child, is that of its mother at the time of the child's birth." *Family Law* (London: Sweet and Maxwell, 1982), 14.

78 The link between homelessness and women's entrapment in abusive relations has been established by legal and sociological analyses, and

the difficulty women experience in securing a safe and independent home has been well documented. In tracing the history of refuges and shelters for women, Rebecca Morley pauses on the important role played by professionals, the National Women's Aid Federation, and abused women-turned-activists in the creation of family and housing legislation to protect women from domestic violence and provide places of safety; see "Domestic Violence and Housing," in *Home Truths about Domestic Violence: Feminist Influences on Policy and Practice, A Reader*, ed. J. Hanmer et al. (London: Routledge, 2000), 231.

79 Jacqueline Barron, *Five Years On: A Review of Legal Protection from Domestic Violence* (Bristol: Women's Aid Federation of England, 2002).

80 As far as establishing a beneficial interest in the matrimonial home is concerned, Patrick Bromley and Nigel Lowe indicate that "at present [in 1987] a spouse [who does not have the legal title to the property] will acquire an interest by indirect contributions only if she can prove that she acted in accordance with an express agreement or that the contributions were substantial and such that, without them, the husband himself would not have been able to make mortgage repayments or pay other expenses in connection with the purchase of the house." *Family Law*, 6th ed. (London: Butterworth, 1987), 535.

81 Before 1976, women who required an eviction injunction to protect themselves from a violent husband had to petition for divorce before being granted the injunction. In other words, their status was determined by the definition of space as matrimonial home and the duty of consortium (living together in a common space). In his annotation of the Domestic Proceedings and Magistrates' Courts Act 1978, Freeman states, "For the first time magistrates are given the power to exclude a husband (or even a wife) from the matrimonial home" (*Dealing with Domestic Violence*, viii).

82 The periods during which occupation orders are in effect vary from one type of relation to another: they can be unlimited in the case of entitled applicants; they cannot exceed six months in the case of former spouses and former civil partners but can be renewed on several occasions; in the case of cohabitants and former cohabitants, they cannot exceed six months and can be renewed only once. The matrimonial template and its notion of commitment is obviously governing these variations.

83 Horton, *Family Homes and Domestic Violence*, 95–6. Not surprisingly, judges in county and magistrates' courts were initially reported to have considered exclusion orders to be "draconian measures" (Barron, *Not Worth the Paper?*, 50), and statistics show that protection orders exceeded exclusion or occupation orders by a long shot. In the 1990s, the reluctance to forbid a man access to his home indicated the persistence of the cultural

link between family head and the social space of the family. Lockton and Ward reported that "judicial statistics reveal that in practice, exclusion orders are granted infrequently. In 1994 there were 25,034 applications under the DVMPA 1976. Of these, 24,566 non-molestations orders were granted and 3,946 exclusion orders" (*Domestic Violence*, 42).

84 Horton, *Family Homes and Domestic Violence*, 2–3.

85 Ibid., 47–8.

86 Family Law Act 1996, subs. 62(3)(c)(c), http://www.legislation.gov.uk/ukpga/1996/27/section/62.

87 Barlow, "Family Law and Housing Law," 11.

88 Family Law Act 1996, Part I, http://www.legislation.gov.uk/ukpga/1996/27/part/I.

89 Rebecca Bailey-Harris elucidates the political origin of this paradox. "Conservative family values ideology did not wholly disappear with the change of government which occurred in 1997. The present government finds itself on the horns of a perceived dilemma: how to promote equality and personal choice in family matters without appearing to undermine the sanctity of marriage?" "New Families for a New Society?" in *Family Law: Essays for the New Millennium*, ed. Stephen Cretney (Bristol: Family Law, 2000), 68.

90 The shift in emphasis from matrimony to parental responsibility as a means of keeping kinship unbroken also operates at the expense of children's safety when the courts enforce contact orders between violent fathers and their children on the assumption that such contact with the genetic father is beneficial to the child.

91 S. 43 of the Family Law Act 1996 states, "Leave of court required for applications by children under sixteen. (1) A child under the age of sixteen may not apply for an occupation order or a non-molestation order except with the leave of the court. (2) The court may grant leave for the purposes of subsection (1) only if it is satisfied that the child has sufficient understanding to make the proposed application for the occupation order or non-molestation order."

92 Ibid., s. 33, http://www.legislation.gov.uk/ukpga/1996/27/section/33. The right of occupation has now been extended to same-sex couples in accordance with the Civil Partnership Act 2004. In 2007, Michael D.A. Freeman noted that "it would seem that more occupation orders are being made (there were more than three times as many in 2003 as in 1996, the last year of the old law)." *Understanding Family Law* (London: Thomson, Sweet and Maxwell, 2007), 73. However, Morley indicates that in a significant number of cases, women prefer to leave the home rather than apply for

an exclusion order. There are three major reasons for this. Staying in the home still exposes the woman to potential retaliatory violence after she receives the order; the home remains associated with memories and fear of violence; and "women without men" have to rely on social housing. "Although we do not know what percentage of women experiencing domestic violence become homeless, we have strong evidence that women escaping violence constitute a substantial proportion of the homeless population." "Domestic Violence and Housing," 230.

93 Horton, *Family Homes and Domestic Violence*, 99.

94 Freeman, however, argues the following: "It is arguable that an *ex parte* occupation order infringes a person's rights under Art. 6 [of the European Convention on Human Rights]. To fall within Art. 6, removal from one's home would have to be interpreted as a punishment. It could be argued that it is not, since the application is brought by an individual, not the state, and the purpose is not to punish the respondent but protect the applicant." *Understanding Family Law*, 77.

95 Glaister, *Honour Thy Father*, 50–1.

96 Ibid., 73.

9. Resistance and Legitimacy

1 Judith Butler, *The Psychic Life of Power* (Stanford, CA: Stanford University Press, 1997), 88–9.

2 For a Foucaultian approach to political resistance to heteronormativity, see Rosie Harding, who argues that "rather than being something external to and different from power, I see resistance as a way of describing a different exercise of power – where those generally conceptualized as 'powerless' seek to produce effects on those conceptualised as 'powerful' in order to change existing power relationships." *Regulating Sexuality: Legal Consciousness in Lesbian and Gay Lives* (London: Routledge, 2011). She distinguishes among stabilizing resistance, moderating resistance, and fracturing resistance.

3 Pierre Bourdieu, *Pascalian Meditations*, trans. Richard Nice (London: Polity Press, 2000), 174.

4 Judith Butler, *Bodies That Matter: On the Discursive Limits of "Sex."* (New York: Routledge, 1993), 12–13.

5 Bourdieu, *Pascalian Meditations*, 232.

6 Ibid., 152.

7 Butler, *Bodies That Matter*, 15.

8 Ibid., 107.

9 Bourdieu, *Pascalian Meditations*, 149.
10 Judith Butler, *Gender Trouble: Feminism and the Subversion of Identity* (New York: Routledge, 1999), 179.
11 Judith Butler, "Imitation and Gender Insubordination," in *The Judith Butler Reader*, ed. Sara Salih and Judith Butler (Malden, MA: Blackwell, 2004), 125.
12 Judith Butler, "Variations on Sex and Gender: Beauvoir, Wittig, Foucault," in *The Judith Butler Reader*, ed. Sara Salih and Judith Butler (Malden, MA: Blackwell, 2004), 27.
13 Bourdieu, *Pascalian Meditations*, 138–9.
14 Ibid., 126.
15 Ibid., 182 (emphasis mine).
16 Ibid., 126.
17 Pierre Bourdieu, *Masculine Domination*, trans. Richard Nice (Stanford, MA: Stanford University Press, 2001), 7–8.
18 Bourdieu, *Pascalian Meditations*, 188.
19 George Orwell, *Animal Farm* (New York: Harcourt, Brace and Company, 1946), 112.
20 Ibid., 141.
21 Ibid., 172.
22 Ibid., 141.
23 Butler, "Imitation and Gender Insubordination," 134.
24 Butler, *Bodies That Matter*, 109.
25 Ibid., 3.
26 Judith Butler, "Competing Universalities," in *Contingency, Hegemony, Universality: Contemporary Dialogues on the Left*, by Judith Butler, Ernesto Laclau, and Slavoj Zižek (London: Verso Books, 2000), 158.
27 Butler, *Bodies That Matter*, 116.
28 Ann Cvetkovich, *An Archive of Feelings: Trauma, Sexuality, and Lesbian Public Cultures* (Durham, NC: Duke University Press, 2003), 10.
29 Ibid., 18.
30 Ibid., 7.
31 For instance, "working-class values are present in butch-femme rejection of middle-class politeness and propriety around sexuality and in the power of the community. What is remarkable about butch-femme culture is how, building on the resourcefulness of working-class culture, it has forged survival strategies for weathering traumatic affective experience without benefit of public recognition or institutional support. … Writing about … emotional and sexual intimacies [of butch-femme culture] becomes a way of forging a public sphere that can accommodate them" (ibid., 82).

32 Butler, *Bodies That Matter*, 109.

33 Ibid., 4.

34 Bourdieu, *Pascalian Meditations*, 235.

35 For instance, Natasha Sandraya Wilson made a study of a queer community in New Orleans, where, through cultural performances in a small nightclub, African American women (female-bodied women, female-bodied men, and male-bodied women) enact and renegotiate economic, political, kinship, and gender relationships; see "A Queer Situation: Poverty, Prisons, and Performances of Infidelity and Instability in the New Orleans Lesbian Anthem," in *Out in Public: Reinventing Lesbian/Gay Anthropology in a Globalizing World*, ed. Ellen Lewin and William L. Leap (Chichester, UK: Wiley-Blackwell, 2009), 104–22.

36 The findings of the report are organized into five areas of concern entitled "My Choices," "My Day," "My Rights," "Me and Others," and "My Wellbeing." For lack of space, I cannot provide the executive summary of the report. Overall, while identifying best practices, the commission provided a dismal report on practices, lack of professional training for staff, reliance on temporary workers, lack of recognition of the residents' autonomy, and absence of advocacy on behalf of residents. See also David Brindle, "Bleak House," *Guardian* (Manchester), 17 January 2007, http://www.guardian.co.uk/society/2007/jan/17/disability.longtermcare.

37 In particular, Butler argues that agency "exceeds the power by which it is enabled. One might say that the purposes of power are not always the purposes of agency. To the extent that the latter diverges from the former, agency is the assumption of a purpose *unintended* by power, one that could not have been derived logically or historically, that operates in relation to contingency and reversal to the power that makes it possible, to which it nevertheless belongs. This is, as it were, the ambivalent scene of agency, constrained by no teleological necessity" (*Psychic Life of Power*, 15).

38 Judith Butler, *Excitable Speech: A Politics of the Performative* (New York: Routledge, 1997), 40.

39 Shauna Van Praagh, "View from the *Succah*: Religion and Neighbourly Relations," in *Law and Religious Pluralism in Canada*, ed. Richard Moon (Vancouver: University of British Columbia Press, 2008), 31–2.

40 Ibid., 33.

41 Ibid., 36–7.

42 Judith Butler, *Precarious Life: The Powers of Mourning and Violence* (London: Verso Books, 2004), xiii–xiv.

43 Butler, *Psychic Life of Power*, 102.

10. Making the Law

1 See exhibition website, http://www.moma.org/interactives/exhibitions/2008/elasticmind/.
2 See http://seedmagazine.com/content/article/design_and_the_elastic_mind/.
3 The statement can be read at http://www.moma.org/interactives/exhibitions/2008/elasticmind/.
4 Hannah Arendt, *The Origins of Totalitarianism* (New York: Harcourt, Brace and World, 1966), 475.
5 See Karl Marx, *Capital*, ed. Friedrich Engels, trans. Samuel Moore and Edward Aveling, vol. 1, chap. 1, sec. 4 (New York: Modern Library, 1936).
6 See Frances Olsen's analysis of the different theories concerning state intervention, "The Myth of State Intervention in the Family," in *Family, State and Law*, ed. Michael D.A. Freeman (Dartmouth, UK: Ashgate Publishing, 1999), 81–110. Susan H. Williams has demonstrated that this public/private dichotomy historically derived from a political theory of civil society that associated the public with the Hobbesian concept of a civil society to protect individuals from state tyranny. In contrast, the private was associated with a state of nature and was the preserve of the family. From this followed the notion that the private sphere was not regulated by the laws of civil society; see "A Feminist Reassessment of Civil Society," *Indiana Law Journal* 72, no. 2 (1997): 417–47. Catherine MacKinnon has made the debatable claim that "women's distinctive experience as women occurs within that sphere that has been socially lived as the personal – private, emotional, interiorized, particular, individuated, intimate – so that what it is to know the politics of women's situation is to know women's personal lives, particularly women's sexual lives." *Toward a Feminist Theory of the State* (Cambridge, MA: Harvard University Press, 1989), 120. Ruth Gavison provides an analytical assessment of the different arguments concerning the public/private dichotomy and contends that radical feminist arguments make the mistake of wanting to remove the distinction when in fact the problem lies with the meanings ascribed to the distinction, not the distinction itself; see "Feminism and the Public/Private Distinction," *Stanford Law Review* 45, no. 1 (1992): 1–45.
7 The link among governmentality, law, and social policies is exemplified by Peter D. Reekie and Richard Tuddenham's analysis of the Child Benefit Act 1975, which allocated child benefits according to the belief that sexual reproduction occurs best within matrimonial pairing. Thus, in 1990, parents received a weekly payment of £7.25. If the parents were married,

the payment went to the wife; if the parents were divorced, it went to the parent with whom the child lived or to the parent who was responsible for child maintenance in this order of priority. In the case of the One-Parent Family benefit, the weekly amount was £5.60 from April 1990, and it applied only to the first child. See *Family Law and Practice* (London: Sweet and Maxwell, 1990), 139.

8 Kristin Savell, "The Mother of the Legal Person," in *Visible Women*, ed. Susan James and Stephanie Palmer (Oxford: Hart Publishing, 2002), 31.

9 Ibid., 31 (footnote omitted).

10 Carole Pateman, "Self-Ownership and Property in the Person: Democratization and a Tale of Two Concepts," *Journal of Political Philosophy* 10, no. 1 (2002): 24–5.

11 Ibid., 25.

12 Ibid., 27.

13 Ibid., 33.

14 Pateman offers an alternative to this process of subordination. "The fiction is that what is offered in the labor market and what has been rented out is a piece of property (labor power, a service, a commodity, a factor of production), not a self-governing person. But once the contract is made and the property is 'employed,' the worker has to use judgment, skills and experience, that is, has to exercise autonomy, or production would be impossible" (ibid., 47). In other words, the worker demonstrates self-governance.

15 Bourdieu, *Pascalian Meditations*, trans. Richard Nice (London: Polity Press, 2000), 103.

16 Arendt, *Origins of Totalitarianism*, 466.

17 Ibid., 465.

18 From a similar perspective, Desmond Manderson envisages the concept of the rule of law as "a set of ideas that institutionally protect the social and dialogic process of exposing and critiquing reasons for decision, rather than as a set of ideas that institutionally entrench the hierarchical or hieratical process of announcing them." *Kangaroo Courts and the Rule of Law: The Legacy of Modernism* (Abingdon, UK: Routledge, 2012), 159.

19 Nicola Lacey, *Unspeakable Subjects: Feminist Essays in Legal and Social Theory* (Oxford: Hart Publishing, 1998), 192–3.

20 In his critique of the dependency of different historical forms of individual and/or human rights on the legitimizing and legalizing power of the state, Roberto Buonamano describes the effects of a monolithic conception of the law in its relation to the legal subject, and he argues that the individual has rights insofar as s/he is a citizen of state power–defined sovereignty;

see "Humanity and Inhumanity: State Power and the Force of Law in the Prescription of Juridical Norms," in *Evil, Law and the State: Perspectives on State Power and Violence*, ed. John T. Parry (Amsterdam: Rodopi, 2006), 159–71.

21 Jack Balkin and Sanford Levinson, "Legal Historicism and Legal Academics: The Roles of Law Professors in the Wake of *Bush v. Gore*," *Georgetown Law Journal* 90, no. 1 (2001): 178 (footnotes omitted).

22 Robert Weisberg goes further and sees in the appropriation of legal language through multiple rhetorical strategies a means of making law productive. Analysing Robert A. Ferguson's analysis of the trial of John Brown, typically represented as a hero of the abolitionist movement in American history, Weisberg underlines the following: "Ferguson's key point is that narrative is multiple and polymorphous, not so much involving competing political narratives (the usual view of the new storyteller-scholars) as eclectically simultaneous narratives. … Though incompetent as a revolutionary, Brown roused visions of both cultural fulfillment and purification, mixed with images of armed invasion. His trial performance blended political, religious, legal, and racial stories in a grand strategy of exaggeration. Drawing largely on Hawthorne's store of romantic tropes, a bungling bankrupt transformed himself into a verbal icon." "Proclaiming Trials as Narratives: Premises and Pretenses," in *Law's Stories: Narrative and Rhetoric in the Law*, ed. Peter Brooks and Paul Gewirtz (New Haven, CT: Yale University Press, 1999), 79–80. Rosemary J. Coombe's argument oscillates between ascribing a legitimizing power to law and underscoring the cultural process of producing new norms of being and practices. "Law generates the signs and symbols – the signifying forms – with which difference is constituted and given meaning. … It invites and shapes (although it does not determine) activities that legitimate, resist, and potentially rework the meanings that accrue to these forms in public spheres. Such processes of institutionalization and intervention are both ongoing and unstable." "Contingent Articulations: A Critical Cultural Studies of Law," in *Law in the Domains of Culture*, ed. Austin Sarat and Thomas R. Kearns (Ann Arbor: University of Michigan Press, 1998), 37.

23 Seyla Benhabib, *Another Cosmopolitanism*, ed. Robert Post, Berkeley Tanner Lectures (Oxford: Oxford University Press, 2008), 22.

24 Ibid., 31.

25 This opening of the legal borders is historically recorded in the Human Rights Act 1998. According to subs. 3(1), and "so far as it is possible," legislation in the United Kingdom "must be read and given effect in a

way which is compatible with the [European Convention of Human Rights]." However, problems arise when, in its universal aspirations, the text of the Convention betrays normative and historical conceptions that have potential exclusionary effects. For instance, Art. 12 reads, "Men and women of marriageable age have the right to marry and to found a family, according to the national laws governing the exercise of this right." Nevertheless, Peter J. Burgess promotes the open-endedness and intercultural conception and significance of the European Community as a legal entity. "The European legal system … has a kind of porosity; it is, not by chance but necessity, contaminated by what is outside it. The sovereign border of EU law, the distinguishing line between what belongs to and what does not, is traversed by flows of cultural meaning, of legitimacy and competence, both nourishing the system and taking nourishment from it." "The New *Nomos* of Europe," *Geopolitics* 14, no. 1 (2009): 154.

26 Benhabib, *Another Cosmopolitanism*, 49.

27 In 2007, Jessica Shepherd reported the following: "An influx of Muslim students is changing university diets across the UK. The Federation of Student Islamic Societies says there are now about 90,000 Muslim students at university in the UK – almost double the number five years ago. It estimates that at least half of all universities now provide halal meat options in their canteens, as opposed to simply a vegetarian alternative." "Halal Is Hot," *Guardian* (Manchester), 30 January 2007, http://www.guardian.co.uk/education/2007/jan/30/highereducation.students.

28 Nicola Lacey, "Responsibility and Modernity in Criminal Law," *Journal of Political Philosophy* 9, no. 3 (2001): 254.

29 Steven DeCaroli, "Giorgio Agamben and the Field of Sovereignty," in *Giorgio Agamben: Sovereignty and Life*, ed. Matthew Calarco and Steven DeCaroli (Stanford, CA: Stanford University Press, 2007), 66.

30 Ibid., 65.

31 Jacques Rancière argues that democratic practices consist in "blurring and displacing the borders of the political. This is what politics means: displacing the limits of the political by re-enacting the equality of each and all *qua* vanishing condition of the political." *Dissensus: On Politics and Aesthetics*, trans. Steven Corcoran (London: Continuum, 2010), 54.

32 Ravit Reichman, "Committed to Memory: Rebecca West's Nuremberg," in *Law and Catastrophe*, ed. Austin Sarat, Lawrence Douglas, and Martha Merrill Umphrey (Stanford, CA: Stanford University Press, 2007), 110.

33 Ibid., 118.

34 Ibid., 123–4.

35 The analysis of deliberative democracy overlaps with that of deliberative justice. This task lies beyond the scope of my argument, but such analysis would have to consider feminist critiques of the concept. Anne Phillips considers the principles of deliberative democracy to be hopelessly utopian and inefficacious because they are fundamentally disconnected from social and economic structures and decision-making processes; see "Equality, Pluralism and Justice: Current Concerns in Normative Theory," *British Journal of Politics and International Relations* 2, no. 2 (2000): 251. Robin West questions the legal humanistic promotion of a communitarian project based on a hermeneutic dialogue around canonical texts of Western culture, which function as criteria of evaluation of well-being and justice; see "Disciplines, Subjectivity, and Law," in *The Fate of the Law*, ed. Austin Sarat and Thomas R. Kearns (Ann Arbor: University of Michigan Press, 138–47. Marion Iris Young argues that the traditional conception of deliberative democracy rests on the use of adversarial strategies and rhetoric, homogenizing consensus, and lack of democratic access. Instead, she promotes a process at the centre of which would lie difference as "a resource for public reason." *Intersecting Voices: Dilemmas of Gender, Political Philosophy, and Policy* (Princeton, NJ: Princeton University Press, 1997), 67. In her analysis of the role of deliberation within the Rawlsian framework of the veil of ignorance, Alison Jaggar attributes an elitist origin to the subject of deliberative democracy. "The method of justifying moral claims by appeal to a postulated but hypothetical agreement is covertly elitist because it requires the construction of elaborate philosophical arguments for which most people have no inclination, time or training. … A method of justification that no ordinary people can use necessarily assigns final moral authority to those few philosophical experts who are able to use it. In Western societies, such people are generally white, male and middle class." "Feminism in Ethics: Moral Justification," in *The Cambridge Companion to Feminism in Philosophy*, ed. Miranda Fricker and Jennifer Hornsby (Cambridge: Cambridge University Press, 2000), 231.

36 John Rawls, *A Theory of Justice* (Cambridge, MA: Harvard University Press, 1971), 139.

37 Ibid., 140.

38 Ngaire Naffine argues that "to imagine that one's true moral self is that which is stripped of all the layers of our social existence is to relegate our social relations to the inessential. In Rawls' scheme of things, my social connections do not shape my view of what is right; they only cloud it." *Law and the Sexes: Explorations in Feminist Jurisprudence* (Sydney: Unwin and Allen, 1990), 62. For a critique of gender blindness in Rawls's

conception of justice as fairness, see Susan Moller Okin, "John Rawls: Justice as Fairness – For Whom?" in *Feminist Interpretations and Political Theory*, ed. Mary Lyndon Shanley and Carole Pateman (University Park: Pennsylvania University Press, 1991): 181–98.

39 Rancière, *Dissensus*, 39.

40 Pateman, "Self-Ownership and Property in the Person," 45. That recent feminist and queer critics subscribe to and promote this principle testifies to Pateman's prescience on the subject. For instance, while agreeing that the "development of an inclusive feminist politics requires remaining truly open to a wide range of diverse and potentially competing perspectives," Anna Carline and Zoe Pearson also suggest that "the reification of difference ... concerns regarding the practicalities of uncritically embracing a plurality of actors in international law and feminist politics." "Complexity and Queer Theory Approaches to International Law and Feminist Politics: Perspectives on Trafficking," *Canadian Journal of Women and the Law* 19, no. 1 (2007): 88, 91. Pateman's conception of the cultural sphere is also akin to Martha Minow's conception of the law as a forum of competing worldviews and perspectives. In her advocacy of a partial justice, Minow refers to the concept of difference in legal doctrine as a means of undermining an autarchic conception of the law; see "Foreword: The Supreme Court, 1986 Term – Justice Engendered," *Harvard Law Review* 110 (1987): 10–95.

41 Elizabeth M. Schneider, "The Dialectics of Rights and Politics: Perspectives from the Women's Movement," in *At the Boundaries of Law: Feminism and Legal Theory*, ed. Martha Fineman and N. Thomadsen (London: Routledge, 1991), 308.

42 Ann Cvetkovich provides a historical perspective on the emergence of the human rights discourse. "Abolitionist movements offer an important way of historicizing the field of trauma studies, representing an early instance of the discourses of human rights that ultimately ground a post–Second World War, post-United Nations perspective on global human rights abuses, which are the public arena of transnational trauma discourse." *An Archive of Feelings: Trauma, Sexuality, and Lesbian Public Cultures* (Durham, NC: Duke University Press, 2003), 37.

43 Lisa C. Bower, "Queer Acts and the 'Politics of Direct Address': Rethinking Law, Culture, and Community," *Law & Society Review* 28, no. 5 (1994): 1011.

44 Lacey argues that "there is a need for commitment to practices which express values and attachments; ... those values themselves proceed from social practices which are open to critique and reconstruction; and ... substantively, one of the most urgent ethical questions has to do with

how diverse peoples, subjectivities, cultures, values, ways of life, can be recognized without abandoning the recognition of a common humanity of interdependence, of the necessity of living together within a variety of co-coordinating institutions such as the legal" (*Unspeakable Subjects*, 230). For an earlier instance of the transformative impact of extra-legal communities, see Mari Matsuda and what she refers to as an outsider jurisprudence in "Public Response to Racist Speech: Considering the Victim's Story," *Michigan Law Review* 87, no. 8 (August 1989): 2320–81.

Bibliography

Abercrombie, Nicholas, and Alan Warde. *Contemporary British Society*. Cambridge: Polity Press, 2003.

Ackelsberg, Martha A. *Resisting Citizenship: Feminist Essays on Politics, Community, and Democracy*. New York: Routledge, 2010.

Agamben, Giorgio. *Homo Sacer: Sovereign Power and Bare Life*. Translated by Daniel Heller-Roazen. Stanford, CA: Stanford University Press, 1998.

Almog, Shulamit. "Healing Stories in Law and Literature." In *Trauma and Memory: Reading, Healing, and Making Law*, edited by Austin Sarat, Nadav Davidovitch, and Michal Alberstein, 289–304. Stanford, CA: Stanford University Press, 2007.

Amsterdam, Anthony G., and Jerome Bruner. *Minding the Law: How Courts Rely on Storytelling, and How Their Stories Change the Ways We Understand the Law – and Ourselves*. Cambridge, MA: Harvard University Press, 2000.

Arendt, Hannah. *The Origins of Totalitarianism*. New York: Harcourt, Brace and World, 1966. First published 1951 by Schocken Books.

Aristodemou, Maria. *Law and Literature: Journeys from Here to Eternity*. Oxford: Oxford University Press, 2000.

Ashe, Marie, and Naomi R. Cahn. "Child Abuse: A Problem for Feminist Theory." In *The Public Nature of Private Violence*, edited by Martha A. Fineman and Roxanne Mykitiuk, 166–94. London: Routledge, 1994.

Auchmuty, Rosemary. "The Married Women's Property Acts: Equality Was Not the Issue." In *Rethinking Equality Projects in Law: Feminist Challenges*, edited by Rosemary Hunter, 13–39. Oñati International Series in Law and Society. Oxford: Hart Publishing, 2008.

———. "Same-Sex Marriage Revived: Feminist Critique and Legal Strategy." *Feminism & Psychology* 14, no. 1 (2004): 101–26.

Auerbach, Nina. "Jane Austen and Romantic Imprisonment." In *Jane Austen in a Social Context*, edited by David Monaghan, 9–27. London: Macmillan, 1981.

Bailey-Harris, Rebecca. "New Families for a New Society?" In *Family Law: Essays for the New Millennium*, edited by Stephen Cretney, 67–77. Bristol: Family Law, 2000.

Bainham, Andrew. "Status Anxiety? The Rush for Family Recognition." In *Kinship Matters*, edited by Fatemeh Ebtehaj, Bridget Lindley, and Martin Richards, 47–65. Oxford: Hart Publishing, 2006.

Baldick, Chris. *In Frankenstein's Shadow: Myth, Monstrosity, and Nineteenth-Century Writing*. Oxford: Clarendon Press, 1987.

Baldick, Chris, and Robert Mighall. "Gothic Criticism." In *A Companion to the Gothic*, edited by David Punter, 209–28. Oxford: Blackwell, 2000.

Balibar, Etienne. "The Invention of the Super-Ego: Freud and Kelsen 1922." Unpublished essay, n.d. Microsoft Word file. http://www.soundandsignifier.com/files/Balibar_The_Invention_of_the_Superego.doc.

Balkin, Jack M., and Sanford Levinson. "Law and the Humanities: An Uneasy Relationship." *Yale Journal of Law & the Humanities* 18, no. 2 (2006): 155–86.

———. "Law as Performance." In *Law and Literature: Current Legal Issues*, edited by Michael D.A. Freeman and Andrew Lewis, vol. 2, 729–51. Oxford: Oxford University Press, 1999.

———. "Law, Music, and Other Performing Arts." *University of Pennsylvania Law Review* 139, no. 6 (1991): 1597–658.

———. "Legal Historicism and Legal Academics: The Roles of Law Professors in the Wake of *Bush v. Gore*." *Georgetown Law Journal* 90, no. 1 (2001): 173–97.

Ballinger, Gill. "Haunting the Law: Aspects of Gothic in Dickens's Fiction." *Gothic Studies* 10, no. 2 (November 2008): 35–50.

Bano, Samia, and Pragna Patel. "*R v Zoora (Ghulam) Shah* – Judgment." In *Feminist Judgments: From Theory to Practice*, edited by Rosemary Hunter, Clare McGlynn, and Erika Rackley, 278–91. Oxford: Hart Publishing, 2010.

Barak, Aharon. *Purposive Interpretation in Law*. Princeton, NJ: Princeton University Press, 2005.

Barbour, Charles. "Sovereign Time: Acts of Creation." *Law, Culture and the Humanities* 6, no. 2 (2010): 143–52.

Barker, Hannah, and Elaine Chalus, eds. *Gender in Eighteenth-Century England: Roles, Representations and Responsibilities*. London: Addison Wesley Longman, 1997.

Barlow, Anne. "Family Law and Housing Law: A Symbiotic Relationship?" In *Family Life and the Law: Under One Roof*, edited by Rebecca Probert, 11–26. Aldershot, UK: Ashgate Publishing, 2007.

Baron, Jane B. "Intention, Interpretation and Stories." *Duke Law Journal* 42, no. 3 (December 1992): 630–78.

———. "Interdisciplinary Legal Scholarship as Guilty Pleasure: The Case of Law and Literature." In *Law and Literature: Current Legal Issues*, edited by

Michael D.A. Freeman and Andrew Lewis, vol. 2, 21–45. Oxford: Oxford University Press, 1999.

———. "Law, Literature, and the Problems of Interdisciplinarity." *Yale Law Journal* 108, no. 6 (1999): 1059–85.

Barron, Anne. "Feminism, Aestheticism and the Limits of Law." *Feminist Legal Studies* 8 (2000): 275–317.

Barron, Jacqueline. *Five Years On: A Review of Legal Protection from Domestic Violence*. Bristol: Women's Aid Federation of England, 2002.

———. *Not Worth the Paper? The Effectiveness of Legal Protection for Women and Children Experiencing Domestic Violence*. Bristol: Women's Aid Federation England, 1990.

Bartky, Sandra Lee. *Femininity and Domination*. New York: Routledge, 1990.

Becker, Susanne. *Gothic Forms of Feminine Fiction*. Manchester: Manchester University Press, 1999.

Belleau, Marie-Claire, and Rebecca Johnson. "I Beg to Differ: Interdisciplinary Questions about Law, Language and Dissent." In *Law, Mystery, and the Humanities*, edited by Logan Atkinson and Diana Majury, 145–66. Toronto: Toronto University Press, 2008.

Benhabib, Seyla. *Another Cosmopolitanism: Hospitality, Sovereignty, and Democratic Iterations*. With contributions by Jeremy Waldron, Bonnie Honig, and Will Kymlicka. Edited by Robert Post. Berkeley Tanner Lectures. Oxford: Oxford University Press, 2008.

Benjamin, Walter. *Selected Writings, Vol. I, 1913–1926*. Edited by Marcus Bullock and Michael W. Jennings. Cambridge, MA: Harvard University Press, 1996.

———. "The Work of Art in the Age of Mechanical Reproduction." In *Illuminations*, edited by Hannah Arendt, 217–51. Translated by Harry Zohn. New York: Schocken Books, 1986.

Bennett, Belinda. "The Economics of Wifing Services: Law and Economics on the Family." In *Family, State, and Law*, vol. 1, edited by Michael D.A. Freeman, 65–77. Dartmouth, UK: Ashgate Publishing, 1999.

Bergvall, Caroline. "Cropper." In *Meddle English*, 137–51. Callicoon, NY: Nightboat Books, 2011.

———. *Jets-Poupée*. Cambridge: Rempress, 1999.

Berlant, Lauren. *The Queen of America Goes to Washington City: Essays on Sex and Citizenship*. Durham, NC: Duke University Press, 1997.

Bevacqua, Maria. "Feminist Theory and the Question of Lesbian and Gay Marriage." *Feminism & Psychology* 14, no.1 (2004): 36–40.

Binder, Guyora. "The Law-as-Literature Trope." In *Law and Literature: Current Legal Issues*, edited by Michael D.A. Freeman and Andrew Lewis, vol. 2, 63–89. Oxford: Oxford University Press, 1999.

Bird, Roger. *Domestic Violence: Law and Practice*. Bristol: Family Law, 2006.

Bix, Brian H. "Legal Positivism." In *The Blackwell Guide to the Philosophy of Law and Legal Theory*, edited by Martin P. Golding and William A. Edmundson, 29–49. Malden, MA: Blackwell, 2005.

Bordo, Susan. *Unbearable Weight: Feminism, Western Culture, and the Body*. Berkeley: University of California Press, 1993.

Botting, Fred. "The Gothic Production of the Unconscious." In *Spectral Readings: Towards a Gothic Geography*, edited by Glennis Byron and David Punter, 11–36. Houndmills, UK: Macmillan, 1990.

———. *Gothic Romanced: Consumption, Gender and Technology in Contemporary Fiction*. London: Routledge, 2008.

———. "In Gothic Darkly: Heterotopia, History, Culture." In *A Companion to the Gothic*, edited by David Punter, 3–14. Oxford: Blackwell, 2000.

———. *Limits of Horror: Technology, Bodies, Gothic*. Manchester: Manchester University Press, 2008.

———, ed. Preface to *The Gothic*, 1–6. Woodbridge, UK: D.S. Brewer, 2001.

Bourassa, Kevin. "Love and the Lexicon of Marriage." *Feminism & Psychology* 14, no. 1 (2004): 57–62.

Bourdieu, Pierre. "The Force of Law: Toward a Sociology of the Juridical Field." *Hastings Law Journal* 38, no. 5 (1987): 814–53.

———. *Language and Symbolic Power*. Edited by John B. Thompson. Translated by Gino Raymond and Matthew Adamson. Cambridge, MA: Harvard University Press, 1991.

———. *Masculine Domination*. Translated by Richard Nice. Stanford, CA: Stanford University Press, 2001.

———. *Outline of a Theory of Practice*. Translated by Richard Nice. Cambridge: Cambridge University Press, 2009.

———. *Pascalian Meditations*. Translated by Richard Nice. London: Polity Press, 2000.

Bower, Lisa C. "Queer Acts and the 'Politics of Direct Address': Rethinking Law, Culture, and Community." *Law & Society Review* 28, no. 5 (1994): 1009–34.

Boyd, Susan. "Family, Law and Sexuality: Feminist Engagements." *Social and Legal Studies* 8, no. 3 (1999): 369–90.

Brabon, Benjamin A. "The Spectral Phallus: Re-Membering the Postfeminist Man." In *Postfeminist Gothic: Critical Interventions in Contemporary Culture*, edited by Benjamin A. Brabon and Stéphanie Genz, 56–67. Houndmills, UK: Palgrave Macmillan, 2007.

Brindle, David. "Bleak House." *Guardian* (Manchester), 17 January 2007. http://www.guardian.co.uk/society/2007/jan/17/disability.longtermcare.

Brodsky, Gwen, Rachel Cox, Shelagh Day, and Kate Stephenson. "*Gosselin v. Québec (Attorney General).*" *Canadian Journal of Women and the Law* 18, no. 1 (2006): 189–249.

Bromley, Patrick. *Family Law*. London: Butterworth, 1957. Reprinted 1966, 1971, 1981.

Bromley, Patrick, and Nigel Lowe. *Family Law*. 6th ed. London: Butterworth, 1987.

Brooks, Peter. "The Law as Narrative and Rhetoric." In *Law's Stories: Narrative and Rhetoric in the Law*, edited by Peter Brooks and Paul Gewirtz, 14–22. New Haven, CT: Yale University Press, 1999.

———. "Law, Therapy, Culture." *Yale Journal of Law & the Humanities* 13, no. 1 (2001): 227–37.

———. "Narrativity of the Law." *Law and Literature* 14, no. 1 (Spring 2002): 1–10.

———. "A Slightly Polemical Comment on Austin Sarat." *Yale Journal of Law & the Humanities* 10, no. 2 (1998): 409–12.

———. "What Is a Monster? (According to Frankenstein)." Chap. 7 in *Body Work: Objects of Desire in Modern Narrative*, 199–220. Cambridge, MA: Harvard University Press, 1993.

Brooks, Rosa Ehrenreich. "The New Imperialism: Violence, Norms, and the 'Rule of Law.'" *Michigan Law Review* 101, no. 7 (June 2003): 2275–340.

Brown, Marshall. "Philosophy and the Gothic Novel." In *Approaches to Teaching Gothic Fiction: The British and American Traditions*, edited by Diane Long Hoeveler and Tamar Heller, 46–57. New York: Modern Language Association, 2003.

Brown, Wendy. *Regulating Aversion: Tolerance in the Age of Identity and Empire*. Princeton, NJ: Princeton University Press, 2008.

Brown, Wendy, and Janet Halley. Introduction to *Left Legalism / Left Critique*, edited by Wendy Brown and Janet Halley, 1–37. Durham, NC: Duke University Press, 2002.

Bruhm, Steven. "Gothic Sexualities." In *Teaching the Gothic*, edited by Anna Powell and Andrew Smith, 93–106. Houndmills, UK: Palgrave Macmillan, 2006.

Bruner, Jerome. *Making Stories: Law, Literature, Life*. Cambridge, MA: Harvard University Press, 2002.

Buckley, Melina. "*Symes v. Canada.*" *Canadian Journal of Women and the Law* 18, no. 1 (2006): 27–66.

Buonamano, Roberto. "Humanity and Inhumanity: State Power and the Force of Law in the Prescription of Juridical Norms." In *Evil, Law and the State: Perspectives on State Power and Violence*, edited by John T. Parry, 159–71. Amsterdam: Rodopi, 2006.

Burgess, J. Peter. "Law and Cultural Identity." ARENA Working Papers Series, WP 97/14. Oslo: ARENA Centre for European Studies, 1997. http://jpeterburgess.com/wp-content/uploads/publications/1997/Law_and_Cultural_Identity.pdf.

______. "The New *Nomos* of Europe." *Geopolitics* 14, no. 1 (2009): 135–60.

Burt, Robert A. "Rethinking Robert Cover's Nomos and Narrative: Robert Cover's Passion." *Yale Journal of Law & the Humanities* 17, no. 1 (2005): 1–8.

Butler, Judith. *Antigone's Claim: Kinship between Life and Death*. New York: Columbia University Press, 2000.

———. *Bodies That Matter: On the Discursive Limits of "Sex."* New York: Routledge, 1993.

———. "Changing the Subject." In *The Judith Butler Reader*, edited by Sara Salih and Judith Butler, 325–56. Malden, MA: Blackwell, 2004.

———. "Competing Universalities." In *Contingency, Hegemony, Universality: Contemporary Dialogues on the Left*, by Judith Butler, Ernesto Laclau, and Slavoj Žižek, 136–81. London: Verso Books, 2000.

———. *Excitable Speech: A Politics of the Performative*. New York: Routledge, 1997.

———. "The Force of Fantasy: Mapplethorpe, Feminism, and Discursive Excess." In *The Judith Butler Reader*, edited by Sara Salih and Judith Butler, 183–203. Malden, MA: Blackwell, 2004.

———. *Gender Trouble: Feminism and the Subversion of Identity*. New York: Routledge, 1999.

———. *Giving an Account of Oneself*. New York: Fordham University Press, 2005.

———. "Imitation and Gender Insubordination." In *The Judith Butler Reader*, edited by Sara Salih and Judith Butler, 119–37. Malden, MA: Blackwell, 2004.

———. "Is Kinship Always Already Heterosexual?" In *Undoing Gender*, 102–30. New York: Routledge, 2004.

———. "Merely Cultural." *New Left Review* 227 (1998): 33–44.

———. *Precarious Life: The Powers of Mourning and Violence*. London: Verso Books, 2004.

———. *The Psychic Life of Power*. Stanford, CA: Stanford University Press, 1997.

———. "Quandaries of the Incest Taboo." In *Undoing Gender*, 152–60. New York: Routledge, 2004.

———. "Variations on Sex and Gender: Beauvoir, Wittig, Foucault." In *The Judith Butler Reader*, edited by Sara Salih and Judith Butler, 21–38. Malden, MA: Blackwell, 2004.

Calhoun, Cheshire. *Feminism, the Family, and the Politics of the Closet: Lesbian and Gay Displacement*. Oxford: Oxford University Press, 2000.

Cameron, Ed. "Ironic Escapism in the Symbolic Spread of Gothic Materialist Meaning." *Gothic Studies* 10, no. 2 (November 2008): 18–34.

Canada. Commission of Inquiry into the Actions of Canadian Officials in Relation to Maher Arar. *Report of the Events Relating to Maher Arar: Analysis and Recommendations*. Cat. No. CP32-88/1-2006E. Ottawa: Minister of Public Works and Government Services, 2006. http://www.sirc-csars.gc.ca/pdfs/cm_arar_rec-eng.pdf.

———. Royal Commission on Electoral Reform and Party Financing. *Reforming Electoral Democracy: Final Report*. Ottawa: Minister of Supply and Services Canada, 1991.

Carline, Anna. "Resignifications and Subversive Transformations: Judith Butler's Queer Theory and Women Who Kill." *Liverpool Law Review* 27, no. 3 (2006): 303–35.

———. "Women Who Kill Their Abusive Partners: From Sameness to Gender Construction." *Liverpool Law Review* 26, no. 1 (2005): 13–44.

———. "Zoora Shah: 'An Unusual Woman.'" *Social and Legal Studies* 14, no. 2 (2005): 215–38.

Carline, Anna, and Zoe Pearson. "Complexity and Queer Theory Approaches to International Law and Feminist Politics: Perspectives on Trafficking." *Canadian Journal of Women and the Law* 19, no. 1 (2007): 73–118.

Case, Sue-Ellen. "Tracking the Vampire." *Differences: A Journal of Feminist Cultural Studies* 3, no. 2 (1991): 1–20.

Castle, Terry. *The Apparitional Lesbian: Female Homosexuality and Modern Culture*. New York: Columbia University Press, 1993.

———. *The Female Thermometer: 18th-Century Culture and the Invention of the Uncanny*. Oxford: Oxford University Press, 1987.

———, ed. *The Literature of Lesbianism: A Historical Anthology from Ariosto to Stonewall*. New York: Columbia University Press, 2003.

Castricano, Jodey. "Cryptomimesis: The Gothic and Jacques Derrida's Ghost Writing." *Gothic Studies* 2, no. 1 (April 2000): 8–22.

Cavarero, Adriana. *Horrorism: Naming Contemporary Violence*. Translated by William McCuaig. New York: Columbia University Press, 2011.

Chaplin, Sue. *The Gothic and the Rule of Law, 1764–1820*. Houndmills, UK: Palgrave Macmillan, 2007.

Cixous, Hélène. "Fiction and Its Phantoms: A Reading of Freud's *Das Unheimliche*." Translated by Robert Dennomé. *New Literary History* 7, no. 3 (Spring 1976): 525–48.

Clery, Emma J. "The Genesis of 'Gothic' Fiction." In *The Cambridge Companion to Gothic Fiction*, edited by Jerrold E. Hogle, 21–39. Cambridge: Cambridge University Press, 2002.

———. "Horace Walpole's *The Mysterious Mother* and the Impossibility of Female Desire." In *The Gothic*, edited by Fred Botting, 23–46. Woodbridge, UK: D.S. Brewer, 2001.

———. *The Rise of Supernatural Fiction 1762–1800*. Cambridge: Cambridge University Press, 1995.

Collier, Richard. *Masculinity, Law and the Family*. London: Routledge, 1995.

Collier, Richard, and Sally Sheldon. *Fragmenting Fatherhood: A Socio-Legal Study*. Oxford: Hart Publishing, 2008.

Commission for Healthcare Audit and Inspection. *A Life like No Other: A National Audit of Specialist Inpatient Healthcare Services for People with Learning Difficulties in England*. London: Healthcare Commission, 2007. http://www.scie-socialcareonline.org.uk/a-life-like-no-other-a-national-audit-of-specialist-inpatient-healthcare-services-for-people-with-learning-difficulties-in-england-easy-read-summary/r/a11G00000017trtIAA.

Conaghan, Joanne. "Reassessing the Feminist Theoretical Project in Law." *Journal of Law and Society* 27, no. 3 (2000): 351–85.

Connolly, William E. "The Complexities of Sovereignty." In *Giorgio Agamben: Sovereignty and Life*, edited by Matthew Calarco and Steven DeCaroli, 23–42. Stanford, CA: Stanford University Press, 2007.

Coombe, Rosemary J. "Contingent Articulations: A Critical Cultural Studies of Law." In *Law in the Domains of Culture*, edited by Austin Sarat and Thomas R. Kearns, 21–64. Ann Arbor: University of Michigan Press, 1998.

———. "Critical Cultural Legal Studies." *Yale Journal of Law & the Humanities* 10. no. 2 (1998): 463–86.

———. "Room for Manoeuver: Toward a Theory of Practice in Critical Legal Studies." *Law and Social Inquiry* 14, no. 1 (Winter 1989): 69–121.

Cooper, David M., and David Ball. *Social Work and Child Abuse*. Houndmills, UK: Macmillan, 1987.

Cooper, Davina. "Like Counting Stars? Equality and the Socio-Legal Space of Same-Sex Marriage." In *Legal Recognition of Same-Sex Partnerships: A Study of National, European and International Law*, edited by Robert Wintemute and Mads Andenaes, 75–96. Oxford: Hart Publishing, 2001.

———. *Sexing the City: Lesbian and Gay Politics within the Activist State*. London: Rivers Oram Press, 1994.

Cormack, Bradin. *A Power to Do Justice: Jurisdiction, English Literature, and the Rise of Common Law, 1509–1625*. Chicago: University of Chicago Press, 2007.

Cossman, Brenda. *Sexual Citizens: The Legal and Cultural Regulation of Sex and Belonging*. Palo Alto, CA: Stanford University Press, 2007.

Cover, Robert. "Nomos and Narrative." In *Narrative, Violence, and the Law: The Essays of Robert Cover*, edited by Martha Minow, Michael Ryan, and Austin Sarat, 95–172. Ann Arbor: University of Michigan Press, 1995.

———. "Violence and the Word." In *Narrative, Violence, and the Law: The Essays of Robert Cover*, edited by Martha Minow, Michael Ryan, and Austin Sarat, 203–38. Ann Arbor: University of Michigan Press, 1995.

Cowan, Sharon. "'Gender Is No Substitute for Sex': A Comparative Human Rights Analysis of the Legal Regulation of Sexual Identity." *Feminist Legal Studies* 13, no. 1 (2005): 67–96.

Cowan, Sharon, and Jacqueline Hodgson. "Violence in a Family Context: The Criminal Law's Response." In *Family Life and the Law: Under One Roof*, edited by Rebecca Probert, 43–60. Aldershot, UK: Ashgate Publishing, 2007.

Crangle, Sara. "You Touch Mine, I'll touch Yours." *Globe and Mail*, 1 March 2000. http://www.walnet.org/csis/news/halifax_2000/gandm-000301.html.

Cretney, Stephen M. "Family Law at the Millennium – Introduction and Overview." In *Family Law: Essays for the New Millennium*, edited by Stephen M. Cretney, 1–9. Bristol: Family Law, 2000.

———. *Principles of Family Law*. London: Sweet and Maxwell, 1984.

———. *Same Sex Relationships: From "Odious Crime" to "Gay Marriage."* Oxford: Oxford University Press, 2006.

Cretney, Stephen M., and Judith M. Masson. *Principles of Family Law*. 6th ed. London: Sweet and Maxwell, 1997.

Cvetkovich, Ann. *An Archive of Feelings: Trauma, Sexuality, and Lesbian Public Cultures*. Durham, NC: Duke University Press, 2003.

Dahlberg, Leif. "Emotional Tropes in the Courtroom: On Representation of Affect and Emotion in Legal Court Proceedings." *Law and Humanities* 3, no. 2 (Winter 2009): 175–205.

Davis, Gwynn. "Love in a Cold Climate – Disputes about Children in the Aftermath of Parental Separation." In *Family Law: Essays for the New Millennium*, edited by Stephen M. Cretney, 127–42. Bristol: Family Law, 2000.

DeCaroli, Steven. "Giorgio Agamben and the Field of Sovereignty." In *Giorgio Agamben: Sovereignty and Life*, edited by Matthew Calarco and Steven DeCaroli, 43–69. Stanford, CA: Stanford University Press, 2007.

de Certeau, Michel. *The Practice of Everyday Life*. Translated by Steven Rendall. Berkeley: University of California Press, 1988.

Deech, Ruth. "Matrimonial Property and Divorce: A Century of Progress?" In *The State, the Law, and the Family: Critical Perspectives*, edited by Michael D.A. Freeman, 245–61. London: Sweet and Maxwell, 1984.

———. "The Work of the Law Commission in Family Law: The First Twenty Years." In *Essays in Family Law*, edited by Michael D.A. Freeman, 57–80. London: Stevens and Sons, 1986.

Derrida, Jacques. "Before the Law." In *Acts of Literature*, edited by Derek Attridge, 181–220. London: Routledge, 1992.

———. "The Law of Genre." Translated by Avital Ronell. *Critical Inquiry* 7, no. 1 (Autumn 1980): 55–81.

DeWaard, Jeanne Elders. "'The Shadow of Law': Sentimental Interiority, Gothic Terror, and the Legal Subject." *Arizona Quarterly: A Journal of American Literature, Culture, and Theory* 62, no. 4 (Winter 2006): 1–30.

Dewar, John, and Stephen Parker. "English Family Law since World War II: From Status to Chaos." In *Cross Currents: Family Law and Policy in the United States and England*, edited by Sanford N. Katz, John Eekelaar, and Mavis Maclean, 123–40. Oxford: Oxford University Press, 2000.

Diduck, Alison, and Felicity Kaganas. "Household Economics," chap. 6 in *Family Law, Gender and the State: Text, Cases and Materials*. Oxford: Hart Publishing, 2006.

Dimock, Wai Chee. "Criminal Law, Female Virtue, and the Rise of Liberalism." *Yale Journal of Law & the Humanities* 4, no. 2 (1992): 209–47.

———. "Introduction: Genres as Fields of Knowledge." *PMLA* 122, no. 5 (October 2007): 1377–88.

———. "Rules of Law, Laws of Science." *Yale Journal of Law & the Humanities* 13, no. 1 (2001): 203–25.

Dobash, Rebecca E., and Russell P. Dobash. "Evaluating Criminal Justice Interventions for Domestic Violence." *Crime and Delinquency* 46 (2000): 252–70.

———. "Violence against Women in the Family." In *Cross Currents: Family Law and Policy in the United States and England*, edited by Sanford N. Katz, John Eekelaar, and Mavis Maclean, 495–510. Oxford: Oxford University Press, 2000.

———. "Violent Men and Violent Contexts." In *Rethinking Violence against Women*, edited by Rebecca E. Dobash and Russell P. Dobash, 141–68. Thousand Oaks, CA: Sage Publications, 1999.

Dobash, Russell P., and Rebecca E. Dobash. "Women's Violence to Men in Intimate Relationships: Working on a Puzzle." In *Domestic Violence*, edited by Michael D.A. Freeman, 41–66. Aldershot, UK: Ashgate Publishing, 2008.

Dolin, Kieran. *Law and Literature: A Critical Introduction*. Cambridge: Cambridge University Press, 2007.

Donnellan, Craig, ed. *Dealing with Domestic Violence*. Cambridge: Independence Educational Publishers, 1999.

Donzelot, Jacques. *The Policing of Families*. New York: Pantheon, 1979.
Dore, Florence. "Law's Literature, Law's Body: The Aversion to Linguistic Ambiguity in Law and Literature." *Law, Culture and the Humanities* 2, no. 1 (2006): 17–28.
Dorfman, Ariel. "The Lost Speech." In *Profession*, edited by Rosemary G. Feal, 40–7. New York: Modern Language Association, 2006.
Douglas, Heather. "The Provocation Defence and Equality." In *Rethinking Equality Projects in Law: Feminist Challenges*, edited by Rosemary Hunter, 41–57. Oñati International Series in Law and Society. Oxford: Hart Publishing, 2008.
Douzinas, Costas, and Ronnie Warrington. *Justice Miscarried: Ethics, Aesthetics and the Law*. Hemel Hempstead, UK: Harvester Wheatsheaf, 1994.
Duder, Cameron. *Awfully Devoted Women: Lesbian Lives in Canada, 1900–65*. Vancouver: University of British Columbia Press, 2010.
Duncker, Patricia. *The Deadly Space Between*. New York: Harper Collins, 2002.
———. "Re-imagining the Fairy Tales: Angela Carter's Bloody Chambers." *Literature and History* 10, no. 1 (Spring 1984): 3–14.
Dworkin, Ronald. *Justice in Robes*. Cambridge, MA: Harvard University Press, 2006.
———. *Law's Empire*. Cambridge, MA: Harvard University Press, 1986.
Eaton, Mary. "Abuse by Any Other Name." In *The Public Nature of Private Violence*, edited by Martha A. Fineman and Roxanne Mykitiuk, 195–223. London: Routledge, 1994.
———. "Homosexual Unmodified." In *Legal Inversions: Lesbians, Gay Men, and the Politics of Law*, edited by Didi Herman and Carl F. Stychin, 46–73. Philadelphia: Temple University Press, 1995.
Eberle-Sinatra, Michael. "Readings of Homosexuality in Mary Shelley's *Frankenstein* and Four Film Adaptations." *Gothic Studies* 7, no. 2 (2005): 185–202.
Eberts, Mary, Sharon McIvor, and Teressa Nahanee. "*Native Women's Association of Canada v. Canada*." *Canadian Journal of Women and the Law* 18, no. 1 (2006): 67–119.
Ebtehaj, Fatemeh, Bridget Lindley, and Martin Richards, eds. *Kinship Matters*. Oxford: Hart Publishing, 2006.
Eekelaar, John. "The End of an Era?" In *Cross Currents: Family Law and Policy in the United States and England*, edited by Sanford N. Katz, John Eekelaar, and Mavis Maclean, 637–55. Oxford: Oxford University Press, 2000.
———. "Family and Social Control." In *Oxford Essays in Jurisprudence*, edited by John Eekelaar and John Bell, 125–44. Oxford: Clarendon Press, 1987.
———. *Family Law and Social Policy*. London: Weidenfeld and Nicolson, 1984.

El Akkad, Omar. "In a Span of Minutes, a Country Goes Off-Line." *Globe and Mail*, 29 January 2011, A16.

Eleftheriadis, Pavlos. "Hart on Sovereignty." In *Reading HLA Hart's "The Concept of Law,"* edited by Andrea Dolcetti, Luis Duarte d'Almeida, and James Edwards, 59–79. Oxford: Hart Publishing, 2013.

Ellis, Kate Ferguson. *The Contested Castle: Gothic Novels and the Subversion of Domestic Ideology*. Urbana: University of Illinois Press, 1989.

Elmer, Jonathan. "Torture and Hyperbole." *Law, Culture and the Humanities* 3, no. 1 (2007): 18–34.

Emerson, Lori. "Materiality, Intentionality, and the Computer-Generated Poem: Reading Walter Benn Michaels with Erin Mouré's *Pillage Laud*." *English Studies in Canada* 34, no. 4 (December 2008): 45–69.

Eskridge, William N. *The Case for Same-Sex Marriage: From Sexual Liberty to Civilized Commitment*. New York: Free Press, 1996.

Ewald, François. "Norms, Discipline, and the Law." In *Law and the Order of Culture*, edited by Robert Post, 138–60. Translated by Marjorie Beale. Berkeley: University of California Press, 1991.

Ewick, Patricia, and Susan S. Silbey. *The Common Place of Law: Stories from Everyday Life*. Chicago: University of Chicago Press, 1998.

Fanon, Frantz. *The Wretched of the Earth*. Translated by Constance Farrington. London: MacGibbon and Kee, 1965.

Farber, Daniel A., and Suzanna Sherry. "Legal Storytelling and Constitutional Law." In *Law's Stories: Narrative and Rhetoric in the Law*, edited by Peter Brooks and Paul Gewirtz, 37–53. New Haven, CT: Yale University Press, 1999.

Fawcett, Barbara. "Women and Violence." In *Addressing Violence, Abuse and Oppression: Debates and Challenges*, edited by Barbara Fawcett and Fran Waugh, 7–16. London: Routledge, 2008.

Felman, Shoshana. "Forms of Judicial Blindness: Traumatic Narratives and Legal Repetitions." In *History, Memory, and the Law*, edited by Austin Sarat and Thomas R. Kearns, 25–93. Ann Arbor: University of Michigan Press, 2002.

———. *The Juridical Unconscious: Trials and Traumas in the Twentieth Century*. Cambridge, MA: Harvard University Press, 2002.

Ferguson, Robert A. "Untold Stories." In *Law's Stories: Narrative and Rhetoric in the Law*, edited by Peter Brooks and Paul Gewirtz, 84–98. New Haven, CT: Yale University Press, 1999.

Finch, Janet. "Kinship as 'Family' in Contemporary Britain." In *Kinship Matters*, edited by Fatemeh Ebtehaj, Bridget Lindley, and Martin Richards, 293–306. Oxford: Hart Publishing, 2006.

Fineman, Martha Albertson. *The Neutered Mother, the Sexual Family, and Other Twentieth Century Tragedies*. New York: Routledge, 1995.

Fiorato, Sidia. "Juridical Issues in Contemporary Fairy Tales: The Case of Angela Carter." *Textus: English Studies in Italy* 21, no. 3 (2008): 647–74.

Fish, Stanley. *Doing What Comes Naturally*. Durham, NC: Duke University Press, 1989.

Fitzgerald, Lauren. "Female Gothic and the Institutionalization of Gothic Studies." In *The Female Gothic: New Directions*, edited by Diana Wallace and Andrew Smith, 13–25. Basingstoke, UK: Palgrave Macmillan, 2009.

Fitzpatrick, Peter. "Why the Law Is Also Nonviolent." In *Law, Violence, and the Possibility of Justice*, edited by Austin Sarat, 142–73. Princeton, NJ: Princeton University Press, 2001.

Fleenor, Juliann E., ed. *The Female Gothic*. Montreal: Eden Press, 1983.

Foakes, Joanne. *Family Violence: Law and Practice*. London: Hemstal Press, 1984.

Foucault, Michel. "Des espaces autres." In *Dits et écrits: 1954–1988. Vol. II, 1976–88*, edited by Daniel Defert and François Ewald, 1571–81. Paris: Éditions Gallimard, 2001.

———. "The Ethics of the Concern of the Self as a Practice of Freedom." In *The Essential Foucault: Selections from the Essential Works of Foucault 1954–1984*, edited by Paul Rabinow and Nikolas Rose, 25–42. New York: New Press, 2003.

———. "L'éthique du souci de soi comme pratique de la liberté." In *Dits et écrits: 1954–1988. Vol. II, 1976–88*, 1527–48. Paris: Éditions Gallimard, 2001.

———. "La technologie politique des individus." In *Dits et écrits: 1954–1988. Vol. II, 1976–88*, 1632–47. Paris: Éditions Gallimard, 2001.

———. *"What Is an Author?"* In *Language, Counter-Memory, Practice*, edited by Donald F. Bouchard and Sherry Simon, 113–38. Ithaca, NY: Cornell University Press, 1977.

Franke, Katherine. "Law." In *A Companion to Gender Studies*, edited by Philomena Essed, David Theo Goldberg, and Audrey Kobayashi, 160–80. Malden, MA: Blackwell, 2005.

Fraser, Laura. "Frankenstein as a Modern Monster: Secrets, Incest and Intrigue Enter a Boy's Life with a Mysterious Stranger." Review of *The Deadly Space Between*, by Patricia Duncker. *SF Gate*, 7 July 2002. http://articles.sfgate.com/2002-07-07/books/17555065_1_patricia-duncker-roehm-tobias.

Fraser, Nancy. "Heterosexism, Misrecognition and Capitalism: A Response to Judith Butler." *New Left Review* 228 (1998): 140–9.

Fredman, Sandra. *Women and the Law*. Oxford: Clarendon Press, 1997.

Freeman, Michael D.A. *Dealing with Domestic Violence*. Bicester, UK: Commerce Clearing House, 1987.

———. *The Domestic Proceedings and Magistrates' Courts Act 1978: With Annotations*. London: Sweet and Maxwell, 1978.

———. "Family Values and Family Justice." In *Family, State, and Law*, vol. 1, edited by Michael D.A. Freeman, 509–53. Dartmouth, UK: Ashgate Publishing, 1999.

———. "Legal Ideologies, Patriarchal Precedents, and Domestic Violence." In *The State, the Law, and the Family: Critical Perspectives*, edited by Michael D.A. Freeman, 51–78. London: Tavistock Publications, 1984.

———. *Understanding Family Law*. London: Thomson, Sweet and Maxwell, 2007.

Freud, Sigmund. "The Uncanny." In *The Complete Psychological Works of Sigmund Freud*, vol. 17, 217–56. Translated by James Strachey. London: Hogarth Press, 1955.

Fricker, Miranda. *Epistemic Injustice, Power and the Ethics of Knowing*. Oxford: Oxford University Press, 2007.

Fuller, Lon. "Positivism and Fidelity to Law – A Reply to Professor Hart." *Harvard Law Review* 71, no. 4 (1958): 630–72.

Gamer, Michael. "Genres for the Prosecution: Pornography and the Gothic." *PMLA* 114, no. 5 (October 1999): 1043–54.

Garrett, Peter K. *Gothic Reflections: Narrative Force in Nineteenth-Century Fiction*. Ithaca, NY: Cornell University Press, 2003.

Gavison, Ruth. "Feminism and the Public/Private Distinction." *Stanford Law Review* 45, no. 1 (1992): 1–45.

Geertz, Clifford. "Local Knowledge: Fact and Law in Comparative Perspective." In *Local Knowledge: Further Essays in Interpretive Anthropology*, 167–234. New York: Basic Books, 1983.

Gentile, Kathy Justice. "Sublime Drag: Supernatural Masculinity in Gothic Fiction." *Gothic Studies* 11, no. 1 (May 2009): 16–31.

Genz, Stéphanie. "(Re)making the Body Beautiful: Postfeminist Cinderellas and Gothic Tales of Transformation." In *Postfeminist Gothic: Critical Interventions in Contemporary Culture*, edited by Benjamin A. Brabon and Stéphanie Genz, 68–84. Houndmills, UK: Palgrave Macmillan, 2007.

Gibson, Colin. "Changing Family Patterns in England and Wales over the Last Fifty Years." In *Cross Currents: Family Law and Policy in the United States and England*, edited by Sanford N. Katz, John Eekelaar, and Mavis Maclean, 31–55. Oxford: Oxford University Press, 2000.

Gilbert, Sandra, and Susan Gubar. *The Madwoman in the Attic: The Woman Writer and the Nineteenth-Century Literary Imagination*. New Haven, CT: Yale University Press, 1979.

Gilchrist, Elizabeth, and Jacqueline Blissett. "Magistrates' Attitudes to Domestic Violence and Sentencing Options." *Howard Journal of Criminal Justice* 41, no. 4 (2002): 348–63.

Glaister, Lesley. *Honour Thy Father*. 1990. London: Bloomsbury Publishing, 1999.

Glaser, Danya, and Stephen Frosh. *Child Sexual Abuse*. Houndmills, UK: Macmillan Press, 1988.

Goddu, Teresa A. *Gothic America: Narrative, History, and Nation*. New York: Columbia University Press, 1997.

Goodrich, Peter. "Antirrhesis: Polemical Structures of Common Law Thought." In *The Fate of the Law*, edited by Austin Sarat and Thomas R. Kearns, 57–102. Ann Arbor: University of Michigan Press, 1991.

———. "The Continuance of the Antirrhetic." *Cardozo Studies in Law and Literature* 4, no. 2 (Autumn 1992): 207–22.

———. "Epistolary Justice: The Love Letter as Law." *Yale Journal of Law & the Humanities* 9, no. 2 (1997): 245–95.

———, ed. *Law and the Unconscious: A Legendre Reader*. Basingstoke, UK: Palgrave Macmillan, 1997.

———. "Law by Other Means." *Cardozo Studies in Law and Literature* 10, no. 2 (Winter 1998): 111–16.

———. *Legal Discourse: Studies in Linguistics, Rhetoric, and Legal Analysis*. London: Palgrave Macmillan, 1987.

———. *Oedipus Lex: Psychoanalysis, History, Law*. Berkeley: University of California Press, 1995.

———. *Reading the Law: A Critical Introduction to Legal Method and Techniques*. Oxford: Basil Blackwell, 1986.

———. "A Theory of the Nomogram." In *Law, Text, Terror*, edited by Peter Goodrich, Lior Barshack, and Anton Schütz, 13–33. Abingdon, UK: Routledge-Cavendish, 2006.

———. "Visive Powers: Colours, Trees and Genres of Jurisdiction." *Law and Humanities* 2, no. 2 (2008): 213–31.

Goodrich, Peter, Lior Barshack, and Anton Schütz, eds. *Law, Text, Terror*. Abingdon, UK: Routledge-Cavendish, 2006.

Gordon, Avery F. *Ghostly Matters: Haunting and the Sociological Imagination*. Minneapolis: University of Minnesota Press, 1997.

Gordon, Malcolm. "Definitional Issues in Violence against Women: Surveillance and Research from a Violence Research Perspective." In *Domestic Violence*, edited by Michael D.A. Freeman, 3–39. Aldershot, UK: Ashgate Publishing, 2008.

Gordon, Randy D. *Rehumanizing Law: A Theory of Law and Democracy*. Toronto: Toronto University Press, 2011.

Graycar, Reg, and Jenny Morgan. "Equality Rights: What's Wrong?" In *Rethinking Equality Projects in Law: Feminist Challenges*, edited by Rosemary Hunter, 105–24. Oxford: Hart Publishing, 2008.

Greenblatt, Stephen. "Invisible Bullets." In *Shakespearean Negotiations: The Circulation of Social Energy in Renaissance England*, 21–65. Berkeley: University of California Press, 1988.

Guillaumin, Colette. "Race and Nature: The System of Marks." Translated by Mary Jo Lakeland. *Gender Issues* 8, no. 2 (1988): 25–43.

Gurnham, David. *Memory, Imagination, Justice: Intersections of Law and Literature*. Farnham, UK: Ashgate Publishing, 2009.

Haggerty, George E. *Queer Gothic*. Urbana: University of Illinois Press, 2006.

Halberstam, Judith. *Skin Shows: Gothic Horror and the Technology of Monsters*. Durham, NC: Duke University Press, 1995.

Hale, Brenda. "The Family Law Act 1996 – Dead Duck or Golden Goose?" In *Family Law: Essays for the New Millennium*, edited by Stephen Cretney, 23–32. Bristol: Family Law, 2000.

Hall, Stuart. "The Meaning of New Times." In *Stuart Hall*, edited by Kuan-Hsing Chen and David Morley, 223–37. Abingdon, UK: Taylor & Francis, 1996. http://lib.myilibrary.com?ID=24019.

Halley, Janet. *Split Decisions: How and Why to Take a Break from Feminism*. Princeton, NJ: Princeton University Press, 2006.

Hamawi, Jack. *Family Law*. London: Stevens and Sons, 1953.

Hamilton, Sheryl. *Impersonations: Troubling the Person in Law and Culture*. Toronto: University of Toronto Press, 2009.

Hanafin, Patrick. "The Writer's Refusal and Law's Malady." In *Law and Literature*, edited by Patrick Hanafin, Adam Gearey, and Joseph Brooker, 3–14. Oxford: Blackwell, 2004.

Hanson, Ellis. "Queer Gothic." In *The Routledge Companion to Gothic*, edited by Catherine Spooner and Emma McEvoy, 174–82. London: Routledge, 2007.

Harding, Rosie. *Regulating Sexuality: Legal Consciousness in Lesbian and Gay Lives*. London: Routledge, 2011.

Harding, Rosie, and Elizabeth Peele. "'We Do'? International Perspectives on Equality, Legality and Same-Sex Relationships." *Lesbian & Gay Psychology Review* 7, no. 2 (2006): 123–40.

Hart, H.L.A. *The Concept of Law*. Oxford: Clarendon Press, 1961.

———. "Positivism and the Separation of Law and Morals." *Harvard Law Review* 71, no. 4 (1958): 593–629.

Heald, Paul J. "The Death of Law and Literature: An Optimistic Eulogy." *Comparatist* 33 (May 2009): 20–8.

Heiland, Donna. *Gothic and Gender: An Introduction*. Malden, MA: Blackwell, 2004.

Heilbrun, Carolyn, and Judith Resnik. "Convergences: Law, Literature, and Feminism." *Yale Law Journal* 99, no. 8 (1990): 1913–56.

Herman, Didi. *Rights of Passage: Struggles for Gay and Lesbian Legal Equality*. Toronto: University of Toronto Press, 1994.

Herman, Didi, and Carl F. Stychin, eds. *Legal Inversions: Lesbians, Gay Men, and the Politics of Law*. Philadelphia: Temple University Press, 1995.

Herman, Judith Lewis. "Justice from the Victim's Perspective." *Violence against Women* 11, no. 5 (2005): 199–230.

Herman, Judith Lewis. With Lisa Hirschman. *Father-Daughter Incest*. Cambridge, MA: Harvard University Press, 2000.

Hoeveler, Diane Long. *Gothic Feminism: The Professionalization of Gender from Charlotte Smith to the Brontës*. University Park: Pennsylvania State University Press, 1998.

Hoeveler, Diane Long, and James D. Jenkins. "Where the Evidence Leads: Gothic Narratives and Legal Technologies." *European Romantic Review* 18, no. 3 (July 2007): 317–37.

Hoff, Lee Ann. *Battered Women as Survivors*. London: Routledge, 1990.

Hogan, Patrick Colm. "On Reading Law as Literature." *College Literature* 25, no. 1 (Winter 1998): 231–6.

Hogle, Jerrold. E. "The Gothic and the 'Otherings' of Ascendant Culture: The Original Phantom of the Opera." In *Spectral Readings: Towards a Gothic Geography*, edited by Glennis Byron and David Punter, 177–201. New York: Macmillan Press, 1999.

———. "The Gothic Ghost of the Counterfeit and the Progress of Abjection." In *A Companion to the Gothic*, edited by David Punter, 293–304. Oxford: Blackwell, 2000.

———. "Introduction: The Gothic in Western Culture." In *The Cambridge Companion to Gothic Fiction*. Cambridge: Cambridge University Press, 2002.

Honoré, Tony. *Making Law Bind: Essays Legal and Philosophical*. Oxford: Clarendon Press, 1987.

Horner, Avril, and Sue Zlosnik. "Female Gothic." In *Teaching the Gothic*, edited by Anna Powell and Andrew Smith, 107–20. Houndmills, UK: Palgrave Macmillan, 2006.

———. *Gothic and the Comic Turn*. Houndmills, UK: Palgrave Macmillan, 2005.

———, eds. Introduction to *Le Gothic: Influences and Appropriations in Europe and America*. Houndmills, UK: Palgrave Macmillan, 2008: 1–11.

———. "Keeping It in the Family: Incest and the Female Gothic Plot in du Maurier and Murdoch." In *The Female Gothic: New Directions*, edited by Diana Wallace and Andrew Smith, 115–32. Basingstoke, UK: Palgrave Macmillan, 2009.

———. "Skin Chairs and Other Domestic Horrors: Barbara Comyns and the Female Gothic Tradition." *Gothic Studies* 6, no. 1 (May 2004): 90–101.

Horton, Michael. *Family Homes and Domestic Violence: The New Legislation*. London: FT Law & Tax, 1996.

Howard, Jacqueline. *Reading Gothic Fiction: A Bakhtinian Approach*. Oxford: Clarendon Press, 1994.

Hughes, William. "'The Taste of Blood Meant the End of Aloneness': Vampires and Gay Men in Poppy Z. Brite's Lost Souls." In *Queering the Gothic*, edited by William Hughes and Andrew Smith, 142–56. Manchester: Manchester University Press, 2009.

Hunter, Nan D. "Marriage, Law, and Gender: A Feminist Inquiry." *Lesbian and Gay Legal Issues* 1, no. 9 (1991): 9–30.

Hunter, Rosemary. "An Account of Feminist Judging." In *Feminist Judgments: From Theory to Practice*, edited by Rosemary Hunter, Clare McGlynn, and Erika Rackley, 30–43. Oxford: Hart Publishing, 2010.

Hunter, Rosemary, Clare McGlynn, and Erika Rackley, eds. *Feminist Judgments: From Theory to Practice*. Oxford: Hart Publishing, 2010.

Hurley, Kelly. *The Gothic Body: Sexuality, Materialism, and Degeneration at the Fin de Siècle*. Cambridge: Cambridge University Press, 1996.

Irigaray, Luce. "The Power of Discourse and the Subordination of the Feminine." In *This Sex Which Is Not One*, 68–85. Translated by Catherine Porter with Carolyn Burke. Ithaca, NY: Cornell University Press, 1985.

———."Women on the Market." In *This Sex Which Is Not One*, 170–91. Translated by Catherine Porter with Carolyn Burke. Ithaca, NY: Cornell University Press, 1985.

Irving, Helen. *Gender and the Constitution: Equity and Agency in Comparative Constitutional Design*. Cambridge: Cambridge University Press, 2008.

Irwin, J., F. Waugh, and M. Bonner. "The Inclusion of Children and Young People in Research on Domestic Violence." *Communities, Families and Children Australia* 1, no. 1 (2006): 17–23.

Jacobs, Francis G. *The Sovereignty of Law: The European Way*. Cambridge: Cambridge University Press, 2007.

Jaggar, Alison. "Feminism in Ethics: Moral Justification." In *The Cambridge Companion to Feminism in Philosophy*, edited by Miranda Fricker and Jennifer Hornsby, 225–44. Cambridge: Cambridge University Press, 2000.

Jakobson, Roman. "Linguistics and Poetics." In *Style in Language*, edited by Thomas A. Sebeok, 350–77. Cambridge, MA: MIT Press, 1960.

Jameson, Fredric. "Postmodernism and Consumer Society." In *The Anti-Aesthetic: Essays on Postmodern Culture*, edited by Hal Foster, 111–25. Port Townsend, WA: Bay Press, 1983.

Jamison, Anne. "Collaboration v. Imitation: Authorship and the Law." *Law and Literature* 18, no. 2 (Summer 2006): 199–224.

Kahn, Paul W. *The Cultural Study of Law: Reconstructing Legal Scholarship.* Chicago: University of Chicago Press, 1999.

———. "Freedom, Autonomy, and the Cultural Study of Law." In *Cultural Analysis, Cultural Studies, and the Law: Moving beyond Legal Realism,* edited by Austin Sarat and Jonathon Simon, 154–87. Durham, NC: Duke University Press, 2003.

———. *Political Theology: Four New Chapters on the Concept of Sovereignty.* New York: Columbia University Press, 2011.

Kapur, Ratna. "Dark Times for Liberal Intellectual Thought." In *Profession,* edited by Rosemary G. Feal, 22–32. New York: Modern Language Association, 2006.

Kayman, Martin A. "Law-and-Literature: Questions of Jurisdiction." In *Law and Literature,* edited by Brook Thomas, 1–20. Vol. 18 of *REAL: Yearbook of Research in English and American Literature.* Tübingen: Gunter Narr Verlag, 2002.

———. "Lawful Writing: Common Law, Statute and the Properties of Literature." *New Literary History* 27, no. 4 (Autumn 1996): 761–83.

Kelsen, Hans. *Introduction to the Problems of Legal Theory.* Translated by Bonnie Litschewski Paulson and Stanley L. Paulson. Oxford: Clarendon Press, 1992.

Kennedy, David. "Law's Literature." In *Field Work: Sites in Literary and Cultural Studies,* edited by Marjorie Garber, Paul B. Franklin, and Rebecca L. Walkowitz, 207–13. New York: Routledge, 1996.

Kennedy, Duncan. *Legal Education and the Reproduction of Hierarchy: A Polemic against the System.* New York: New York University Press, 2007.

Kilgour, Maggie. *The Rise of the Gothic Novel.* London: Routledge, 1995.

Kitzinger, Celia, and Sue Wilkinson. "The Re-branding of Marriage: Why We Got Married Instead of Registering a Civil Partnership." *Feminism & Psychology* 14, no. 1 (2004): 127–50.

Korobkin, Laura Hanft. "Narrative Battles in the Courtroom." In *Field Work: Sites in Literary and Cultural Studies,* edited by Marjorie Garber, Paul B. Franklin, and Rebecca L. Walkowitz, 225–36. New York: Routledge, 1996.

Kristeva, Julia. *Power of Horrors: An Essay in Abjection.* New York: Columbia University Press, 1982.

———. "Thinking in Dark Times." In *Profession,* edited by Rosemary G. Feal, 13–21. New York: Modern Language Association, 2006.

Lacey, Nicola. "Analytical Jurisprudence versus Descriptive Sociology Revisited." *Texas Law Review* 84, no. 4 (2006): 945–82.

———. "Responsibility and Modernity in Criminal Law." *Journal of Political Philosophy* 9, no. 3 (2001): 249–76.

———. "Theories of Justice and the Welfare State." In *Family, State and Law*, edited by Michael D.A. Freeman, 197–218. Dartmouth, UK: Ashgate Publishing, 1999.

———. *Unspeakable Subjects: Feminist Essays in Legal and Social Theory*. Oxford: Hart Publishing, 1998.

———. "Violence, Ethics and Law: Feminist Reflections on a Familiar Dilemma." In *Visible Women*, edited by Susan James and Stephanie Palmer, 117–36. Oxford: Hart Publishing, 2002.

———. *Women, Crime, and Character*. Oxford: Oxford University Press, 2008.

Laclau, Ernesto. "Bare Life or Social Indeterminacy." In *Giorgio Agamben: Sovereignty and Life*, edited by Matthew Calarco and Steven DeCaroli, 11–22. Stanford, CA: Stanford University Press, 2007.

Lahey, Kathleen A. "Women, Substantive Equality, and Fiscal Policy: Gender-Based Analysis of Taxes, Benefits, and Budgets." *Canadian Journal of Women and the Law* 22, no. 1 (2010): 27–106.

Levin, Jennifer. *Family Law*. London: Sweet and Maxwell, 1982.

Lewis, Jane. "Family Policy in the Post-War Period." In *Cross Currents: Family Law and Policy in the United States and England*, edited by Sanford N. Katz, John Eekelaar, and Mavis Maclean, 81–10. Oxford: Oxford University Press, 2000.

Lewis, Ruth, Russell P. Dobash, Rebecca E. Dobash, and Kate Cavanagh. "Protection, Prevention, Rehabilitation or Justice? Women's Use of the Law to Challenge Domestic Violence." In *Domestic Violence*, edited by Michael D.A. Freeman, 171–97. Aldershot, UK: Ashgate Publishing, 2008.

Lockton, Deborah, and Richard Ward. *Domestic Violence*. London: Cavendish Publishing, 1997.

Loizidou, Elena. *Judith Butler: Ethics, Law, Politics*. Abingdon, UK: Routledge-Cavendish, 2007.

Lovell, Terry. "Resisting with Authority: Historical Specificity, Agency and the Performative Self." *Theory, Culture & Society* 20, no. 1 (2003): 1–17.

Lowe, N.V. "English Adoption Law: Past, Present, and Future." In *Cross Currents: Family Law and Policy in the United States and England*, edited by Sanford N. Katz, John Eekelaar, and Mavis Maclean, 307–39. Oxford: Oxford University Press, 2000.

Lysyk, Stephanie. "Love of the Censor: Legendre, Censorship and the Basoche." In *Law, Text, Terror*, edited by Peter Goodrich, Lior Barshack, and Anton Schütz, 119–29. Abingdon, UK: Routledge-Cavendish, 2006.

Mackay, James. "Family Law Reform – A Lord Chancellor's View." In *Family Law: Essays for the New Millennium*, edited by Stephen Cretney, 11–16. Bristol: Family Law, 2000.

MacKinnon, Catherine. *Toward a Feminist Theory of the State*. Cambridge, MA: Harvard University Press, 1989.

Maloutas, Maro Pantelidou. *The Gender of Democracy: Citizenship and Gendered Subjectivity*. London: Routledge, 2006.

Manderson, Desmond. *Kangaroo Courts and the Rule of Law: The Legacy of Modernism*. Abingdon, UK: Routledge, 2012.

Manderson, Desmond, and Richard Mohr. "From Oxymoron to Intersection: An Epidemiology of Legal Research." *Law Text Culture* 6 (2003): 165–83.

Marcus, Isabel. "Terrorism in the Home." In *The Public Nature of Private Violence*, edited by Martha A. Fineman and Roxanne Mykitiuk, 11–35. London: Routledge, 1994.

Marx, Karl. *Capital*. Edited by Friedrich Engels. Translated by Samuel Moore and Edward Aveling. Vol. 1. New York: Modern Library, 1936.

———. *"Grundrisse."* In *Karl Marx: Selected Writings*, edited by David McLellan, 345–87. Oxford: Oxford University Press, 1977.

Massé, Michelle A. *In the Name of Love: Women, Masochism and the Gothic*. Ithaca, NY: Cornell University Press, 1992.

Matsuda, Mari J. "Public Response to Racist Speech: Considering the Victim's Story." *Michigan Law Review* 87, no. 8 (August 1989): 2320–81.

McCandless, Julie. "Recognising Family Diversity: The 'Boundaries' of Re G." *Feminist Legal Studies* 13, no. 3 (2005): 323–36.

McCue, Margi Laird. *Domestic Violence: A Reference Handbook*. Santa Barbara, CA: ABC-CLIO, 2008.

McEwan, Ian. *Atonement*. London: Vintage, 2002. First published 2001 by Jonathan Cape.

McLoughlin, Kate, and Carl Gardner. "When Is Authorial Intention Not Authorial Intention?" *European Journal of English Studies* 11, no. 1 (April 2007): 93–105.

Meyer, Linda Ross. "Plowing Up the Ground of Reason." In *Law and Catastrophe*, edited by Austin Sarat, Lawrence Douglas, and Martha Merrill Umphrey, 19–32. Stanford, CA: Stanford University Press, 2007.

Meyers, Helene. *Femicidal Fears: Narratives of the Female Gothic Experience*. New York: State University of New York Press, 2001.

Mezey, Naomi. "Law as Culture." In *Cultural Analysis, Cultural Studies, and the Law: Moving beyond Legal Realism*, edited by Austin Sarat and Jonathan Simon, 37–72. Durham, NC: Duke University Press, 2003.

Mighall, Robert. *A Geography of Victorian Gothic Fiction*. Oxford: Oxford University Press, 1999.

Milbank, Alison. *Daughters of the House: Modes of the Gothic in Victorian Fiction*. Houndmills, UK: Macmillan, 1992.

Miles, Robert. "Abjection, Nationalism and the Gothic." In *The Gothic*, edited by Fred Botting, 47–70. Cambridge: D.S. Brewer, 2001.

———. "The Gothic and Ideology." In *Approaches to Teaching Gothic Fiction: The British and American Traditions*, edited by Diane Long Hoeveler and Tamar Heller, 58–65. New York: Modern Language Association, 2003.

———. *Gothic Writing 1750–1820: A Genealogy*. London: Routledge, 1993.

———. "'Mother Radcliff': Anne Radcliffe and the Female Gothic." In *The Female Gothic: New Directions*, edited by Diana Wallace and Andrew Smith, 42–59. Basingstoke, UK: Palgrave Macmillan, 2009.

———. "The 1790s: The Effulgence of Gothic." In *The Cambridge Companion to Gothic Fiction*, edited by Jerrold E. Hogle, 41–62. Cambridge: Cambridge University Press, 2002.

Mill, Catherine. "Biopolitics, Liberal Eugenics, and Nihilism." In *Giorgio Agamben: Sovereignty and Life*, edited by Matthew Calarco and Steven DeCaroli, 180–202. Stanford, CA: Stanford University Press, 2007.

Minow, Martha. "Foreword: The Supreme Court, 1986 Term – Justice Engendered." *Harvard Law Review* 110 (1987): 10–95.

Mnookin, Robert, and Lewis Kornhauser. "Bargaining in the Shadow of the Law: The Case of Divorce." *Yale Law Journal* 88, no. 5 (1979): 950–97.

Moran, Leslie J. "Dangerous Words and Dead Letters: Encounters with Law and *The Love That Dares to Speak Its Name*." *Liverpool Law Review* 23, no. 2 (2001): 153–65.

———. "Gothic Law." *Griffith Law Review* 10, no. 2 (2001): 75–100.

———. "The Homosexualization of English Law." In *Legal Inversions: Lesbians, Gay Men, and the Politics of Law*, edited by Didi Herman and Carl F. Stychin, 3–28. Philadelphia: Temple University Press, 1995.

———. "Law and the Gothic Imagination." In *The Gothic*, edited by Fred Botting, 87–109. Woodbridge, UK: D.S. Brewer, 2001.

Morley, Rebecca. "Domestic Violence and Housing." In *Home Truths about Domestic Violence: Feminist Influences on Policy and Practice, A Reader*, edited by J. Hanmer, C. Itzin, Sheila Quaid, and Debra Wigglesworth, 228–45. London: Routledge, 2000.

Mulvey-Roberts, Laura. "The Corpse in the Corpus: Frankenstein, Rewriting Wollstonecraft and the Abject." In *Mary Shelley's Fictions: From Frankenstein to Falkner*, edited by Michael Eberle-Sinatra and Nora Crook, 197–210. Houndmills, UK: Macmillan, 2000.

———. "From Bluebeard's Bloody Chamber to Demonic Stigmatic." In *The Female Gothic: New Directions*, edited by Diana Wallace and Andrew Smith, 98–114. Basingstoke, UK: Palgrave Macmillan, 2009.

Munford, Rebecca. "'The Desecration of the Temple'; or, 'Sexuality as Terrorism'? Angela Carter's (Post-)Feminist Gothic Heroines." *Gothic Studies* 9, no. 2 (2007): 58–70.

———. "Dracula's Daughters: Angela Carter and Pierrette Fleutiaux's Vampiric Exchanges." In *Le Gothic: Influences and Appropriations in Europe and America*, edited by Avril Horner and Sue Zlosnik, 116–33. Houndmills, UK: Palgrave Macmillan, 2008.

Munt, Sally R. *Queer Attachments: The Cultural Politics of Shame*. Aldershot, UK: Ashgate Publishing, 2007.

Murphy, Mark C. "Natural Law Theory." In *The Blackwell Guide to the Philosophy of Law and Legal Theory*, edited by Martin P. Golding and William A. Edmundson, 15–28. Malden, MA: Blackwell, 2005.

Murphy, W.T., and Hilary Clark. *The Family Home*. London: Sweet and Maxwell, 1983.

Musgrave, L. Ryan. "Liberal Feminism, from Law to Art: The Impact of Feminist Jurisprudence on Feminist Aesthetics." *Hypatia* 18, no. 4 (Fall–Winter 2003): 214–35.

Musiol, Marie-Jeanne. "Inclure/Exclure." Exhibition of photographs at Festival X In/Out: Contemporary Photography and the Politics of Difference, Ottawa, 2 October 2010.

Naffine, Ngaire. "Can Women Be Legal Persons?" In *Visible Women*, edited by Susan James and Stephanie Palmer, 69–90. Oxford: Hart Publishing, 2002.

———. *Law and the Sexes: Explorations in Feminist Jurisprudence*. Sydney: Unwin and Allen, 1990.

Negri, Antonio. "The Discreet Taste of the Dialectic." In *Giorgio Agamben: Sovereignty and Life*, edited by Matthew Calarco and Steven DeCaroli, 109–25. Stanford, CA: Stanford University Press, 2007.

Nussbaum, Martha. *Poetic Justice: The Literary Imagination and Public Life*. Boston: Beacon Press, 1995.

O'Donovan, Katherine. *Family Matters*. London: Pluto Press, 1993.

———. "A New Settlement between the Sexes? Constitutional Law and the Citizenship of Women." In *Feminist Perspectives on the Foundational Subjects of Law*, edited by Anne Bottomley, 243–59. London: Cavendish Publishing, 1996.

O'Grady, Kathleen. "Guardian of Language: An Interview with Hélène Cixous." *Women's Education des femmes* 12, no. 4 (Winter 1996–97): 6–10. Reprinted at http://bailiwick.lib.uiowa.edu/wstudies/cixous/.

Okin, Susan Moller. "John Rawls: Justice as Fairness – For Whom?" In *Feminist Interpretations and Political Theory*, edited by Mary Lyndon Shanley and

Carole Pateman, 181–98. University Park: Pennsylvania University Press, 1991.

Olsen, Frances. "The Myth of State Intervention in the Family." In *Family, State and Law*, edited by Michael D.A. Freeman, 81–110. Dartmouth, UK: Ashgate Publishing, 1999.

O'Rourke, Michael, and David Collings. "Introduction: Queer Romanticisms: Past, Present, and Future." *Romanticism on the Net* 36–37 (November 2004–February 2005).

Orwell, George. *Animal Farm*. New York: Harcourt, Brace and Company, 1946.

Ost, François. "The Law as Mirrored in Literature." *SubStance* 35, no. 1 (2006): 3–19.

Pahl, Jan. "The Allocation of Money within the Household." In *State, Law, and Family: Critical Perspectives*, edited by Michael D.A. Freeman, 36–50. London: Tavistock, 1984.

Palmer, Paulina. *Lesbian Gothic: Transgressive Fictions*. London: Cassell, 1999.

Pan, David. "Against Biopolitics: Walter Benjamin, Carl Schmitt, and Giorgio Agamben on Political Sovereignty and Symbolic Order." *German Quarterly* 82, no. 1 (Winter 2009): 42–62.

Pateman, Carol. *The Disorder of Women*. Stanford, CA: Stanford University Press, 1989.

———. "Self-Ownership and Property in the Person: Democratization and a Tale of Two Concepts." *Journal of Political Philosophy* 10, no. 1 (2002): 20–53.

———. *The Sexual Contract*. London: Polity Press, 1988.

Paxman, John M. *Law and Planned Parenthood*. London: International Planned Parenthood Federation, 1980.

Perkins, William. *Christian Oeconomie: Or a Short Survey of the Right Manner of Erecting and Ordering a Family, according to the Scripture*. Cambridge: Legge, 1609.

Peters, Julie Stone. "Law, Literature, and the Vanishing Real: On the Future of an Interdisciplinary Illusion." *PMLA* 120, no. 1 (March 2005): 442–53.

———. "Legal Performance Good and Bad." *Law, Culture and the Humanities* 4, no. 2 (2008): 179–200.

Pether, Penelope. "Is There Anything Outside the Class? Law, Literature, and Pedagogy." *Cardozo Law Review* 26, no. 6 (May 2005): 2415–23.

Peucker, Brigitte. "The Fascist Choreography: Riefenstahl's Tableaux." *Modernism/Modernity* 11, no. 2 (2004): 279–97.

Phelan, Shane. *Sexual Strangers: Gays, Lesbians, and Dilemmas of Citizenship*. Philadelphia: Temple University Press, 2001.

Phillips, Anne. "Equality, Pluralism and Justice: Current Concerns in Normative Theory." *British Journal of Politics and International Relations* 2, no. 2 (2000): 237–55.

———. "Feminism and the Politics of Difference. Or, Where Have All the Women Gone?" In *Visible Women: Essays on Feminist Legal Theory and Political Philosophy*. Edited by Susan James and Stephanie Palmer, 11–28. Oxford: Hart Publishing, 2002.

———. *Which Equalities Matter?* Cambridge: Polity Press, 1999.

Piper, Christine. "Commentary on *Re L (a Child) (Contact: Domestic Violence)*." In *Feminist Judgments: From Theory to Practice*, edited by Rosemary Hunter, Clare McGlynn, and Erika Rackley, 114–33. Oxford: Hart Publishing, 2010.

Pizzey, Erin. *Scream Quietly or the Neighbours Will Hear*. London: Penguin, 1974.

Plato. *Republic*. Translated by Robin Waterfield. Oxford: Oxford University Press, 1994.

Polikoff, Nancy D. *Beyond (Straight and Gay) Marriage: Valuing All Families under the Law*. Boston: Beacon Press, 2008.

Post, Robert C. "Who's Afraid of Jurispathic Courts? Violence and Public Reason in *Nomos and Narrative*." *Yale Journal of Law & the Humanities* 17, no. 1 (2005): 9–16.

Punter, David. *Gothic Pathologies: The Text, the Body and the Law*. Houndmills, UK: Macmillan Press, 1998.

———. *The Literature of Terror: A History of Gothic Fictions from 1765 to the Present Day*. London: Longman, 1980.

———. "Scottish and Irish Gothic." In *The Cambridge Companion to Gothic Fiction*, edited by Jerrold E. Hogle, 105–23. Cambridge: Cambridge University Press, 2002.

———. "The Uncanny." In *The Routledge Companion to Gothic*, edited by Catherine Spooner and Emma McEvoy, 129–36. London: Routledge, 2007.

Punter, David, and Elisabeth Bronfen. "Gothic: Violence, Trauma and the Ethical." In *The Gothic*, edited by Fred Botting, 7–21. Woodbridge, UK: D.S. Brewer, 2001.

Rae, Maggie. "Fair, Just and Reasonable?" In *Family Law: Essays for the New Millennium*, edited by Stephen Cretney, 163–8. Bristol: Family Law, 2000.

Rancière, Jacques. *Aesthetics and Its Discontents*. Translated by Steven Corcoran. Cambridge: Polity Press, 2009.

———. *Dissensus: On Politics and Aesthetics*. Translated by Steven Corcoran. London: Continuum, 2010.

———. *The Politics of Aesthetics*. Translated by Gabriel Rockhill. London: Continuum, 2004.

Rawls, John. *A Theory of Justice*. Cambridge, MA: Harvard University Press, 1971.

Raz, Joseph. *The Authority of Law: Essays on Law and Morality*. Oxford: Clarendon Press, 1979.

Reekie, Peter D., and Richard Tuddenham. *Family Law and Practice*. London: Sweet and Maxwell, 1990.

Reichman, Ravit. "Committed to Memory: Rebecca West's Nuremberg." In *Law and Catastrophe*, edited by Austin Sarat, Lawrence Douglas, and Martha Merrill Umphrey, 91–130. Stanford, CA: Stanford University Press, 2007.

Resnik, Judith. "Living Their Legal Commitments: Paideic Communities, Courts, and Robert Cover." *Yale Journal of Law & the Humanities* 17, no. 1 (2005): 17–54.

Rigby, Mair. "'Do You Share My Madness?' Frankenstein's Queer Gothic." In *Queering the Gothic*, edited by William Hughes and Andrew Smith, 36–54. Manchester: Manchester University Press, 2009.

———. "Uncanny Recognition: Queer Theory's Debt to the Gothic." *Gothic Studies* 11, no. 1 (May 2009): 46–57.

Robson, Ruthann. *Sappho Goes to Law School: Fragments in Lesbian Legal Theory*. New York: Columbia University Press, 1998.

Rountree, William. "Contract and the Legal Mooring of Same-Sex Intimacy." In *Regulating Sex: The Politics of Intimacy and Identity*, edited by Elizabeth Bernstein and Laurie Schaffner, 19–34. New York: Routledge, 2005.

Royle, Nicholas. *The Uncanny*. New York: Routledge, 2003.

Rubin, Gayle. "The Traffic among Women: Notes on the 'Political Economy' of Sex." In *Toward an Anthropology of Women*, edited by R.R. Reiter. New York: Monthly Review, 1975.

Samson, Rémi. "Language and Law as Objects of Scientific Study." In *Law, Mystery, and the Humanities: Collected Essays*, edited by Logan Atkinson and Diana Majury, 121–42. Toronto: University of Toronto Press, 2008.

Samuel, Raphael. *Island Stories: Unravelling Britain*. Vol. 2. of *Theatres of Memory*. London: Verso Books, 1999.

Samuels, Alec, ed. Introduction to *Social Security and Family Law with Special Reference to the One-Parent Family: A Comparative Survey*. United Kingdom Comparative Law Series, vol. 4. London: British Institute of International and Comparative Law, 1979.

Sandland, Ralph. "Feminism and the Gender Recognition Act 2004." *Feminist Legal Studies* 13, no. 1 (2005): 43–66.

Sarat, Austin, ed. *Pain, Death, and the Law*. Ann Arbor: University of Michigan Press, 2001.

———. "Traditions and Trajectories in Law and Humanities Scholarship." *Yale Journal of Law & the Humanities* 10, no. 2 (1998): 401–7.

Sarat, Austin, Lawrence Douglas, and Martha Merrill Umphrey. "A Jurisprudence of Catastrophe." In *Law and Catastrophe*, edited by Austin Sarat, Lawrence Douglas, and Martha Merrill Umphrey, 1–18. Stanford, CA: Stanford University Press, 2007.

Sarat, Austin, Cathrine Frank, and Matthew Anderson, eds. *Teaching Literature and Law.* MLA Approaches to Teaching Series. New York: Modern Language Association, 2010.

Sarat, Austin, and Thomas R. Kearns. "A Journey through Forgetting: Toward a Jurisprudence of Violence." In *The Fate of the Law*, edited by Austin Sarat and Thomas R. Kearns, 209–73. Ann Arbor: University of Michigan Press, 1991.

———. "Making Peace with Violence: Robert Cover on Law and Legal Theory." In *Law, Violence, and the Possibility of Justice*, edited by Austin Sarat, 49–84. Princeton, NJ: Princeton University Press, 2001.

Savarese, Josephine L. "'Doing No Violence to the Sentence Imposed': Racialized Sex Worker Complainants, Racialized Offenders, and the Feminization of the *Homo Sacer* in Two Sexual Assault Cases." *Canadian Journal of Women and the Law* 22, no. 2 (2010): 365–96.

Savell, Kristin. "The Mother of the Legal Person." In *Visible Women*, edited by Susan James and Stephanie Palmer, 29–67. Oxford: Hart Publishing, 2002.

Savoy, Eric. "The Rise of American Gothic." In *The Cambridge Companion to Gothic Fiction*, edited by Jerrold E. Hogle, 167–88. Cambridge: Cambridge University Press, 2002.

———. "Spectres of Abjection: The Queer Subject of James's 'The Jolly Corner.'" In *Spectral Readings: Towards a Gothic Geography*, edited by Glennis Byron and David Punter, 161–74. Houndmills, UK: Macmillan, 1990.

Scheppele, Kim Lane. "Foreword: Telling Stories." *Michigan Law Review* 87, no. 8 (1989): 2073–98.

Schmitt, Carl. *Political Theology: Four Chapters in the Concept of Sovereignty.* Translated by George Schwab. Cambridge, MA: MIT Press, 1985.

Schneider, Elizabeth M. "The Dialectics of Rights and Politics: Perspectives from the Women's Movement." In *At the Boundaries of Law: Feminism and Legal Theory*, edited by Martha Fineman and N. Thomadsen, 301–19. London: Routledge, 1991.

Seal, Vivien. *Whose Choice: Working Class Women and the Control of Fertility.* London: Fortress Books, 1991.

Sedgwick, Eve Kosofsky. *Between Men: English Literature and Male Homosocial Desire.* New York: Columbia University Press, 1985.

———. *The Coherence of Gothic Conventions.* New York: Methuen, 1986.

Seidman, Steven. "From Outsider to Citizen." In *Regulating Sex: The Politics of Intimacy and Identity*, edited by Elizabeth Bernstein and Laurie Schaffner, 225–45. New York: Routledge, 2005.

Sharpe, Andrew N. "Endless Sex: The Gender Recognition Act 2004 and the Persistence of a Legal Category." *Feminist Legal Studies* 15, no. 1 (2007): 57–84.

———. "England's Legal Monsters." *Law, Culture and the Humanities* 5, no. 1 (2009): 100–30.

Shepherd, Jessica. "Halal Is Hot." *Guardian* (Manchester), 30 January 2007. http://www.guardian.co.uk/education/2007/jan/30/highereducation.students.

Shipman, Beccy, and Carol Smart. "'It's Made a Huge Difference': Recognition, Rights and the Personal Significance of Civil Partnership." *Sociological Research Online* 12, no. 1 (2007). http://www.socresonline.org.uk/12/1/shipman.html.

Shipway, Lyn. *Domestic Violence: A Handbook for Professionals*. London: Routledge, 2004.

Simon, Jonathan. "The Vicissitudes of Law's Violence." In *Law, Violence, and the Possibility of Justice*, edited by Austin Sarat, 17–48. Princeton, NJ: Princeton University Press, 2001.

Smart, Carol. "Divorce in England 1950–2000: A Moral Tale?" In *Cross Currents: Family Law and Policy in the United States and England*, edited by Sanford N. Katz, John Eekelaar, and Mavis Maclean, 363–86. Oxford: Oxford University Press, 2000.

———. *Feminism and the Power of the Law*. London: Routledge, 1989.

———. *Law, Crime, and Sexuality: Essays in Feminism*. London: Sage Publications, 1995.

———. *The Ties That Bind: Law, Marriage and the Reproduction of Patriarchal Relations*. London: Routledge and Kegan Paul, 1984.

Smith, Marie Hockenhull. "The Children Will Be 'Subject to the Infamy of Their Deluded and Unfortunate Mother': Rhetoric of the Courtroom, a Gothic Fantasy and a Plain Letter to the Lord Chancellor." *Law and Literature* 18, no. 3 (2006): 403–30.

Somerville, Siobhan. "Queer Loving." *GLQ: A Journal of Gay and Lesbian Studies* 11, no. 3 (2005): 335–70.

Sommerlad, Hilary. "That Obscure Object of Desire: Sex Equality and the Legal Profession." In *Rethinking Equality Projects in Law: Feminist Challenges*, edited by Rosemary Hunter, 171–94. Oñati International Series in Law and Society. Oxford: Hart Publishing, 2008.

Stanko, Elizabeth A. "Theorizing about Violence: Observations from the Economic and Social Research Council's Violence Research Program." *Violence against Women* 12, no. 6 (2006): 105–17.

Sterne, Abigail, and Liz Poole. With Donna Chadwick, Catherine Lawler, and Lynda W. Dodd. *Domestic Violence and Children: A Handbook for Schools and Early Years Settings*. London: Routledge, 2010.

Stetson, Dorothy M. *A Woman's Issue: The Politics of Family Law Reform in England*. Westport, CT: Greenwood Press, 1982.

Stevenson, Helen. "*The Deadly Space Between* by Patricia Duncker: This Oedipus Is Too Complex." *Independent* (UK), 2002. Accessed 23 March 2007. http://www.independent.co.uk/arts-entertainment/books/reviews/the-deadly-space-between-by-patricia-duncker-657411.html.

Strathern, Marilyn. "Displacing Knowledge: Technology and the Consequences for Kinship." In *Conceiving the New World Order: The Global Politics of Reproduction*, edited by Faye D. Ginsburg and Rayna Rapp, 346–63. Berkeley: University of California Press, 1995.

Stychin, Carl F. "Family Friendly? Rights, Responsibilities and Relationship Recognition." In *Feminist Perspectives on Family Law*, edited by Alison Diduck and Katherine O'Donovan, 21–37. Abingdon, UK: Routledge-Cavendish Publishing, 2006.

———. *Governing Sexuality: The Changing Politics of Citizenship and Law Reform*. Oxford: Hart Publishing, 2003.

———. "Not (Quite) a Horse and Carriage: The Civil Partnership Act 2004." *Feminist Legal Studies* 14, no. 1 (2006): 79–86.

Sutcliff, Robert. *Travels in Some Parts of North America, in the Years 1804, 1805, and 1806*. York: C. Peacock, 1811.

Tamanaha, Brian Z. *On the Rule of Law: History, Politics, Theory*. Cambridge: Cambridge University Press, 2004.

Teubner, Gunther. *Law as an Autopoietic System*. Edited by Zenon Bankowski. Translated by Anne Bankowska and Ruth Adler. Oxford: Blackwell, 1993.

Thiong'o, Ng g wa. "For Peace, Justice, and Culture: The Intellectual in the Twenty-First Century." In *Profession*, edited by Rosemary G. Feal, 33–9. New York: Modern Language Association, 2006.

Thomas, Brook. "Reflections on the Law and Literature Revival." *Critical Inquiry* 17, no. 3 (Spring 1991): 510–39.

Thurschwell, Adam. "Reading the Law." In *The Fate of the Law*, edited by Austin Sarat and Thomas R. Kearns, 275–332. Ann Arbor: University of Michigan Press, 1991.

Townshend, Dale. *The Orders of Gothic: Foucault, Lacan, and the Subject of Gothic Writing, 1764–1820*. New York: AMS Press, 2007.

Triumph of the Will. Film directed and produced by Leni Riefenstahl. Synapse Films, 2001.

Unger, Roberto Mangabeira. "Liberal Political Theory." In *Critical Legal Studies*, edited by Allan Hutchinson, 15–35. Totowa, NJ: Rowman and Littlefield, 1989.

United Kingdom. "Domestic Violence: A National Report." London: Home Office, 2005.

United Kingdom. Law Commission. *Family Law: Domestic Violence and Occupation of the Family Home*. Law Com. No. 207. London: HMSO, 1992.

———. "Partial Defences to Murder: Consultation." Consultation Paper No. 173. 31 October 2003.

Vaihinger, Hans. *The Philosophy of "As If": A System of the Theoretical, Practical and Religious Fictions of Mankind*. Translated by C.K. Ogden. London: Kegan Paul, Trench, Trubner, 1924.

Valverde, Mariana. *Law's Dream of a Common Knowledge*. Princeton, NJ: Princeton University Press, 2003.

Van Praagh, Shauna. "View from the *Succah*: Religion and Neighbourly Relations." In *Law and Religious Pluralism in Canada*, edited by Richard Moon, 21–40. Vancouver: University of British Columbia Press, 2008.

Vara, Maria. "Gothic Permutations from the 1790s to the 1970s: Rethinking the Marquis de Sade's Legacy." In *Le Gothic: Influences and Appropriations in Europe and America*, edited by Avril Horner and Sue Zlosnik, 100–15. Houndmills, UK: Palgrave Macmillan, 2008.

Wachspress, Megan. "Rethinking Sovereignty with Reference to History and Anthropology." *International Journal of Law in Context* 5, no. 3 (2009): 315–30.

Walker, L.E. *The Battered Woman*. New York: Harper Colophon Books, 1979.

———. *The Battered Woman Syndrome*. New York: Springer, 1984.

Wallace, Diana. "'The Haunting Idea': Female Gothic Metaphors and Feminist Theory." In *The Female Gothic: New Directions*, edited by Diana Wallace and Andrew Smith, 26–41. Basingstoke, UK: Palgrave Macmillan, 2009.

Walsh, Sue. "Gothic Children." In *The Routledge Companion to Gothic*, edited by Catherine Spooner and Emma McEvoy, 183–91. London: Routledge, 2007.

Ward, Ian. *Law and Literature: Possibilities and Perspectives*. Cambridge: Cambridge University Press, 1995.

———. "Towards a Poethics of Terror." *Law, Culture and the Humanities* 4, no. 2 (2008): 248–79.

Ward, Richard, and Roger Bird. *Domestic Violence, Crime and Victims Act 2004: A Practitioner's Guide*. Bristol: Jordan Publishing, 2005.

Warner, Michael. "Beyond Gay Marriage." In *Left Legalism / Left Critique*, edited by Wendy Brown and Janet Halley, 259–89. Durham, NC: Duke University Press, 2002.

Warrington, Ronnie, and Costas Douzinas. *Justice Miscarried: Ethics, Aesthetics and the Law*. Hemel Hempstead, UK: Harvester Wheatsheaf, 1994.

———. "The Trials of Law and Literature." *Law and Critique* 1, no. 6 (1995): 135–65.

Weisberg, Richard H. "The Codification of Western Law and the Poethics of Disclosure." *Cardozo Studies in Law and Literature* 6, no. 2 (Autumn–Winter 1994): 157–70.

———. *Poethics and Other Strategies of Law and Literature*. New York: Columbia University Press, 1992.

Weisberg, Robert. "The Law-Literature Enterprise." *Yale Journal of Law & the Humanities* 1, no. 1 (1989): 1–67.

———. "Proclaiming Trials as Narratives: Premises and Pretenses." In *Law's Stories: Narrative and Rhetoric in the Law*, edited by Peter Brooks and Paul Gewirtz, 61–83. New Haven, CT: Yale University Press, 1999.

Weisberg, Robert, and Guyora Binder. *Literary Criticisms of Law*. Princeton, NJ: Princeton University Press, 2000.

West, Robin. *Caring for Justice*. New York: New York University Press, 1997.

———. "Communities, Texts, and Law: Reflections on the Law and Literature Movement." *Yale Journal of Law & the Humanities* 1, no. 1 (1989): 129–56.

———. "Disciplines, Subjectivity, and Law." In *The Fate of the Law*, edited by Austin Sarat and Thomas R. Kearns, 119–57. Ann Arbor: University of Michigan Press, 1991.

———. "Jurisprudence as Narrative: An Aesthetic Analysis of Modern Legal Theory." *New York University Law Review* 60, no. 2 (1985): 145–211.

———. *Narrative, Authority, and Law*. Ann Arbor: University of Michigan Press, 1993.

White, Hayden. "The Historical Text as Literary Artifact." In *Tropics of Discourse: Essays in Cultural Criticism*, 81–100. Baltimore: Johns Hopkins University Press, 1978.

White, James Boyd. *Heracles' Bow: Essays in the Rhetoric and Poetics of the Law*. Madison: University of Wisconsin Press, 1985.

———. "Imagining the Law." In *The Fate of the Law*, edited by Austin Sarat and Thomas R. Kearns, 29–55. Ann Arbor: University of Michigan Press, 1991.

———. *Justice as Translation: An Essay in Cultural and Legal Criticism*. Chicago: University of Chicago Press, 1990.

———. "Writing and Reading in Philosophy, Law, and Poetry." In *Law and Literature*, vol. 2 of *Current Legal Issues*, edited by Michael D.A. Freeman and Andrew Lewis, 1–20. Oxford: Oxford University Press, 1999.

Williams, Anne. *Art of Darkness: A Poetics of Gothic*. Chicago: University of Chicago Press, 1995.

Williams, Melanie. "Laws, Morals, Marriage and Cohabitation: Virtuous Individuals and Venal Laws – Hardy's Eternal Message for Attitudes to Marriage and Cohabitation." In *Secrets and Law: Collected Essays in Law, Lives and Literature*, 103–22. London: Cavendish Publishing, 2005.

Williams, Susan H. "A Feminist Reassessment of Civil Society." *Indiana Law Journal* 72, no. 2 (1997): 417–47.

Wilson, Natasha Sandraya. "A Queer Situation: Poverty, Prisons, and Performances of Infidelity and Instability in the New Orleans Lesbian Anthem." In *Out in Public: Reinventing Lesbian/Gay Anthropology in a Globalizing World*, edited by Ellen Lewin and William L. Leap, 104–22. Chichester, UK: Wiley-Blackwell, 2009.

Wisker, Gina. "Devouring Desires: Lesbian Gothic Horror." In *Queering the Gothic*, edited by William Hughes and Andrew Smith, 123–41. Manchester: Manchester University Press, 2009.

———. "Love Bites: Contemporary Women's Vampire Fictions." In *A Companion to the Gothic*, edited by David Punter, 167–79. Oxford: Blackwell, 2000.

Wolfreys, Julian. *Victorian Hauntings: Spectrality, Gothic, the Uncanny and Literature*. New York: Palgrave, 2002.

Woolf, Virginia. *Between the Acts*. St Albans, UK: Granada Publishing, 1978.

Wright, Angela. "'To Live the Life of Hopeless Recollection': Mourning and Melancholia in Female Gothic, 1780–1800." *Gothic Studies* 6, no. 1 (May 2004): 19–29.

Young, Marion Iris. *Intersecting Voices: Dilemmas of Gender, Political Philosophy, and Policy*. Princeton, NJ: Princeton University Press, 1997.

———. "Throwing like a Girl: A Phenomenology of Feminine Comportment, Motility, and Spatiality." In *The Thinking Muse: Feminism in Modern French Philosophy*, edited by Marion I. Young and Jeffner Allen, 51–71. Bloomington: Indiana University Press, 1989.

Index

www.ingramcontent.com/pod-product-compliance
Lightning Source LLC
LaVergne TN
LVHW090148080826
844660LV00013B/713/J

* 9 7 8 1 4 4 2 6 4 9 0 3 3 *